Second Edition

PSYCHED

ELISA SETMIRE

Kendall Hunt
publishing company

Kendall Hunt
publishing company

www.kendallhunt.com
Send all inquiries to:
4050 Westmark Drive
Dubuque, IA 52004-1840

Copyright © 2014, 2017 by Kendall Hunt Publishing Company

ISBN 978-1-5249-2403-4

Published in the United States of America

Contents

Warm-ups   365

Handouts and Activities   437

Study Guides and Extra Credit   475

Chapter 1
History and Scope of Psychology

Outline

© stockshoppe/Shutterstock.com

Introduction to the Chapter (Summary)

Psychology's roots are largely based in Philosophy. Since the time of Plato and Aristotle, people have been wondering about and writing about human behavior and mental processes. A dramatic change came in the 1800's when the scientific method was applied to those ponderings making psychology a separate and distinct discipline. Most agree that psychology was born in 1879 when Wilhelm Wundt founded the first psychological laboratory in Germany. Since becoming a distinct field, psychology has been through several paradigm shifts. While the early psychologists were largely white middle class European men, the field has changed considerably and is currently marked by a much greater diversity of professionals.

The history of psychology is full of several prominent model or paradigm shifts as psychologists strived to explain human thought and behavior. Psychology started out with a very philosophical emphasis which was followed by a shift to Edward Titchener's structuralism and the functionalism of William James. Gestalt psychologists followed with a focus on patterns and forms followed shortly by Freudian Psychology in the late 1800s. Freud's theories are often regarded as some of the most prominent and influential within the field and they sparked several other models and viewpoints in the years that followed. Psychology shifted to behaviorism with prominent psychologists like Pavlov, Watson, and Skinner followed by Humanistic theorists that emphasized the more goal-oriented and positive aspects of psychology. Cognitive theories were dominant in the mid-1950s followed by evolutionary theories, behavioral genetics, and then cross-cultural perspectives as we neared the 2000s. Psychology is an ever-changing discipline with new theories constantly being developed. We will discuss several of these key theories within the field in more detail later in the class during the unit on personality.

Currently, psychology is defined as the scientific study of behavior and mental processes. There are many different perspectives and branches within the field of psychology and many issues and questions that psychology attempts to tackle. One large question within the field of psychology is that of nature vs. nurture; do our human traits and/or personality develop through experience or do we come equipped with them? This is an ancient debate dating back to Plato and Aristotle and still does not have a definitive answer with most things being believed to be the result of a combination of both influences. Psychology also attempts to examine phenomena from different levels of analysis including looking at how biological, psychological, and social-cultural influences can contribute to our behaviors or mental processes.

There are many different subfields in psychology including Developmental Psychology, Physiological Psychology, Experimental Psychology, Personality Psychology, Industrial and Organizational Psychology, Social Psychology, Clinical and Counseling Psychology, and many others. With such a great variety of subfields and areas of focus, there is also a great range of careers. Different levels of college degrees play a large role in dictating the available positions with many careers in psychology requiring graduate degrees or above.

The Roots of Psychology

Psychology's roots are largely based in Philosophy. Since the time of Plato and Aristotle, people have been wondering about and writing about human behavior and mental processes. A dramatic change came in the 1800's when the scientific method was applied to these ponderings making psychology a separate and distinct discipline. Most agree that psychology was born in 1879 when Wilhelm Wundt founded the first psychological laboratory in Germany. Wundt was primarily interested in memory and selective attention, but it was his insistence on measurement and experimentation that moved psychology out of the realm of philosophy and into the realm of science.

The History of Psychology

Psychology went through several paradigm shifts in its early years and there are many important pioneers within the field. While the early psychologists were largely white, middle class, European men, the field has changed considerably and is currently marked by a much greater diversity of professionals.

As mentioned above, Psychology's roots lie deep in the realm of philosophy. Originally, psychology was defined as the study of the soul, spirit or mind but transitioned to more of a science in the late 1800s due to the work and focus of Wilhelm Wundt. Once psychology was established as a science separate from philosophy, the debate about how to describe and explain human behavior began! The early days of the field of psychology were focused on **Structuralism** and **Functionalism**. Structuralism was formally established by psychologist Edward Titchener who was a student of Wilhelm Wundt and seeks to analyze the mind in terms of the simplest definable components and then to find how those components fit together to form more complex experiences as well as how they correlate to physical events. The major tool of structuralism is introspection which helps to reduce normal conscious experience into basic elements. From a structuralist perspective, consciousness is an accumulation of all your experiences throughout your life. In response to structuralism, William James proposed an alternate perspective called functionalism. Functionalism was more concerned with the capability of the mind than with the process of thought. From a functionalist approach, mental life and behavior are considered in terms of active adaptation to the environment. Our brain is inherently neutral but produces different behaviors depending on the signal it receives. These two approaches are very commonly confused. One way that I always kept them separate was to remember that functionalism looks to the brain but structuralism looks more at the mind and consciousness.

© art4all/Shutterstock.com

Following structuralism and functionalism was **Gestalt Psychology**. Gestalt translates to mean form or pattern and looks at something in its entirety. From a Gestalt perspective, the mind is not just a compilation of different parts like in structuralism but rather operates on the premise that the whole is greater than (or other than) the sum of its parts. Complex stimuli are not just reducible to their parts in this perspective. Gestalt psychology is all about how our minds create entire concepts, not the individual pieces.

Following Gestalt psychology came the work of Sigmund Freud; probably the most well-known psychologist to this day. Before Freud, psychology focused largely on conscious experiences. Freud proposed a new idea that emphasized the importance of the unconscious mind and content that we are not normally aware of. Freud's work with patients convinced him that many nervous ailments were psychological instead of physiological. The main premise behind his **Psychodynamic Theory** was that behavior results from psychological factors that interact within the individual, often outside conscious awareness. His theories focus heavily on childhood experiences, intrapsychic conflict, and sexuality.

© Everett Historical/Shutterstock.com

The approaches mentioned so far focus mainly on mental aspects and things that cannot be seen or measured. In response to limitations and concerns about these approaches, **Behavioral Psychology** was formed and became the next leading paradigm. Until the beginning of the 20th century psychology was defined as the study of mental processes and the primary method of collecting data was introspection or self-observation. Behaviorism studies only observable and measurable behavior and marked a new approach. Some of the prominent psychologists in this approach were Ivan Pavlov, John Watson, and later, B.F. Skinner. Watson believed that you can't see or define consciousness any more than you can observe a soul and if you cannot locate or measure something it can't be the object of scientific study.

Another field that was growing in psychology was **Humanistic Psychology**; a more holistic approach to psychology developed by Abraham Maslow and later Carl Rogers which included a focus on feelings and yearnings. Maslow called this the 3rd force (beyond Freud's theories and behaviorism). The main components of this theory include the emphasis on human potential, the importance of love, belonging, self-esteem, self-expression, and self-actualization. In general, this branch of psychology focuses more on mental health instead of mental illness.

Cognitive Psychology, the study of mental processes such as attention, language, memory, perception, and thinking, gained popularity in the late 1950s and early 1960s. The "cognitive revolution" of the 1950s sought to bring psychology back to a focus on mental processes. Next came **Evolutionary Psychology** which seeks to identify which human traits are evolved adaptations or the product of natural selection. Evolutionary psychology is a theoretical approach to psychology that attempts to explain useful mental and psychological traits such as memory, perception, or language as the functional products of natural selection. In short, evolutionary psychology is focused on how evolution has shaped the mind and behavior. Very closely related to evolutionary psychology, the 1980s were dominated by a focus on biological factors and **Behavior Genetics**.

Evolutionary psychology focuses on how humans are alike because of our common biology and evolutionary history while behavioral genetics focuses on how we are different and diverse because of our differing genes and environment.

The 1990s saw another shift to focusing on **Cross-Cultural Psychology** which is a branch of psychology that looks at how social and cultural factors influence human behavior. Because we exist within a sea of people, cultural influences can have a powerful effect on us. **Culture** is the enduring behaviors, ideas, attitudes, values, and traditions shared by a group of people and passed from one generation to the next. While many aspects of human thought and behavior are universal, cultural differences can often lead to differences in how people think, feel, and act. Some cultures, for example, might stress individualism and the importance of personal autonomy. Other cultures, however, may place a higher value on collectivism and cooperation among members of the group. Such differences can play a powerful role in many aspects of life. Cross-cultural psychology strives to understand both the differences and similarities among people of various cultures throughout the world.

As we move into our current time, psychology is a blend of all the models that have existed over the years. The definition of **Psychology** as it stands today is the scientific study of behavior and mental processes; a little different than the soul spirit or mind! Currently the field of psychology is focused more on biological and evolutionary factors such as epigenetics, but psychology is an ever-changing discipline with new theories constantly being developed. There are several other theories within the field which we will discuss later in the class during the unit on personality.

Psychology's Big Question: Nature vs. Nurture?

Do our human traits (gender, IQ, sexual orientation, mental illness, etc.) develop through experience or do we come equipped with them? This is an ancient debate dating back to Plato and Aristotle. Some philosophers such as Plato and Descartes suggested that certain things are inborn, or that they simply occur naturally regardless of environmental influences. Other well-known thinkers such as John Locke believed in what is known as **Tabula Rasa**, which suggests that the mind begins as a blank slate; everything that we are and all of our knowledge is determined by our experience. There is no definitive answer to this question and most things are believed to be the result of a combination of both influences. We also often add another element to the analysis of behavior and mental processes by including the role of social and cultural influences which can directly impact our thoughts and behaviors.

The Subfields of Psychology

Just as there are many different models and ways of approaching psychology, there are many different subfields. **Developmental Psychology** examines human growth and change (physical, mental, and emotional) from the prenatal period through old age. Developmental psychologists are interested in the emotional, physical, and psychological changes and growth individuals experience over their lifespans. They work in schools, hospitals, clinics, and universities, as well as in private practices. **Biological Psychology** focuses on the biological basis of human behavior, thoughts, and emotions. It looks at the impact of genetics, brain structures, and neurotransmitters on our behavior and mental processes.

Another subfield is **Experimental Psychology** which focuses on conducting experiments on basic psychological processes including learning, memory, sensation, perception, thinking, motivation, and emotion with a primary goal of searching for answers to research questions. Experimental psychologists use scientific methods to collect data and perform research. They can work in varied settings, including universities, research centers, the government and private businesses. **Personality Psychology** studies the differences among individuals in traits such as sociability, conscientiousness, emotional stability, self-esteem, and openness to new experiences. Personality psychologists attempt to explain the factors

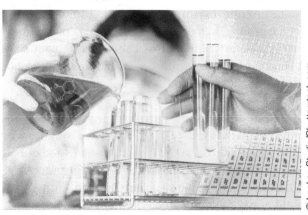

© Looker_Studio/Shutterstock.com

that have contributed to a person's personality and/or to describe the personality of an individual. **Industrial and Organizational Psychology** applies the principles of psychology to the workplace and is concerned with practical issues such as selecting and training personnel, improving productivity, and examining working conditions. **Social Psychology** examines how social influences are exerted and the effects they have. Social psychologists seek to understand and explain how the thoughts, feelings, and behavior of individuals are influenced by the actual, imagined, or implied presence of other people. **Abnormal Psychology** deals with the assessment, diagnosis, treatment, and prevention of psychopathology or mental illness.

Another large area of psychology's subfields deals with the clinicians of the field. **Clinical Psychologists** are interested primarily in the diagnosis, causes, and treatment of psychological disorders (such as depression or anxiety) while **Counseling Psychologists** are concerned mainly with the "normal" everyday problems of adjustment that most of us face at some point in life (such as coping with a troubled relationship or making a difficult decision). The work that these two groups perform tends to be similar but their training, background, and focus differ slightly. Closely related to these two professions is a **Psychiatrist**, a medical doctor who in addition to 4 years of medical training has completed 3 years of residency training in psychiatry specializing in diagnosis and treatment along with prescribing medications. The focus of a psychiatrist tends to be on

© Garneteyed/Shutterstock.com

medication and how well the patient is tolerating the side effects of drugs. While a psychiatrist might offer some traditional "therapy", they typically will refer clients to a counseling or clinical psychologist that they can work with while also being on medication.

Chart: Comparing Counseling Psychologists, Clinical Psychologists, and Psychiatrists

	Counseling	Clinical	Psychiatrist
Education	Master's Degree	PhD	Medical Degree
Focus	Every Day Problems	Psychological Disorders	Medication
Appointment Length	50 minutes	50 minutes	20 minutes
Yearly Salary (Average)	$62,000	$87,000	$144,000

The American Psychological Association

The American Psychological Association (APA) is the largest scientific and professional organization of psychologists in the United States. Educators, clinicians, students, researchers, and scientists studying psychology are all members of the APA. The American Psychological Association was first founded in 1892 at Clark University by a small group of thirty men but quickly grew in the following years with the first president of the APA being G. Stanley Hall. Currently the APA has over 115,000 members and more information about it can be found at www.apa.org.

© Panptys/Shutterstock.com

Truths and Myths about Psychology

There are several common myths about the field of psychology. In the chart below, I will provide some of the myths and then counter them with the corresponding fact.

Myths about Psychology	Facts about Psychology
Psychology is simply common sense	Psychology uses scientific methods
Psychology focuses only on abnormal behavior	Psychology studies both normal and abnormal behavior
Psychologists all share similar perspectives and approaches to analyzing information	Psychology embraces many different perspectives and has many different subfields.
Psychology is all old theories in textbooks	Psychology is ever-changing and all around you
If you want to work in the field of psychology, you want to be a therapist	Psychology is not just therapy; psychology offers a wide range of career options

Careers in Psychology

With such a great variety of subfields and areas of focus, there is a great range of careers within the field of psychology. Different levels of college degrees play a large role in dictating the available positions and many careers in psychology require graduate degrees or above. With an *Associates Degree,* some of the common career options include paraprofessional positions in state hospitals, correctional facilities, and other human service settings. *Bachelor's Degrees* open up the employment field a little bit with common jobs including working in correctional centers, assisting psychologists in mental health centers, research assistants, teaching psychology in high school, or working with the government or in business. With a *Master's Degree* and/or a *Doctorate* (Ph. D), careers typically include working in colleges and universities as professors and other capacities, researchers, educational psychologists, management and consulting positions, and counselors or therapists.

© Yuttana Jaowattana/Shutterstock.com

With my Associates Degree in psychology, I managed a Warehouse Music (way back before they all went out of business)! Having a degree gave me an advantage over people who did not have a degree. With my Bachelor's Degree, I managed an REI, worked at Starbucks, and was a teaching assistant. It wasn't until I entered a Master's Degree program that I actually started working within the field of psychology! During my Master's program, I was a therapeutic behavioral aid for children with behavioral disorders, a teaching assistant, and I still worked at Starbucks! Once I received my Master's Degree, the options were incredible. I was a Marriage and Family Therapist Intern working toward the required hours to take the licensing exam, I worked part-time as an EOPS counselor, I taught part-time at the college level, and also worked as an academic advisor.

In Popular Culture

Psychology and its many topics constantly find its way into popular culture. In films and television, you see everything from therapists to ESP to debunking myths to portrayals of mental illness. The examples are so vast that it would be nearly impossible to list them all! A few popular examples of television shows, movies, and texts include:

- *Lie to Me* (2009-2011) – a television show highlighting the effects of emotions on the body as it relates to lying.

- *Criminal Minds* (2005 to present) – a television show about profilers analyzing criminal minds and relating to forensic psychology.

- *My Strange Addiction* (2010-2015) – a television show about addictions to odd behaviors.

- *Hoarders: Buried Alive* (2009-2013) – a television show about obsessive compulsive disorder and hoarding behaviors.

- *Dexter* (2006-2013) – a television show about a character with antisocial personality disorder.

- *Bates Motel* (2013-2017) – a television show about Norman Bates and his battle with dissociative identity disorder.

- *The Biggest Loser* (2004-2016) – a television show about weight loss.

- *Curiosity* (2008-200) – a television show with the aim of uncovering the truths behind life's most challenging questions.

- *Mythbusters* (2003-2016) – a television show that conducts investigations using the scientific method to debunk common myths.

- *Girl, Interrupted (1999)* - a movie and book about a young woman with borderline personality disorder.

- *Shutter Island (2010)* – a movie featuring a portrayal of dissociative identity disorder.

- *The Soloist (2009)* - a movie about a man suffering from schizophrenia.

- *Black Swan* (2010) - a movie about a ballet dancer struggling with schizophrenia.

- *Silver Linings Playbook (2012)* - a movie featuring a main character suffering from bipolar disorder and several other characters also struggling with mental illness.

- *Split* (2016) – a movie about a character with 23 different personalities (dissociative identity disorder).

- *Psychology Today* – a popular psychology magazine featuring the latest mental health news and archives, as well as articles on dealing with anxiety, parenting, personality, and relationships.

- *American Psychologist* – a journal featuring selected articles on current issues in psychology; official journal of American Psychological Association (APA).

- *Scientific American Mind* – a quarterly magazine focusing on the workings of the mind and brain. Topics covered include autism, depression, schizophrenia, neuroscience, perception, brain development, intelligence, psychology and more.

- *In-Mind* - Online quarterly magazine for social psychology. Explores every day concerns such as love, motivation, or religion.

Psyched with Setmire

"A Brief History of Psychology"
https://www.youtube.com/watch?v=qwjNliVO2cA

In this lecture presentation video (adapted from lecture content from my PSY M01 classes), I will very briefly cover some of the big perspectives and paradigm shifts in the history of the field of Psychology. While entire courses could be taught on this topic, we will review it together in just a few minutes! I hope it is helpful.

Application: Degrees and Careers

As mentioned in the summary and in the textbook, there are countless careers and areas of emphasis available in the field of psychology. For more information about psychology majors, careers, salary, education requirements, or job responsibilities, here are some websites that you can visit!

© michaeljung/Shutterstock.com

- *American Psychological Association* (http://www.apa.org/) – the homepage for the American Psychological Association which has information about different educational and career paths, salary, requirements, and much more . . .

- *All Psychology Careers* (http://www.allpsychologycareers.com/) – this website contains information about schools, programs, careers, salaries, and becoming a licensed counselor.

- *Careers in Psychology* (http://careersinpsychology.org/) – this website has information about different areas of emphasis and the top schools offering those degree paths.

Key Terms

Structuralism: a school of thought that seeks to analyze the mind in terms of the simplest definable components and then to find how those components fit together to form more complex experiences as well as how they correlate to physical events.

Functionalism: a school of thought exploring mental life and behavior in terms of active adaptation to the environment; more concerned with the capability of the mind than with the process of thought.

Gestalt Psychology: a branch of psychology asserting that the mind is not just a compilation of different parts like in structuralism but rather operates on the premise that the whole is greater than (or other than) the sum of its parts.

Psychodynamic Theory: a branch of psychology that believes behavior results from psychological factors that interact within the individual, often outside conscious awareness; focus heavily on childhood experiences, intrapsychic conflict, and sexuality.

Behavioral Psychology: a branch of psychology that studies only observable and measurable behavior.

Humanistic Psychology: a branch of psychology that emphasizes human growth and potential; often called the 3rd force in psychology.

Cognitive Psychology: a branch of psychology that emphasizes the exploration of how we perceive, process, and remember information.

Evolutionary Psychology: the study of the evolution of behavior and the mind using principles of natural selection.

Behavior Genetics: the study of the relative power and limits of genetic and environmental influences on behavior.

Cross-Cultural Psychology: a branch of psychology that looks at how social and cultural factors influence human behavior.

Culture: the enduring behaviors, ideas, attitudes, values, and traditions shared by a group of people and passed from one generation to the next.

Psychology: the scientific study of behavior and mental processes.

Tabula Rasa: suggests that the mind begins as a blank slate; everything that we are and all our knowledge is determined by our experience.

Developmental Psychology: examines human growth and change (physical, mental, and emotional) from the prenatal period through old age.

Biological Psychology: focuses on the biological basis of human behavior, thoughts, and emotions.

Experimental Psychology: focuses on conducting experiments on basic psychological processes including learning, memory, sensation, perception, thinking, motivation, and emotion with a primary goal of searching to answers to research questions.

Personality Psychology: studies the differences among individuals in traits such as sociability, conscientiousness, emotional stability, self-esteem, and openness to new experiences.

Industrial and Organizational Psychology: applies the principles of psychology to the workplace and is concerned with practical issues such as selecting and training personnel, improving productivity, and examining working conditions.

Social Psychology: examines how social influences are exerted and the effects they have.

Abnormal Psychology: deals with the assessment, diagnosis, treatment, and prevention of psychopathology.

Clinical Psychologists: interested primarily in the diagnosis, causes, and treatment of psychological disorders (such as depression or anxiety).

Counseling Psychologists: concerned mainly with the "normal" everyday problems of adjustment that most of us face at some point in life.

Psychiatrist: a medical doctor who in addition to 4 years of medical training has completed 3 years of residency training in psychiatry specializing in diagnosis and treatment along with prescribing medications.

Outline

© Andrey_Kuzmin/Shutterstock.com

Introduction to the Chapter (Summary)

This chapter focuses on research strategies and the various ways that psychologists ask and answer questions. Most people rely on pseudoscientific approaches for asking and answering questions such as intuition and common sense. While intuition and common sense can provide us with valuable information, they can also result in errors such as the hindsight bias or overconfidence. In contrast to intuition, psychology relies on the scientific attitude (composed of curiosity, skepticism, and humility), critical thinking (not accepting arguments and conclusions blindly), and the scientific method when seeking to answer questions. The scientific method is an approach to knowledge that relies on collecting data, generating a theory to explain the data, producing testable hypotheses based on the theory, and then testing those hypotheses empirically. Using this method, scientists take facts and organize them into theories and then make hypotheses which are then tested empirically.

Psychologists use a variety of research methods to collect data systematically and objectively. One method is naturalistic observation which studies animal or human behavior in natural settings rather than in the laboratory. Another type of research method is the case study which involves intensive analysis of a single individual or just a few individuals of interest. Another commonly used research method is survey research where questionnaires or interviews are administered to a selected group of people; typically, a random sample. Correlational research is also used frequently and examines the naturally occurring relationship between two or more variables. Since correlations are naturally occurring it doesn't allow us to determine cause (the phrase to remember is "correlation does not imply or equal causation") but they can often be helpful despite this limitation. Finally, the experimental method is another technique in which an investigator deliberately manipulates selected events or circumstances and then measures the effects of those manipulations in subsequent behavior. There are several components within any given experimental design including the independent variable (what is manipulated), dependent variable (what is being measured), the experimental group (the group subjected to a change), and the control group (the group that is used for comparison).

In an effort to protect research participants, the American Psychological Association has put forth guidelines to ensure that participants' rights are not violated. In the past, these guidelines didn't exist and people often suffered psychological harm as a result of participation in research. Some examples of current guidelines include participation being voluntary, needing to get informed consent from participants, not exposing participants to harmful or dangerous procedures, not violating the privacy of participants, not performing unnecessarily cruel research on animals, and several others. There can be harsh consequences for violating these ethical standards including monetary fines, loss of a license, and even jail time depending on the severity of the infraction.

Imperfect Methods: Intuition, Common Sense, and Pseudoscience

Intuition and Common Sense

Most of us have an interest in asking and answering questions about our world. In a way, we are all like little scientists collecting data informally and analyzing our experiences in an effort to better understand and predict outcomes. For example, if a romantic relationship of three years fails, we might try to understand what specifically were the factors that lead to its downfall. Was it a certain personality type? Was it a lack of shared interests? That our partner was of a certain astrological sign that clearly wasn't compatible with ours? Hair color? The possible contributors are endless! While all (or some) of these factors might have played a role, the complete picture and accurate answer to the question of why the relationship

failed might be difficult to ascertain without a more detailed and formalized inquiry.

When the average person is trying to gather information, they rely on things like common sense, intuition, and personal experiences when drawing conclusions. **Common Sense** can be defined as what people would typically agree on or what can reasonably be expected without any need for debate. **Intuition** is commonly described as a gut feeling or an ability to sense or know immediately without reasoning. Our personal experiences would be just that; events and knowledge we have gained through our own experiences and learning. These resources can give us some valuable information but are not free from error or bias. One common tendency we have when relying on more subjective sources of information is the **Hindsight Bias**; the tendency to believe, after learning an outcome, that one would have foreseen it or that the event was predictable. This is sometimes called the "I knew it all along phenomenon" or even creeping determinism. Going back to our failed relationship example, committing the hindsight bias would have us saying "I knew it would fail all along". If this were truly the case, why did you date the person for three years? Another great example of the hindsight bias is the idea of the "Monday Morning Quarterback"; a person

© tmcphotos/Shutterstock.com

who, after the event (in this case a football game), offers advice or criticism concerning decisions made by others. Of course the call to go for it on fourth down seems like a mistake now or the decision to go for two points instead of one was a brilliant one because it paid off. It is always easier to think we knew the right or wrong course of action in retrospect.

The other mistake that we might be vulnerable to is **Overconfidence** or overestimating our knowledge based on personal experiences. Our experiences don't always generalize to everyone and the accuracy of our judgements is often lower than our confidence in our knowledge. The most common way in which overconfidence has been studied is by asking people how confident they are of specific beliefs they hold or answers they provide. For example, how confident are you that you could get to a certain location without directions or how confident are you that you could spell a certain word correctly? The data show that confidence systematically exceeds accuracy, implying that people are often more sure that they are correct than they deserve to be. In other words, we often think that we know more than we actually do!

© airdone/Shutterstock.com

Pseudoscience

The takeaway here is that sometimes our everyday thinking that relies on common sense and intuition, can lead us to incorrect conclusions. Both the hindsight bias and overconfidence can lead us to overestimate our personal experiences and intuition. When we rely too heavily on our intuition and personal experiences, and believing them to be reality and truth, we are approaching a closely related concept of pseudoscience. **Pseudoscience** is a body of knowledge, methodology, belief, or practice that is claimed to be scientific or is made to appear

scientific, but does not adhere to the scientific method or lacks a scientific status; sometimes known as "fringe science". Pseudoscience ignores the scientific method. It makes conclusions and then looks for facts to support the conclusions. In pseudoscience, there is no healthy skepticism about fantastic claims, in fact there is an enthusiasm to accept untested personal testimony as a public truth. Pseudoscience includes quite a few very common and popular topics such as the belief in astrology, the existence of aliens, extrasensory perception (ESP), ghosts, and many others. People are drawn to pseudoscience because it tends to be more approachable, interesting, and easier than real science which can be more time consuming to digest and is often difficult to understand. Pseudoscientific assertions and topics are often fascinating to contemplate but the misinformation that can be perpetuated can become harmful and even dangerous when people take items as facts, truths, or scientific when they are in fact only pseudoscientific in nature.

Box: Have Aliens Landed?

Aliens are one of the more common pseudo-scientific topics discussed in popular culture! There are thousands of "first-hand accounts" of UFO sightings, alien abductions, mysterious crop circles, and other phenomenon supporting the existence of aliens. Area 51, Roswell in New Mexico, the pyramids, and many other pieces of "evidence" are often cited by those who believe!

As we transition away from the ideas of intuition, common sense, and pseudoscience to start thinking more like a psychologist, hopefully a more skeptical mentality will emerge. Psychologists and scientists might ask questions like: How do we define alien? Are we talking about little green or gray men or just something foreign to us? What else could explain the creation of crop circles? What else could a UFO be? Might there be an agenda or motivation behind alien abduction stories? While logic would say that we aren't alone due to the sheer size of the universe, blindly accepting testimonials and anecdotal claims as truths, is firmly within the realm of pseudoscience!

Embracing a Scientific Attitude and Critical Thinking

What is Science?

Dating back to the work of Wilhelm Wundt in the 1800's, Psychology identifies as a science. Psychologists use the *science* of behavior and mental processes to better understand why people think, feel, and act the way that they do. In direct contrast to Pseudoscience, **Science**, coming from Latin *scientia*, meaning "knowledge", is a systematic enterprise that builds and organizes knowledge in the form of testable explanations and predictions about the universe. When describing science, a few key words come to mind:

- **Observable** – Science embraces that which is observable or able to be seen and measured.

- **Objective** – Rather than being subjective, science strives to be impartial and free of bias.

- **Empirical** – Science is dependent on evidence and data produced by observation.

- **Testable** – When we embrace a scientific mentality, we are able to generate and test hypotheses.

- **Falsifiable** – That something is "falsifiable" does not mean it is false, rather it means that *if* it is false, then observation or experiment will at some point demonstrate its falsehood. For example, the assertion that "all cakes have frosting" is falsifiable, because it is logically possible that a cake can be found that does not have frosting. Personally, that is not a cake I want to eat!

- **Replicable** – Scientific studies can be re-created and re-tested for accuracy.

- **Systematic** – Refers to organized and formalized inquiries.

- **Peer-Reviewed** – To help ensure accuracy, other experts in the field have reviewed the information.

A Scientific Attitude

Collectively, the words above capture the essence of science and are embraced by Psychologists who are striving to answer questions about behavior and mental processes. When we embrace science and a **Scientific Attitude**, we are defined by curiosity (a passion for exploration), skepticism (doubting and questioning) and humility (the ability to accept responsibility when wrong). Scientists are curious, constantly seeking to find answers and are hungry to know more. The curiosity is also fueled by skepticism of sources of information. Finally, humility permits us the opportunity to start over if we don't feel we have reached a satisfactory conclusion. For example, if I wanted to know more about a topic such as depression, I could conduct a basic web search for depression to gather data. Maybe the first site I click on will answer my questions about depression but I would want to look at who authored it. What is their level of expertise? Credentials? Do they have something to gain from the article or information being shared? I'm skeptical and maybe check several sites to make sure that the information is consistent. And if I don't get the answer I seek, I'm back to the drawing board and will start over; I'm ready to change my mind as the evidence changes.

Principles of Critical Thinking

Another important element of embracing science and a scientific attitude is **Critical Thinking**; not accepting arguments and conclusions blindly. When we think critically we examine assumptions, try to discern hidden values, evaluate evidence, and assess conclusions. The essence of thinking critically is not so much on answering questions but on questioning answers and not accepting information at face value. It involves questioning, probing, analyzing, and evaluating. Psychologists use critical thinking so that they aren't misled by research findings. Using critical thinking will not only allow you to evaluate information in this class but also information in the media, in conversations with others, and in all areas of your life allowing you to be a critical consumer of information. Let's look at *seven key principles of critical thinking*:

1. **Be Skeptical** – as we discussed earlier, always ask questions with an open mind before assuming something is true. Who conducted the study? Is there an agenda behind the study? What does the person publishing this research or data have to gain?

2. **Examine Definition of Terms** – it is important to have clearly defined terms so that we know what are we referring to in our studies. If an article claims that a product is successful, what do they mean by successful? Defining and clarifying terms might lead to different interpretations of results.

3. **Be Cautious in Drawing Conclusions from Evidence** – we must look at things more deeply than on the surface. For example, if a friend told you that they took Echinacea to treat their cold and that they felt better within a few days, should you run out and buy Echinacea? Maybe; but before you jump to conclusions, see the principle below!

4. **Consider Alternative Interpretations of Research Findings** – Considering the Echinacea example, what else besides the Echinacea could have explained your friend's recovery? Could it have been a matter of time, other medications, or the placebo effect from expecting it to work? Always look for other possible reasons that might explain research findings.

5. **Do Not Oversimplify** – be suspicious of single factor explanations! For example, after the Columbine shootings in Littleton, Colorado, experts came up with single factor explanations such as blaming listening to Marilyn Manson or wearing trench coats. Human behavior is generally more complicated than one factor so be sure to not make your explanations overly simplistic.

6. **Do Not Overgeneralize** – on the flip side, you also have to question claims that generalize to populations not studied. A good survey will have a random sample of participants and be inclusive of everyone of interest. Look at the sample for every research finding to evaluate if it can be applied to everyone or if it is only true of a small portion of the population.

7. **Avoid Making Belief Changes Based on the Findings from One Study** – replication of studies is extremely important and allows us to have confidence in our results. Finding one article to support an assertion might be easy enough but to ensure validity, it is always better to find multiple articles asserting the same thing. When I was in college, my dorm mate was taking a nutrition class where her instructor gave her an article about how horrible butter is for you to consume and that margarine is much healthier. When she shared this information with us, we promptly got rid of our butter and ran out to buy margarine (convinced that we were now making healthy choices in life). The next class session, her teacher gave her an article on why margarine is horrible for you and that you should eat butter instead! You can always find an article that will argue against the findings of another one so be sure to avoid changing your mind from one study alone!

Box: Being a Critical Consumer of Information: "Your Baby Can Read"

Several years ago, prior to becoming a parent of three little girls, I remember walking through a store and seeing a product called "Your Baby Can Read". One of my first thoughts when seeing this product, was thinking that it would be great to give my child an edge and to help him or her learn the very difficult task of learning to read that much faster and easier! I also remember thinking that babies should be free to be babies and not feel pressure to read faster than their baby peers! In the end, I didn't buy the product and knowing what I know now, I'm grateful!

© Kamila Starzycka/Shutterstock.com

(Continued)

For those of you who are unfamiliar with this product, Your Baby Can Read made promises of teaching babies to read even before they could walk using a system of picture cards and videos. The product made comments about not missing the window of opportunity to give your child a major advantage in life. Thousands of people purchased this product trying to give their children the lifelong success and advantages promised in the infomercial but recent interviews have caused this company to go out of business after debunking some of their claims and discovering that the "research" on which the product was based, was largely comprised parent testimonials and other non-scientific findings.

Here's where critical thinking and being a critical consumer of information comes into play! When you see products like this, think about them using a scientific lens. What else could explain the results? What does the company have to gain from the claims they are making? What is the evidence in support of the product? When you think critically and embrace a scientific attitude, you become a critical consumer of information!

The Scientific Method

Putting it all together, scientists (and psychologists) use the **Scientific Method** to ask and answer questions within the field. The scientific method is an approach to knowledge that relies on collecting data, generating a theory to explain the data, producing testable hypotheses based on the theory, and testing those hypotheses empirically. An integral part of the scientific method process is the concept of a **Fact**; an objective and verifiable observation or something that truly exists or has happened. Facts lead us to **Theories** or systematic explanations of a phenomenon. Theories organize known facts and allow us to predict new facts. Theories then allow us to form **Hypotheses** which are specific testable predictions or educated guesses derived from a theory. For example, if I were to take my pen, hold it up at eye level, and then drop it, it would fall to the floor. If people were watching this incredibly exciting event, they would be able to observe this occurrence as a fact. From the fact that my pen fell, I could create a theory of gravity and relativity to explain why my pen fell and the rate at which it fell (luckily someone has already done this for me)! From that theory, I could then make a prediction (hypothesis) that if I were to hold up my phone at eye level and drop it, that it would also fall!

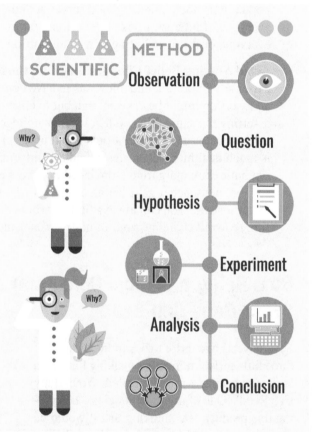

© Becris/Shutterstock.com

at eye level and drop it, that it would also fall! Though in the interest of not breaking my phone, it might be better if I chose a different object! If my phone or other object didn't fall or fell at a different rate, I might go back and change my theory or generate a new hypothesis and round and round this scientific method process goes until we answer the question at hand.

Box: Using the Scientific Method and Conducting Research – *The Nightmare Before Christmas*

In Tim Burton's *The Nightmare Before Christmas*, the main character, Jack Skellington, uses scientific methods to help understand Christmas. Jack is the king of Halloween Town and one day stumbles upon Christmas Town by accident. After singing a whole song asking himself "what's this?", Jack wishes to understand Christmas in hopes of recreating it in Halloween Town where he resides. To understand Christmas, he collects data (candy canes, holly berries, teddy bears, and so on) and takes them to his laboratory to conduct experiments on them. He also does what could be called a "literature review" and reads all the Christmas books he can find to better understand Christmas. In the end, Jack collects enough knowledge to create his own Halloween version of Christmas (which goes horribly wrong) and we have a fun popular culture example of using science and the scientific method to answer questions and gain knowledge!

Research Methods

Psychologists use a variety of research methods to collect data systematically and objectively. Each of the methods we will discuss has advantages and disadvantages and these methodologies are sometimes combined to create a more multifaceted research design. Science aims to describe, predict, and explain various phenomena and we can boil the various research methods down into three basic categories: descriptive methods, correlational methods, and experimental methods.

© Dusit/Shutterstock.com

Descriptive Methods

Descriptive Methods have the goal of describing situations or creating a snapshot of the people who take part in the study. One commonly used descriptive method is **Naturalistic Observation**. Naturalistic observation is the systematic study of animal or human behavior in a natural setting rather than in a laboratory or other artificial environment. Using this method, one might observe children playing on an outdoor playground and record the number of times someone goes down the slide or maybe the frequency of arguments over a piece of play equipment. You could observe typical behavior in a school, office, mall, or other defined setting and look for patterns or frequencies of whatever target behavior has been defined. A huge advantage of this type of research is that the recorded behavior is more natural and spontaneous than if it were to be studied in

© Vaclav Volrab/Shutterstock.com

a laboratory. When people know they are being observed, they tend to not act naturally! A few disadvantages of this approach are that you have to take behaviors as they come and that you often will not know the reasons or motivations behind behaviors since you aren't directly interacting with research participants. There is also the possibility that the expectations or biases of the observer might influence or distort the interpretation of what was observed; this is known as the **Observer Bias**.

Another method of investigation is the case study. **Case Studies** involve an intensive description and analysis of a single individual or even a small group of interest. Typically, information in a case study is gathered using a variety of methods such as observation and interviews. Case studies can potentially last for extended periods of time following people over the course of years to track developments. Because case studies employ multiple methods of data col-

© Maksim Kabakou/Shutterstock.com

lection, some argue that it is not a distinct research modality by itself. Despite this assertion, we typically reference it as they are widely used in the field of psychology. One advantage of the case study is that it can provide detailed information that can lead to great insights into a certain topic or population. A main disadvantage is that the information gathered might not be generalizable to larger groups or populations depending on the sample or topic studied.

© jannoon028/Shutterstock.com

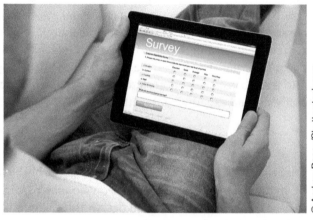

© Andrey_Popov/Shutterstock.com

One of the most popular methods in psychological research is the survey. In **Survey Research** a questionnaire or interview is administered to a selected group of people with the intent of gathering information about a specified topic or group of individuals. Surveys allow researchers to gather large amounts of information rather quickly and they are often quite easy to administer either as an oral interview in-person or on the phone, a written questionnaire filled out in-person or through the mail, and even as an online survey. When using a survey method, researchers are interested in a certain **Population**. The population is the complete collection to be studied; it contains all subjects of interest. Often it is impossible to reach every participant within a defined population so researchers will instead take a **Sample** or smaller part of the population of interest; a sub-collection selected from a population. For example, if we are interested in finding out the most common type of frosting used on cakes, then the statistical population is the set of all cakes that exist now, ever existed, or will exist in the future. Since in this case and many others it is impossible to observe the entire statistical population, due to time limitations, constraints of geographical accessibility, and maybe the extent of the researcher's resources, a researcher would instead observe a statistical sample from the population to attempt to make inferences about and learn something about the population as a whole. There is no chance that we would be able to access the entire population of cakes. I know this as a fact since I myself have eaten quite a few of them over the years thereby removing their ability to be studied! But again, it isn't actually necessary to survey an entire population, just a solid sample of that population.

When choosing a sample, it is important that psychologists and researchers use what is called a **Random Sample**. In a random sample, each member of a population has an equal chance of inclusion into the sample and is chosen at random. If the sample isn't random, then the information gathered and the conclusions made from the survey, may not be accurate. For example, let's say that I wanted to find out more about the average sexual behaviors of women such as how often they have sex, the average number of sexual partners, frequency of orgasms, and so on. If I only ask women that are prostitutes, the information that I gather will likely not apply to women in general! If I want to know about the sexual behaviors of women I need to ask a wide variety of women including different ages, ethnicities or racial backgrounds, sexual orientation, women who have taken vows of chastity and those who are prostitutes, those that are married and those that are single, and so on. The variety in a random sample gives me the richness I need to make accurate conclusions from the data collected.

© etraveler/Shutterstock.com

Correlational Methods

Another commonly used research method is **Correlational Research** in which psychologists examine the naturally occurring relationship between two or more variables. A **Variable** is anything that can have different values between different individuals or over time; an element, feature, or factor that is liable to vary or change. Literally anything can be a variable from GPA to the average number of hours spent studying to the number of hot dogs eaten on the Fourth of July and so on. In correlational research, psychologists select two or more variables and investigate the relationship between them. The strength of the relationship between two factors can be indicated by what is known as the **Pearson Product-Moment Correlation Coefficient** or for short, *Pearson's r*. *Pearson's r* is a measure of the linear correlation or strength between two variables and ranges in value between +1 and −1. This numerical indicator was developed by an English mathematician and biostatistician named Karl Pearson with roots going back to the ideas of Sir Francis Galton. Pearson contributed heavily to the field of statistics with his Pearson product moment correlation coefficient being one prominent example of his long-lasting contributions.

Correlation Coefficient
Shows strength & Direction of correlation

Strong ← Weak | Weak → Strong

| −1.0 | −0.5 | 0.0 | +0.5 | +1.0 |

Negative correlation   Zero   Positive correlation

Correlations can be classified as negative, positive, and zero in nature and can be represented not only numerically but also in the form of a graph as seen in the image to the right. **Negative Correlation** is a relationship between two variables in which one variable increases as the other decreases; sometimes referred to as an inverse relationship. For example, if a psychologist was examining the relationship

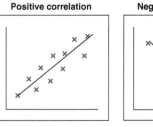

Positive correlation

As one variable increases, the other variable increases (they move in the same direction).

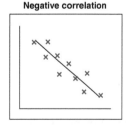

Negative correlation

As one variable increases, the other variable increases (they move in different direction).

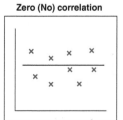

Zero (No) correlation

There appears to be no connection (correlation) between the two variables; the data points are random.

between time spent watching television and GPA, it might be reasonable to find that as the number of hours watching television goes up, GPA goes down. A negative correlation would have a Pearson's r value that is negative and the stronger the relationship, the closer the number would be to -1. So, a correlation of -.90 would be stronger than a correlation of -.25. A **Positive Correlation** is a relationship between two variables in which they both move in the same direction; as one increases, so does the other. One example of a positive correlational relationship might be that as the number of cakes eaten by an individual increases, so does their weight. Or as class attendance increases, so does exam scores. Positive correlations have a Pearson's r value that is positive or greater than zero. A correlation of .85 would be stronger than a correlation of .35 since it is closer to positive one on the -1 to +1 scale. A **Zero Correlation** would indicate that there is no relationship between two variables. Typically, there will be some relationship between any two factors but the closer that r is to zero, the weaker the strength of that correlation. For example, it seems logical to propose that there is likely little to no relationship between the number of moldy containers in your refrigerator and the number of packs of cigarettes smoked in one day.

Correlation Does Not Imply Causation

I remember in my first psychology statistics class learning the phrase "correlation does not equal or imply causation". At the time, I didn't really know what that meant but as I took more psychology and statistics courses, I began to understand how headlines and many popular research studies appearing in the media are often misleading. Recently I saw the headline "Eating Pizza Cuts Cancer Risk". Reading that headline implies eating more pizza reduces your chances of getting cancer. I wish this were true as it would justify all the pizza I eat! Maybe there is some truth to this statement and maybe not. Remember our discussion earlier about being a critical consumer of information and thinking critically? Many media headlines suggest causal relationships when, upon closer reading of the article itself, one finds that the research was correlational in nature, and the headline is not justified which is likely the case with the pizza and cancer article.

© THPStock/Shutterstock.com

© g-stockstudio/Shutterstock.com

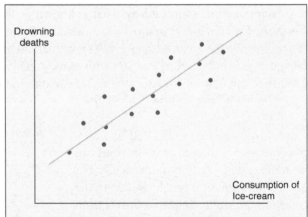

Correlation does not equal or imply causation. Just because there is a relationship present between two variables, it doesn't mean that they cause each other. Just because ice cream sales and drownings have a strong positive correlation doesn't mean that eating ice cream will cause you to drown or make you more prone to drowning. It is possible, and likely, that there are other factors in play like for example, weather! When it is hot outside, people are more likely to eat ice cream and are also more likely to go swimming which might increase the number of drowning incidents. So maybe ice cream consumption doesn't connect to drowning as much as weather or time of year. The examples of this are endless! Many headlines suggest a causal relationship between two variables but unfortunately, the headlines of articles in the popular media often misrepresent the research on which they are based. Always remember to be a critical consumer of information!

Experimental Method

The **Experimental Method** is a technique in which an investigator deliberately manipulates selected events or circumstances and then measures the effects of those manipulations on subsequent behavior. In an experiment, researchers identify and define key variables and then scientifically test a hypothesis (or hypotheses) through manipulating the variables involved and then collecting data. Researchers attempt to control the various variables involved, measure outcomes and manipulations objectively, and this allows us to imply causal relationships. Experiments are a powerful research tool for this very reason; they can allow us to draw conclusions about cause and effect relationships whereas other methods (like correlational research that we just discussed) cannot. On the other hand, artificial lab settings might influence subjects and change their natural behaviors along with possibly being difficult or expensive to set-up.

© venimo/Shutterstock.com

Experimental designs vary widely and can get quite complicated but it is safe to say that on a very basic level, each experiment contains a few different elements and variables that need to be furthered discussed and defined. If we keep it simple, in any experiment, there will be an **Independent Variable** and a **Dependent Variable**. The independent variable in an experiment is the item or variable that the experimenter manipulates to test its effects on the dependent variable. The dependent variable is the variable that is being measured to see how it is changed or affected by the manipulations in the independent variable. For example, if I am interested in how caffeine consumption affects a person's ability to sleep, caffeine

© TypoArt BS/Shutterstock.com

would be my independent variable and the ability to sleep would be my dependent variable. A little trick that I learned long ago in a research methods class is to ask the following sentence when trying to figure out which variable is which: *What is the effect of the IV on the DV?* Then replace the words independent variable and dependent variable with the actual items in the experiment and you have your factors! So, if I ask: What is the effect of caffeine on sleep? Caffeine would be my independent variable and sleep the dependent one; it is that simple!

Another designation to be made in an experimental design has to do with who gets the change in the independent variable versus who will serve as a baseline for comparison. In an experiment, the **Experimental Group** is the group subjected to the independent variable; it is the group that receives the variable being tested. The **Control Group** is the group in an experiment that does not receive the variable being tested or in other words, is not subjected to a change in the independent variable. A control group allows for direct comparison with the experimental group because it isolates out the independent variable's effects on the experiment. While not every experiment has a control group and some experiments might have more than just two groups, it is common to see these elements

appear in an experimental design. Revisiting the previously given example of how caffeine affects sleep, I could divide my experiment participants into two groups; one group would drink a cup of caffeinated coffee prior to going to bed and the other group will drink a cup of decaffeinated coffee prior to going to bed. The group that drinks the caffeine would be the experimental group and the group that does not get caffeine would be the control group. I can then make comparisons between the amount of sleep of the participants in the two groups and possibly attribute the differences in scores to the effects of caffeine.

Box: Schachter's Affiliation Experiment

In the 1950's, Stanley Schachter conducted an experiment examining the effects of anxiety and fear on affiliation. In his experiment, Schachter divided participants into two groups and told both groups that they were participating in a study on the physiological effects of electric shock. One group of female participants were told that they would be receiving painful but harmless electric shocks (no permanent damage) while the other group of female participants were told that they would be given painless electrical shocks. Schachter then told both groups that they would have to wait for ten minutes prior to the procedure while everything was getting setup in the room and that during the ten-minute wait, they could choose to wait either with the other participants or alone. In reality, no shocks were to be given; the threat of shocks was just to instill fear or anxiety. The results showed that a significantly higher number of women in the group of high fear (those who were going to receive the painful shocks), chose to wait with other women while those in the low fear group (those who would receive the painless shocks) chose to wait alone.

Can you figure out the variables and the groups? If you ask yourself, what is the effect of the IV on the DV then hopefully you could come up with the independent variable being fear/anxiety and the dependent variable being affiliation. The experimental group was the one with the high fear conditions and the control group would be the low fear condition!

Ethical Concerns and Guidelines

When conducting research, psychologists have a moral and ethical obligation to protect participants. With that being said, ethical guidelines are complicated and rarely have simple black and white answers. It is important to protect the rights of participants and the integrity of the research but it is also important to consider the costs of not conducting the research. Maybe there is a potential for harm in the study but the

knowledge to be gained far outweighs the potential damages or harm that could be caused. These are the ethical considerations that are debated by review boards and psychologists who work to uphold ethical concerns and guidelines. It is important to note that these guidelines have not always been in existence and several studies such as John Watson's conditioning of "Little Albert", Stanley Milgram's study of obedience, and the Stanford Prison Experiment were conducted prior to their implementation and would be questionable if not extremely unlikely to be approved today. These experiments and several others, lead to the development of ethical guidelines by the American Psychological Association that protect the rights of those that participate in research.

One basic but key ethical guideline is that participation in research should always be voluntary. Those who engage in a research study as a participant should never be coerced into contributing, should have the freedom to withdraw at any time, and should always be informed in advance of any aspects of the study that might influence their willingness to participate. Letting research participants know about any potential risks involved in participating in the study is known as **Informed Consent**. This is another basic but crucial ethical guideline but it can be a little bit tricky as in some cases, revealing the full nature of the study might directly impact the results. Deceiving participants is allowed under certain circumstances but if there is deception of participants involved in the study, the researcher must correct any misunderstandings as soon as possible which is known as debriefing.

Another ethical guideline involves not violating a participant's right to privacy. Maintaining **Confidentiality** or ensuring that information acquired during the study must be kept confidential or secret, helps to protect the research participant. It is also required that prior to conducting studies, approval must be gained from host institutions or reviewed by committees. When host institutions or committees review potential research projects, they are looking for the benefits and drawbacks involved in the study and weighing both sides before deciding if the study is appropriate to be conducted. Other ethical guidelines include not exposing participants to harmful or dangerous research procedures, that all results should be reported fully and accurately, and that harmful or painful procedures imposed on animals must be thoroughly justified in terms of the knowledge to be gained. Violating these ethical guidelines can lead to severe penalties including losing a license, monetary fines, loss of status in the psychological community, and even imprisonment depending on the nature of the violation.

In Popular Culture

- **The Demon-Haunted World: Science as a Candle in the Dark** by Carl Sagan. This book aims to encourage people to embrace skeptical thinking as it explains methods to help distinguish between ideas that are considered valid science and ideas that can be considered pseudoscience.

- **Lost Tapes** - A television series on Animal Planet that explores encounters with some of the mysterious creatures that science doesn't recognize.

- **Mythbusters** - A television show on the Discovery Channel that uses a scientific attitude to test the validity of rumors, myths, movie scenes, adages, Internet videos and news stories.

- **Curiosity** - A television show on the Discovery Channel that uses a spirit of curiosity and discovery to uncover the truths behind life's most challenging questions.

Psyched with Setmire

"Correlation versus Causation" (11:52)

https://www.youtube.com/watch?v=bZSy5ymQC4E

In this presentation, I have adapted a lecture from my Introduction to Psychology class reviewing the topic of correlation vs. causation. I will define correlational research, variables, and Pearson's r and then explore how the media can use correlation to manipulate our conclusions via headlines such as "Pirates and Global Warming", "Ice Cream and Drowning", "Pizza Cuts Cancer Risk", and a few others. I hope you find this video helpful in understanding this somewhat challenging concept in Psychology and that you enjoy the pop culture and food references throughout the lesson!

Application

Be a critical consumer! The headline "Eating Chicken on the Bone Makes Kids More Aggressive" permeated the Psychological community after a study performed by researchers at Cornell University found that kids who eat chicken on the bone tended to be more aggressive than kids who ate cut up chicken. The experiment contained twelve children between the ages of 6-10 who were served either chicken on the bone or chicken that was pre-cut into small bite sized pieces. The findings were that children who ate their chicken on the bone were twice as likely to disobey adults (the most common form of disobedience was noncompliance with requests) and also to be aggressive toward other children. These findings suggest a connection between how children eat and how they behave which could have implications for developmental psychologists as well as for educators and parents.

© Jacek Chabraszewski/Shutterstock.com

Using a scientific attitude and critical thinking, how can you apply what you have learned to this study? Hint: *Think critically about correlation versus causation, the number of children in the study, and what else could possibly explain the findings!*

Key Terms

Common Sense: what people would typically agree on or what can reasonably be expected without any need for debate.

Intuition: commonly described as a gut feeling; an ability to sense or know immediately without reasoning.

Hindsight Bias: the tendency to believe, after learning an outcome, that one would have foreseen it or that the event was predictable.

Overconfidence: overestimating our knowledge based on personal experiences.

Pseudoscience: a body of knowledge, methodology, belief, or practice that is claimed to be scientific or is made to appear scientific, but does not adhere to the scientific method or lacks a scientific status; sometimes known as "fringe science".

Science: a systematic enterprise that builds and organizes knowledge in the form of testable explanations and predictions about the universe.

Scientific Attitude: embracing a mentality of curiosity, skepticism, and humility.

Critical Thinking: not accepting arguments and conclusions blindly.

Scientific Method: an approach to knowledge that relies on collecting data, generating a theory to explain the data, producing testable hypotheses based on the theory, and testing those hypotheses empirically.

Fact: an objective and verifiable observation or something that truly exists or has happened.

Theory: a systematic explanation of a phenomenon.

Hypothesis: specific testable predictions or educated guesses derived from a theory.

Descriptive Methods: research methods with the goal of describing situations or creating a snapshot of the people who take part in the study.

Naturalistic Observation: the systematic study of animal or human behavior in a natural setting rather than in a laboratory or other artificial environment.

Observer Bias: the phenomenon where the expectations or biases of the observer might influence or distort the interpretation of what was observed.

Case Study: a research method involving an intensive description and analysis of a single individual or even a small group of interest.

Survey Research: a research method in which a questionnaire or interview is administered to a selected group of people with the intent of gathering information about a specified topic or group of individuals.

Population: the complete collection to be studied; it contains all subjects of interest.

Sample: a smaller part of the population of interest, a sub-collection selected from a population.

Random Sample: each member of a population has an equal chance of inclusion into the sample.

Correlational Research: a research method in which psychologists examine the naturally occurring relationship between two or more variables.

Variable: is anything that can have different values between different individuals or over time; an element, feature, or factor that is liable to vary or change.

Pearson Product Moment Correlation Coefficient (Pearson's r): a measure of the linear correlation or strength between two variables; ranges in value between $+1$ and -1.

Negative Correlation: a relationship between two variables in which one variable increases as the other decreases; sometimes referred to as an inverse relationship.

Positive Correlation: a relationship between two variables in which they both move in the same direction; as one increases, so does the other.

Zero Correlation: indicates that there is no relationship between two variables.

Experimental Method: a research method in which an investigator deliberately manipulates selected events or circumstances and then measures the effects of those manipulations on subsequent behavior.

Independent Variable: in an experiment, the item or variable that the experimenter manipulates to test its effects on the dependent variable.

Dependent Variable: in an experiment, the variable that is being measured to see how it is changed or affected by the manipulations in the independent variable.

Experimental Group: in an experiment, the group subjected to the independent variable; it is the group that receives the variable being tested.

Control Group: in an experiment, the group that does not receive the variable being tested; the group not subjected to a change in the independent variable.

Informed Consent: an ethical guideline involving letting participants know about any potential risks involved in participating a research study.

Confidentiality: an ethical guideline that requires the researcher to keep secret all information related to a research participant.

Outline

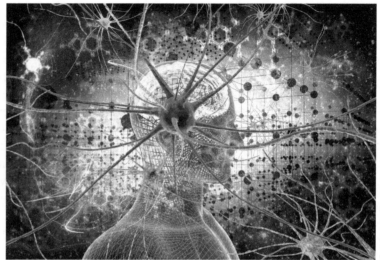

© vitstudio/Shutterstock.com

Introduction to the Chapter (Summary)

The focus of this chapter is on biological psychology. A critical part of our psychobiology are neurons; individual cells that are the smallest unit of the nervous system and allow us to react with speed and complexity to our environment. Neurons vary in size and shape but all are specialized to receive and transmit information. The nervous system also contains a vast number of glial cells which perform quite a few supportive functions. There are three main types of neurons: sensory neurons, motor neurons, and interneurons which all work together to take in information and carry out actions. Neurons communicate in a simple yes-no, on-off language consisting of electrochemical impulses. The electrical portion of communication is controlled by electrically charged particles called ions which exist both inside and outside of a neuron. A change in the electrical charge of a neuron will cause it to fire generating an action potential. Neurons are separated by a tiny gap called the synapse. For the neural impulse to move on to the next neuron it must cross the space between neurons; this transfer is made by chemicals called neurotransmitters released from the terminal buttons. Neurotransmitters make up the chemical portion of electrochemical communication.

We have several systems within our body that allow us to take the information gathered by our neurons, process it, and then conduct the required actions. The Central Nervous System includes the brain and spinal cord and the Peripheral Nervous System consists of nerves that connect the brain and spinal cord to every other part of the body. There are two main parts to the peripheral nervous system: The Somatic Nervous System and the Autonomic Nervous System which further divides into the Sympathetic Nervous System and the Parasympathetic Nervous System. The Endocrine System also plays a key role in helping to coordinate and integrate complex psychological reactions. Endocrine glands release hormones which help to regulate bodily activities, activate behaviors, and influence mood. Hormones are carried throughout the body by the bloodstream and therefore travel slower than neurotransmitters.

The brain is the command center of the nervous system and is the most complex organ in the human body. We often talk about the brain in terms of three main divisions including the hindbrain, midbrain, and forebrain which together are responsible for our personality, memories, movements, and how we perceive and interact with the world. The brain is also commonly discussed as being divided into a left and right brain with the primary connection between the two being the corpus callosum which allows the two hemispheres to work as a coordinated unit. Each hemisphere has a set of tasks that it controls and despite popular opinion, research does not support the idea of a left right brain difference. We know an incredible amount about the brain due to the availability of several brain imaging techniques such as EEGs, CAT scans, MRIs, and PET scans along with cases of damage to the brain. Luckily, we are born with an amazing plasticity meaning that our brain responds to changes in the environment and does so in a feedback loop; experiences leads to changes in the brain, which facilitates new learning, which leads to further change. The brain also has an incredible ability to compensate for and persevere in cases of injury as we saw in the famous case of railroad foreman Phineas Gage.

Biological Psychology

Biological Psychology (sometimes referred to as behavioral neuroscience or psychobiology) involves the scientific study of the links between biological and psychological processes. Biological psychology examines the physiological bases of behavior including genetic, hormonal, neural, and anatomical influences. Every thought, feeling, and behavior that we carry out is influenced and controlled by biological elements so it is important to understand how these various structures work together within our system to make

© Lightspring/Shutterstock.com

it all possible. We will begin by looking at the basic building blocks of the nervous system which allows us to react with speed and complexity to the events around us and then build from there by discussing the various systems that work together within our body along with the brain and its major structures and components.

Neurons

What Are Neurons?

Neurons are individual cells that are the smallest unit of the nervous system. Neurons are often called the building blocks of the nervous system as the brain of an average human contains as many as 100 billion neurons with billions more being found in other parts of the nervous system. Neurons vary in size and shape but all are specialized to receive and transmit information. Neurons respond to stimuli (such as touch, sights, sounds, and so on), conduct impulses, and communicate with each other via electrochemical impulses.

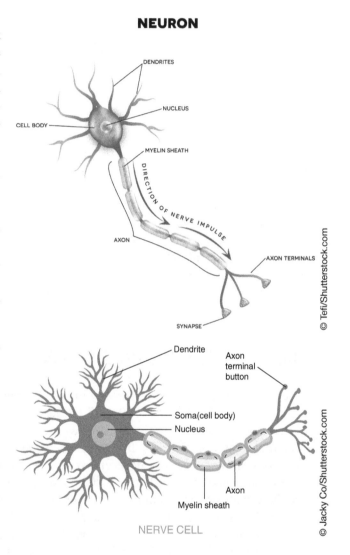

While there isn't necessarily a typical neuron since there are several different types of neurons within our system, there are several key structures that play a crucial role in allowing neurons to function and communicate with each other. Each neuron possesses a **Cell Body** or soma which is the life support center of a cell. This spherical part of a neuron contains the **Nucleus** which can be thought of like the command or administrative center of a cell that contains our chromosomes and genetic information. Branching out from the cell body are the **Dendrites** which are the short bushy branch-like fibers that pickup incoming messages from adjoining cells. Once a message is received by the dendrites and passes through the cell body, it continues along the **Axon**. Axons are the long slender fibers extending from the cell body that carry away outgoing messages. Axons can be myelinated or unmyelinated depending on the type or function of the neuron. If an axon is myelinated, it is covered by a **Myelin Sheath** or a fatty white covering that looks like a string of microscopic sausages. The myelin sheath has two main functions: 1) providing insulation so that signals from adjacent neurons do not interfere with each other and 2) increasing the speed at which signals are transmitted. As a message nears the end of an axon, it reaches what are referred to as the terminal branches. These terminal or end branches contain **Terminal Buttons** which are little structures at the ends of the branches that extend from axons and are responsible for helping to carry messages on to neighboring neurons via a process we will discuss shortly.

Types of Neurons

As mentioned previously, there are multiple types of neurons that exist within our system and work together to make our actions possible. One way of classifying neurons is by the number of extensions that come out of the cell body; in other words, categorizing them by shape. According to this system of classification, neurons can be unipolar, bipolar, pseudounipolar, and multipolar. Unipolar neurons have one primary projection that serves as both the dendrites and axon, bipolar neurons have two processes extending from the cell body, pseudounipolar neurons have two axons with one extending toward the spinal cord and the other toward the skin or muscle, and multipolar neurons have multiple processes extending from the cell body.

Neurons can also be classified based on their function or the direction that they send information. Looking at this method of classification there are three different types of neurons: sensory (afferent) neurons, motor (efferent) neurons, and interneurons (association neurons). **Sensory (Afferent) Neurons** carry messages from the various sense organs toward the spinal cord and brain. **Motor (Efferent) Neurons** carry messages away from the spinal cord and brain to the muscles and glands and **Interneurons (Association Neurons)** carry messages from one neuron to another (between sensory and motor neurons) helping to facilitate the

· **Basic Neuron Types** ·

© Silbervogel/Shutterstock.com

Box: ALS Ice Bucket Challenge

ALS was first discovered in 1869 by French neurologist Jean-Martin Charcot, but it wasn't until 1939 that Lou Gehrig brought national and international attention to the disease (which is why it is sometimes referred to as Lou Gehrig's disease). **Amyotrophic Lateral Sclerosis** (ALS) is a progressive neurodegenerative disease that affects nerve cells in the brain and the spinal cord. Motor neurons reach from the brain to the spinal cord and from the spinal cord to the muscles throughout the body (as we just discussed). The progressive degeneration of the motor neurons in ALS eventually leads to their death and once the motor neurons die, the ability of the brain to initiate and control muscle movement is lost. With voluntary muscle action progressively affected, patients in the later stages of the disease may become totally paralyzed.

© Marcos Mesa Sam Wordley/Shutterstock.com

In the summer months of 2014, the ALS Ice Bucket Challenge was started as a social movement to raise awareness and money for ALS. The movement is thought to have been inspired by a man named Pete Frates who challenged a wide range of people via social media to film themselves pouring a bucket of ice water on their heads, post it on social media, and then to nominate others to do the same. The nominated parties typically had 24 hours to comply or forfeit by way of a charitable financial donation to ALS. Thousands participated in the challenge helping to raise support both financially and in terms of a greater awareness for the disease.

whole process of communication. Let's take the example of some really hot freshly baked chocolate chip cookies and an over-excited person to see how these three types of neurons work together! If someone were to try to take a chocolate chip cookie that just came out of the oven off the cooking tray too early, sensory neurons would register the heat from the cookie and send that message away from the sensory receptors on the fingers back to the spinal cord and brain. Once the message reached the spinal cord and brain, motor neurons would carry the messages away from the central nervous system to the muscles allowing the hand to swiftly retract and sadly for the cookie to be dropped or put down. Interneurons would help to facilitate this whole communication process. The three types of neurons work closely together to allow us to react swiftly and accurately to our environment and hopefully, to eventually eat that chocolate chip cookie once it has cooled down!

Glial Cells

The nervous system also contains a vast number of **Glial Cells** sometimes referred to as neuroglia or even just glia. Glial comes from the Greek word meaning "glue" which reflects the 19th century notion that these cells held the nervous system together in some way; that glial cells were like the glue of the nervous system. While this notion hasn't been shown to be true, the word has endured over the years and is still used today.

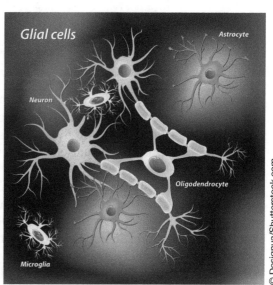

There are a vast number of glial cells in the brain and it is currently estimated that there are about 10-50 times more glial cells than neurons! Glial cells help to maintain homeostasis, they form the myelin sheath, and provide support for neurons by helping to hold them in place, provide nourishment, and remove waste. Glial cells also help prevent harmful substances from passing from the bloodstream into the brain by helping to support the blood brain barrier. The blood brain barrier protects the brain from "foreign substances" in the blood that may injure the brain, protects the brain from hormones and neurotransmitters in the rest of the body, and maintains a constant environment for the brain. So, while glial cells might not be the "glue cells" that we once thought, they do in fact have quite a few supportive functions!

The Neural Impulse

How Neurons Communicate

Neurons exist in clusters or networks and must communicate with each other in order to accomplish their goals. When a neuron is stimulated by a signal from one of our sense organs or from a neighboring neuron, it will transmit a message by firing an impulse called an **Action Potential** that will travel from the cell body, down the axon, and to the terminal buttons that will then release neurotransmitters to stimulate the next neuron. Neurons speak to each other in a simple yes-no, on-off language consisting of *electrochemical impulses*. When a neuron is resting, the semipermeable membrane surrounding the cell forms a partial barrier between the fluids that are inside and outside the neuron. Both solutions (inside and outside) contain Ions which are electrically charged particles. **Ions** make up the electrical element of the electrochemical communication process that occurs both within and between neurons. Sodium and potassium are two of the most common and important positive ions in our system while chloride is the most prominent negatively charged ion. When a neuron is not sending a signal, it is "at rest" which we refer to as the **Resting Potential**; the inside of the neuron is negative in electrical charge relative to the outside of the neuron.

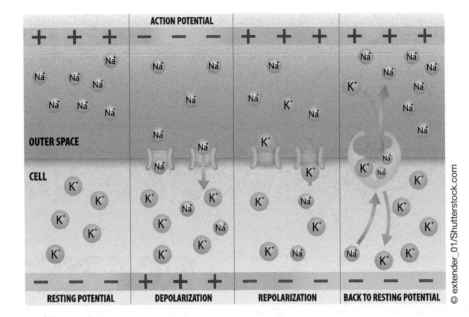

When a small area on the cell membrane is stimulated by an incoming message, pores or small channels in the membrane at the stimulated area open allowing a sudden inflow of positively charged sodium ions to flood inside. This process is called **Depolarization**. As a result of this process, the inside of the neuron becomes positively charged relative to the outside which sets off a chain reaction; more points on the cell membrane open allowing even more sodium ions to flow in. This process continues along the entire length of the neuron and the resulting electrical change creates the previously mentioned action potential also known as the firing of a nerve cell.

For a neuron to fire, the change in the electrical composition must exceed a certain minimum called the **Threshold of Excitation.** Just as a light switch requires a minimum amount of pressure to be flipped on, neurons require a certain electrical threshold to be crossed for the neuron to fire. Neurons react according to the **All-or-None Law** which dictates that the action potential of a neuron does not vary in strength; either the neuron fires at full strength or it does not fire at all. Again, going back to the light switch analogy, the light is either on or off; there is no middle ground.

The Synapse and Neurotransmitters

To complicate things a little bit, neurons are not directly connected to each other but rather are separated by a tiny gap called the **Synapse**. The synapse or synaptic cleft as it is sometimes called is the junction or narrow space

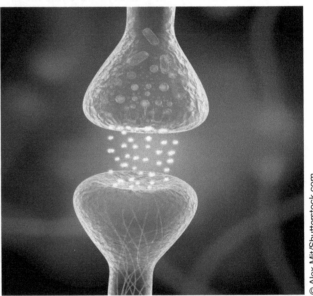

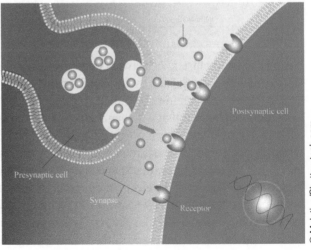

between the axon terminals of one neuron and the dendrites and cell body of the next neuron. For the neural impulse to move on to the next neuron it must somehow cross the synaptic space and this is where the chemical portion of the electrochemical communication process comes into play. When the action potential reaches the terminal buttons, it triggers the release of chemical messengers that will allow the neural impulse to be transferred across the synapse; these chemical messengers are called **Neurotransmitters.** Neurotransmitters are released by the synaptic vesicles and travel across the synapse to chemically stimulate the adjacent neuron by causing the channels in the receiving site to unlock thereby allowing positively charged ions to flow in. Once the neurotransmitter reaches the other side of the synapse, it connects to **Receptor Sites** which are locations on a receptor neuron into which a specific neurotransmitter fits like a key into a lock. The specificity of receptor sites ensures that the neurotransmitters don't randomly stimulate other neurons. Once a neurotransmitter's job is complete, it detaches from the receptor site and in most cases, is either reabsorbed into the axon terminals to be used again in a process called **Reuptake**, is broken down and recycled to make new neurotransmitters, or is disposed of by the body as waste. There are dozens of different neurotransmitters within our system and each one plays a role in certain typical actions, behaviors, and processes along with having a prominent influence on our system when they are out of balance; see the chart below for brief descriptions of their typical functions and what they influence when they are malfunctioning.

Examples of Neurotransmitters

Neurotransmitter	Function	Examples of Malfunctions
Acetylcholine (Ach)	Enables muscle action, learning, and memory.	Ach producing neurons deteriorate in Alzheimer's disease.
Dopamine	Influences movement, learning, attention, and emotion.	Excess dopamine receptor activity is linked to schizophrenia.
Serotonin	Affects mood, hunger, sleep, and arousal.	Low levels of Serotonin are linked to depression.
Norepinephrine	Helps control alertness and arousal.	Low levels can lead to depressed mood.
gamma-Aminobutric acid (GABA)	A major inhibitory neurotransmitter.	Low levels are linked to seizures, tremors, and insomnia.
Glutamate	A major excitatory neurotransmitter; involved in memory.	Oversupply can lead to migraines and seizures.

The Nervous System

As we discussed previously, neurons do not exist in isolation but rather in bunches that communicate with each other making up our nervous system. The body is made up of complex networks of **Nerves** that work together allowing messages to be carried to and from the brain and spinal cord to different parts of the body. A nerve is an enclosed, cable-like bundle of axons that provides a common pathway for electrochemical impulses. There are countless nerves within our body constantly registering and sending information to and from the brain.

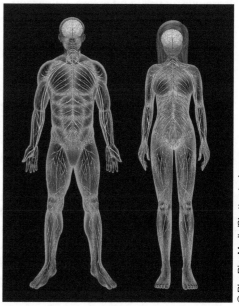

© BlueRingMedia/Shutterstock.com

Our nervous system contains two main divisions, the **Central Nervous System** and the **Peripheral Nervous System**. The Central Nervous System includes the brain and spinal cord which together contain more than 90% of the body's neurons. We will get to the brain shortly! **The Spinal Cord** is our communication superhighway connecting the brain to most of the rest of the body. It is a complex cable of neurons that runs down the spine made up of soft, jelly-like bundles of axons, wrapped in insulation (myelin) and surrounded and protected by the bones in the spine.

Box: Spinal Cord Injury and Paralysis

Knowing what you now know about the function of the brain and spinal cord in relaying information to the body in response to information from the sensory neurons, you can have a better understanding of the impact of spinal cord injury on movement and behavior. The spinal cord is the communication superhighway connecting the brain to most of the rest of the body. The spinal cord allows motor messages from the brain to be carried out by the muscles and sensations from the body to be processed by the brain. When someone has an accident or physical trauma damaging the spinal cord, paralysis from the point of injury downward can occur resulting in the inability to have sensation or movement below the point of trauma. One example of such an injury was the case of Christopher Reeve (the actor made famous for his role as Superman) who became a quadriplegic after being thrown from a horse in an equestrian competition in Virginia. Reeve suffered a cervical spinal injury that paralyzed him from the waist down which caused him to require a wheelchair and breathing apparatus for the rest of his life.

© 360b/Shutterstock.com

© Featureflash Photo Agency/Shutterstock.com

The Peripheral Nervous System consists of nerves that connect the brain and spinal cord to every other part of the body, carrying messages back and forth between the central nervous system and the sense organs, muscles, and glands. The peripheral nervous system further divides into the Somatic Nervous System which controls the external actions of skin and muscles and the **Autonomic Nervous System** which controls the internal activities of organs and glands acting largely unconsciously or automatically to control functions like heart rate, digestion, respiration, and many others. The autonomic nervous system divides an additional time into the **Sympathetic Nervous System** which oversees arousing us to fight off a threat (fight or flight reactions) and the **Parasympathetic Nervous System** which helps to calm us down after a threat has passed (rest and digest reactions). Despite each of these divisions having their own specialty and controlled tasks, the nervous system works together as a coordinated unit to process information from our internal and external environments.

The Endocrine System

The **Endocrine System** is a collection of glands that produce hormones that regulate an incredible number of bodily processes including metabolism, growth and development, tissue function, sexual and reproductive functions, sleep, mood, and many others. The endocrine system works closely with the nervous system; they are in a constant chemical conversation with each other. The endocrine system plays a key role in helping to coordinate and integrate complex psychological reactions and is made up of a network of glands including the pituitary gland, thyroid gland, adrenal glands, pancreas, and the gonads (the ovaries in women and the testes in men). Endocrine glands affect almost every organ and cell in the body through the release of **Hormones** which are chemical

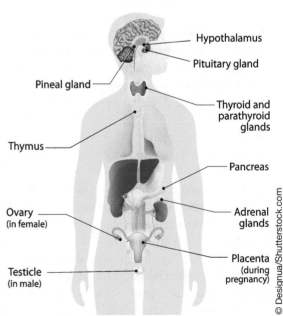

Hypothalamus
Pituitary gland
Pineal gland
Thyroid and parathyroid glands
Thymus
Pancreas
Ovary (in female)
Adrenal glands
Placenta (during pregnancy)
Testicle (in male)

© Designua/Shutterstock.com

substances that help to regulate bodily activities, carried throughout the body by the bloodstream. A few commonly known and referenced hormones are testosterone which is the dominant male hormone, estrogen the dominant female hormone, and cortisol which plays a large role in our stress responses.

Hormones versus Neurotransmitters

Hormones and neurotransmitters work together to accomplish the countless demands of our internal and external environments. The release mechanism of a chemical determines if it is a neurotransmitter or a hormone. Take the hormone adrenaline and the neurotransmitter norepinephrine for example. These bodily chemicals are incredibly similar to the point of sometimes having their names being used interchangeably and both play a role in the fight or flight short-term stress response. In the case of adrenaline for example, it is a hormone when the adrenal gland releases it into the bloodstream and it goes to the heart or the lungs but it is a neurotransmitter when it is released from a stimulated nerve cell and acts on a neighboring cell. While their end goals may be similar, there are many key differences between hormones and neurotransmitters; see the chart below.

	Neurotransmitters	**Hormones**
System	Belong to the nervous system	Belong to the endocrine system
Transmission	Transmitted across the synapse	Transmitted through the blood
Production	Produced by neurons	Produced by the endocrine glands
Target	Target can be specific neurons or other cells	Target can be at a distance from the gland
Speed	Action is fast (milliseconds)	Action can last for a long period of time (few seconds to a few days)

The Brain

The brain is the command center of the nervous system and is the most complex organ in the human body. It influences an incredible number of functions and helps to control our other organs allowing for rapid and coordinated responses to internal and external environments. Weighing an average of about 3.3 pounds, the brain takes up about 2% of our body weight and is about 15 cm long. The brain is what makes us human, giving us the capacity for art, language, moral judgments, and rational thought. It's also responsible for our personality, memories, movements, and how we perceive and interact with the world.

We often discuss the brain in terms of three main divisions, the hindbrain, midbrain, and the forebrain. Another

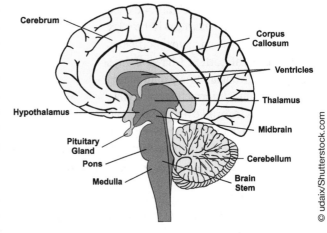

HUMAN BRAIN -SIDE VIEW

Cerebrum — Corpus Callosum — Ventricles — Thalamus — Midbrain — Cerebellum — Brain Stem — Medulla — Pons — Pituitary Gland — Hypothalamus

© udaix/Shutterstock.com

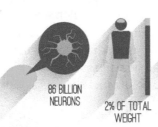
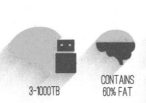

Amazing facts about the brain: 86 BILLION NEURONS — 2% OF TOTAL WEIGHT — 3-1000TB — CONTAINS 60% FAT — CONSUMES 20% OF ENERGY — AVERAGE WEIGHT IS 1300 g

© Macrovector /Shutterstock.com

way of thinking about the divisions would be to talk about the brain as older or more primitive structures, the limbic system, and then the cerebral cortex or higher level systems and functions.

Older Brain Structures

The older or more primitive parts of the brain include the brainstem, pons, medulla, and the cerebellum. The **Brainstem** is responsible for automatic survival functions including heart rate, breathing, maintaining consciousness, and regulating the sleep cycle. Making up the brainstem are the pons and medulla. The **Pons** which is Latin for "bridge", contains nuclei that deal primarily with sleep, respiration, swallowing, and equilibrium. The **Medulla** or Medulla Oblongata is the lower half of the brainstem and is often referred to as simply the medulla. The medulla deals with autonomic, involuntary functions, such as breathing, heart rate and blood pressure. Finally, the **Cerebellum**, sometimes referred to as the "little brain" due to its shape and size, regulates reflexes and balance along with coordinating movement.

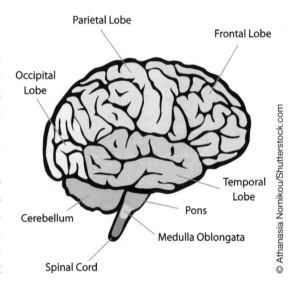

The Limbic System

The **Limbic System** is a system of structures that control our emotions such as fear and aggression, influences our drives, and plays a role in the formation of memories. The major structures in the limbic system are the thalamus, hypothalamus, hippocampus, and amygdala. Located between the cerebral cortex and the brainstem, the **Thalamus** is the relay station for sensory and motor information to the cerebral cortex. I have always thought of the thalamus as a train station within the brain. Information comes into the thalamus from all over the body and then is routed out via the connections to other limbic system structures much like trains would arrive at a central hub and then travel away to various locations. The thalamus also plays a role in our sleep and wake cycles and states of consciousness.

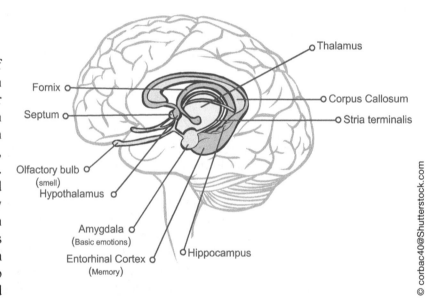

The **Hypothalamus** has quite a few responsibilities and is a very busy part of the brain and limbic system! The hypothalamus plays a role in our metabolic processes and controls body temperature, hunger, thirst, fatigue, sleep, and circadian cycles. This part of the brain is often compared to a thermostat in that it is constantly regulating our system to try and keep us at a set point or what we call **Homeostasis**. The hypothalamus receives information from sources throughout the body and then sends out instructions to our system to maintain homeostasis. Another key function of the hypothalamus is that it links the nervous system to the endocrine system via the pituitary gland which plays a large role in our stress response and our automatic functions such as blood pressure, digestion, and other functions of the autonomic nervous system.

The **Hippocampus** plays an important role in the consolidation of information from short-term memory to long-term memory and spatial navigation. It aids in the forming, organizing, and storing of memories acting as a memory index by sending out memories to the appropriate parts of the cerebral cortex. When damage occurs to the hippocampus, people struggle to build new memories. The almond shaped **Amygdala** lies deep within the limbic system and controls our emotional reactions, motivations, and memories. The amygdala is thought to play a big role in all emotions but especially our fear reactions and the conditioning that takes places with feared stimuli. It also plays a role in our sense of smell as it receives input from the olfactory bulb which can lead to smell memories (something we will talk more about in the sensation and perception unit).

The Cerebral Cortex

Ballooning out and over the central core of the brain is the cerebrum which is divided into two hemispheres and is covered by a thin layer of gray matter called the **Cerebral Cortex**. This is the part of the brain that regulates most complex behavior such as thought and awareness, vision, language, memory, and emotions. The cerebral cortex is composed of **Gray Matter** which contains most of the brain's neurons and is involved in the countless functions of the cerebral cortex. The cortex is gray because the neurons in this area are unmyelinated. It also contains many bulges and valleys giving it a very distinct appearance. The folds are probably what most people notice first when they look at an actual brain. Because the cerebral cortex is where so many of the higher level processes take place in the brain, the folds and fissures help to maximize this very important part of the brain. The cortex is only about 3.4 mm thick so to maximize the amount of surface area in a relatively fixed space, it is folded. If we unfolded the cortex of our brains it would stretch out to roughly 2.5 square

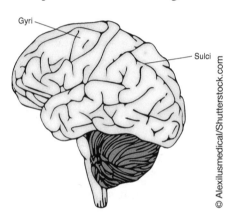

© Alexilusmedical/Shutterstock.com

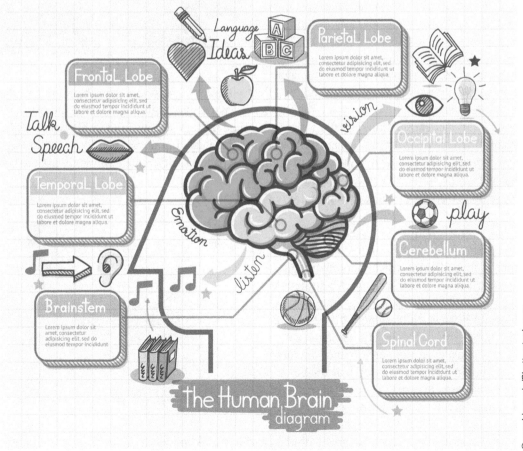

© graphixmania/Shutterstock.com

feet. The folds in the brain have technical names; the higher ridges are called **Gyri** (Gyrus for singular) and the lower valleys are called **Sulci** (Sulcus for singular).

The cerebral cortex is divided into four lobes which are separated by deep fissures; the frontal lobe, parietal lobe, occipital lobe, and the temporal lobe. The **Frontal Lobe**, which is conveniently located in the front part of the brain, is responsible for voluntary movement, attention, goal-directed behavior, decision making, and emotional experiences. It contains our motor cortex which helps to initiate voluntary muscle activity and Broca's Area which is primarily responsible for speech production. The **Parietal Lobe** contains our somatosensory cortex (which processes information such as hot cold, and pain from the skin) and plays a large role in receiving and processing sensory information. The parietal lobe receives and processes sensory information from the skin, muscles, joints, organs, taste buds, and many others along with having a part in spatial abilities. Located at the back of the brain, the **Occipital Lobe** has one job and that is to receive and interpret visual information to allow us to make sense of all that we see. Finally, the **Temporal Lobe**, which is located near the temples and ears, helps to regulate hearing, balance, and equilibrium, certain emotions and motivations, and also plays a role in understanding language. The temporal lobe contains our auditory cortex along with Wernicke's Area which plays a role in comprehension of language.

Tools for Studying the Brain

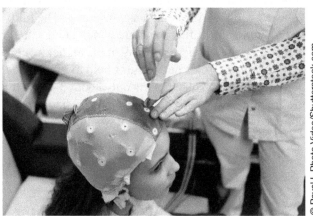

How do we know what all the different parts of the brain control? We have several different methods of studying the brain depending on the goal or purpose of our study. There are four basic groups of techniques for studying the brain: microelectrode techniques, macroelectrode techniques, structural imaging, and functional imaging. *Microelectrode Techniques* are used to study the functions of individual neurons. A microelectrode technique might be used if psychologists or scientists were looking at action potentials or the effects of certain drugs or toxins. The method for this is to take a tiny tube smaller in diameter than a human hair, fill it with a conducting fluid, and then place the tip inside a neuron and record the results. *Macroelectrode Techniques* are used to capture the activity in a particular region of the brain almost as if we were listening to the brain. The most commonly used macroelectrode technique is an EEG or **Electroencephalogram**. When neurons communicate with each other through electrochemical communication (as we discussed earlier), that electrical energy can be recorded in the form of brain wave patterns. EEGs are commonly used to study sleep and epilepsy and are performed by putting small electrodes on the scalp to measure and record brain activity.

Structural Imaging techniques are used to map the structures in a living brain (or other parts of the body). There are quite a few different structural brain imaging methods that are used with the most common being either a CAT scan or Computerized Axial Tomography and an MRI or Magnetic Resonance Imaging. **Computerized Axial Tomography (CAT) Scans** involve taking a series of x-ray images from a variety of angles which are then combined together to create cross-sectional images of the structure being investigated. CAT scans are incredibly common in medical practice and are often used to examine an internal injury. In the case of the brain, CAT scans are often used to evaluate the structures within the brain to look for masses, bleeding, abnormality in blood vessels, and sometimes to examine the skull.

Magnetic Resonance Imaging (MRI) is an imaging test that uses a magnetic field and pulses of radio wave energy to capture images of the structures and organs within the body. The area of interest is placed within a machine that typically looks like a large tunnel or tube with a table in the middle. The patient will lay on the table and then slide into the tube before the procedure begins. MRIs work via incredibly strong magnets which act on the hydrogen and oxygen atoms within the water molecules in our body. The magnetic fields are turned on and off in a series of pulses that cause our hydrogen atoms to alter their alignment and then return to their original relaxed state creating a cross-sectional image which can then be interpreted.

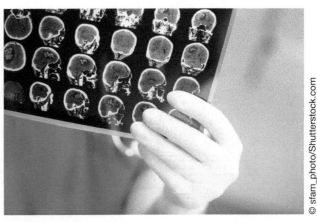

The loud thumping and knocking sounds that a person hears during this procedure are the vibrations caused by the pulses of the magnetic fields. MRIs of the head are often looking for tumors, aneurysms, nerve injury, damage from a stroke, and bleeding in the brain. This test can be done with or without contrast. If it is done with contrast, the patient receives an injection of the contrast materials into the bloodstream which will help to make certain tissues or abnormalities more clearly visible. Other than the injection, this is a relatively painless procedure though many find it uncomfortable due to being in a small confined/enclosed machine; especially those who struggle with claustrophobia.

Functional Imaging involves capturing activity in the brain as it responds to various stimuli such as pain, words, tones, and so on. Functional techniques measure activity on a millisecond by millisecond basis recording how the brain is using energy. The most commonly used functional imaging technique is a **Positron Emission Tomography or a (PET) Scan** which is a type of nuclear medicine imaging test that allows psychologists and doctors to examine how tissues and organs are functioning. PET scans measure functions such as blood flow, oxygen use, and glucose metabolism to help doctors to evaluate the functioning of an organ or tissue. In the brain, this scan is commonly used to look for brain abnormalities, tumors, neurocognitive disorders such as Alzheimer's disease, and sometime seizures. This scan works by using a radioactive tracer that shows activity within the structure of interest. The tracer can be swallowed, injected, or even inhaled as a gas depending on what area of the body is being studied and then collects in areas that have a high level of

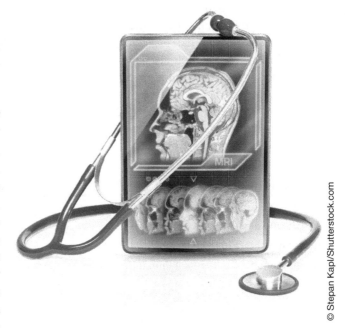

chemical activity thereby showing up as bright spots on the scan. So instead of showing anatomy or structures, the focus here is on hot spots or cold spots which indicate high or low levels of chemical or metabolic activity and can therefore be diagnostic. Other than the injection of the tracer, this procedure is relatively painless.

Hemispheric Specialization

The human brain is also commonly discussed in terms of the right half of the brain and the left half of the brain with the primary connection between the two being the **Corpus Callosum**; a thick band of nerve fibers that

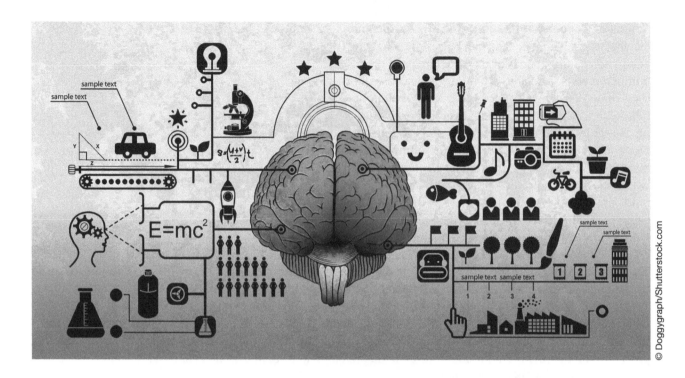

connects the left and right cerebral hemispheres allowing them to work together as a coordinated unit. Since the left and right brains are connected and work together, the idea of being left or right brained is more of a popular culture notion that is pseudoscientific in nature than scientific. It is popularly referenced but not really held to be true by psychologists and scientists. In a two-year study done at the University of Utah in 2013, this popular idea was debunked after careful investigation of brain scans examining the specific mental processes taking place in either side of the brain (functional lateralization). The results indicated that individual differences don't favor one hemisphere or the other so again, while the left and right brains do have different skill sets and tasks that they control, but again, work as a team to accomplish their actions.

Left Brain	Right Brain
Language	Visual and spatial tasks
Analyzing details	Holistic processing
Speaking	Facial recognition
Logic (numbers and critical thinking)	Creativity (music and art)

In rare cases, a person might have the corpus callosum severed. This is primarily done in cases of severe epilepsy to isolate the two hemispheres thereby minimizing the damage that can occur during seizures. In cases where this procedure has been done, we have learned quite a bit about the functions of the two hemispheres. We know that the left hemisphere receives and controls information from the right side of the body and right half of the visual field while the right hemisphere receives and processes information and actions from the left side of the body and left side of the visual field. The right side of the brain also controls our visual and spatial tasks, operates on holistic processing, controls facial recognition, and deals with our creativity (music, art, and so on). The left side of the brain controls our language, analyzing details, is in charge of our ability to speak, and is oriented toward logic (numbers and critical thinking). While not everyone shows the same pattern of differences between right and left hemispheres there is again not thought to be such a thing as being right or left brained.

Brain Damage and Neural Plasticity

In addition to brain imaging techniques, we know an incredible amount about the brain and the functions of its structures from cases of brain trauma. One of the most famous incidents of brain trauma ever studied in psychology is that of American railroad foreman Phineas Gage. Gage was railroad construction foreman who was injured on the job in 1848 when an explosion sent an iron rod straight through the left side of his brain from an upward direction. The rod passed behind the left eye through the left side of the brain and clear out the top of his skull. Miraculously, Gage survived the accident but had severe damage to his brain (namely the frontal lobe) which completely changed his personality. "Gage's survival would have ensured him a measure of celebrity, but his name was etched into history by observations made by John Martyn Harlow, the doctor who treated him for a few months afterward. Gage's friends found him "no longer Gage," Harlow wrote. The balance between his intellectual faculties and animal propensities seemed gone. He could not stick to plans, uttered the grossest profanity and showed little deference for his fellows.

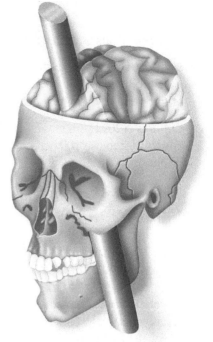

BSIP/Contributor/Getty

Gage's accident and the countless brain traumas and subsequent studies that have occurred since 1848 have taught us about the brain's amazing talent of **Neural Plasticity**. Our brain has the ability to change in response to experiences and form new neural connections throughout the course of our lives. A classic set of experiments by American Psychologist M.R. Rosenzweig involving baby rats helped to further this notion of plasticity and brain changes throughout the lifespan. Rosenzweig divided the rats into two groups; one in an impoverished environment isolated in barren cages and one in an enriched environment living with other rats and toys that provided opportunities for exploration and social interaction. The rats in the enriched environment had larger neurons with more synaptic connections than those in the impoverished one indicating that the brain responds to changes in the environment. His findings along with those of many others, supports the notion that experiences lead to changes in the brain and that our brain doesn't stop growing during childhood.

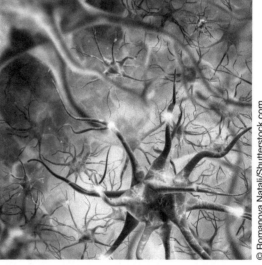

© Romanova Natali/Shutterstock.com

We often reference this plasticity as it relates to the synaptic pruning that occurs when we are young and developing our brain as it experiences our environments but it also refers to the ability of the brain to compensate for injuries. It is thought that after a traumatic brain injury, the brain makes every effort to relearn how to function and to regenerate.

In Popular Culture

- *The Walking Dead* (2010 to present) – One popular culture example highlighting the topic of neurons comes from the AMC television series *The Walking Dead*. In season 1, a group of survivors reach a branch of the CDC (Center for Disease Control) and are shown a recording of a patient who was bitten by a "walker" and died only to later come back as a zombie. In this episode, there is a discussion of neurons and the role that they play in determining our life and personality. As we are watching the test subject's brain, we see "ripples of life" which represent action potentials or the firing of neurons. This portion of the episode also discusses what comprises life versus death as it relates to brain and neuron activity and of course, deals with an interesting topic of zombies and the parts of the brain reactivated in the undead!

- *Lucy* (2014) – a movie starring Scarlett Johansson who portrays the title character, a woman who gains psychokinetic abilities from a drug being absorbed into her bloodstream. The movie discusses the 10% of our brain myth and the idea of our brain's capacity if we could "access 100%".

- *Limitless* (2011) – a movie starring Bradley Cooper about a writer who takes an experimental drug that allows him to use 100 percent of his brain (based on the popular notion that we only have access to 10% of our brain's ability).

Psyched with Setmire

"The 10% Myth (Lucy and Limitless)"
https://www.youtube.com/watch?v=6q6chuFlmvk

This Psychology presentation (adapted from my PSY M01 class lecture and activities) is a discussion of the myth that we only use 10% of our brain. I will describe the myth, cover its origins, show a brief clip from the trailers for the films Lucy and Limitless (two of several pop culture movies perpetuating the myth), and then cover the reasons why the myth is false.

Application

While the left and right brain work together thereby negating the idea that someone is left or right brained, it is still a very popular pseudoscientific idea that can be fun to think about! Below are links to a few websites that have a right versus left brain quizzes that you can take to find out which side of your brain is more dominant (just for fun)!

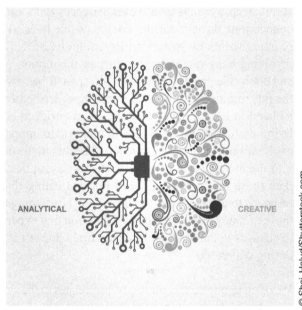

ANALYTICAL   CREATIVE

VS

© Shai_Halud/Shutterstock.com

- http://www.hect.org/images/workshop/2015-16/Child_Development/Jana_Din/Right_Left_brain_dominance_test.pdf

- http://www.angelfire.com/wi/2brains/test.html

- https://www.biologycorner.com/anatomy/nervous/dominance_test.html

Key Terms

Biological Psychology: involves the scientific study of the links between biological and psychological processes; sometimes referred to as behavioral neuroscience or psychobiology.

Neurons: individual cells that are the smallest unit of the nervous system; the building blocks of the nervous system.

Cell Body: the life support center of a cell; sometimes called the soma.

Nucleus: the command or administrative center of a cell that contains our chromosomes and genetic information.

Dendrites: the short bushy branch-like fibers that pickup incoming messages from adjoining cells.

Axon: the long slender fibers extending from the cell body that carry away outgoing messages.

Myelin Sheath: a fatty white covering that encases and insulates axons to help speed up neural impulses.

Terminal Buttons: structures at the ends of the terminal branches that are responsible for helping to carry messages on to neighboring neurons.

Sensory Neurons: neurons that carry messages from the various sense organs toward the spinal cord and brain; sometimes called afferent neurons.

Motor Neurons: neurons that carry messages away from the spinal cord and brain to the muscles and glands; sometimes called efferent neurons.

Amyotrophic Lateral Sclerosis (ALS): is a progressive neurodegenerative disease that affects nerve cells in the brain and the spinal cord.

Glial Cells: from the Greek word meaning "glue", glial cells help to maintain homeostasis, form the myelin sheath, and provide support for neurons.

Action Potential: the firing of a neuron; a neuron sending a message from the cell body, down the axon, and to the terminal buttons that will then release neurotransmitters to stimulate the next neuron.

Ions: electrically charged particles such as sodium, potassium, and chloride; make up the electrical element of electrochemical communication in neurons.

Resting Potential: the inside of the neuron is negative in electrical charge relative to the outside of the neuron; the neuron is "at rest".

Depolarization: a sudden change within a neuron resulting in a reversal in the electrical charge of a cell which in turn causes an action potential.

Threshold of Excitation: the critical level to which a neuron must be depolarized to cause an action potential to occur.

All-or-None Law: the principle that dictates that the action potential of a neuron does not vary in strength; either the neuron fires at full strength or it does not fire at all.

Synapse: the junction or narrow space between the axon terminals of one neuron and the dendrites and cell body of the next neuron.

Neurotransmitters: chemical messengers that are released by the synaptic vesicles and travel across the synapse to chemically stimulate the adjacent neuron; make up the chemical portion of electrochemical communication in neurons.

Receptor Sites: locations on a receptor neuron into which a specific neurotransmitter fits like a key into a lock.

Reuptake: a process in which neurotransmitters are reabsorbed back into the sending (pre-synaptic) neuron.

Nerve: an enclosed, cable-like bundle of axons that provides a common pathway for electrochemical impulses.

Central Nervous System: one of the two main divisions of the human nervous system; contains the brain and spinal cord.

Spinal Cord: our communication superhighway connecting the brain to the rest of the body.

Peripheral Nervous System: one of the two main divisions of the human nervous system; consists of nerves that connect the brain and spinal cord to every other part of the body.

Autonomic Nervous System: a division of the peripheral nervous system which controls the internal activities of organs and glands.

Sympathetic Nervous System: a division of the autonomic nervous system which is in charge of activating the fight or flight response.

Parasympathetic Nervous System: a division of the autonomic nervous system which helps to calm us down after a threat has passed; in charge of rest and digest responses.

Endocrine System: the collection of glands that produce hormones that regulate numerous body activities and functions.

Hormones: chemical substances that help to regulate bodily activities and are carried throughout the body by the bloodstream.

Brainstem: region of the brain connecting the cerebrum to the spinal cord; responsible for automatic survival functions including heart rate, breathing, maintaining consciousness, and regulating the sleep cycle.

Pons: Latin for "bridge", contains nuclei that deal primarily with sleep, respiration, swallowing, and equilibrium.

Medulla: the lower half of the brainstem; responsible for autonomic, involuntary functions, such as breathing, heart rate and blood pressure.

Cerebellum: sometimes referred to as the "little brain" due to its shape and size; regulates reflexes and balance along with coordinating movement.

Limbic System: a system of structures that control our emotions such as fear and aggression, influences our drives, and plays a role in the formation of memories.

Thalamus: located between the cerebral cortex and the brainstem; relay station for sensory and motor information to the cerebral cortex.

Hypothalamus: a structure in the limbic system that plays a role in our metabolic processes and controls body temperature, hunger, thirst, fatigue, sleep, and circadian cycles.

Homeostasis: a state of balance, stability, or constancy.

Hippocampus: a structure in the limbic system that plays an important role in the consolidation of information from short-term memory to long-term memory along with spatial navigation.

Amygdala: an almond shaped structure deep within the limbic system that controls our emotional reactions, motivations, and memories.

Cerebral Cortex: part of the brain that regulates most complex behavior such as thought and awareness, vision, language, memory, and emotions.

Gray Matter: makes up the cerebral cortex, contains most of the brain's neurons, and is involved in the processing of information in the brain; so named because of its appearance to the naked eye.

Gyri (Gyrus): in the cerebral cortex, the higher ridges or peaks.

Sulci (Sulcus): in the cerebral cortex, the lower valleys or grooves.

Frontal Lobe: one of the lobes of the brain responsible for voluntary movement, attention, goal-directed behavior, decision making, and emotional experiences; contains the motor cortex.

Parietal Lobe: one of the lobes of the brain responsible receiving and processing sensory information; contains the somatosensory cortex.

Occipital Lobe: one of the lobes of the brain responsible for receiving and interpreting visual information.

Temporal Lobe: one of the lobes of the brain responsible for regulating hearing, balance and equilibrium, certain emotions and motivations, and playing a role in understanding language; contains the auditory cortex.

Electroencephalogram (EEG): a macroelectrode technique for studying the brain that measures the electrical energy emitted by the brain in the form of brain wave patterns.

Computerized Axial Tomography (CAT) Scan: a structural imaging test that involves taking a series of x-ray images that can be combined to create cross-sectional images of the structure being investigated.

Magnetic Resonance Imaging (MRI): a structural imaging test that uses a magnetic field and pulses of radio wave energy to capture images of the structures and organs within the body.

Positron Emission Tomography (PET) Scan: a functional imaging technique that allows for the study of tissue and organ functioning through measuring blood flow, oxygen use, and glucose metabolism.

Corpus Callosum: a thick band of nerve fibers that connects the left and right cerebral hemispheres allowing them to work together as a coordinated unit.

Neural Plasticity: the ability of the brain to change in response to experiences and to form new neural connections throughout the course of our lives.

Chapter 4

Sensation and Perception

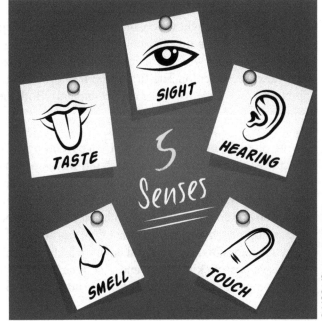

© MSSA/Shutterstock.com

Introduction to the Chapter (Summary)

In this chapter we will look at the processes of sensation and perception. Sensation begins when energy from an external source or from inside the body stimulates a receptor cell in one of the sense organs while perception involves organizing and interpreting our sensations. We exist in a sea of energy and in order to receive and pick up this energy, we are equipped with countless receptor cells. When there is sufficient energy, the receptor cell fires and sends the brain a coded signal in a process called transduction. Stimuli that are below our absolute thresholds are not consciously detected but are thought to potentially have a degree of influence, under certain conditions. The most common example of this would be subliminal messages.

The first sense we will look at is vision. There are several important parts of the eye including the cornea, pupil, iris, lens and the retina which contains the rods and cones which are our receptor cells for vision. Rods are responsible for night vision and the perception of brightness and cones are responsible for color vision and vision during the daytime. Visual information entering the eye must travel to the brain in order for a visual experience to occur which is accomplished via specialized neurons and the optic nerve. There are two theories about how we see color. The first is the trichromatic (three color) theory and the second theory is called the opponent-process theory (three opposing pairs). Both theories are viewed as valid but at different stages of the visual process.

Moving on to the other senses, sound is a psychological experience created by the brain in response to changes in air pressure. Sound exists due to sound waves which can vary in both frequency and intensity or loudness. The skin is our largest sense organ and protects us from the environment, holds in body fluids, regulates our internal temperature, and contains receptors for our sense of touch which plays an important role in human interaction and emotion. Taste is another sense that we possess. We have five basic taste qualities which include sweet, sour, salty, bitter, and umami. Often working with taste is our sense of smell which is gathered by 1000's of tiny receptors high in the nasal cavity which are sent to the olfactory bulb or the smell center in the brain. Finally, we possess kinesthetic and vestibular senses which are our senses of muscle movement, posture, and strain on muscles and joints and also equilibrium and body position in space.

Our senses provide us with raw data about the external world but it must then be interpreted. Perception involves deciphering meaningful patterns, using various principles of grouping as proposed by Gestalt psychologists, and is the brain's process of organizing and making sense of sensory information. We use perception to interpret visual cues such as gauging depth, to process auditory information, and movement. Sometimes our perpection can lead us astray and result in illusions. Perception is the result of sensation and cognition; the interaction of physical stimuli and our thoughts, experiences, and expectations.

A final topic is extrasensory perception (ESP) which is the ability to perceive or acquire information without using the ordinary senses. As it stands today, despite its popularity, no reliable scientific evidence has been found to suggest that any of these phenomena exist!

Sensation and Perception

We exist within a sea of energy with countless stimuli surrounding us at every moment. If you were to take a few seconds, you might be surprised how many sensory items you could detect in any given moment when you pay attention to your environment. Right now I am aware of the temperature in the room, the sound of the air conditioning humming in the background, the sensation of being hungry and ready for lunch, and so much more. All of the sensory stimulation occuring around us must first be detected in order to then be interpreted and given meaning. **Sensation** begins when energy from an external source or from inside the body stimulates a receptor cell in one of the sense organs. When our skin detects a change in pressure or temperature, our eyes react to differing levels of light, or our nose detects the faint smell of something being cooked in the kitchen, all of those involve the process of sensation. **Perception** involves organizing and interpreting our sensations. That faint smell in the kitchen, what could it be? Is it a cake that I should be excited to eat or vegetables that I should dread? When we perceive our world, we make sense of the sensations that we have detected and interpret them according to our experiences and expectations. The second that I recognize that faint smell as a cake, my mind will form expectations about that cake filling me with excitement! Sensation and perception work together which is why two people might detect the same physical stimuli in their environments but react to them quite differently. Take for example a song. Two people driving in a car together will both have their auditory systems detect the same physical information but one person might feel happy due to their connections and experiences with the song while the other might respond with sadness.

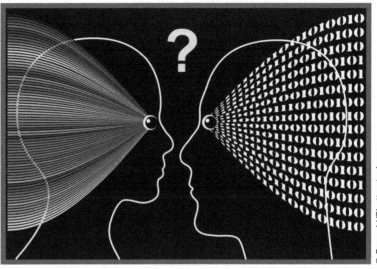

Receptor Cells, Thresholds, and Subliminal Messages

We are equipped with countless **Receptor Cells**; specialized cells that respond to a particular type of energy such as light waves or the vibration of air molecules. When there is sufficient energy, receptor cells will fire and send a coded signal to the brain. The process of converting physical energy such as light or sound into an electrochemical code is called **Transduction**. The specific sensation produced depends on how many neurons fire, which neurons fire, and how rapidly they fire. For example, very bright light is coded differently than dim light. The differences in coding ensures that when the messages reach the brain they are precise and detailed.

In order to produce any sensation, the physical energy reaching a receptor must achieve a minimum intensity known as an **Absolute Threshold**. An absolute threshold is the least amount of energy that can be detected as a stimulation 50% of the time. Anything below the threshold will not be experienced. In order to calculate a person's threshold, psychologists present stimuli at different intensities and ask people whether they see or hear it and the absolute threshold is when people can detect the stimulus 50% of the time. Think of a hearing test. The

person administering the test will play sounds of various tones and loudness into the test subject's ears and are looking for the point at which the person can hear the sounds 50% of the time.

Absolute thresholds differ from person to person and even from moment to moment. A big reason for that is **Adaptation**. Under normal conditions the thresholds vary according to the level and nature of the stimulus. For example your threshold for the taste of salt would be considerably higher after you ate salty chips. Thresholds rise and fall because our senses automatically adjust to the overall level of stimulation in a particular setting. Go back to the chips example. When you open a brand new bag of chips and start eating them, the first chips are incredibly salty. As you get deeper into the bag, you might experience the chips as being less salty because your taste buds have adapted to the salt. The same is true of our skin. When you first put a bandaid on your skin, you are very aware of its prescence. After a few hours of having it on, you almost forget that it is there! Your skin has adapted to its prescence. Our senses are much less sensitive when there is a great deal of stimulation than when overall stimulation is low. This allows our senses to be keenly attuned to environmental cues without being overloaded.

There are quite a few things that we don't consciously notice and that fall into the realm of **Subliminal Perception or Subliminal Messages**. If something is subliminal, it is below our level of awareness and not consciously attended to by our mind. The classic reference with subliminal messages occurred in the 1950's when a market researcher named James Vicary inserted the phrases "Eat Popcorn" and "Drink Coca-Cola" into movies for a single frame. The idea was to have the messages be brief enough that viewers wouldn't consciously attend to them but that they would be picked up by the unconscious mind. Vicary claimed that the messages resulted in an increase in sales of both Coca-Cola and popcorn but his results were later shown to be fraudlent and unable to be replicated. So do subliminal messages affect us? There is some evidence that in a controlled laboratory setting people can process and respond to information outside of awareness but this in no way means that people automatically or mindlessly obey

subliminal messages. In general, the effects of subliminal messages are often fleeting rather than enduring. Current research shows that they might increase the likelihood of you doing something that you already wanted you to do but not cause you to do something out of the blue. So in theory, if I were sitting in a movie theater and was thinking about getting popcorn, subliminal messages might have a chance of pushing me to go to the concession stand. Much more powerful would be seeing and smelling the popcorn that other people were eating!

Our Five Senses

On a very basic level that we are taught early in life, humans posses five different senses; sight, sound, taste, smell, and touch. Many experts and neurologists have identified additional senses often asserting that we have somewhere between nine to twenty-one senses in all. A **Sense** refers to any system that consists of a group of sensory cells that responds to specific physical phenonemon, and that corresponds to a particular group of regions within the brain where the signals are received and then interpreted. In general, what constitutes a sense is a matter of debate so for the purpose of being traditional, we will stick to the basic five in our discussion!

Vision and the Eyes

Sight or vision is our most dominant sense and involves the capability of the eyes to focus and detect light. Our eyes receive light energy from the environment and then transduce it into neural messages that our brain will then process into what we actually see. There are two physical characteristics that help to determine what we see and experience, **Wavelengths** and **Intensity**. Wavelengths are the distance from the peak of one light wave to the peak of the next and help to determine the **Hue** or color that we see and experience. The human eye can only see a small portion of the whole spectrum of light waves which we refer to as the visble spectrum. Long wavelengths are found at the red end of the visible spectrum of light while shorter wavelenghts are found at the blue end of the spectrum. Intensity on the other hand, is the amount of enegy in a light wave which influences our perception of brightness and is determined by the wave's height (amplitude).

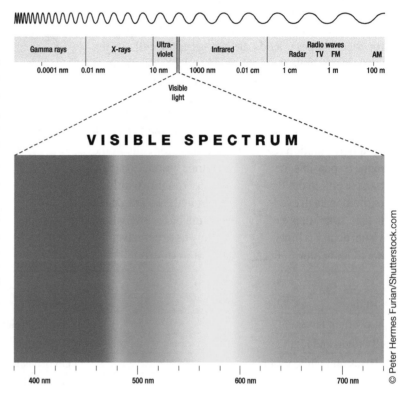

The eyes are the sense organs of vision. Light enters the eye through the **Cornea** which is the transparent protective coating over the front part of the eye. Light then passes through the **Pupil** which is a small opening in the iris through which light enters the eye. The **Iris** is the colored part of the eye that regulates the size of the pupil. In bright light the muscles in the iris contract to make the pupil smaller and thus protect the eye from damage. In dim light the muscles relax to open the pupil wider and let in more light. If you want to watch this process in action, stand in front of a mirror and turn the lights on and off! Behind the pupil is the **Lens**; the transparent part of the eye behind the pupil that focuses light onto the retina. Normally the lens is focused on a middle distance and it changes shape

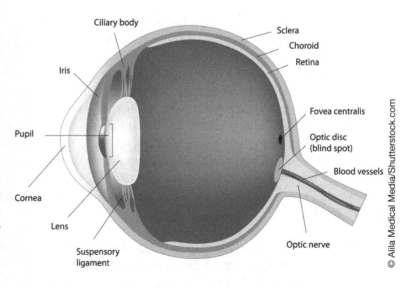

Human Eye Anatomy

to focus on objects that are closer or farther away by changing its curvature and thickness in a process called **Accommodation**. The final stop for light within the eye is the **Retina**; the light-sensitive inner surface of the eye, containing the receptor cells that are sensitive to electromagnetic energy and process visual information.

Photoreceptors

The retina contains three layers; ganglion cells, bipolar cells, and photorecptors. We have two different types of photoreceptors, **Rods** and **Cones** (which are named for their shapes). Rods are the receptor cells in the retina responsible for night vision and the perception of brightness. Rods are highly sensitive to light and there are roughly 120 million of them in each eye located in the peripheral regions of the retina. Rods allow us to perceive black and white, faint light, and help with peripheral motion. Cones are the receptor cells in the retina responsible for color and daytime vision. Cones are most useful in daytime and there are roughly 6 million of them in each eye located mainly in the **Fovea** which is thea small depression in the retina of the eye where visual acuity is highest. Cones allow us to perceive fine detail and color (which we will get to shortly).

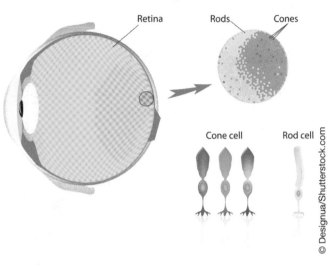

Photoreceptor cell

© Designua/Shutterstock.com

Rods	Cones
Low light levels	High light levels
Twilight and night vision	Daytime vision
Black and white vision	Color vision
Low acuity	High activity
120 million	6 million
Peripheral regions of the retina	Located in the fovea

From the Eye to the Brain

Messages from the eye must travel to the brain in order for a visual experience to occur. The rods and cones connect to specialized neurons that eventually join with the **Optic Nerve** which is the bundles of axons of ganglion cells that carries neural messages from each eye to the brain. The place on the retina where the axons of all the ganglion cells leave the eye and where there are no receptors is called the **Blind Spot**. The blind spot causes there to be a small blank area in the visual field; similar to what we experience with our rear view mirrors when driving execpt that we don't see our blind spot since our brain fills that gap in for us!

After the nerve fibers that make up the optic nerves leave the eyes, they separate and some of them cross to the other side of the head at the **Optic Chiasm**. The optic chiasm is the point near the base of the brain where some fibers in the optic nerve

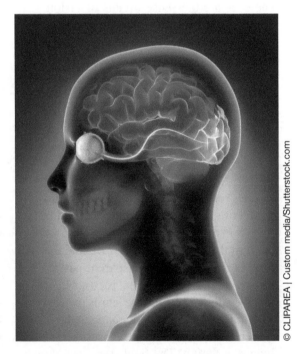

© CLIPAREA | Custom media/Shutterstock.com

from each eye cross to the other side of the brain. The optic nerve carries messages to various parts of the brain but mainly to the occipital lobe where the messages are registered and interpreted.

Theories of Color Vision

How do we see color? If you look closely at a television screen (especially an older one), you see that the picture is actually made up of tiny red, green, and blue dots that blend together to give all possible hues; the same principle is at work in our bodies. There are two main theories of color vision, the **Trichromatic (Three Color) Theory** and the **Opponent-Process Theory**. The trichromatic (three color) theory is the theory of color vision that holds that all color perception derives from three different color receptors (usually red, green, and blue). This theory is based on additive color mixing; there are three primary colors of light so there must be three types of cones and color experiences come from mixing the signals from the three receptors. The other theory is the opponent-process theory which holds that three sets of color receptors (yellow-blue, red-green, and black-white) respond to determine the color you experience. The members of each pair work in opposition of each other; the yellow-blue pair can only relay messages about yellow or blue, but not yellow and blue at the same time. Both of these theories are viewed as valid but at different stages of the visual process. The trichromatic theory matches what exists in the retina but the opponent-process theory reflects what happens along the neural pathways connecting the eye and brain.

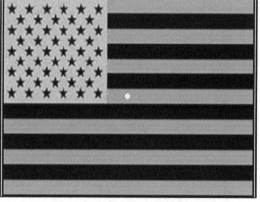

CICCARELLI; SAUNDRA; WHITE, J. NOLAND, PSYCHOLOGY WITH DSM-5 UPDATE, 3rd Ed., ©2014. Reprinted by permission of Pearson Education, Inc., New York, New York.

One interesting effect related to color vision is that of **Color Afterimages** which are an image continuing to appear in one's vision after exposure to the original image has ceased; explained by opponent-process theory. The most popular example of a color afterimage is the American flag. Looking at the flag image, stare at the white dot for about 30 seconds and then look at the white box beneath it and although the flag is printed in green, yellow, and black, its afterimge will appear in red, blue and white. This can be explained by the opponent process theory. While looking at the green strips, the red-green receptors were sending green messages to your brain but were adapting to the stimulation and becoming less sensitive to green light. When you looked at the white page, the red-green receptors responded vigourously and you saw red! The receptors become fatigued causing you to see the opposite color of the color pair.

Box – Stereograms:

A stereogram is a picture within a picture. I don't know if these are still popular, but when I was a little younger, these posters could be found most anywhere (I had one with a hidden image of a surfer in my bedroom)! Stereograms work on planes or layers; an image is sliced from front to back into 256 layers. The depth map is interpreted by special Stereogram software to create the hidden image. While this is a bit of a side note, it is fun and interesting and yet another example of sensation and perception! Here are some tips for viewing in case you are having some difficulty.

1. Pick a spot on the picture (the middle seems to work best) and just stare at it.

2. Allow your eyes to relax, don't just stare AT the image, try to stare THROUGH it. You'll notice your eyes will go slightly out of focus. This is normal.

3. Keep staring, don't give up, once you begin to see the first image, it gets much easier

Hopefully you were able to see the hidden image! If not, don't feel bad, these often take some practice!

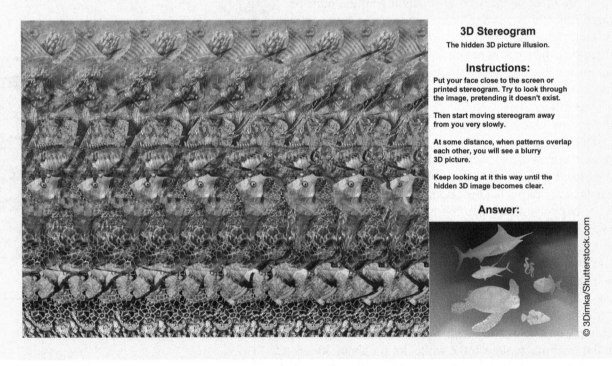

3D Stereogram
The hidden 3D picture illusion.

Instructions:
Put your face close to the screen or printed stereogram. Try to look through the image, pretending it doesn't exist.

Then start moving stereogram away from you very slowly.

At some distance, when patterns overlap each other, you will see a blurry 3D picture.

Keep looking at it this way until the hidden 3D image becomes clear.

Answer:

© 3Dimka/Shutterstock.com

Hearing and the Ears

Hearing or audition is the sense of perceiving **Sound**. Sound is a psychological experience created by the brain in response to changes in air pressure that are received by the auditory system. Sound is our brain's interpretation of air molecules pounding on our eardrums. **Sound Waves** are changes in pressure caused when molecules of air or fluid collide with one another and then move apart again. There are two main characteristics of sound. The first is frequency which is the number of cycles per second in a wave. In sound, this is the primary determinant of pitch and is commonly expressed in a unit called Hertz or cycles per second. The second characteristic is intensity or loudness and the primary determinant of loudness is amplitude or the magnitude of a wave. Loudness is expressed in decibels.

Hearing begins when sound waves are gathered by the outer ear and passed along to the eardrum causing it to vibrate. The vibration of the eardrum causes three tiny bones (hammer, anvil, and stirrup) in the middle ear to vibrate. The ear contains thousands of tiny hair cells that move from the vibrations causing them to send a signal that joins with the **Auditory Nerve** which is a bundle of axons that carries signals from each ear to the brain which then pools the information from thousands of hair cells to create sounds. The messages go to higher parts of the brain but primarily the temporal lobes.

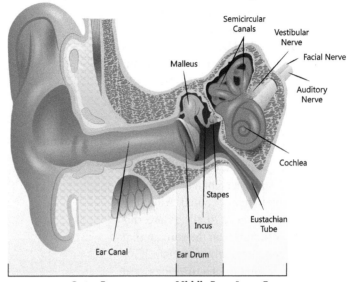

Touch and the Skin

The skin is our largest sense organ; a person who is six feet tall has about twenty-one square feet of skin! Our skin protects us from the environment, holds in body fluids, regulates our internal temperature, and contains receptors for our sense of touch which plays an important role in human interaction and emotion (hugging, kissing, handshakes, and so on). Touch or tactition involves the perception of information from the skin and our skin receptors give us four distinct sensations: pressure, warmth, cold, and pain. More people visit doctors for pain relief than for any other reason and yet pain still remains a puzzle to doctors and psychologists. A common thought or belief is that pain is nature's way of telling us that there is something wrong but physical injury is not always accompanied by pain. Scientists have great difficulty even finding pain receptors which violates the reasonable assumption that pain occurs when a pain receptor is stimulated. Individuals vary widely in their pain threshold or the amount of stimulation that is required in order to feel pain and also their pain tolerance which is the amount of pain someone can cope with. There are even incredibly rare cases and conditions in which individuals feel no pain at all. One example of that is Congenital Insensitivity to Pain with Anhidrosis (CIPA). CIPA is present from birth and people with this condition don't experience any pain, can't differentiate extreme temperatures, and also commonly lack a body sweating response. Because people with this condition don't experience the caution that pain can bring on, they often suffer injuries and might even have shortened lifespans.

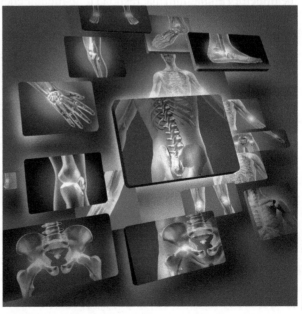

Taste and the Mouth

Taste or gustation is our capability to detect the taste of substances such as food. Taste must be distinguished from flavor which is a complex interaction of taste and smell. This is why if you hold your nose while you eat, much of the flavor will disappear (a technique that often helped me eat my vegetables when I was younger).

We posses five **Basic Taste Qualities** which include sweet, sour, salty, bitter, and umami (meat and protein heavy foods). Allowing us to experience these qualities are our **Taste Buds**; structures on the tongue that contain the receptor cells for taste. Our taste buds are found on the tip, sides, and back of the tongue and are embedded in the tongue's papillae (small bumps on your tongue). Taste buds are able to differentiate among different tastes through detecting interaction with different molecules or ions. The chemical substances in the food dissolve in saliva, go into the crevices between the papillae, and come into contact with the taste buds which release neurotransmitters that causes adjacent neurons to fire sending nerve impulses to the parietal lobe of the brain and to the limbic system.

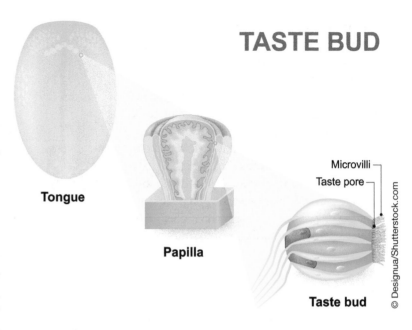

TASTE BUD

Tongue

Papilla

Microvilli
Taste pore
Taste bud

© Designua/Shutterstock.com

Smell and the Nose

Smell or olfaction is our ability to detect and process odors. Exactly how we smell is still an open question. We have 1000's of tiny receptors high in the nasal cavity and the axons of these receptors go directly to the **Olfactory Bulb** which is the smell center in the brain. Hair cells are the receptors in the olfactory epithelium that respond to particular chemicals. These cells have small hairs called cilia on one side and an axon on the other side. In humans, there are about 40 million olfactory receptors. The olfactory tract transmits the signals to the brain to areas such as the hippocampus, amygdala, and hypothalamus; many of these brain areas are part of the limbic system. The limbic system is involved with emotional behavior and memory. That's why when you smell something, it often brings back memories associated with the object. This phenomenon is known as smell memories (something that will be discussed in the application portion of the chapter).

© Khamidulin Sergey/Shutterstock.com

OLFACTORY SYSTEM

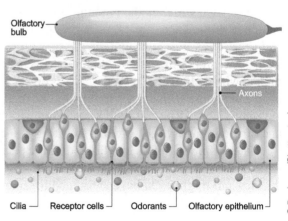

Olfactory bulb

Axons

Cilia   Receptor cells   Odorants   Olfactory epithelium

© Designua/Shutterstock.com

Other Senses (Kinesthetic and Vestibular)

In addition to sight, sound, touch, taste, and smell, we also posess **Kinesthetic Senses** and **Vestibular Senses**. Our kinesthetic senses are our senses of muscle movement, posture, and strain on muscles and joints. Kinesthesia is the sense which helps us detect weight, body position, or the relationship between movements in our body parts such as joints, muscles and tendons. In short, it is the muscle sense. The vestibular senses are our senses of equilibrium and body position in space. We use this information to determine which way is up and which way is down. Awareness of body balance and movement are monitored by the vestibular system. The vestibular senses (the sensations of body rotation and of gravitation and movement) arise in the inner ear; the sense organs are the hair cells that send out signals over the auditory nerve. When there is a discrepancy between visual information and vestibular senses some people will have motion sickness.

© leungchopan/Shutterstock.com

Box: Vertigo and Motion Sickness

Vertigo is a very specific kind of dizziness often described as a sensation of spinning or swaying movement. Vertigo is a medical condition where a person feels as if they or the objects around them are moving when they are not. This may be associated with nausea, vomiting, sweating, or difficulties walking. The dizziness that defines vertigo has one of two causes: most commonly it is thought to be caused by disturbances in the balance organs of the inner ear but it is also thought to be caused by a problem in parts of the brain/sensory nerve pathways that process information to and from the thalamus. Vertigo is often treated through repositioning exercises, therapies, and sometimes medications for short-term relief.

© pathdoc/Shutterstock.com

In contrast to vertigo, motion sickness is a condition in which a disagreement exists between visually perceived movement and the vestibular system's sense of movement. People commonly experience motion sickness in cars, on boats, and airplanes and the sensations accompanying it include dizziness, fatigue, and nausea which can lead to vomiting. Common treatments for motion sickness include getting fresh air, lying down and/or keeping your head still, and drinking something fizzy such as ginger ale. There are also several medications that are available to help with motion sickness. Certain antihistamines like Dramamine are often taken to reduce symptoms or people might use patches behind the ear like Scopolamine.

Perceptual Organization

We have talked a lot about sensation and now will shift more to the perceptual side of the coin! Our senses provide us with raw data about the external world but it must then be interpreted. Perception involves deciphering meaningful patterns in the jumble of sensory information and is the brain's process of organizing and making sense of sensory information.

In the early 20th century, a group of German psychologists calling themselves Gestalt psychologists set out to discover the principles through which we interpret sensory information. Gestalt roughly translates to mean "whole" "form" or "pattern". Gestalt Psychologists believed that our brains create a coherent perceptual experience that is more than simply the sum of the available sensory information and that it does so in predictable ways. One example of this is Figure-Ground. Sometimes when we look at an image, there aren't enough cues to allow us to distinguish the figure from the ground; they blend into each other in a sort of camouflage. We alternate back and forth between the two images because of the ambiguity of the cues.

Another example of Gestalt principles is the concept of **Grouping**; the perceptual tendency to organize stimuli into coherent groups. There are four principles of perceptual organization or grouping: proximity, similarity, closure/connectedness, and continuity. Proximity involves grouping nearby items together, similarity involves clumping similar or like items, closure/connectedness involves seeing items as a single or connected unit, and finally, continuity is seeing things as a smooth continuous pattern. Grouping usually broadens our understanding of the world as our brain tries to fill in missing information rather than seeing things as random bits and pieces of raw data.

© Christos Georghiou/Shutterstock.com

Depth Perception and Illusions

We are constantly judging the distance between ourselves and other objects in a process known as depth perception. Depth perception can be accomplished with one eye (monocular cues) or both eyes (binocular cues) and sometimes our visual cues can lead us astray and cause illusions. Visual illusions result from false and misleading depth cues and can be either physical or perceptual in nature.

© Ioskutnikov/Shutterstock.com

Physical Illusions are caused by the behavior of the light before it reaches the eye causing us to see something that isn't physically there. The classic example of this is seeing a mirage or water on the road in the distance. There isn't actually water but the eyes perceive it due to misleading cues. **Perceptual Illusions** occur because the stimulus contains misleading cues that give rise to inaccurate or impossible perceptions. These illusions can be ambiguous in nature like the Necker Cube or the result of a distortion like the Muller-Lyer Illusion where two separate lines with arrows at either end of each line appear to be of different length because on one line, the arrows point out, while on the other line, the arrows point in. Illusions can also be from impossible figures like the famous Penrose Stairs.

© Darq/Shutterstock.com

Box: Forced Perspectives

In the Peter Jackson directed *Lord of the Rings* movies, the perceptual concept of forced perspective was used quite heavily to make the characters appear larger or smaller to match the descriptions laid out in the books. Have you ever wondered how hobbit Frodo Baggins looked so much smaller than Gandalf the wizard? There were obviously some CGI tricks used but the main technique was to trick viewers with optical illusions using forced perspective. Forced perspective is is a technique which employs optical illusion to make an object appear farther away, closer, larger or smaller than it actually is. It manipulates human visual perception through the use of scaled objects and the correlation between them and the vantage point of the spectator or camera. Through manipulating the location and distance between characters and also through using scaled objects, Jackson was able to make characters appear to be drastically different sizes. For example, in the beginning of the first film, there is a scene where Gandalf rides into town on a wagon with Frodo sitting next to him. From the viewpoint of the movie watcher, the two characters are sitting side by side but if you watch the making of the movies extras, the wagon was specially constructed to distort perception. Frodo and Gandalf are not sitting side by side at all but rather at a distance to manipulate perception!

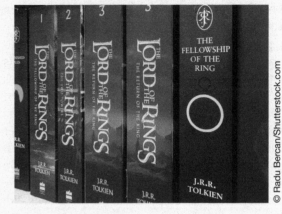

© Radu Bercan/Shutterstock.com

Perception of Movement

The perception of movement is a complicated process involving both visual information from the retina and messages from the muscles around the eyes as they follow an object. Just as with vision, we can have tricks played on us where we think we perceive movement when the objects we are looking at are in fact stationary. Just as there are two different types of visual illusions, we must distinguish between real and apparent movement. **Real Movement** is the physical displacement of an object from one position to another. This is perceived by observing how the positions of objects change in relation to the background

© Master1305/Shutterstock.com

that is perceived as stationary (if we move our head or eyes, the room around us will still appear motionless). **Apparent Movement** is when we perceive movement in objects that are actually standing still. A couple of examples of illusions or tricks with apparent movement include **Stroboscopic Motion** and the **Phi Phenomenon**. Stroboscopic motion is apparent movement that results from a series of still pictures in rapid succession such as you might find in a motion picture. The phi phenomenon is apparent movement caused by flashing lights in sequence. Las Vegas is a great place to witness the phi phenomenon as the lights appear to be moving or chasing each other but are not actuall moving, they are just flashing in succession.

Perceptual Set

Is perception innate or learned? As with most things in Psychology, it is both. Perception is the result of sensation and cognition; physical stimuli and our thoughts, experiences, and expectations. Experience

guides, sustains, and maintains the brain's neural organization and points to the existence of a critical period shortly after birth (an optimal time when certain events must take place) for normal sensory and perceptual development. A lack of visual stimulation during critical periods can cause the cells not to develop their normal connections; our eyes and brain need variety. We are heavily influenced by our experiences, assumptions, and expectations when perceiving the world which can be further evidenced through what is called **Perceptual Set**. Perceptual set is a mental predisposition to perceive one thing and not another; heavily influenced by our experiences, assumptions, and expectations. We often perceive what we expect to perceive and are heavily influenced by context. For example, looking at the image to the right, do you see clouds or do you see a flying saucer (UFO)?

Extrasensory Perception

One final topic related to sensation and perception is **Extrasensory Perception or ESP** which is the ability to perceive or acquire information without using the ordinary senses. In psychology, Parapsychology is the field of

study focusing on extrasensory perception (ESP) and other psychic phenomenon. Are there people who can read minds? See the future? Claims of extrasensory perception include astrological predictions, psychic healing, communication with the dead, and out of body experiences. **Telepathy** is mind-to-mind communication with one person sending thoughts and the other receiving them. **Clairvoyance** is the perception of remote events, such as sensing a friend's house on fire. **Precognition** involves perceiving future events before they have happened. And finally, the other commonly claimed ESP ability is **Psychokinesis** which is mind over matter where people claim to be able to levitate objects or influence the movement of an object with their mind.

No psychic to date has been able to predict the outcome of the lottery or make billions on the stock market and vague predictions are often retrofitted to match events that have occurred. Chance alone would guarantee that some stunning coincidences are bound to occur. As of right now, no reliable scientific evidence exists to suggest that any of these phenomenon exist! In order to give these ideas credibility, they need to be reproducible in controlled experiments. The search for a valid and reliable test for ESP has lead to thousands of experiments and while some have produced results that were greater than chance, when repeated, the experiments failed to produce them again.

In Popular Culture

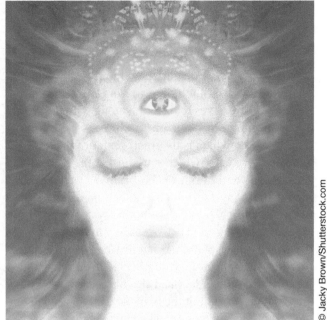

- *The Eye* (2008) – a movie about an eye transplant and the idea of cellular memory.

- *Blindness* (2008) – film where the whole world falls victim to an epidemic of blindness.

- *At First Sight* (1999) – a love story featuring a character who is blind.

- *Ray* (2004) – story of the musician Ray Charles who went blind at the age of seven.

- *The Village* (2004) – a thriller about inhabitants (one of which is blind) who live in fear of the creatures inhabiting the woods beyond it.

- *Daredevil* (2003) – movie about a blind super-hero whose other senses are enhanced.

- *Mr Holland's Opus* (1995) – a story about a music teacher and his son who has a hearing impairment.

- *Lord of The Rings* (2001–2003) – a triology of movies that used foced perspective as a technique to make characters look bigger or smaller.

- *Ghostbusters* (1984) – the original Ghostbusters film features an ESP experiment using flashcards to test precognition abilities.

- *Final Destination* (2000) – a movie featuring themes of precognition to cheat death.

- *Push* (2009) – a film centering on a group of characters with superhuman powers and ESP abilities.

- *Pain by Three Days Grace* (2009) – A song featuring the theme of pain and posing the question: If you could never feel pain again, would you want that?

Psyched with Setmire

"Color Afterimages"
https://www.youtube.com/watch?v=PigN5KVDTJk&t=101s

In this lecture presentation video, we will explore the topic of color afterimages (what are they, why do they occur, and some examples). Prepare your eyes - they are about to have a flag, a bird, and a fish burned into your retinas (at least for a few seconds)!

Application: Smell Memories

Our sense of smell plays a powerful role in several of our behaviors including influencing our sense of taste, perception of flavor, our mood, and also our memories and associations. Have you ever noticed that certain smells can trigger powerful memories? The smell of pumpkin pie instantly transports me to memories of Thanksgiving celebrations with family, certain lotions and perfumes remind me of the people in my life who wear them, and even items as small as sunscreen remind me of summer and trips to the beach!

All of these associations and connections are not accidental or coincidental but rather are the result of several factors including the organization and location of structures in the brain along with the role of conditioning. Smells are first processed by the olfactory bulb which is the smell center of the brain. The olfactory bulb, which starts inside the nose and runs along the bottom of the brain, is part of the brain's limbic system which is sometimes referred to as the "emotional brain". The limbic system contains several structures critical to our ability to interact with the world but of particular interest to this topic are two areas that are strongly implicated in emotion and memory; the amygdala and the hippocampus. The amygdala is an area of the brain strongly associated with emotional memories and the hippocampus plays

© pathdoc/Shutterstock.com

a role in associative learning and is a sort of memory index in the brain. Because the olfactory bulb is so closely connected to the amygdala, smells are commonly linked to emotional memories. When we smell something for the first time, our brain makes connections between the smell and the corresponding events. This is why smells and memories can be so intimately connected with each other and even the smallest of scents can bring up powerful memories.

Conditioning also plays a major role in smell memories. In classical conditioning, we learn to associate one item with another and smell memories are a great example of this process occurring. Classical conditioning, discovered by Ivan Pavlov, links a formerly neutral stimulus with something meaningful thereby creating an association. For Pavlov, it was associating a bell with the presentation of food but in talking about smell and memory, it would be learning to associate an event with a particular smell. For example, before getting married years ago, someone gave me the suggestion that my wife and I give each other a new perfume or cologne on our wedding day as a gift so that we would forever associate that smell with our wedding. Thinking this was not only a great suggestion but also an opportunity to be romantic, I jumped all over it and we exchanged new scents as gifts on that day. Our brains formed links between those smells and the emotional events of the day and now whenever either of us wears one of those scents, those powerful emotional memories are brought back to the surface!

Key Terms

Sensation: the detection of energy from an external source or from inside the body; the physical detection of information from one of the five sense organs.

Perception: the process of organizing and interpreting our sensations.

Receptor Cells: specialized cells that respond to a particular type of energy such as light waves or the vibration of air molecules.

Transduction: the process of converting physical energy such as light or sound into an electrochemical code.

Absolute Threshold: the least amount of energy that can be detected as a stimulation 50% of the time.

Adaptation: a change over time in the responsiveness of the sensory system to a constant stimulus.

Subliminal Messages (Perception): sensory information that is below our level of awareness and therefore not consciously attended to by our mind.

Sense: a group of sensory cells that responds to specific physical phenonemon and that corresponds to a particular group or region within the brain where the signals are received and then interpreted.

Wavelength: the distance from the peak of one light wave to the peak of the next; help to determine the color that we see and experience.

Intensity: the amount of enegy in a light wave which influences our perception of brightness; determined by the wave's height (amplitude).

Hue: the dimension of color determined by the wavelength of light.

Cornea: the transparent protective coating over the front part of the eye.

Pupil: a small opening in the iris through which light enters the eye.

Iris: the colored part of the eye that regulates the size of the pupil.

Lens: the transparent part of the eye behind the pupil that focuses light onto the retina.

Accommodation: the process by which the lens of the eye changes in curvature or thickness to focus on objects that are far away or close.

Retina: The light-sensitive inner surface of the eye, containing the receptor cells that are sensitive to electromagnetic energy and process visual information.

Rods: the receptor cells in the retina responsible for night vision and the perception of brightness.

Cones: the receptor cells in the retina responsible for daytime and color vision.

Fovea: a small depression in the retina of the eye where visual acuity is highest.

Optic Nerve: the bundles of axons of ganglion cells that carries neural messages from each eye to the brain.

Blind Spot: the place on the retina where the axons of all the ganglion cells leave the eye and where there are no receptors.

Optic Chiasm: the point near the base of the brain where some fibers in the optic nerve from each eye cross to the other side of the brain.

Trichromatic (Three Color) Theory: the theory of color vision that holds that all color perception derives from three different color receptors (usually red, green, and blue).

Opponent-Process Theory: theory of color vision that holds that three sets of color receptors (yellow-blue, red-green, and black-white) respond to determine the color you experience.

Color Afterimages: an image continuing to appear in one's vision after exposure to the original image has ceased; explained by the opponent-process theory.

Sound: a psychological experience created by the brain in response to changes in air pressure that are received by the auditory system.

Sound Waves: changes in pressure caused when molecules of air or fluid collide with one another and then move apart again.

Auditory Nerve: a bundle of axons that carries signals from each ear to the brain which then pools the information from thousands of hair cells to create sounds.

Taste Buds: structures on the tongue that contain the receptor cells for taste.

Olfactory Bulb: the smell center in the brain.

Kinesthetic Senses: senses of muscle movement, posture, and strain on muscles and joints.

Vestibular Senses: the senses of equilibrium and body position in space.

Grouping: the perceptual tendency to organize stimuli into coherent clusters or groups.

Physical Illusions: illusions that occur because of the behavior of the light before it reaches the eye causing us to see something that isn't physically there.

Perceptual Illusions: illusions that occur because the stimulus contains misleading cues that give rise to inaccurate or impossible perceptions.

Real Movement: the physical displacement of an object from one position to another.

Apparent Movement: the perception of movement in objects that are actually standing still.

Stroboscopic Motion: apparent movement that results from a series of still pictures in rapid succession as in a motion picture.

Phi Phenomenon: apparent movement caused by flashing lights in sequence.

Perceptual Set: a mental predisposition to perceive one thing and not another; heavily influenced by our experiences, assumptions, and expectations.

Extrasensory Perception (ESP): the ability to perceive or acquire information without using the ordinary senses.

Parapsychology: the field of study focusing on ESP and other psychic phenomenon.

Telepathy: a form of ESP involving mind-to-mind communication; one ne person sending thoughts and the other receiving them.

Clairvoyance: a form of ESP involving the perception of remote events, such as sensing a friend's house on fire.

Precognition: a form of ESP involving the percption of future events.

Psychokinesis: a form of ESP nvolving the ability to levitate objects or influence the movement of an object with one's mind.

Chapter 5
States of Consciousness

Outline

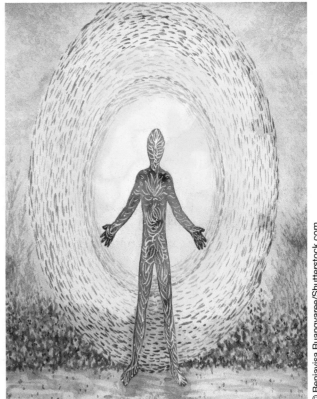

© Benjavisa Ruangvaree/Shutterstock.com

Introduction to the Chapter (Summary)

This unit will explore the topic of consciousness; the relationship between the mind and the world with which it interacts. Even when we are fully awake and alert we are only consciously aware of a small portion of what is going on around us and use selective attention to focus in on what we deem important. Since we process only a tiny amount of the stimuli bombarding us, we sometimes fail to notice certain things and can fall victim to inattentional blindness and/or change blindness.

Daydreams are a common form of altered consciousness and typically occur when we would rather be somewhere else or doing something else. Another state of consciousness is sleep, a natural state of rest characterized by a reduction in voluntary body movement and decreased awareness of our surroundings. We spend almost 1/3 of our lives sleeping! Nobody knows for sure why we sleep but we do know that sleepiness appears to be triggered by several bodily chemical along with our biological rhythms. While we sleep we progress through several different stages, each marked by characteristic patterns of brain waves, muscular activity, blood and body temperature. Rapid-Eye Movement (REM) is when dreams typically occur and while there are a number of posited explanations as to why we dream, dreams continue to remain a great mystery!

Another form of consciousness is hypnosis which is typically described as a social interaction in which one person (the hypnotist) suggests to another (the subject) that certain perceptions, feelings, thoughts, or behaviors will spontaneously occur. Individuals vary in their susceptibility to hypnosis, in how well they respond to suggestions made during hypnosis, and to posthypnotic commands. Hypnosis can be helpful for pain relief and getting rid of unwanted behaviors but contrary to popular belief, cannot force someone to act against their will. In general, hypnosis is a controversial state and there is no universal definition of what it means to be hypnotized.

Consciousness can also be altered through the use of psychoactive drugs which are chemical substances that change mood and perception. Most people can use drugs moderately and not suffer ill effects but for some it can escalate into a substance use disorder or can create a substance induced disorder. In general, the causes of substance use disorders are a complex combination of biological (genetic basis), psychological, and social factors (peer pressure and cultural norms) that vary for each individual and for each substance.

Drugs can affect the mind and body as agonists or antagonist and there are three general categories of drugs: depressants, stimulants, and hallucinogens. Depressants are chemicals that slow down behavior or cognitive processes and include substances such as alcohol, the opiates, and benzodiazepines. Stimulants excite the sympathetic nervous system and produce feelings of optimism and boundless energy and include caffeine, nicotine, cocaine, amphetamines, and ecstasy. Hallucinogens are psychedelic drugs that distort visual and auditory perception evoking sensory images in the absence of sensory input; the most common examples are LSD and marijuana.

Consciousness

The field of Psychology began with studying and explaining the various states of consciousness and this topic has played a role in the theories of many prominent psychologists over time. The idea of **Consciousness** can be a hard one to pinpoint but generally refers to our awareness of various cognitive processes such as sleeping, dreaming, concentrating, and making decisions. Another way of putting it might be to say that it refers to the relationship between the mind and the world with which it interacts.

© Benjavisa Ruangvaree/Shutterstock.com

Selective Attention

Our conscious mind, even when we are fully awake and alert, is only aware of a small portion of what is going on around us. Because we are constantly being bombarded with sensory information, in order to make sense of our environment, we select only the most important information to attend to and filter the rest out. This focusing of our conscious awareness on particular stimuli is known as **Selective Attention** (which is sort of like selective hearing where we only hear what we want or choose to hear). For example, we are not consciously aware of our blood pressure or respiration, we can ride a bike or walk without consciously thinking about it, and we might even travel a route so many times that it becomes almost automatic. Because we only attend to a small amount of sensory information, we sometimes fail to notice things in our environments in a phenomenon called **Inattentional Blindness**; failing to see visible objects because our attention is directed elsewhere. Very closely related to this is **Change Blindness** which occurs when we fail to notice changes in stimuli or in our environment.

© Charles Amundson/Shutterstock.com;
© Luis Molinero/Shutterstock.com

One of the most well-known examples of inattentional blindness is the invisible gorilla test which has been conducted through several different variations over time. The essence of this experiment is that participants are asked to focus in on the number of times a basketball is passed back and forth between players wearing yellow jerseys. Also present in the experiment, as distractions, are several basketball players wearing a dark blue jersey and participants are told to ignore them and to focus in only on the yellow jersey players. Since the players in dark colored jerseys are ignored, when a person in a gorilla costume walks in the middle of the court, most of the participants fail to notice it! After the experiment, very few members reported seeing anything strange or odd while they watched the film and only once they are told to watch it as if it were a show on television, do they notice the gorrilla! It is incredible to think that we could miss so much in our visual field simply because we weren't directly paying attention to it!

Daydreams

Before we cover the topic of sleep, there is a dream-like state of altered consciousness worth mentioning and that is **Daydreams**; apparently effortless shifts in attention away from the here and now into a private world of make-believe. When we daydream, we have a short-term detachment (during wakefulness) from one's immediate surroundings, during which a person's contact with reality is blurred and partially substituted by a visionary fantasy. A Freudian psychological perspective would interpret daydreaming as an expression of repressed instincts or wishes similar to those revealed in night-

time dreams while other persepctives view daydreams as nothing more than a retreat from the real world. We typically daydream when we would rather be somewhere else or doing something else and they often represent images of unfilfilled thoughts or wishes. In general, daydreams are considered normal and aren't thought to be harmful unless they start to interfere with productive activities, replace human interaction, or become extensive.

Sleep

Sleep is a natural state of rest characterized by a reduction in voluntary body movement and decreased awareness of our surroundings. It is wild to think that if we sleep eight hours a night, we will spend 1/3 of our lives sleeping! While some people claim that they never sleep, when studied in a lab, their brain waves show otherwise.

Sleep Theories

For something that takes up almost a third of our lifetimes, it is shocking how little we know about sleep and why we do it! Nobody knows for sure why we sleep but of course we have some theories and it is probably some combination of all of them that explains our need for sleep.

One theory of sleep is the *Restorative theory* which says that sleep helps our bodies save and restore energy by slowing down our metabolism, helping to replenish our stores of neurotransmitters (neurons decrease their activity during sleep), and serving to "restore" what is lost in the body while we are awake by providing an opportunity for the body to repair and rejuvenate itself. Many major restorative functions like muscle growth and tissue repair occur mostly during sleep which further supports this idea. Another theory is that of *Learning and Memory*. During sleep, we can reorganize and store information and Rapid Eye Movement (REM) sleep plays a role in memory retention and consolidation.. This can be further supported if we looks at the effects of not getting enough sleep on memory and learning. Sleep deprivation has been shown to lead to reduced attention and impairment of short-term or working memory. This in turn influences what gets saved as long-term episodic memories, but it also impacts the performance of higher-level cognitive functions such as decision-making and reasoning *Developmental /Brain Plasticity Theories* correlate sleep to changes in the structure and organization of the brain. REM sleep is a major component of sleep for babies both in utero and after birth and is thought to activate visual, motor and sensory areas in the brain increasing the ability of neurons to make the correct connections and function properly. We also sometimes reference *Adaptive/Evolutionary/Inactivity Theories* which view sleep as an adaptive behavior to keep us away from trouble at night asserting that we refrain from being active at night when our vision is poor. Another way of saying this would be that inactivity at night is an adaptation that served a survival function by keeping organisms out of harm's way at times when they would be particularly vulnerable.

What makes us sleepy?

We may not be certain about why we sleep, but we know quite a bit more about what makes us sleepy. Each one of us possesses a **Circadian Rhythm** which is a regular biological rhythm with a period of approximately 24 hours. Circadian rhythm

comes from the Latin expression "circa diem" meaning about a day and is an ancient and fundamental adaptation to the 24 hour solar cycle of light and dark found not only in humans but also in animals and plants. The **Suprachiasmatic Nucleus (SCN)** is a cluster of neurons in the hypothalamus that receives input from the retina regarding light and dark cycles and is involved in regulating our biological clock or circadian rhythms. In response to light and dark cycles the SCN releases neurotransmitters that control the body's temperature, metabolism, blood pressure, hunger, and so on. Our bodily rhythms can function and be influenced even without cues from the cycle of night and day (the SCN is not the only determinant) and

we often notice our natural rhythms the most when they are disrupted such as in cases of jet lag. If you have ever traveled more than an hour or two forward or backward in time, you know the feeling of jet lag. For my honeymoon I went on a cruise out of Puerto Rico which was absolutely amazing! The cruise ship had soft serve ice cream machines everywhere and must have gained ten pounds that week! I digress! The point of the story was that when I traveled to Puerto Rico, which is a five hour time difference from California, I struggled with the difference and suffered from jet lag. I only struggled a little bit going there but it was coming home that I really noticed the disruption with the timing of my hunger for meals and my need to sleep being off my usual schedule. I was able to readjust after just a few days but it was a glaring example of my typical bodily rhythms!

In addition to our natural rhythms and the SCN, there are several bodily chemicals that play a role in our sleepiness with two of the most prominent being melatonin and adenosine. **Melatonin** is a hormone that contributes to the regulation of the sleep-wake cycle by chemically causing drowsiness and lowering body temperature. When darkness falls, the biological clock triggers the production of

© Grigory Lugovoy/Shutterstock.com

melatonin which makes you feel sleepy. **Adenosine** is a neurotransmitter that plays a role in promoting sleep and suppressing arousal, with levels increasing with each hour an organism is awake. Adenosine builds up in your system as time awake increases and then while you sleep, your body breaks down the adenosine to start over the next day.

The Rhythms of Sleep

We have learned about sleep largely through sleep studies conducted in sleep labs where electrodes are attached to the skull to monitor brain waves. In these studies, significant differences in sleep behavior between people have been noted but almost everyone goes through the same stages of sleep with each stage being marked by characteristic patterns of brain waves, muscular activity, blood, and body temperature.

One of the biggest misconceptions about sleep is that sleep is just a matter of our bodies "turning off" for several hours, followed by our bodies "turning back on" when we awake. Most of us think of sleep as a passive and relatively constant and unchanging process when in fact, sleep is a very active state. As discussed previously, the brain is an electrochemical organ with electrical activity emanating from the brain

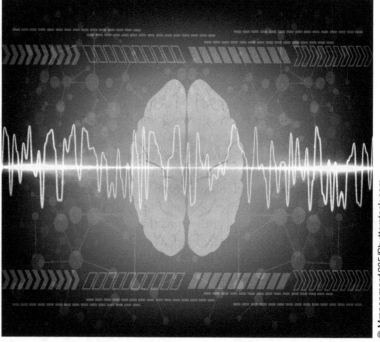

© Mrspopman1985/Shutterstock.com

being displayed in the form of brainwaves. Each type of brain wave represents a different speed of oscillating electrical voltages in the brain and characterizes a different stage of sleep.

When we are wide awke, our brain wave patterns are characterized as **Beta Waves**; waves that are the highest in frequency and lowest in amplitude (averaging 13 to 40 cycles per second). As we lay our head on the pillow and prepare to fall asleep, we are in an awake but relaxed state sometimes referred to as the Twilight Stage. In the **twilight stage** we display irregular slow low **Alpha Waves** (slower waves that are higher in amplitude ranging from 9 to 14 cycles per second). It is relatively commonly for people to see flashing lights, patterns, floating or falling sensations, and visions of landscapes while in this state.

Once we actually fall asleep, we enter **Stage 1 of Sleep** which is marked by **Theta Waves** (tight waves of low amplitude averaging 4 to 7 cycles per second). Theta waves resemble those of when a person is alert and excited but our pulse is starting to slow and our muscles relax. Stage one of sleep is considered light sleep, usually lasts just a few minutes, and a person is easily aroused or awakened at this stage by any changes in the environment such as a sound. Stage 2 of Sleep is also considered light sleep and is characterized by theta waves but with two distinct patterns; **Sleep Spindles** and **K-Complexes** (short rhythmic bursts of brain wave activity). Stages one and two involve us transitioning from being awake into being asleep, are considered light sleep, and a person can eaasily be awakned by changes in the environment.

Normal Adult Brain Waves

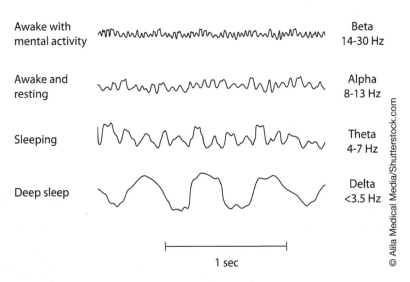

© Allia Medical Media/Shutterstock.com

Box: Power (Cat) Naps

Power or cat naps are a growing trend not only in large businesses but also among what has become an increasingly sleep deprived population! A **Power Nap** is a short sleep taken during the working day to restore one's mental alertness; a short sleep that ends before slow-wave sleep (deep sleep) occurs. Sometimes these short naps are referred to as a cat nap and got that name because cats tend to fall asleep randomly for brief periods of time.

A power nap of about 10-20 minutes can help to improve mood, alertness, lift productivity, lower stress, and

© BONNINSTUDIO/Shutterstock.com

improve a person's memory and learning without leaving you feeling groggy or interfering with nighttime sleep. 20 minutes seems to be the ideal amount of time for a power nap. If you wake up after 20 minutes you will likely feel refreshed and the benefits discussed above but waking up after 30 minutes or more can result in **Sleep Inertia** which is the feeling of grogginess and disorientation than can come from waking from a deep sleep. In general it is better to nap for either 20 minutes or less or to nap for 90 minutes and complete an entire sleep cycle if you want to avoid the cranky and groggy feelings of waking from a deep sleep.

When power napping, there are a few key things to remember! One important thing is to not nap too late in the day so that you don't make it harder to fall asleep at night. In general, mid to late morning seems to be ideal or even in the early afternoon. Another important thing is to fall asleep quickly. Make the room dark if possible, eliminate all distractions like cell phones or other things that might keep you from focusing on sleep, make sure that the room is a comfortable temperature, and consider playing soothing music in the background or investing in a white noise machine.

Information from: http://www.nationalsleepfoundation.org

Next we progress to **Stages 3 & 4 of Sleep** which are considered deep sleep. Stages 3 and 4 are marked by **Delta Waves** (0 to 4 cycles per second) which are the slowest and highest amplitude brain waves. There is no real division between stages 3 and 4 except that, typically, stage 3 is considered delta sleep in which less than 50 percent of the waves are delta waves, and in stage 4 more than 50 percent of the waves are delta waves. In deep sleep, a person is harder to wake, doesn't respond to lights or noises, and heart rate, blood pressure, and temperature continues to drop.

Rapid-Eye Movement (REM) or Paradoxical Sleep is an additional sleep stage characterized by rapid eye movements and dreaming. This stage is called paradoxical sleep because although brain activity, heart rate, blood pressure, and other physiological functions resemble waking consciousness, the sleeper is deeply asleep and incapable of moving; our voluntary muscle are essentially paralyzed.

In a normal night's sleep, a sleeper begins in stage 1 and then progressively moves down through the stages to stage 4 and then back up through the stages toward stage 1 again though it becomes replaced with REM sleep as we go through the night. So the sleeper goes: 1, 2, 3, 4, 3, 2, 1, and then REM. One cycle, from stage 1 to REM takes approximately ninety minutes. This is repeated throughout the night, with the length of REM periods increasing, and the length of delta sleep decreasing, until during the last few cycles there is no delta sleep at all.

© Luis Molinero/Sutterstock.com

Sleep Disorders

Many people suffer from chronic, long-term sleep disorders ranging from insomnia to narcolepsy. One of the most common occurrences during sleep are **Nightmares**; frightening dreams that occur during REM sleep. Nightmares can affect anyone at any age; they are simply a frightening dream. There is quite a bit of history or lore on nightmares. Nightmares were originally considered to be the work of demons which were thought to sit on the chest of sleepers. In Old English the name for these beings was *mare* and since they generally occurred at night, the name nightmare was formed. The term "nightmare" was originally classified by Dr. Samuel Johnson as referring to sleep paralysis but has since evolved into our modern definition. Over time, nightmares have been closely connected to myths, monsters, and other influences across time and cultures. In Swedish folklore, sleep paralysis is caused by a Mare, a supernatural creature related to the werewolf. The Mare is a damned woman, who is cursed and her body is carried mysteriously during sleep and without her noticing. In this state, she visits villagers to sit on their rib cages while they are asleep, causing them to experience nightmares. In Fiji the experience is interpreted as "kana tevoro" being 'eaten' or possessed by a demon. In many cases the 'demon' can be the spirit of a recently dead relative who has come back for some unfinished business, or has come to communicate some important news to the living. In 19th century Europe, diet was thought to be responsible for nightmares. For example, in Charles Dickens 's A Christmas Carol, Ebenezer Scrooge attributes the ghost he sees to ". . . an undigested bit of beef, a blot of mustard, a crumb of cheese, a fragment of an underdone potato . . .".

Nightmares occur during REM sleep, are generally remembered upon waking, and are very common. In contrast to nightmares, **Night Terrors** are frightening, often terrifying dreams that occur during NREM sleep (stages 1–4) from which a person is difficult to awaken and doesn't remember the content. When people have night terrors, they often sit up in bed suddenly screaming out of fear. Night terrors are much more common in children than adults with the most common age of occurrence being in children ages 5–12. While they are relatively rare, we do know that they seem to have a genetic component to them and are often brought on by sleep deprivation or disruption of a routine. It can be incredibly difficult to snap a child out of a night terror and they are often quite scared and confused which only adds to to difficulty.

Nightmares	Night Terrors
Common	Rare
Occurs in all ages	Occurs mainly in children (ages 5–12)
Remembered upon waking	Not typically remembered upon waking
Occur during REM sleep	Occur during NREM sleep

Another sleep issue that is quite common is **Insomnia**. Insomnia is a sleep disorder characterized by difficulty in falling asleep or remaining asleep throughout the night. Insomnia can affect not only your energy level and mood but also your health, work performance, and quality of life. Most people will struggle with insomnia at some point in their life as it is often stress related or due to poor sleep habits. Finding ways to reduce and cope with stress along with having better sleep habits (sometimes called sleep hygeine) can reduce insomnia. Some tips for better sleep hygeine include: avoiding substances like caffeine, nicotine, and alochol which may interfere with the ability to fall asleep or the quality of sleep, avoiding excessive stimulation in bed or prior to bed, trying to go to bed at the same time each evening, and having a routine prior to going to bed.

Other sleep issues that people face include **Sleeptalking** and **Sleepwalking**. Talking or walking in your sleep occurs during stage 4 when we are in our deepest sleep of the night. These two things are more common in children than adults and while they can be confusing for not only the sleeper but also those around them, contrart to popular opinion it is not dangerous to awaken a sleepwalker; it is just difficult! **Sleep Apnea** is another relatively common sleep disorder characterized by breathing difficulty during the night and feelings of exhaustion during the day. And finally, **Narcolespy** is a hereditary sleep disorder characterized by sudden nodding off and loss of muscle tone following moments of emotional arousal. With narcolepsy, a person isn't sleepy all the time as popular opinion tends to believe. Someone suffering from narcolepsy immediately enters into REM sleep which causes the lose of muslce tone and can produce frightening hallucinations.

Dreams and Dream Theories

Earlier we mentioned that we dream during REM sleep. **Dreams** are vivid visual and auditory experiences that occur primarily during REM periods of sleep. An average person has 4-5 dreams per night (1-2 hours of sleep) with each typically containing a storyline or sequence of events. Dreams can be affected by stimuli (internal and external) and can be incredibly vivid and hard to distinguish from reality.

We don't know why we dream but of course, as Psychologists, we have several posited explanations and it is most likely some combination of these theories that fully captures why it is we dream every night. One commonly referenced theory is that *dreams are unconscious wishes*. Sigmund Freud called dreams the "royal road to the unconscious" and believed they represented unfulfilled wishes. In dreams, he believed that people permit themselves to express primitive desires relatively free of moral control. Another theory explains *dreams as information processing*; in our dreams we reprocess information gathered during the day as our way of strengthening memories of information. Our brain is bombarded with sensory material during the day and we need a "time-out" to decide what is valuable and where that information should be stored or if it should be erased. From this perspective, dreams seem illogical because the brain is rapidly scanning old files.

Another theory is that dreams serve a *physiological function* and help with developing and preserving neural pathways. In this theory, dreams are almost like a mental house keeping or a defragmenting our mental hard drive. Through dreams we are shuffling old connections and erasing inefficient links to streamline our system. The *activation-synthesis theory* views dreams as neural activity. Using advanced brain imaging techniques research has shown that the limbic system which is involved in emotions, motivations, and memories, is widely active during dreams which might explain the emotional content

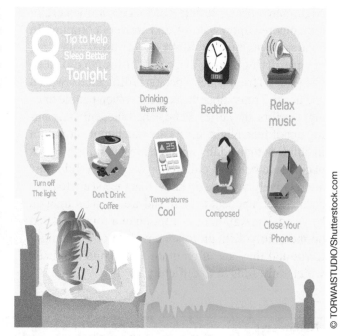

© TORWAISTUDIO/Shutterstock.com

© Milkovasa/Shutterstock.com

© Victor Brave/Shutterstock.com

of dreams. So while the limbic system and the mind are functioning and active during dreams, the dreams themselves are just random firings of the brain and it is only in our conscious mind that we want to find or create a deeper meaning in them. In other words, dreams are random firings of nerves in the brain that we then attempt to make sense of when we wake up. Another theory is that dreams allow for *cognitive development* and brain maturation to occur. Newborn babies sleep an absurd twenty or so hours a day (though it sadly is not all at once but rather occurs in 20–30 minute chunks of time). In the periods of sleep, it is thought that an incredble amount of brain and cogniive development is occurring. Finally, we can also explain *dreams as an extension of waking life.* According to this theory, we extend the concerns of our waking life in altered form and dreams often reflect a person's unique conceptions, concerns, and interests from that day. I have had many dreams that fit this theory! Too many times have I watched *The Walking Dead* just before going to sleep and then find myself dreaming about walkers and post-apocalyptic society! Again, all of these theoires may be true on some level or for certain dreams, we just don't know!

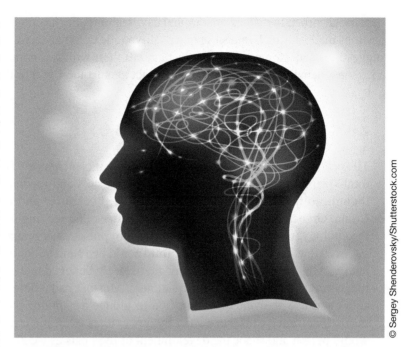

© Sergey Shenderovsky/Shutterstock.com

© Diana.Bahrin03/Shutterstock.com

Hypnosis

Hypnosis, named after Hypnos the Greek God of sleep, is a trancelike state in which a person responds readily to suggestions. Another way of describing it might be to say that is is a social interaction in which one person (the hypnotist) suggests to another (the subject) that certain perceptions, feelings, thoughts, or behaviors will spontaneously occur. A person who is hypnotized is not sleeping but rather is relaxed and alert the whole time in a state that is often compared to daydreaming.

Everyone can be hypotized but there is an incredible variety between individuals in their susceptibility to hypnosis which is thought to be related to our ability to

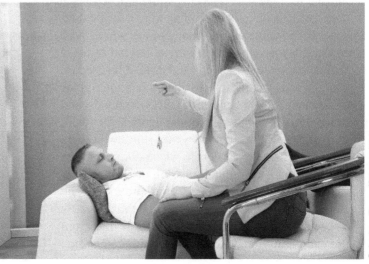

© Andrey_Popov/Shutterstock.com

become absorbed in reading, music, and daydreaming. Each person also varies in how well they respond to suggestions made during hypnosis and to posthypnotic commands. Contrary to popular opinion and film, hypnotic suggestions can't force someone to act against their will. It is completely possible for a hypnotist to influence a person's behavior but not cause them to act against their will or do something they didn't want to do.

Box: Brief History of Hypnosis

The use of hypnosis seems to stretch back into ancient history. Hieroglyphics found on ancient Egyptian tombs depict the use of hypnosis in religious rites and medical procedures, the Ancient Greeks were thought to have used hypnosis for surgical procedures and healing, and ancient texts from Egypt, China, Greece, and Rome all describe practices that we might now regard as hypnosis. In the field of Psychology, one of the first people to use hypnosis was Franz Anton Mesmer (1734–1815). Mesmer believed that an invisible magnetic fluid could be found not only in the human body, but also throughout nature; a theory he called animal magnetism. He believed that magnets could help restore the balance of magnetic fluid and therefore cure sickness. Mesmer had a flare for theater and showmanship and would chant and use an eye fixation method to induce a hypnotic trance in his patients. The idea of animal magnetism failed to be supported by any evidence but his trance-inducing and suggestion techniques would persist and shape the development of hypnosis as we know it today. Mesmer was the first to lead hypnosis out of the realms of the occult and supernatural into scientific study though some might say that he didn't lead it very far!

As the belief in animal magnetism and an ethereal magnetic fluid faded away, the idea of suggestion began to gain ground as several other prominent psychologists and physicians experimented with the idea of mesmerism. Dr. Jean-Martin Charcot (1825–1893) was another prominent contribution in the field of psychology to the progression of hypnosis. Charcot, widely recognized for his expertise in neurology, attempted to categorize and label various depths of trance and was well-known for his interests in female hysteria. Scottish doctor James Braid (1795–1860) was the first to coin the term "hypnosis". Braid is often regarded as the "Father of Hypnosis" and studied the topic extensively through a scientific lens. Braid would use eye-fixation and attention related techniques to induce a trance-like state. He could put people into a sleep-like trance by having them focus on candle flames or small mirrors. In fact, the sleep like states that he induced inspired the name hypnosis after Hypnos the Greek God of sleep.

Dr. Sigmund Freud (1856–1939) used hypnosis to release the emotions of his patients by putting them into a trancelike state. Working with Dr. Joseph Breuer, a master hypnotist who believed that he could address patients directly while they were in a hypnotic state, Freud came up with many of the premises of modern day psychoanalysis. Freud fell out of favor with hypnotherapy methods and instead focused on using free association to reach the unconscious minds of his clients. Clark Hull (1884-1952), a scientist and academic, was another important figure in the realm of hypnosis. Hull is best known for starting the state vs. non-state hypnosis debate which dominated the academic and scientific discussion of hypnosis for much of the 20th century and even into today. The state side of the debate argues that hypnotic trance is a special state of consciousness that is distinct from the everyday. Non-state theorists on the other side

© Milles Studio/Shutterstock.com

(Continued)

argue that there is no special state of consciousness associated with trance and that hypnotic phenomenon can be accounted for by everyday psychological mechanisms such as suggestibility.

Another prominent individual was American Psychiatrist Dr. Milton Erickson (1901–1980) who embraced a very naturalistic approach to the induction of hypnosis using the power of metaphor and symbolic story telling. Above all, Erickson was interested in the therapeutic value of hypnosis and helped to establish hypnosis as an important therapeutic tool through the smuggling in of messages to the unconscious which he believed contained all of the resources necessary to bring about a cure for an individual in the present moment.

Hypnosis has been controversial throughout its history and remains debated even today. Despite all the controversy, hypnosis can be viewed as simply a method for focusing attention inwards and is thought to be something that we all experience rather than being some magical or mysterious phenomenon. Advances in neurological science and brain imaging along with linking hypnosis to REM (Rapid Eye Movement) have also helped to add credibility to hypnosis and resolve the state vs. non-state debate that has existed since the early 1900s.

Hypnosis can be used to help with undesired behaviors, pain relief, reducing anxiety, and quite a few other therapeutic applications. The cornerstone of how hypnosis works is through the use of **Posthypnotic Suggestions** which are suggestions, made during a hypnosis session, to be carried out after the subject is no longer hypnotized. For example, a posthypnotic suggestion could be given to a person that the next time they are craving a cigarette, they will reach for a carrot instead. Through the use of these suggestions, hypnosis can help to remove unwanted behaviors such as smoking, eating problems, anxiety and so on. We also often hear of hypnosis being used to help

© Image Point Fr/Shutterstock.com

retrieve memories and while this might be a common usage, it doesn't always guarantee an accurate retrieval. We often combine fact with fiction and the hypnotist can unintentionally plant memories which is why memories retrieved through hypnosis are not accepted in courts as testimony.

Throughout its history and into today, hypnosis has been a controversial state. There is no universal definition of what it means to be hypnotized as everyone describes it in different ways. While the commonality of some form of hypnotic induction exists, the specifics of the procedure are often different from practionioner to practitioner. The bigger problem is that it is not really known what hypnosis is. Some believe hypnosis is just a social phenomenon where people act and feel in ways appropriate for "good hypnotic subjects". Another commonly proposed theory is that hypnosis involves a divided consciousness or a split in our awareness that allows some thoughts and behaviors to occur simultaneously with others. For example, with pain control, this theory proposes that hypnosis allows a dissociation of the sensation of pain from the emotional suffering that defines the experience of pain. Hypnosis is most likely an extension of the normal principles of social influence and of everyday dissociations between our conscious awareness and our automatic behaviors but again, this lack of clarity, tends to make it controversial.

Drug Altered Consciousness

Another form of altered consciousness can be discussed in relationship to the impact of drugs on behavior and consciousness. A **Psychoactive Drug** is a chemical substance that changes moods and perceptions. In nearly every culture throughout time people have sought ways to alter their consciousness. Alcohol has the longest history of widespread use (stone-age groups making mead, wine being a gift from the gods to Greeks and Romans, and so on). While drugs have been around throughout time, drug use today has a few key differences compared to drug use in the past. One big difference over time is that drug use in the past was often more spiritual or as a medicine

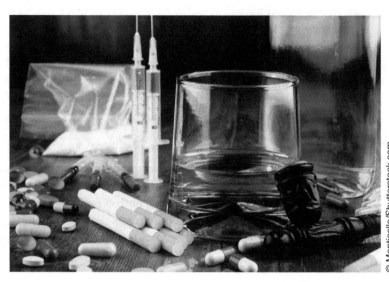

© Monticello/Shutterstock.com

or tonic compared to being more recreational in motivation in current times. Drugs have also changed to stronger and more addictive substances than were previously available with many popular substances now being synthetic drugs with unpredictable effects. And finally, we know more now about the harmful and also helpful effects of drugs. Go back 100 years and Freud thought cocaine was going to be the next wonder drug. He would send it in the mail to his fiancé and take heavy doses of it himself. At the time, we were unaware of the strong addictive tendencies that come with the use of cocaine. In a different spirit, we also know now that there are helpful medicinal qualities to drugs like marijuana which can be prescribed to help relieve anxiety, pain, nausea, and several other implications. We have definitely learned a lot about the various psychoactive substances in use today!

Typical Use Versus Substance Use Disorder

The average person can use a drug every now and then or even moderately and not suffer any ill effects from doing so. Now this obviously depends on the substance and the person using it, but many people drink coffee without developing a problematic relationship with it or even use marijuana without becoming dependent on the drug. But for some, the use of a substance, even once, can escalate into a long-term problematic pattern or relationship known as a Substance Use Disorder. **Substance Use Disorder** combines the previously separate disorders that were substance abuse and substance dependence (addiction) and also adds the element of being on a continuum from mild to severe. In order to have a substance use disorder, a person must display multiple problematic symptoms that cause significant distress and impairment in their personal,

© napocska/Shutterstock.com

social, or occupational life for a period of at least twelve months. Some of the symptoms include having a craving or strong desire to use the substance, recurrent use of the substance despite posing physical hazards or causing problems, a cessation or reduction of important activities because of the use of the substance, failure to fulfill responsibilities because of the use of the substance, and also experiencing **Tolerance** and **Withdrawal** reactions to the drug. Tolerance is a diminishing effect with regular use of the same dose of a drug; a person requires higher and/or stronger doses to produce the original effects or to prevent withdrawal. Withdrawal involves unpleasant physical or psychological effects following the discontinuance of a substance. As a person's body becomes used to having a drug, their chemistry changes causing these two reactions to occur which only intensifies the difficulty of stopping the use of the drug.

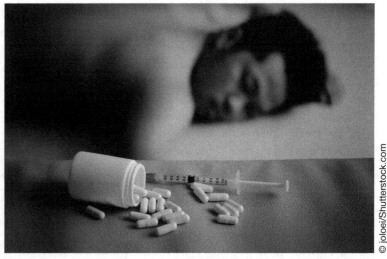

How Drugs Work in the Body

There are several different mechanisms of action when it comes to how drugs work in the body but many addictive drugs can be grouped into one of two categories based on their method of action. Drugs can often be classified as being either an **Agonist** or an **Antagonist** though it might not always be this simple as they can often be further divided into direct and indirect mechanisms of action. An agonist is a chemical that binds to some receptor of a cell and triggers a response by that cell. Agonists often trigger a response and/or mimic the effect of a neurotransmitter in the brain. One example of an agonist might be morphine which mimics the actions of endorphins in our body. An antagonist is a type of drug that does not provoke a biological response itself upon binding to a receptor, but blocks or dampens neurotransmitters in the brain. An example of an antagonist is Haloperidol which blocks dopamine to help control symptoms of schizophrenia. In summary, whereas an agonist causes or triggers an action, an antagonist blocks an or dampens an action. Again, it is not always as simple as this classification. It is important to look at the specific neurotransmitters and also the systems being affected when deciding how to classify the method of action of a drug.

Three Main Categories of Drugs

When talking about specific drugs, we typically boil them down to three main categories: depressants, stimulants, and hallucinogens.

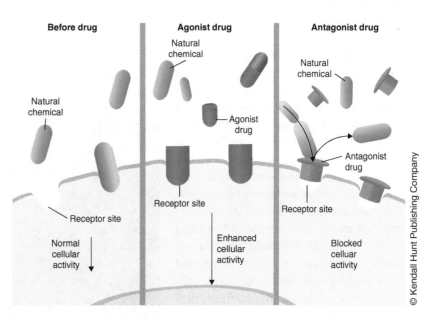

Depressants

Depressants are chemicals that slow down behavior or cognitive processes and are often taken to reduce tension, forget troubles, or relieve feelings of inadequacy, loneliness, or boredom. **Alcohol** is the most commonly used depressant and is the intoxicating ingredient in whiskey, beer, wine, and other fermented or distilled liquors. Alcohol is the most frequently used drug in the U.S. and can be highly addictive with many long-term effects. Excessive alcohol abuse can harm virtually every organ in the body (brain, kidneys, liver, heart, etc) and alcohol is commonly involved in violent and accidental deaths, automobile accidents, suicides, and domestic violence. Alcohol affects the frontal lobes of the brain which regulate impulse control, reasoning, and judgment, the cerebellum which controls motor control and balance, and then the spinal cord and medulla which control our involuntary functions. It works by interfering with the communication between nerve cells by interacting with the receptors on some cells. It inhibits Glutamate (causes relaxation of muscles), enhances GABA (creates feelings of calm and reduced anxiety), increases dopamine (feelings of excitement and stimulation), and increases endorphins which kills pain and leads to a high feeling.

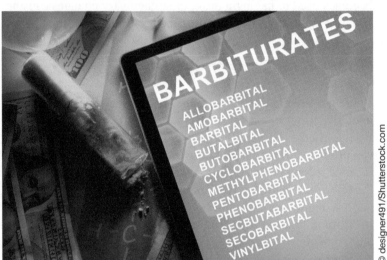

Barbiturates are another group within the depressants and are drugs that depress the activity of the central nervous system, reducing anxiety but often also impairing memory and judgment. As a group, these depressants were first used for their sedative and anticonvulsant properties but are now used only to treat such conditions as epilepsy and arthritis. They are commonly known as downers and can cause dependence when used for long periods. **Benzodiazepines** are similar to the barbiturates but in general are a slightly safer and more commonly used group of drugs. Benzodiazepines typically work on the neurotransmitter

GABA (gamma-aminobutyric acid) and are commonly prescribed to help with anxiety and to work as a sleep-aid. The most common drugs in this categoy are Valium and Xanex which are typically prescribed for short-term use. As a group, these drugs can lead to dependence and have several side effects including causing sleepiness and tolerance.

The **Opiates** are another group of depressants drugs and include substances such as opium, morphine, codeine, and heroin, derived from the opium poppy, that dull the senses and cause feelings of euphoria, well-being, and relaxation. Opiates depress nerve transmission in sensory pathways of the spinal cord and brain that signal pain by binding to mu receptors in brain and medulla. Regular use of the opiates often leads to tolerance and dependence and withdrawal symptoms.

Stimulants

Stimulants are the second main category of drugs including amphetamines, cocaine, nicotine and several others that stimulate the sympathetic nervous system and produce feelings of optimism and boundless energy. One of the most commonly used stimulants is **Caffeine** which occurs naturally in coffee, tea, and cocoa, and is used to maintain alertness and wakefulness often making it more difficult for a person to fall asleep. Caffeine works by increasing adrenaline, and Acetylcholine along with blocking the effects of adenosine, a brain chemical involved in sleep. Thinking the body is in an emergency, the pituitary gland initiates the "fight or flight" response by releasing adrenaline which causes the liver to release extra sugar into the bloodstream for energy. Caffeine also affects dopamine levels (a chemical in the brain's pleasure center) which can make you feel as though you have more energy. Caffeine is generally considered a benign drug but high doses may cause caffeinism, anxiety, headaches, and insomnia with chronic use leading to tolerance and withdrawal symptoms or crashing, irritability, and depression.

Amphetamines which are drugs that initially produce "rushes" of euphoria often followed by sudden crashes and sometimes severe depression, are another group of stimulants. Amphetamines are widely used for recreational purposes and narrowly used for medical purposes though their use originated as a nasal spray for asthma relief and they were also formerly used as diet pills. Amphetamines are very addictive habit forming drugs with dangerous side effects and work by blocking the reuptake of dopamine to create more dopamine. **Ecstasy** or MDMA is a synthetic stimulant and a mild hallucinogen that produces feelings of euphoria and social intimacy, but with short-term health risks and longer term harm to serotonin producing neurons and to mood and cognition. The major effect of ecstasy is releasing stored serotonin which results in emotional elevation and connectedness with people around them and a "I love everyone" feeling. MDMA is often a club drug for raves and night clubs and can causes severe dehydration and overheating which can result in death when coupled with the environment in which it is used.

Cocaine is another stimulant derived from the coca plant that, although producing a sense of euphoria by stimulating the sympathetic nervous system, also leads to anxiety, depression, and addictive cravings. Freud was a big user of cocaine until realizing its addictive properties. Cocaine affects our dopamine receptors by blocking its reuptake which is why it produces a feeling of euphoria. Another stimulant is **Nicotine** which is the psychoactive ingredient in tobacco and is probably the most dangerous and addictive stimulant in use today. It is estimated that about 250 million packs a day of cigarettes are consumed worldwide and nearly 5 million deaths each year. When

© Victoria 1/Shutterstock.com

smoked, nicotine arrives at the brain all at once resulting in a high in less than seven seconds as it affects our Acetylcholine receptors. The resulting effects are a diminished appetite, a boost of mental alertness and efficiency, calming people down, and reducing sensitivity to pain. Symptoms of withdrawal include nervousness, difficulty concentrating, insomnia, headaches, irritability, and intense cravings which can continue for months or even years after a smoker has quit. Because of all the withdrawal symptoms, nicotine is one of the harder substances to quit! In addition to being difficult to quit, nicotine is also a relatively dangerous drug with common negative effects including increased heart rate, causing cancer, and accelerating the process of aging.

Often containing caffeine, **Energy Drinks** are another commonly used stimulant. Energy drinks generally contain a mix of substances such as caffeine, vitamin B and various herbs. Other common ingredients are guarana, acai, and taurine, plus various forms of ginseng, carbonated water, and ginkgo biloba but the central ingredient in most energy drinks is caffeine, the same stimulant found in coffee or tea. In the past ten or so years, energy drinks such as Red Bull, Monster, Amp, Rockstar, and countless others have become incredibly popular and widely available at grocery stores, gas

© Keith Homan/Shutterstock.com

stations, and on college campuses. The obvious advantage to energy drinks is that they often result in significant improvements in mental and cognitive performances as well as increased subjective alertness. As far as drawbacks to energy drinks are concerned, consumption of a single energy beverage will not lead to excessive caffeine intake; however, consumption of two or more beverages in a single day can. Other stimulants such as ginseng are often added to energy beverages and may enhance the effects of caffeine, and ingredients such as guarana themselves contain caffeine. Negative effects associated with caffeine consumption in amounts greater than 400 mg can include nervousness, irritability, sleeplessness, increased urination, abnormal heart rhythms (arrhythmia), and stomach upset. Another danger comes in mixing energy drinks and alcohol. Energy drinks are stimulants and alcohol is a depressant so mixing them can be particularly hazardous as energy drinks can mask the influence of alcohol and a person may misinterpret their actual level of intoxication.

Hallucinogens

Hallucinogens are psychedelic drugs, such as marijuana, LSD and marijuana that distort visual and auditory perception evoking sensory images in the absence of sensory input. One of the most commonly used (and abused) hallucinogens is **Marijuana**; a mild hallucinogen that consists of the leaves and flowers of the hemp plant. Whether eaten or smoked, its major active ingredient **THC (delta-9-tetrahydrocannabinol)** produces a ranges of effects that sometimes make this drug hard to classify. Marijuana produces a "high" often characterized by feelings of euphoria, a sense of well-being, and swings in mood from relaxation to anxiety and paranoia along with heightening a person's

sensitivity to colors, sounds, tastes, and smells. Marijuana is the most frequently used illegal drug in U.S. and laws about its use vary greatly from state to state. Using marijuana can cause distortion of time and memory loss with the most dangerous side effects including respiratory and cardiovascular damage. We have high

concentrations of cannabinoid receptors in the hippocampus, cerebellum, and basal ganglia and when the THC binds with the cannabinoid receptors inside the hippocampus, it interferes with the recollection of recent events. THC also affects coordination, which is controlled by the cerebellum. The basal ganglia controls unconscious muscle movements, which is another reason why motor coordination is impaired when under the influence of marijuana. Many people think of marijuana as not being "dangerous" or even a real drug but there are mixed findings and opinions on this topic. While there are many negative side effects that are possible and this drug can definitely be abused, it is also sometimes used for pain

reduction as the THC sensitive receptors in the brain may be related to pain control. Many people have medical marijuana prescriptions to help reduce pain, help with relaxation and anxiety, and numerous other conditions.

LSD (Lysergic Acid Diethylamide) is another commonly used psychedelic drug. LSD was created artificially by a chemist and produces hallucinations and delusions similar to those occurring in a psychotic state. This drug works by mimicking the effects of serotonin leading to abnormal activity that can cause good and/or bad "trips" ranging from intensification of sensory experiences and feeling like you are watching yourself from a distance to terrifying nightmarish visions causing panic. There doesn't appear to be withdrawal effects associated with the use of LSD but tolerance builds up rapidly causing a person to need higher and/or stronger doses to achieve the same result.

Influences on Drug Use

As mentioned earlier, many factors play a role in a person's use and/or abuse of a substance. While many people can use a drug every now and then and not develop a problematic relationship with the drug, there are several factors that tend to play a role in leading to long-term problematic patterns of substance use. There are thought to be several *biological factors* that might make someone more vulnerable to drug use or abuse. These might include a genetic predispostition or tendency to use a substance or a person might use a substance because of issues with their dopamine reward circuit in the brain. Many *psychological factors* are also thought to play a role and include things such as using drugs as a coping mechanism for stress, anxiety, or mental illness or even lacking a significant sense of purpose in life. When people feel like life is meaningless or purposeless, it often increases the liklihood for drug use as a way of filling the void or coping. *Social influences* might also contribute to a person's liklihood of using and abusing drugs. Social and peer pressure,

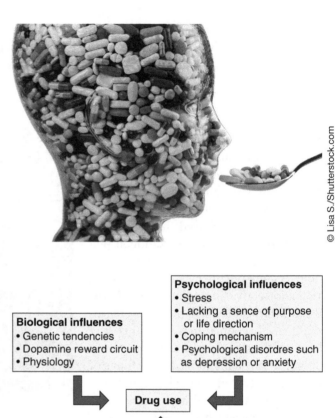

© Lisa S./Shutterstock.com

Psychological influences
• Stress
• Lacking a sence of purpose or life direction
• Coping mechanism
• Psychological disordres such as depression or anxiety

Biological influences
• Genetic tendencies
• Dopamine reward circuit
• Physiology

Drug use

Social-Cultural influences
• Peer pressure or influences
• Social environment
• Belonging to a drug-using cultural group

especially in teenagers and college populations, can contribute heavily to a person's liklihood to use a substance. Often times people are pressured to use drugs to fit in or be part of a certain culture, again very common in college settings. The media also plays a prominent role in the popular opinions about drugs and their use. In the media, drug use increased in the 1970s and then decreased after drug education campaigns and negative media depictions of drug use. We saw another increase again in early 1990's when anti-drug voices softened and drugs were again glamorized in the media. Television shows, actors, singers, movies, and other popular culture media, can directly shape the substances that are popular and being used along with the attitudes about drug use in our culture.

Box - Getting Help for Substance Use Disorder

While some people are able to use drugs moderately and not suffer any ill effects, many people struggle with substance related problems. If you notice signs of a substance use disorder in yourself, a friend, or a family member, there are several nation-wide resources that can help provide you with information and/or support. Help is just a mouse-click or telephone call away. Check out these resources!

• *Alcoholics Anonymous* - Alcoholics Anonymous (AA) is a fellowship of men and women who share their experience, strength, and hope with each other that they may solve their common problem and help others to recover from alcoholism. The only requirement for membership is a desire to stop drinking. There are no dues or fees for AA membership. Web site: www.aa.org (Local meeting information)alanon.png

- *Al-Anon/Alateen* - For over 50 years, Al-Anon (which includes Alateen for younger members) has been offering hope and help to families and friends of alcoholics. It is estimated that each alcoholic affects the lives of at least four other people . . . alcoholism is truly a family disease. No matter what relationship you have with an alcoholic, whether they are still drinking or not, all who have been affected by someone else's drinking can find solutions that lead to serenity in the Al-Anon/Alateen fellowship. For meeting information in Canada, the U.S., and Puerto Rico: 1-888-4AL-ANON Monday through Friday, 8:00am to 6:00pm ET. Web site: www.al-anon.alateen.org

- *Mothers Against Drunk Driving (MADD)* - MADD is a 501(c)(3) non-profit grass roots organization with more than 400 entities nationwide. MADD is not aMAAD.png crusade against alcohol consumption— MADD's mission is to stop drunk driving, support the victims of this violent crime and prevent underage drinking. Web site: www.madd.org

- *Students Against Destructive Decisions (SADD)* - SADD's Mission is to provide students with the best prevention and intervention tools possible to deal with the issues of underage drinking, other drug use, impaired driving and other destructive decisions. Web site: www.sadd.org

In Popular Culture

Sleep, Dreams, and Sleep Disorders

- *Nightmare on Elm Street* (2010) – both the classic and modern versions of this film depict common fears and myths related to nightmares.

- *Inception* (2010) – this film is all about extracting information from a person's unconscious mind during their dreams.

- *Stepbrothers* (2008) – one topic comically covered in this film is sleepwalking.

- *Deuce Bigalow* (1999) – this film depicts a character suffering with narcolepsy.

Hypnosis

- *The Fourth Kind* (2009) – this movie features hypnosis as a means of memory retrieval.

- *Stir of Echoes* (1999) – this movie features a unique twist on hypnosis and a great example of a hypnotic induction.

Drugs

- *Blow* (2001) – a film starring about the famous cocaine smuggler George Jung.

- *Traffic* (2000) – film exploring the illegal drug trade from many perspectives: a user, an enforcer, a politician and a trafficker.

- *Requiem for a Dream* (2000) – a powerful film depicting different forms of addiction.

- *Yes Man* (2008) – contains a great example of abusing energy drinks (specifically Red Bull).

- *Fear and Loathing in Las Vegas* (1998) – a cult classic depicting a journey to Las Vegas and psychedelic drug use.

- *Trainspotting* (1996) – a movie that follows a group of heroin addicts.

Psyched with Setmire

"Remembering Your Dreams"
https://www.youtube.com/watch?v=Id2pjcMkTp0

Every single one of us dreams but we don't always remember our dreams when we wake up! In this video presentation, I will highlight some tips for remembering your dreams! I hope this is helpful; happy dreaming!

Application

Why do we dream and what do dreams mean? There are an incredible number of theories about why we dream and what our dreams mean ranging from wish fulfillment to the random firings of our brain while we sleep. While different dreams might fit different theories, I personally tend to think that dreams at least have the potential to be incredibly meaningful!

When interpreting your dreams, you can think about them symbolically, at surface value, or even as disguised or hidden representations of something in your unconscious. While the best way to figure out what your dreams mean is to think about what it means to you personally, there are some great (and free) resources on the Internet if you want to look up the symbolic meanings of items in your dreams. As Freud would have said, "sometimes a cigar is just a cigar" but sometimes, it might represent something more. To find out more about common symbolic meanings of various objects, visit one of the following websites:

- www.sleeps.com – contains information about sleep and dreams along with a dream dictionary of common dream items and their symbolic meanings.

- www.dreammoods.com – this website has an incredible dream dictionary detailing common meanings for objects in dreams along with a history of dream interpretation and common dreams.

- www.dreambible.com – contains a dream dictionary, various types of dreams, and information and things like lucid dreaming and nightmares.

Key Terms

Consciousness: refers to the relationship between the mind and the world with which it interacts.

Selective Attention: the focusing of our conscious awareness on particular stimuli.

Inattentional Blindness: failing to see visible objects because our attention is directed elsewhere.

Change Blindness: occurs when we fail to notice changes in stimuli in our environment because our attention was directed elsewhere.

Daydreams: apparently effortless shifts in attention away from the here and now into a private world of make-believe.

Sleep: a natural state of rest characterized by a reduction in voluntary body movement and decreased awareness of our surroundings.

Circadian Rhythms: a regular biological rhythm with a period of approximately 24 hours; comes from the Latin expression "circa diem" meaning about a day.

Suprachiasmatic Nucleus (SCN): a cluster of neurons in the hypothalamus that receives input from the retina regarding light and dark cycles and is involved in regulating our biological clock or circadian rhythms.

Melatonin: a hormone that contributes to the regulation of the sleep-wake cycle by chemically causing drowsiness and lowering body temperature.

Adenosine: a neurotransmitter that plays a role in promoting sleep and suppressing arousal, with levels increasing with each hour an organism is awake.

Beta Waves: brain waves displayed when we are wide awake that are the highest in frequency and lowest in amplitude (averaging 13 to 40 cycles per second).

Twilight Stage: the stage of the sleep cycle where we are awake but relaxed and brain wave patterns display alpha waves.

Alpha Waves: brain wave patterns displayed during the twilight stage of sleep that range from 9 to 14 cycles per second.

Stage 1 of Sleep: the first stage of sleep that is marked by theta waves; light sleep where the sleeper can easily be woken up.

Theta Waves: brain wave patterns displayed during stage 1 of sleep that range from 4 to 7 cycles per second.

Stage 2 of Sleep: the second stage of sleep that is marked by two distinct patterns of brainwaves, sleep spindles and k-complexes.

Sleep Spindles: a burst of brain wave activity visisble on an EEG during stage 2 of sleep.

K-Complexes: a sharp, negative EEG wave followed by a high-voltage slow wave that occurs during stage 2 of sleep and is ofen accompanied by sleep spindles.

Power Nap: a short sleep taking during the working day to restore one's mental alterness; sometimes called a cat nap.

Sleep Inertia: the feeling of grogginess and disorientation that can come from waking up from a deep sleep.

Stages 3 & 4 of Sleep: the third and fourth stages of sleep in which the sleeper is in a deep sleep and showing delta brain wave patterns.

Delta Waves: brain wave patterns displayed in stages 3 and 4 of sleep that range from 0 to 4 cycles per second.

Rapid Eye Movement (REM) or Paradoxical Sleep: a sleep stage characterized by rapid eye movements and dreaming; called paradoxical sleep because although brain activity, heart rate, blood pressure, and other physiological functions resemble waking consciousness, the sleeper is deeply asleep and incapable of moving.

Nightmares: a frightening dream that occurs during REM sleep and can be remembered upon waking.

Night Terrors: frightening, often terrifying dreams that occur during NREM sleep from which a person is difficult to awaken and doesn't remember the content.

Insomnia: a sleep disorder in which a person has difficulty falling or staying asleep.

Sleepwalking: also known as somnambulism, involves getting up and walking around while in a state of sleep; occurs in stages 3 or 4 of sleep.

Sleeptalking: also known as somniloquy, involves talking during sleep; occurs in stages 3 or 4 of sleep.

Sleep Apnea: a sleep disorder characterized by breathing difficulty during the night and feelings of exhaustion during the day.

Narcolepsy: a hereditary sleep disorder characterized by sudden nodding off and loss of muscle tone following moments of emotional arousal.

Dreams: vivid visual and auditory experiences that occur primarily during REM periods of sleep.

Hypnosis: named after Hypnos the Greek God of sleep, a trancelike state in which a person responds readily to suggestions.

Posthypnotic Suggestions: suggestions, made during a hypnosis session, to be carried out after the subject is no longer hypnotized.

Psychoactive Drugs: a chemical substance that changes moods and perceptions.

Substance Use Disorder: a long-term problematic pattern or relationship with a substance.

Tolerance: a diminishing effect with regular use of the same dose of a drug; a person requires higher and/or stronger doses to produce the original effects or to prevent withdrawal.

Withdrawal: involves unpleasant physical or psychological effects following the discontinuance of a substance.

Agonist: a chemical that binds to some receptor of a cell and triggers a response by that cell; trigger a response and/or mimic the effect of a neurotransmitter in the brain.

Antagonist: a type of drug that does not provoke a biological response itself upon binding to a receptor, but blocks or dampens neurotransmitters in the brain.

Depressants: one of the three main categories of drugs; chemicals that slow down behavior or cognitive processes and are often taken to reduce tension, forget troubles, or relieve feelings of inadequacy, loneliness, or boredom.

Alcohol: the most commonly used depressant and is the intoxicating ingredient in whiskey, beer, wine, and other fermented or distilled liquors.

Barbiturates: are a group of depressant drugs known as sedative-hypnotics, which generally describes their sleep-inducing and anxiety-decreasing effects.

Benzodiazepines: are a group of depressant drugs used to treat a range of conditions, including anxiety and insomnia.

Opiates: a group of depressants drugs including substances such as opium, morphine, codeine, and heroin, derived from the opium poppy, that dull the senses and cause feelings of euphoria, well-being, and relaxation.

Stimulants: a category of drugs including amphetamines, cocaine, nicotine and several others that stimulate the sympathetic nervous system and produce feelings of optimism and boundless energy.

Caffiene: a stimulant that occurs naturally in coffee, tea, and cocoa, and is used to maintain alertness and wakefulness; works by increasing adrenaline, and Acetylcholine along with blocking the effects of adenosine, a brain chemical involved in sleep.

Amphetamines: a potent group of stimulants affecting the central nervous system and commonly used in the treatment of attention deficit hyperactivity disorder, narcolepsy, and obesity.

Ecstasy (MDMA): a synthetic stimulant and a mild hallucinogen that produces feelings of euphoria and social intimacy, but with short-term health risks and longer term harm to serotonin producing neurons and to mood and cognition.

Cocaine: a stimulant derived from the coca plant that, although producing a sense of euphoria by stimulating the sympathetic nervous system, also leads to anxiety, depression, and addictive cravings.

Nicotine: a stimulant that is the psychoactive ingredient in tobacco.

Energy Drinks: a stimulant used to increase alertness and energy generally containing a mix of substances such as caffeine, vitamin B and various herbs.

Hallucinogens: are psychedelic drugs, such as marijuana, LSD and marijuana that distort visual and auditory perception evoking sensory images in the absence of sensory input.

Marijuana: a mild hallucinogen that consists of the leaves and flowers of the hemp plant.

THC (delta-9-tetrahydrocannabinol): the primary psychoactive ingredient in marijuana; ne of many chemical compounds known as cannabinoids found inside the glands of the cannabis flower.

LSD (Lysergic Acid Diethylamide): a potent synthetically created, mood-changing, hallucinogen manufactured from lysergic acid, which is found in the fungus that grows on rye and other grains.

Outline

© VLADGRIN/Shutterstock.com

Introduction to the Chapter (Summary)

Learning is the process by which experience or practice results in a relatively permanent change in behavior or potential behavior. There are three main types of learning: classical conditioning, operant conditioning, and observational learning.

Classical Conditioning was discovered by Russian Psychologist Ivan Pavlov and is a form of learning in which a response naturally elicited by one stimulus comes to be elicited by a different, formerly neutral stimulus. Pavlov is famous for his research which was originally on digestion but quickly changed when he made the observation that the dogs in his experiment were salivating before they even tasted the food. Before any type of conditioning had occurred, the presentation of food (unconditioned stimulus) to the dogs lead to the automatic reaction of salivating (unconditioned response). After conditioning had occurred, the dogs would salivate (conditioned response) to a bell (conditioned stimulus). The bell was originally neutral but through pairing with the food became meaningful. In order for a conditioning process to occur successfully, repeated pairings are typically needed in a phase known as acquisition. There are several other important conditioning processes that occur in classical conditioning and they are extinction, spontaneous recovery, generalization, and discrimination.

The second type of learning is called Operant Conditioning in which behaviors are emitted to earn rewards or avoid punishments. Edward Thorndike, an American psychologist, began his research by using a "puzzle box" to study how cats learn. B.F Skinner, one of behaviorism's most influential and controversial figures, continued Thorndike's research principle of the Law of Effect by developing what became known as a Skinner Box or an Operant Chamber. Through the process of shaping, Skinner was able to teach animals to perform lengthy sequences and elaborate behaviors. Shaping is accomplished via one of the most important concepts of operant conditioning, consequences (events following a behavior). There are two main types of consequences; 1) reinforcers which increase the likelihood that a behavior will be performed again and 2) punishers which decrease the likelihood of a behavior occurring again. Through the use of these consequences, we learn to perform or stop performing behaviors accordingly.

The third type of learning is observational (vicarious) learning which is learning by observing other people's behavior. We often learn by modeling what we have seen or heard or as a result of vicarious reinforcement or punishment. Neuroscientists have even discovered a neural basis for observational learning called mirror neurons which are frontal lobe neurons that fire when performing certain actions or when observing another doing so. Social learning theorists emphasize that we use our powers of observation and thought to interpret our own experiences and those of others when deciding how to act. One of the most well-known social learning theorists is Albert Bandura who among other things, conducted experiments with children studying the effects of modeling on aggression. He came to the conclusion that observational learning can lead to prosocial behaviors or antisocial behaviors. We often discuss this concept in psychology with one very prominent example being the potential effect of playing violent video games on one's liklihood to display violent behavior.

Learning

Learning is the process by which experience or practice results in a relatively permanent change in behavior or potential behavior. Human life would be impossible without learning as it is involved in virtually everything we do. We can learn things by association as we connect events that occur closely together in sequence, we can learn to repeat behaviors that are rewarded or avoid ones that lead to undesired consequences, or we can learn by watching others. In this unit, we will talk about those three methods of learning: classical conditioning, operant conditioning, and observational learning.

Classical Conditioning

Ivan Pavlov and His Dogs

Classical Conditioning was discovered by a Russian Psychologist named Ivan Pavlov and is a form of learning in which a response naturally elicited by one stimulus comes to be elicited by a different, formerly neutral stimulus. Pavolv wasn't actually interested in the idea of conditioning at all, he was studying digestion and the salivatory responses of dogs and stumbled across this concept in the process. In this type of learning, we learn to associate something that used to be neutral or have no meaning with another stimulus which leads to changes in bodily responses, thoughts, feelings, and reactions. At its core, this often involuntary form of learning is all about learning through association and involves **Respondent Behaviors** which are behaviors that occur as an auomatic response to some stimulus in our environment.

We can learn an incredible number of things through classical conditioning from phobias to emotional responses to food aversions! I have a particularly strong food aversion to chili that was aquired through classical conditioning! Years ago my mother-in-law made a batch of chili for all of us for dinner one night. It was early in my relationship and while I knew that my mother-in-law was a very sweet and selfless woman, I did not know that she wasn't the best cook! I ate her seemingly wonderful chili and then spent the entire night throwing it all up! Now, every time I smell chili, I instantly feel nauseous and like I'm going to throw up! That is classical conditioning; I learned to associate chili with getting sick. Luckily, we can also unlearn behaviors aquired this way (more on that later) so there is hope for me enjoying chili again one day!

Hulton Archive/Stringer/Getty

© vm2002/Shutterstock.com

There are several terms to describe the various elements of classical conditioning that we need to discuss and define! A common term that you will hear over and over again in this section is **Stimulus**. A stimulus is any event or situation that evokes or brings on a response in an organism. A stimulus can literally be anything from chili to the food in Pavlov's experiment to a song, smell, or other sensory item. In this type of learning, there is an **Unconditioned Stimulus (US)** which is a stimulus that invariably causes an organism to respond in a specific way; it automatically elicits a reflex reaction without any learning taking place. Notice that this is a "un" conditioned stimulus which means that it isn't taught and no conditioning has taken place yet. When you present someone with an unconditioned stimulus, it leads to an **Unconditioned Response (UR)** which is a response that takes place in an organism whenever an unconditioned stimulus occurs. Again, the unconditioned response isn't taught or conditioned, it is before any learning has occurred. Once we start the conditioning process, we have what is called a **Conditioned Stimulus (CS)** an originally neutral stimulus that is paired with an unconditioned stimulus and eventually produces the desired response in an organism when presented alone. Our goal is to take a neutral stimulus or item of some sort, and through conditioning, make it meaningful in some way. The conditioned stimulus is always the item that was neutral or lead to no response in the beginning of this process. After repeated pairings, we end up with a **Conditioned Response (CR)** which after conditioning, is the response an organism produces when a conditioned stimulus is present.

Ivan Pavlov's Experiment

Before conditioning

Food (Unconditioned stimulus) → Salivating (Unconditioned response)

During conditioning

Bell (Neutral stimulus) → Food (Unconditioned stimulus) → Salivating (Conditioned response)

After conditioning

Bell (Conditioned stimulus) → Salivating (Unconditioned response)

© Yayayoyo/Shutterstock.com

Let's look at a specific example to see how they all work together! In Pavlov's experiments with the dogs, he would present the dogs with food which would cause them to salivate. The food in this case is the unconditioned stimulus and the salivating is the unconditioned response. You don't have to teach a dog (or person) to salivate to food, it is an inherent or automatic reaction or response. So far, no conditioning has taken place whatsoever; it is all unlearned and automatic. From here, Pavlov would ring a bell and then present the food to the dogs. In the beginning of this experiment, the bell was meaningless and caused no reaction in the dogs but through repeatedly pairing it with the presentation of the food, the dogs learned that the bell signaled that food was on the way and they began to respond to the bell as they would to the food! The bell in Pavlov's experiment, was the conditioned stimulus; it was neutral or meaningless at the beginning but through repeated pairings, it became meaningful and elicited a response. The response of salivating to the bell is the conditioned response or the response that was taught through this whole process. Notice the the UR and the CR are the same (salivating in this case). They will always be the same so if you can figure out one, you have them both!

Let's look at another example that is near and dear to my heart; ice cream! Whenever I hear the sound of an ice cream truck passing through my neighorhood, I get a rush of excitement. That response, was taught through classical conditioning many years ago when I was a child! As a child, when the ice cream truck came around, we were allowed to get one item (which for me was typically an ice cream sandwich). After multiple times of hearing the iconic song coming from the ice cream truck passing through the neighborhood and then running outside to buy ice cream, by brain formed a link between that song and the ice cream sandwich. Initially, the song was completely meaningless to me but after multiple

© painterr/Shutterstock.com

pairings, I learned that the sound signaled that the truck was nearby and that ice cream was coming so I got excited! Initially the ice cream itself made me excited but now the sound of the song made me excited. If we take this example, the easiest place to start (for me) is with the conditioned stimulus. If you can ask yourself, what was it in the beginning of this example that started out meaningless and then was given meaning, you have the conditoned stimulus (CS) and the hardest element. In this example, the CS is the song from the ice cream truck which leads to the conditioned response (CR) of excitement. Then you ask yourself, what originally made me feel excited which in this case, was the ice cream. The ice cream is the unconditioned stimulus (US) leading the unconditioned response (UR) of excitement.

Here are the questions (step-by-step process) to figure out the four elements in a classical conditioning example:

1. What was it in this example that started out neutral or meaningless and gained meaning through conditioning? (CS)

2. What is the response to that formerly neutral item? (CR)

3. Now that you have the CR you also have the UR since they are always the same! (UR)

4. What initally lead to that response? (US)

> **Unconditioned Stimulus (US)** = Ice cream
>
> **Unconditioned Response (UR)** = Excitement
>
> **Conditioned Stimulus (CS)** = Ice cream truck song
>
> **Conditioned Response (CR)** = Excitement

Classical Conditioning Elements

In most cases of classical conditioning, you need repeated pairings in order for an association to be formed and the likelihood and strength of the conditioned response increases each time the two stimuli are paired together. It is also critical that two events follow each other very rapidly in order for the association to take place. The initial stage in classical conditioning where a neutral stimulus becomes associated with an unconditioned stimulus so that the neutral stimulus comes to elicit a conditioned response is called **Acquisition**. In some cases, only one pairing can be strong enough to cause an association to occur (as with my chili example) but most commonly, conditioning occurs over repeated pairings. If we were to stop pairing two stimuli together, **Extinction** can occur. Extinction is the diminishing of a conditioned response and occurs in classical conditioning when an unconditioned stimulus (US) does not follow a conditioned stimulus (CS). For example, if Pavlov were to ring the bell but not present the food, the dogs would eventually stop salivating to the bell. If food no longer follows the bell, the bell begins to lose its power to elicit a response. With my chili aversion, for example, if I were to ea chili and not get sick, the conditioned response would be weakened and evenually become extinct. We can very easily cause the response to reoccur through **Spontaneous Recovery** however if we re-pair the bell and food together. Back to the chili example, if I had another bad batch of chili and got sick, that conditioned response would reappear and I might struggle with chili again.

Other things that can occur in classical conditioning include **Generalization** and **Discrimination**. Generalization is the tendency, in classical conditioning, once a response has been conditioned, for stimuli similar to the conditioned stimulus to elicit similar responses. Continuing to run with Pavlov's experiment, generalization would occur if the dogs salivated to sounds similar to the bell. Discrimination, on the other hand, is the learned ability to distinguish between a conditioned stimulus and stimuli that do not signal an unconditioned stimulus. For example, if you were confronted by a pit bull your heart might race but confronted by a Chihuahua your heart probably would not race and your panic levels will be much lower.

John Watson and "Little Albert"

Ivan Pavlov's work heavily influenced another prominent psychologist named John Watson. Watson followed the school of **Behaviorism** which views human behavior to be exclusively the result of conditioning; we are a bundle of conditioned responses. Watson's research centered aroud the idea that human emotions and behavior are mainly a bundle of conditioned responses that can be heavily influenced. He is famous for saying: "*Give me a dozen healthy infants, well-formed, and my own specified world to bring them up in and I'll guarantee to take any one at random and train him to become any type of specialist I might select – doctor, lawyer, artist, and, yes, even beggar-man and thief, regardless of his talents, tendencies, abilities, and race of his ancestors.*"

Watson tested this theory on an eleven month old child who became known as "Little Albert". Watson, along with his assistant Rosalie Rayner, were trying to demonstrate how specific fears could be conditioned. Before beginning the experiment, "Little Albert" was given a battery of baseline tests and was exposed to several different stimuli to make sure that no prior fears were present. Like most children his age, "Little Albert" feared loud noises (but not the white rats that were to be involved in the study). Through pairing loud noises with the presentation of white rats, Watson was able to condition "Little Albert" to become afraid of rats. Albert's fear was even conditioned to be generalized to other fluffy objects such as a rabbit, a furry dog, and even a Santa Claus mask. Watson considered the experiment a great success. Interestingly, little is known about "Little Albert's" fate after the experiment and the long-term implications of Watson's work.

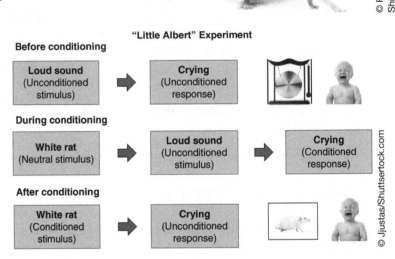

Pavlov and Watson had great disdain for mentalistic concepts such as consciousness but behaviorists since them have more appreciation for cognitive processes such as our thought, perceptions, and expectations on our learning capacity. In other words, we aren't mindless, we can predict events and form expectations (something looked at extensively by the social learning theorists we will talk about later in this chapter).

Operant Conditioning

In contrast to classical conditioning, **Operant Conditioning** is a type of learning in which behaviors are emitted (in the presence of specific stimuli) to earn rewards or avoid punishments. Operant conditioning is much more active and voluntary and relies on **Operant Behaviors**. Operant behaviors operate on the environment as a person decides how to change a specific behavior in response to the consequences that follow that behavior.

Edward Thorndike and Puzzle Boxes

Edward Thorndike was an American psychologist who had a powerful impact on ideas related to reinforcement and behavioral psychology.

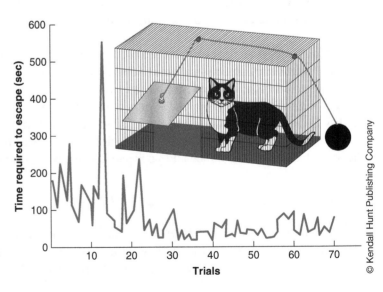

Thorndike was interested in the posibility of animals learning through imitation and observatio which lead to his creation of the "puzzle box" to study how cats learn. His puzzle box had a door that could be pulled open by a weight attached to a string that ran over a pulley and was attached to the door. When the cat pushed on a lever, the door would open. He confined a hungry cat in the puzzle box with food outside the box where the cat could see and smell it. To get the food, the cat had to figure out how to open the latch on the door. Whenever the animal successfully performed the desired response, it was allowed out of the cage and given a food reward. Thorndike time the trials and noticed that with each trial it took less and less time for the cat to escape. In the beginning the cats would wander the box meowing and act aimlessly but once they performed a behavior by chance and were rewarded, the rate of their learning seemed to increase. From his research, Thorndike came up with the **Law of Effect** which stated that rewarded behavior was likely to occur again.

B.F. Skinner and Operant Chambers

Advancing Thorndike's principle of the Law of Effect was one of behaviorism's most influential figures B.F. Skinner. Burrhus Frederic Skinner was an American psychologist and behaviorist who believed that free will was just an illusion and that all of our actions are the direct result of consequences; an idea known as radical behaviorism. Skinner developed what he called a **Skinner Box or Operant Chamber**. Skinner's operant chambers were boxes often used in operant conditioning of animals and operated by limiting the number of available responses and thus increasing the likelihood that the desired response will occur. These boxes were an enclosed apparatus that contained a bar or key that an animal could press or manipulate in order to obtain food as a reinforcement. Skinner taught pigeons to "read" by training them to turn in a circle to a one word prompt and to also to peck at the box wall to a different word prompt. He was able to accomplish this through **Shaping** which involves reinforcing successive approximations to a desired behavior. When the pigeon would turn, Skinner would reward the pigeon with a food pellet. Through building up gradually one step at a time, he was able to teach animals to perform various behaviors and elaborate sequences.

Nina Leen/Contributor/Getty

Another example of how shaping might be used can be found in potty training! I have three little girls and at this point have successfully potty trained all three of them (which was a huge task)! When my oldest, Kaiya, was first starting to transition away from diapers, we would reward her with a single piece of chocolate for just going in the bathroom and sitting on the toilet. We did this for several days to help her make a positive association with the bathroom (and more specifically the toilet). Once she was comfortable with that step, we would give her a piece of chocolate for sitting on the toilet and trying to go potty. After that stage, it was a piece of chocolate for keeping her

© Saklakova/Shutterstock.com

roos (underwear) dry and not having an accident. We slowly kept increasing the amount expected of her to earn a piece of chocolate and to get her closer to using the toilet like a big girl. Eventually, in order to get a piece of chocolate, she had to go into the bathroom, take off her roos, go potty on the toilet, wipe, flush, and pull her pants back up! We had to shape or work up to that behavior slowly but we got there through operant conditioning!

Consequences

I mentioned several times in the potty training example, that we rewarded our daughter for certain behaviors in order to shape them in the desired direction. Operant conditioning works based on **Consequences** which are events following a behavior such as a child earning a treat for a desired behavior or even being put in time out for an undesired one. There are two main types of consequences that are used in operant conditioning, **Reinforcement** and **Punishment**. To reinforce something is to strengthen it and the same idea applies here. When we refer to reinforcement in operant conditioning, we are talking about any stimulus following an action, that will strengthen or increase the liklihood of a behavior occuring again. Punishment on the other hand, is a stimulus that follows an action with the intent of decreasing the liklihood of a behavior occuring. To complicate things slightly, reinforcement and punishment can be either positive or negative in nature. These terms are very confusing as most people think of positive and negative meaning good and bad which is not the case in operant conditioning. In order for the positive and negative to make sense, you must almost think about this concept mathematically. When we refer to positive, we are talking about adding something and negative refers to taking something away.

So with the inclusion of positive and negative, we end up with four different types of consequences: positive reinforcement, negative reinforcement, positive punishment, and negative punishment. **Positive Reinforcement** involves adding something desired or pleasant with the goal of increasing a behavior. A very common example of positive reinforcement might be giving an allowance to someone for completing their chores or a treat to a dog for performing a desired trick. By giving a person (or animal) something desired as a consequence for a behavior, we hope to increase the liklihood that behavior will occur again in the future.

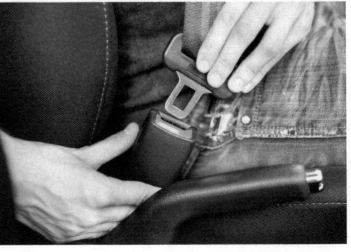

Negative Reinforcement involves removing something unpleasant or undesired following a target behavior with the goal of increasing that behavior in the future. This is probably the trickiest one for most people to understand and again, it comes back to the word negative which people think means "bad". The negative here means to take away or remove and since it is reinforcement, the goal is to increase a behavior. One great example of negative reinforcement would be the seatbelt alarm in my truck! When I get into my truck and start the ignition, if I start driving without my seatbelt on, the truck will ding at me. The dinging gets progressively louder and longer the more I ignore it and becomes quite unpleasant and annoying. The second I put my seatbelt on, the loud dinging alarm goes away to reward me for proper behavior; this is negative reinforcement! The annoying loud sound, which is undesired, is removed to encourage me to wear my seatbelt! In theory, in the future, I would just put my seatbelt on immediately to avoid the sound all together!

	Reinforcement (Increasing Behavior)	**Punishment (Decreasing Behavior)**
Positive (Adding)	**Add Something Pleasant/Desired** *Examples: Ice cream for good grades, allowance for chores, candy.*	**Add Something Unpleasant** *Examples: spanking, timeout, extra chores for bad behavior.*
Negative (Taking Away)	**Remove Something Unpleasant/Undesired** *Examples: years from a jail sentence for good behavior, car beeping when don't put on your seatbelt.*	**Remove Something Pleasant/Desired** *Examples: take away phone or television (or desserts) for bad behavior.*

Just as with reinforcement, the positive and negative apply to punishment as well. **Positive Punshiment** is the adding of something unpleasant or undesired following a target behavior with the goal of decreasing that behavior in the future. Positive punishment sounds strange because we again associate positive with "good" but in this case positive means adding something to the scenario. An example of positive punishment might be adding extra chores because someone didn't get their original chores completed in time or maybe putting a child in timeout for an undesired behavior. The goal here is to decrease the liklihood that the behavior will occur again in the future. **Negative Punishment** is the taking away or removing of something desired or pleasant following a target behavior with the goal of decreasing the liklihood of the behavior occuring again in the future. Some examples might include taking away a person's television privledges because they failed an exam or taking away dessert after dinner because someone didn't eat their vegetables! This was a very common occurrence in my house growing up! By removing something that is desired, the hope is that the person will not be as likely to perform the behavior again in the future since they were punished for doing so.

Punishment can be a little bit tricky so when possible, it is better to reinforce desired behaviors than to punish undesired ones. In order for punishment to be effective it must be imposed properly; it must be swift, sufficient, and consistent. If the punishment does not immediately follow the undesired behavior and also occur consistently, the connection between the two events might not be percieved. My in-laws have a dog named Buster and Buster loved to chew on shoes when he was a puppy. Whenever he chewed shoes in front of my mother-in-law, she would smack him with the shoes and yell at him immediately. But if he chewed shoes around my father-in-law, he would roughly pet his head and not do much else. That sort of inconsistency will lead to the behavior continuing. It is really important that all parties involved in punishment are on the same page with their actions or children (and even pets) will know how to manipulate and beat the system!

Punishment can also have drawbacks! When we punish behaviors, we can teach unwanted ones. Punishment works by attempting to suppress the unwanted behavior rather than forcing someone to learn a more desireable one. Punishment can also backfire by leading to negative feelings and in some cases, it can teach aggression. Harsh punishment may encourage the learner to copy that same harsh and aggressive behavior toward other people. So again, it is always better to reward when possible!

© Anneka/Shutterstock.com

To review, here are some key differences between operant and classical conditioning:

Classical Conditioning	Operant Conditioning
Involuntary and passive in nature	Voluntary and active in nature
Relies on association	Relies on consequences
Mental, emotional, and physical changes occur as a result of conditioning.	Behavioral changes occur as a result of conditioning.
Pavlov and Watson	Thorndike and Skinner
US, UR, CS, CR	Punishment and reinforcement

Observational Learning

In addition to classical and operant conditioning, we also learn quie a bit of behaviors through **Observational Learning** which involves learning by observing other people's behavior through modeling what we have seen or heard. This type of learning is sometimes called vicarious learning as witnesing vicarious reinforcement or punishment might affect our willingness to perform behaviors. For exaample, before you got behind the wheel of a car to drive for the first time, you were most likely a passenger for many years. In those years as a passenger, you observed some of the rules of the road, street signs, and soaked

© bubutu/Shutterstock.com

up quite a bit of information about the process of driving. While you may not yet have known how to operate the pedals or shift gears, you learned quite a bit of what to do (or not do) from waching other people drive. That **Modeling** is a key part of this type of learning. When we model others we observe and imitate their behaviors. As people, especially children, we are natural mimics! My girls will imitate me for better or for worse so I always have to be careful of what I say around them.

The theorists that study observational learning are called **Social Learning Theorists**. Social learning theorists are psychologists whose view of learning emphasizes the ability to learn by observing a model or receiving instructions, without firsthand experience. As a group, they place an emphasis on expectations, insights, and information and study how it broadens our understanding of how we learn. According to social learning theorists, we use our powers of observation and thought to interpret our own experiences and those of others when deciding how to act.

Mirror Neurons

There are several intersting studies and pieces of information that support this type of learning. Neuroscientists have discovered a neural basis for observational learning called **Mirror Neurons**. Mirror neurons are frontal lobe neurons that fire when performing certain actions or when observing another doing so. It is proposed that the brain's mirroring of another's actions may enable imitation and empathy. These type of neurons were discovered in a lab in Italy when researchers noticed that the monkeys in their experiment were showing brain activty when watching the researchers or other monkeys performing an action (moving a peanut to their mouths). Expanding on what was learned in this experiment, we have learned that mirror neurons are not just present in monkeys but are also present in people and are thought to be a foundational part of how we empathize and respond to the behavior of others.

Albert Bandura and Bobo Dolls

A key experimental finding that supports this type of learning can be found in the work of social learning theorist Albert Bandura. Bandura has been a prominent name in the field of psychology, education, and social learning theory for decades and is well known for hi experiments on observational learning conducted in the 1960s. Bandura conducted was became known as the "Bobo Doll Experiment" in 1961 in an attempt to demonstrate that children learn behaviors through modeling. Bobo dolls toys aren't all that common any more (I had a Ninja Turtle one as a child). They are a weighted inflatable toy that will spring back up once you knock

it over. In his experiment, Bandura had preschool age children observe an adult being aggressive to a Bobo doll ; hitting it, kicking it, and even yelling at it. The child was then left alone in a room with the Bobo doll and Bandura observed that child's actions. The children that observed the adults being aggressive to the dolls were more likely to model that behavior and yell, hit, and kick the dolls as they had observed. the modeling reactions of children after they watched researchers interact with the dolls. His experiment, although deemed to be controversial for modeling aggression to children, was incredibly influential in the field of learning and heavily contributed to the understanding of vicarious learning and the field of psychology in general.

Observational learning can lead to prosocial behaviors which are positive, constructive, helpful behaviors or also to antisocial behaviors which are negative, aggressive, or harmful behaviors. For example, watching violent television shows or playing violent video games has been found to be correlated with an increase in aggressive behavior or acceptance of aggressive attitudes. This has been a highly researched and discussed topic in the field of observational learning for several decades but remember what we talked about back in chapter two, correlation does not equal causation! Just because there is a connection between violent television or video games and aggressive behavior doesn't necessarily mean that there is a causal link between them so we have to take these findings lightly!

In Popular Culture

- *America's Funniest Home Videos* – this show constantly features brief examples of conditioning.

- *The Big Bang Theory* – in the episode entitle "The Gothowitz Deviation" from season 3, several different methods of learning are highlighted in addition to being quite comical.

- *The Office* – there are often comical pranks on this show related to conditioning.

- *Meet the Parents* (2000) – in this movie, the dad trains his cat to wave, jump into his arms, and even to use the toilet instead of the litter box; all through conditioning.

- *Brave New World* by Aldous Huxley – a fiction novel featuring a dystopian society in which the citizens are conditioned from birth into specific roles.

- *The Giver* by Lois Lowry – a fiction novel featuring principles of conditioning to create "sameness" within the futuristic society.

Psyched with Setmire

"Classical vs Operant Conditioning (Key Differences)"
https://www.youtube.com/watch?v=A0CdTzjQKYs

In this brief lecture presentation video, I will review some of the key differences between classical and operant conditioning in the field of psychology. Enjoy!

Application

Now that you understand the three different approaches to learning, you can teach your pets, friends, or family members to perform desired behaviors using a variety of methods. Here are some examples of ways that you could use this information:

- *Training Pets* – many people train their pets to perform tricks such as sitting, lying down, rolling over, and many others through the principles of operant conditioning. If you give your dog a reward such as food or praise when they do something, they will be more likely to continue performing that behavior.

- *Games* – like the game "hot and cold", you could come up with a behavior that you want a person to perform and without telling them what it is, get them to perform it using simple reinforcers and punishers. For example, if you wanted someone to turn the lights off in a room, you would clap to reinforce them when they move toward the light switch. The closer they get to the switch, the louder you clap. You could also "boo" at them when they do not make movement toward the light switch. It may take a few minutes but they will eventually figure it out!

- *Smell Memories* – as we talked about in the unit on perception, we often make intense associations with smells. Buy your partner a special lotion, perfume, cologne or product with a distinct smell (or you could also buy it for yourself to create an association for them). After wearing it for a period of time, you will begin to associate that smell with that person!

- *Desired Behaviors* – in general, people do things to earn rewards or avoid punishments. The way that you respond to the behavior of people around you will directly influence their future actions. Rewarding someone for a behavior will mean they are likely to do it again. For example, if my partner vacuums the house for me without me asking and I am thankful and appreciative, the likelihood that it will happen again is high. If my partner vacuums and I say nothing or even worse comment that she missed a spot, the likelihood that she will vacuum again is quite low. Respond according to the direction you seek in the desired behavior!

- *Pranks* – countless people have used classical conditioning to play a trick or prank on others. You can build an association with a sound or smell (or other stimulus of your choice) without a person realizing it.

- *The list goes on and on* – how will you use this knowledge in your personal life?

Key Terms

Learning: the process by which experience or practice results in a relatively permanent change in behavior or potential behavior.

Classical Conditioning: discovered by a Russian Psychologist named Ivan Pavlov; a form of learning in which a response naturally elicited by one stimulus comes to be elicited by a different, formerly neutral stimulus.

Respondent Behaviors: behaviors that occur as an auomatic response to some stimulus in our environment.

Stimulus: any event or situation that evokes or brings on a response.

Unconditioned Stimulus (US): a stimulus that invariably causes an organism to respond in a specific way; it automatically elicits a reflex reaction without any learning taking place.

Unconditioned Response (UR): a response that takes place in an organism whenever an unconditioned stimulus occurs.

Conditioned Stimulus (CS): an originally neutral stimulus that is paired with an unconditioned stimulus and eventually produces the desired response in an organism when presented alone.

Conditioned Response (CR): after conditioning, is the response an organism produces when a conditioned stimulus is present.

Acquisition: the initial stage in classical conditioning where a neutral stimulus becomes associated with an unconditional stimulus so that the neutral stimulus comes to elicit a conditioned response.

Extinction: the diminishing of a conditioned response that occurs in classical conditioning when an unconditioned stimulus (US) does not follow a conditioned stimulus (CS).

Spontaneous Recovery: in classical conditioning, the reapperance of a learned response after extinction has occurred.

Generalization: the tendency, in classical conditioning, once a response has been conditioned, for stimuli similar to the conditioned stimulus to elicit similar responses.

Discrimination: in classical conditioning, the learned ability to distinguish between a conditioned stimulus and stimuli that do not signal an unconditioned stimulus.

Behaviorism: a branch of psychology that views behavior as the result of conditioning without regard to mental processing.

Operant Conditioning: a type of learning in which behaviors are emitted (in the presence of specific stimuli) to earn rewards or avoid punishments.

Operant Behaviors: behavior that operates on the environment resulting in consequences.

Law of Effect: a principle proposed by Edward Thorndike stating that if an action is followed by a pleasurable consequence, it will tend to be repeated.

Skinner Box (Operant Chamber): a laboratory apparatus created by B.F. Skinner to study and manipulate animal behavior.

Shaping: the reinforcement of successive approximations toward a desired more complex behavior.

Consequences: events, such as reinforcers or punishers, following a behavior.

Reinforcement: any event or stimulus following a response or behavior that increases the liklihood that the response or behavior will occur again.

Punishment: any event or stimulus following a response or behavior that decreases the liklihood that the behavior or response will occur again.

Positive Reinforcement: the strengthening of a behavior or response through the addition of something desired or pleasant.

Negative Reinforcement: the strengthening of a behavior or response through the taking away of something undesired or unpleasant.

Positive Punishment: the weakening of a behavior or response through the addition of something unpleasant or undesired.

Negative Punishment: the weakening of a behavior or response through the taking away of something desired or pleasant.

Observational Learning: the learning of behavior through watching other people perform that behavior; sometimes called vicarious learning.

Modeling: the process of observing and imitating a specific behavior.

Social Learning Theorists: a group of psychologists that study how people learn through the observing of others.

Mirror Neurons: frontal lobe neurons that fire when observing other people performing certain actions; thought to play a role in imitation and empathy.

Chapter 7

Memory

Outline

© TypoArt BS/Shutterstock.com

Introduction to the Chapter (Summary)

Memory is the ability to store, retain, and recall information and experiences. Most contemporary psychologists perceive memory as a series of steps in which we process information much like a computer. This model is known as the information processing model and involves three main processes; encoding, storage, and retrieval.

Short-term memory (STM) is our working memory that briefly stores and processes selected information from the sensory registers. Short-term memory holds the information that we are thinking about or aware of at any given moment and has two primary tasks 1) to store new information briefly and 2) to work on that (and other) information. Short-term memory has a very limited capacity. Through chunking or the grouping of information into meaningful units, we allow ourselves to process an even greater amount of information in our STM. We can also use rote rehearsal to hold information in our STM for slightly longer periods of time.

Long-term memory (LTM) is the portion of memory that is more or less permanent, corresponding to everything we "know". We can store a vast amount of information in our LTM for many years. Just as with STM, there are processes used to hold information in LTM including rote rehearsal, elaborative rehearsal, using mnemonics, and using schema or schemata. Information in LTM can take many forms including episodic memory, semantic memory, procedural memory, and emotional memory.

Psychologists still don't know all the specifics about how we store memories but one theory is that when we learn new things, new connections are formed in the brain and when we review or practice previously learned things, old connections are strengthened. This increase in the number of connections among neurons is known as long-term potentiation. Psychologists know more information about the storage of memories than how they are stored and the consensus is that they are stored not all in one place but rather that different parts of the brain are specialized for the storage of memories.

Why is it that once memories are formed, they don't remain in the brain forever? The answer is partly due to biology of memory and partly due to experiences that we have before and after learning. Biological factors related to forgetting include time and the decay theory, disruption of storage process, and head injuries or brain damage due to accidents, surgeries, poor diet, and disease. Experience related factors in forgetting include inadequate learning, interference (both retroactive and proactive interference), and situational factors such as state-dependent memory and the role of context.

There are several special topics within memory including autobiographical memory, childhood amnesia, extraordinary memory such as eidetic memory (commonly called photographic memory), and flashbulb memories which involve the experience of remembering vividly a certain event. Eyewitness testimony is another special topic in memory. Psychologist Elizabeth Loftus has done extensive research in this area and in general found eyewitness testimony to be unreliable because of source error. Finally, déjà vu is another special topic in memory and one that we struggle to explain.

Memory

The ability to store, retain, and recall the things that we have experienced, imagined, and learned is known as **Memory**. Without this ability, life would be incredibly difficult! Imagine if every time we all got behind the wheel of our car, we had to relearn how to drive because you couldn't remember what you had learned previously. Nobody would ever get anywhere and accident rates would skyrocket! Our ability to remember information allows us to learn and adapt and function in the world.

Information Processing Model

Psychologists perceive memory as a series of steps in which we process information much like a computer in what is called the **Information Processing Model**. There are three main steps involved in this computer-like model, encoding, storing, and retrieving information. When we are **Encoding** information into our brain, this is the first step toward creating a new memory. Information can be encoded in visual, acoustic, tactical, and semantic forms and this process begins with the senses. Our sensory registers are entry points for raw data information from the senses like waiting rooms where the information enters and stays for only a short period of time. Through attention we select some of the incoming information for further processing. We consciously attend to very little of the information in our sensory registrars

and select only some information to process further and this information enters our short-term memory. If we run with the computer analogy, encoding would be analogous to typing the information into the computer on a keyboard. Information must be converted into a form that can be stored in the brain and that is the essence and goal of encoding.

The second part of the information processing model involves storing or retaining the information that has been encoded. Where the information is stored will determine how long we can remember it (more on this in a moment). Continuing with the computer model, this might be compared to saving information on a flash drive or computer hard drive. Retrieval is the third process involved in memory and refers to accessing and getting the information out of storage to be used. This could be compared to opening a file on the computer. If we don't encode and/or store information properly, we might struggle to retrieve it when we need it later.

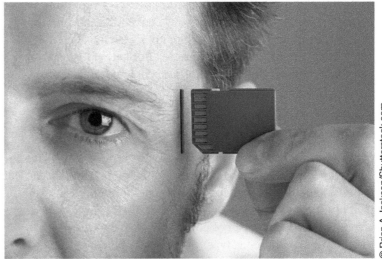

Short-Term Memory

Once information has been processed by our senses and given attention, it enters into our **Short-Term Memory** which is sometimes called our working memory. Short-term memory briefly stores and processes selected information from the sensory registers and can hold 7 +/- 2 pieces of information (5-9 pieces of information). We call this our working memory because of how active it is and because it is working at any given point; for this reason it is sometimes referred to as the brain's Post-it note or scratch pad! Short-term memory holds the information that we are thinking about or aware of in the current moment and has a very limited capacity. It can only hold about the amount of information that can be repeated in roughly 10 to 15 seconds. If we don't make some sort of conscious effort to hold onto information being processed in our short-term memory, it will quickly disappear.

One way that we can increase the capacity of our short-term memory is a method called **Chunking**. Chunking involves the grouping of information into meaningful units for easier handling by our short-term memory. Putting things into smaller chunks makes them easier to remember than a long string of unrelated letters or digits and allows us to process an even greater amount of information in our working memory. Phone numbers are a great example of chunking. A phone number is chunked into three sets of numbers to help us remember it rather than one long strand. On top of chunking a phone number, it also has a sort of cadence to it which might also aid in remembering.

Another method that might assist with maintaining information in our short-term memory is **Rote Rehearsal** or the repeating of information over and over again either silently or out loud. If you are out on a Friday night and meet someone who wants to give you their phone number but you don't have any way of recording it, rote rehearsal is your new best friend! You will try to repeat the number over and over as if you were trying to burn it into your mind. This can be effective for a short period of time but in order to master complex skills and remember personal experiences, we need to store information longer than a few minutes and have it transition into our long-term memory.

Long-Term Memory

Different from short-term memory, our **Long-Term Memory** is the portion of memory that is more or less permanent, corresponding to everything we "know". Long-term memory can store a vast amount of information for many years or even indefinitely. If the information in our short-term memory is consolidated and given a meaningful association, it will become part of our long-term memory. There are several different types of long-term memory that have been distinguished. **Episodic Memory** is the portion of our long-term memory that stores our personally experienced events. You can think about this type of memory being like a diary or journal of all our personal memories. **Semantic Memory** is the portion of our long-term memory that stores general facts and information almost like a dictionary or encyclopedia filled with facts and concepts that we have acquired. People who are good at trivia games and shows like Jeopardy have strong semantic memories and are able to retain and recall those little factoids. **Procedural Memory** is the portion of long-term memory that stores information relating to skills, habits, and other

perceptual-motor tasks. Knowing how to ride a bike or swim which are sequences of coordinated movements often learned through repetition and deliberate practice, make up this type of memory. When I was in middle school and high school, I played the clarinet. After graduating high school, I stopped playing and a few year ago, found my clarinet in my parent's basement. Even though it had been almost ten years, I still remembered how to hold and play my instrument from the countless times I had played it years before. Procedural memories tend to be durable like that. **Emotional Memories** are our learned emotional responses to various stimuli such as our loves, hates, fears, and so on. Memories that are especially emotional might be remembered more vividly and for longer than those without strong emotional content. And speaking of that notion, when we combine the different types of long-term memory together, we might be even more likely to remember something (which is what we will talk about next).

Maintaining Long-Term Memory

Most of the information in long-term memory is encoded in terms of meaning often extracting the main points and retaining those rather than verbatim accounts or exact words. In order to maintain information in our long-term memory and to hold on to it indefinitely, we can rely on several different methods or processes. Just like with short-term memory, we can use rote rehearsal which is a standard method for storing conceptually meaningless material such as phone numbers, social security number, passwords, birthdates, and so on. Repetition without any intent to learn generally has little effect on subsequent recall so this might work in the short run but in order to hold onto something more effectively **Elaborative Rehearsal** is the technique to use. Elaborative rehearsal is the linking of new information in short-term memory to familiar material stored in long-term memory. You are basically extracting the meaning of new information and relating it to material already in your long-term memory. This process of making associations makes the information more likely to be remembered. One common usage of elaborative rehearsal is to use **Mnemonics** which are techniques that make material easier to remember. For example, if you had to remember the five great lakes, you might use the mnemonic of HOMES. The letters in the

Box: More on Mnemonic Devices

Clues of any kind that help us remember something, usually by helping us associate the information we want to remember with a visual image, a sentence, or a word are known as mnemonics. Here are a few examples:

Acrostic - Make up a sentence in which the first letter of each word is part of or represents the initial of what you want to remember.	The sentence "Every good boy does fine" to memorize the lines of the treble clef, representing the notes E, G, B, D, and F.
Acronym – An acronym is a word that is made up by taking the first letters of all the key words or ideas you need to remember and creating a new word out of them.	The word "HOMES" to remember the names of the Great Lakes: Huron, Ontario, Michigan, Erie, and Superior.
Rhymes and alliteration - Rhymes, alliteration (a repeating sound or syllable), and even jokes are a memorable way to remember facts.	The rhyme "Thirty days hath September, April, June, and November" to remember the months of the year with only 30 days.
Chunking – Chunking breaks a long list of numbers or other types of information into smaller, more manageable chunks.	Remembering a 10-digit phone number by breaking it down into three sets of numbers: 555-867-5309 (as opposed to 5558675309).

mnemonic would hopefully be enough to trigger your memory for what they stand for (Huron, Ontario, Michigan, Erie, and Superior). Use these whenever you can as they are often helpful for remembering information!

Another elaborative rehearsal technique is to use **Schema or Schemata** which are a set of beliefs or expectations about something that is based on past experience. Another way of putting this might be to say that schema are like a script that past experience has begun writing for you and the details will be filled in by your present experience. Schema are mental representations of events, objects, situations, people, processes, relationships that lead you to have certain expectations. They work by providing the framework into which incoming information in fitted which then helps us to fill in missing information.

Making information meaningful is one of the best ways to keep it in long-term memory. Whenever you can add a layer of meaning to information, you will be more likely to remember it. Another way to do this is to use as many senses as possible when trying to remember information. I always suggest to my students that they take notes in my classes. Note taking is a good strategy in general but in this instance, it allows for another layer of encoding and multiple senses to be utilized during a lecture. If you are listening to an instructor lecture, looking at the Power Point slides, and also writing down notes, that involves three

different senses and might prove helpful when it comes to remembering the information. Every little bit helps and multiple senses definitely increase your chances of long-term retention.

Finally, another way to help maintain information in long-term memory is the **Spacing Effect**. When it comes to remembering something, there is a tendency for distributed study or practice to yield better long-term retention; we more easily remember or learn items when they are studied over a long time span rather than repeatedly studied in a short span of time. When studying for a test, it is better to study a little bit at a time rather than to cram it all in at once; especially if you want to remember it beyond the test! If you can break up your studying into several 10 to 15 minutes chunks of time each day and study that way for a week, you will hold onto that information much more successfully than trying to cram it all in the night before.

The Biology of Memory

Memory, like so many other psychological concepts, is still a bit of a mystery. Psychologists don't have an accurate and complete answer to the question of how memories are stored. When we learn new things, new connections are formed in the brain and when we review or practice previously learned things, old connections are strengthened. This increase in the number of connections among neurons increases the likelihood that cells will excite one another through electrical discharges in a process known as **Long-Term Potentiation (LTP)**.

This long-lasting change in the structure or function of a synapse, increases the efficiency of neural transmission and is thought to be related to how information is stored by neurons. So at the most basic level, memories are stored as microscopic chemical changes at the connecting points between neurons in the brain. Going one step farther than that, it is proposed that memories are stored throughout the brain as groups of neurons that are primed to fire together in the same pattern that created the original experience and as we will get to in a second, each component is then stored in the brain area that initiated it.

So if we don't quite know how memories are stored, we must at least know where they are stored right? Well we do know that memories are not all stored in one place in the brain; different parts of the brain are specialized for the storage of different types of memories. Our short-term working memory (which is actively being used right now) is thought to be stored in the frontal and parietal lobes of the brain. Procedural memories like how to ride a bike or play a musical instrument are thought to be stored in the cerebellum which plays an important role in motor skills. The amygdala plays a large role in storing emotional memories and the hippocampus is crucial for episodic memories. Together, all of these parts of the brain (and then some) work together to allow us to store, reconstruct, and retrieve our memories.

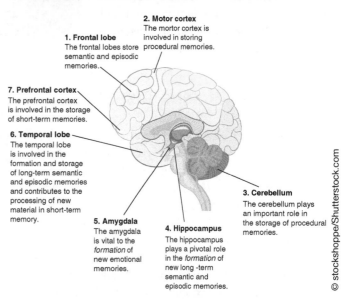

1. Frontal lobe
The frontal lobes store semantic and episodic memories.

2. Motor cortex
The mortor cortex is involved in storing procedural memories.

7. Prefrontal cortex
The prefrontal cortex is involved in the storage of short-term memories.

6. Temporal lobe
The temporal lobe is involved in the formation and storage of long-term semantic and episodic memories and contributes to the processing of new material in short-term memory.

5. Amygdala
The amygdala is vital to the *formation* of new emotional memories.

4. Hippocampus
The hippocampus plays a pivotal role in the *formation* of new long -term semantic and episodic memories.

3. Cerebellum
The cerebellum plays an important role in the storage of procedural memories.

Why Do We Forget?

Why do memories once formed, not remain in the brain forever? In other words, why do we forget? The answers to these questions are partly explained by the biology of memory and also partly by the experiences that we have before and after learning.

Biology and Forgetting

The number one biological reason that we forget is due to the passage of time and the **Decay Theory**. According to the decay theory, memories deteriorate from our short-term memory due to the passage of time. When information isn't used, it tends to fall away. Remember that our short-term memory has a very limited capacity and it we don't actively use or do something with that incoming information, as time passes it will just slip away.

Another biological factor might involve some some of disruption of the storage process occuring. If the information isn't saved properly due to some sort of condition, problem, or disruption, it won't be easy to recall it. One instance of this can be found in **Retrograde Amnesia** which occurs when people are not able to remember what happened to them shortly before an injury. The thought is that memories are not fully consolidated in the brain which leads to an inability to remember them. A similar example to this might be working on a document on a computer and having a power outage occur resulting in loss of information not saved to the hard drive; you only retireve up until the last save or restore point. Other biological factors that can interfere with memory recall are head injuries or brain damage, poor diet, diseases, and the neurocognitive disorders such as Alzheimer's Disease.

© lassedesigner/Shutterstock.com

Box: Alzheimer's Disease

Alzheimer's Disease is the most common neuro-cognitive disorder (formerly called dementias), usually occurring after the age of 65. The time-frame between onset and death in someone with Alzheimer's is typically 8 to 10 years. This disease usually begins with mild memory problems, lapses of attention, and difficulties in language and communication but as symptoms worsen people eventually have trouble with simple tasks and changes in personality often become noticeable. People tend to be unaware of their difficulties as they worsen and sometimes withdraw from others and may become confused about the time and place. They may even lose all recognition of familiar faces and become completely reliant on others for care as they near the end of their lives. Alzheimer's disease is named after Alois Alzheimer who identified the first case in 1901.

© Lightspring/Shutterstock.com

Experiences and Forgetting

In addition to biology, environmental factors and inadequate learning play a role in forgetting. We can't expect to remember information for long if we have not learned it well in the first place! One example of an environmental variable that might lead to forgetting is interference. Learning itself can actually cause forgetting when the information gets mixed up with, or pushed aside by other information thereby making it harder to remember. There are two different types of interference that can occur, **Retroactive Interference** and **Proactive Interference**.

© Kunst Bilder/Shutterstock.com

Retroactive Interference occurs when new information interferes with information that is already in our memory. For example, let's say a person knows Spanish but is having difficulty trying to recall a word in Spanish because he or she is currently taking French. The Spanish word is in long-term memory somewhere, but he or she can't pick it out because the new information is interfering with the old information. Proactive Interference occurs when information already in our memory interferes with new information. An example of this might be a lifelong baseball player who suddenly begins to take up golf might have difficulty learning the correct golf swing, as the previously learned way of swinging a baseball bat may be getting in the way. Both of these types of interference can wreak havoc on your ability to remember something clearly and commonly cause students issues durng finals week when they are studying for multiple exams at one time!

Situational Factors can also play a role in remembering and forgetting. Whenever we learn something, we unintentionally pick up information about the context in which the learning is taking place. In fact, people who

learn material in a certain physiological state tend to recall that material better if they return to the same state they were in during learning; a phenomenon known as **State-Dependent Memory**. For example, if you are drinking coffee while studying for an exam, you should drink coffee when you take the test. Recreating the physical state and conditions in which you learned something, might help you in your recall of that information. This phenomenon is often referenced or related to substance use – the idea that if you are drunk when you learn something and can't remember it sober, you might be more likely to remember it the next time you drink alcohol. There is some support for this notion but don't think that this could help you with exam preparation! Studying under the influence of a drug will probably not be all that helpful in earning you a good grade on the next exam. State dependent memory is different from **Context-Dependent Memory** which refers to improved recall of specific information when the *context* present at encoding and retrieval are the same. The easiest example of this might be trying to remember where you put your keys that are currently lost and the idea of retracing your steps. As you go back through all the places that you were looking for your keys, the context often triggers the recall of where they might have been put (or at least that is the hope).

Special Topics in Memory

Childhood Amnesia

There are quite a few interesting side notes and special topics in memory. One of them concerns our **Autobiographical Memory** or our recollection of events that happened in our life and when those events took place. One interesting phenomenon that occurs with our autobiographical memory is **Childhood Amnesia** which is the inability of adults to remember personally experienced events prior to the age of two. If you try to think back in time, when is your earliest memory? I am pretty sure that I remember a few random images and things from preschool but even those memories are a little blurry! It is hard to know for sure if I actually remember my preschool or if I am remembering pictures and stories of preschool. Unless an early experience was incredibly strong or even traumatic, we tend to not remember anything before the age of around two. There are a few reasons why psychologists think this occurs with one of them being that a

© Jeanette Dietl/Shutterstock.com

child's brain is not fully developed so it isn't fully capable of storing and processing information. Another big factor might be that very young children lack a clear sense of self which might make remembering events difficult. Finally, our language skills when we are quite young are not very developed. If we don't have the language skills necessary to encode, strengthen, and consolidate early experiences, it makes them difficult to recall later!

Extraordinary Memory

Some people are lucky enough to have extraordinary memories! One example of that is called **Eidetic Memory** which is the ability to reproduce unusually sharp and detailed images of something one has seen; commonly called photographic memory. In experiments studying eidetic memory, individuals are commonly asked to look at an image for a matter of seconds and then once it has been removed, are asked to either recreate or describe that image in great detail. Consistently, some people seem to be better able to do this than others! But does this mean that those better at this task have a photographic memory? Does a truly photographic memory actually exist?

© Sangoiri/Shutterstock.com

In most of the experiments, people claiming to have eidetic memory did not remember the pictures they were shown in perfect detail. Many people would fail to remember some details and often would even invent details that were never in the original image. This might suggest that eidetic images are not neccesarily photographic in nature but instead are reconstructed from our memory and can be influenced by cognitive biases and expectations. While some level of eidetic memory may exist, psychologists still do not know why it occurs, what brain mechanisms may be responsible, or why it is found in such a small proportion of the population. Nevertheless, it is an incredibly interesting idea and something that many of us wish we could possess!

Another interesting form of memory recall often referenced are **Flashbulb Memories** which refer to the experience of remembering vividly a certain event and the incidents surrounding it even after a long time has passed. This has often been compared to watching a home video of an event in your life from many years ago. The events that we tend to remember vividly are often those events that are shocking or significant in some way. Your wedding day might be an excellent example of a flashbulb memory or even a cultural event such as 9/11. In either example, you would replay the events of the day in your mind almost as if you were re-experiencing them. Interestingly though, flashbulb memories are not always accurate. Just like anything else in our memory, they can be influenced by other memories or pieces of information occurring after the fact. Our memories are incredibly malleable and can be heavily influenced by context (more on this next)!

Eyewitness Testimony

Eyewitness testimony is one area of memory that commonly demonstrates how inaccurately we might remember an event. The research of Psychologist Elizabeth Loftus sheds some light on the inaccurate nature of eyewitness testimony. Her main focus in research has been on the influence of (mis)leading information in terms of both visual imagery and wording of questions in relation to eyewitness testimony.

© Monkey Business Images/Shutterstock.com

In her experiments, Loftus show research participants several short films (in random order) depicting a traffic accident. After watching the film, the research participants were asked to describe what had happened as if they were eyewitnesses to the accident. They were also asked specific questions, including "About how fast were the cars going when they (smashed/collided/bumped/hit/contacted) each other?" What she found in her experiment was that the estimated speed of the car was directly affected by the verb used in the question. The verb implied information about the speed, which systematically affected the participants' memory of the accident. Those who were asked the "smashed" question thought the cars were going faster than those who were asked the "hit" question.

The takeaway from this is that if someone is exposed to new information during the interval between witnessing an event and recalling it, this new information may have noticeable effects on what they recall. The original memory can be modified, changed or supplemented and eyewitness testimony might be biased by the way the questions are asked. Very closely related to this is the idea of Source Error which is the misattribution of the source of a memory; people are sometimes unable to tell the difference between what they witnessed and what they heard about or imagined. For example, individuals may learn about a current event from a friend, but later report having learned about it on the local news, thus reflecting an incorrect source attribution. Again, our memories are not fixed but rather are easily manipulated by context and later information!

DEJA VU

© Nobelus/Shutterstock.com

Déjà vu

Déjà vu is a French term coined by a French psychic researcher, Émile Boirac literally meaning "already seen". Deja vu is the experience of feeling that one has already witnessed or experienced a current situation, even though the exact circumstances of the previous encounter are uncertain and were perhaps imagined. The experience of déjà vu is usually accompanied by a compelling sense of familiarity, and also a sense of "eeriness", "strangeness", or "weirdness". The "previous"experience is most frequently attributed to a dream, although in some cases there is a firm sense that the experience has genuinely happened in the past. While the exact nature of deja vu is unknown, several theories have been posited. One commonly referenced but unsupported theory is that déjà vu results from reincarnation and therefore from events experienced in a former life. Dreams and precognition are other proposed ideas and would explain déjà vu being the result of dreaming about the current situation previously or as an extrasensory perceptual cause like viewing something in your mind before you experienced it. None of the theories mentioned so far have any scientific merit to support them and the most supported and current thought is that déjà vu is the result of the cues in a current situation unconsciously retrieving an earlier, similar experience. We take in vast amounts of information some of which is forgotten rapidly or hardly noticed and sometimes the current experience might awaken a shadow of an earlier experience. While this explanation is the best we currently have in psychology, it isn't very satisfying when you have a déjà vu experience.

How to Improve Your Memory

Most of us wish that we had a better memory (I know that I wish this often)! A strong memory depends on the health and vitality of your brain and there are lots of things you can do to improve your memory and mental performance.

One factor playing a large role in impriving memory is sleep. When we are sleep deprived, our brain simply does not operate a full capacity. We also know that sleep plays an important role in memory consolidation. Getting a good night of sleep is therefore important for allowing your brain the rest it needs to operate efficiently and store memories. Exercise is another thing you can to do to improve memory. When you exercise the body, you also exercise the brain. Treating your body well can help with your ability to process and recall information as physical exercise increase the oxygen levels in your brain helps to reduce your risk levels for certain medical problems that might correlate with memory loss such as diabetes and cardiovascular disease.

Finding ways to keep stress in check can also help with memory as stress can cause significant impairments to our memory abilites and system. If left unchecked, chronic stress can destroy brain cells and damage the hippocampus, the region of the brain involved in the formation of new memories and the retrieval of old ones. Methods of stress reduction such as yoga, guided relaxation exercises, and meditation can help to improve focus, concentration, creativity, memory, and learning and reasoning skills.

Just as the body needs fuel, so does the brain. Maintaining a proper diet can go a long with with brain health and memory. Trying to limit calories and saturated fats will reduce risk of

BENEFITS OF RUNNING

STRENGTHENS MUSCLE

STRENGTHENS LUNGS

WEIGHT CONTROL

STRONG IMMUNE SYSTEM

REDUCED RISK OF HEART DISEASE

IMPROVED BLOOD PRESSURE

IMPROVED BRAIN FUNCTION

dementia and help with concentration. Being sure to get omega-3s into your diet (foods such as fish, spinach, broccoli, certain beans, nuts, and soybeans) will also help to increase brain health. Other diet tips for memory include eating more fruits and vegetables, drinking green tea, and refraining from abusing alcohol and other drugs.

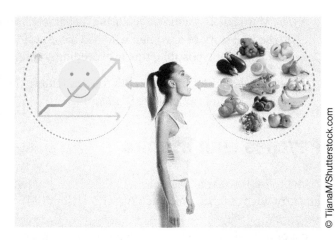

Giving your brain a workout through mental activities and exercises is also important for memory. The more you work out your brain, the stronger it will be and the better it will be at processes and remembering information. Playing instruments, activities that require hand-eye coordination, and creativity are some of the best ways to work out your brain. Do new things and break the routine! Learning new things outside of your comfort zone pushes the brain to make new connections. Play puzzles like Sudoku, learn a new language, follow the road less traveled, involve as many senses as possible, pay attention, and try to have fun with it! There are tons of apps on your smart phone that are free and fun games to play that will boost your memory skills so consider trying one out to help improve your memory.

In Popular Culture

- *The Butterfly Effect* (2004) – a movie featuring memory manipulation through altering and erasing memories to thereby change the future.

- *Eternal Sunshine of the Spotless Mind* (2004) – a movie exploring memory loss and love through a couple who have erased each other from their memories through memory manipulation.

- *50 First Dates* (2004) – a movie featuring a character who has a fictional condition called amnesia Goldfield Syndrome which causes her to lose memory every time she goes to sleep at night. True anterograde amnesia affects either short-term memory, which can last minutes or seconds, or intermediate-term memory, which can last days or weeks. Falling asleep has nothing to do with the condition, and sleep actually intensifies many chemical effects which help memory.

- *Finding Nemo/Finding Dory* (2003/2016) – both movies feature a great character who claims to suffer from short-term memory loss but most likely just has an extremely poor memory!

- *The Matrix* (1999) – a movie about an alternate reality and featuring a short section highlighting deja vu as a glitch in the matrix. While it is entertaining and thought provoking (along with many of the concepts of the movie), again, we still don't completely understand the nature of déjà vu.

- *Memento* (2000) – a movie featuring a character suffering from anterograde amnesia and short-term memory loss.

- *The Notebook* (2004) – a movie featuring a character suffering from Alzheimer's disease; a progressive dementia primarily affecting those over the age of 65.

- *Paycheck* (2003) – a movie featuring a character who has his memory wiped after each job he completes in order to protect his clients.

- *The Vow* (2012) – a movie featuring a character who has memory loss due to trauma. This film is based on the true story of a woman who had a car accident and lost her memories of the 18 months before the accident. While possible, this is exceedingly rare.

- *Total Recall* (1990/2012) – both movies feature themes of implanting false memories and having repressed memories emerge in dreams.

Psyched with Setmire

"How to Improve Your Memory"
https://www.youtube.com/watch?v=GY-1HItnYPM

Most of us wish we had a better memory! Imagine how much easier our lives would be if we could easily hold onto the information that we have experienced and/or learned! In this lecture presentation, I will highlight some tips for improving your memory including lifestyle oriented tips and tips related to attention and learning. Hopefully this presentation will prove to be useful and will help you to remember things better in your daily life!

Application

How can you use all this information on memory to help you study and do well on exams? Here are some memory tips for studying for exams:

- *Start Early* – remember that when you space information out over longer periods of time, you tend to remember it longer and stronger. Try to start studying at least a week or more before your exam to increase your long-term retention of the information.

- *A Little at A Time* – when studying, it is better to study a little at a time rather than in one long session. Your brain can only handle so much information and your attention span will start to waiver if you try to focus for too long. Have you ever been reading a chapter in a textbook and suddenly you realize that you have no memory of what you were reading? We can only attend to so much before our brain shuts down!

- *Change Up the Order* – if you are studying with flashcards, don't always study the cards in the same order! Similar to the suggestion above, you will find that you remember the first and last cards but that the middle is a blur. This is known as the serial position effect (we tend to remember information at the beginning and end and forget the middle sections). By changing up the order of the cards, you start with new ones each time and will hopefully have a better mastery of all the cards rather than just the beginning and end.

- *Use State and Context Dependent Memory* – I always like to study with coffee so ideally, when I go to take the exam, I should take it with coffee! If you can recreate the physiological conditions in which you learned the information, you might be ever so slightly more likely to remember it. You could also try to repeat the context and see if that helps you. If you studied listening to music, listen to music while you take the test. All these little connections just might help you to remember!

- *Study Before Bed and When You Wake Up* – if only putting the index cards under your pillow was enough to memorize information! While you can't soak up information through physically sleeping on your studying materials, reviewing notes or cards just before bed might help you remember it better as memory is consolidated and strengthened during sleep. If you study before bed and then again when you wake up in the morning, it might help with retention.

- *Sleep, Eat, and Reduce Stress* – try to find ways to embrace the tips given earlier related to getting enough sleep, eating well, and reducing stress! Exams are stressful and studying is hard work so find ways to reward yourself and take breaks to keep the stress in check!

Key Terms

Memory: the ability to store, retain, and recall the things that we have experienced, imagined, and learned.

Information Processing Model: a computer-like model used to describe the way humans encode, store, and retrieve information.

Encoding: the intial learning of information and the process of putting it into the brain and memory.

Short-Term Memory: our working memory; briefly stores and processes selected information from the sensory registers.

Chunking: the grouping of information into meaningful units for easier handling by short-term memory.

Rote Rehearsal: repeating information over and over again either silently or out loud.

Long-Term Memory: the portion of memory that is more or less permanent, corresponding to everything we "know".

Episodic Memory: the portion of long-term memory that stores personally experienced events.

Semantic Memory: the portion of long-term memory that stores general facts and information.

Procedural Memory: the portion of long-term memory that stores information relating to skills, habits, and other perceptual-motor tasks.

Emotional Memory: the portion of long-term memory that stores learned emotional responses to various stimuli.

Elaborative Rehearsal: the linking of new information in short-term memory to familiar material stored in long-term memory.

Mnemonics: techniques such as a pattern of letters, ideas, or associations that make material easier to remember.

Schema (Schemata): a set of beliefs or expectations about something that is based on past experience.

Spacing Effect: the tendency for distributed study or practice to yield better long-term retention.

Long-Term Potentiation (LTP): a long-lasting change in the structure or function of a synapse that increases the efficiency of neural transmission and is thought to be related to how information is stored by neurons.

Decay Theory: the theory of forgetting stating that memories deteriorate from short-term memory due to the passage of time.

Retrograde Amnesia: the phenomenon of not being able to remember what happened shortly before an injury.

Retroactive Interference: new information interfering with information already in memory.

Proactive Interference: information already in memory interfering with new information.

State-Dependent Memory: refers to the tendency to better recall information in a certain physiological state if a person returns to the same state they were in during learning.

Context-Dependent Memory: refers to the improved recall of specific information when the context present at encoding and retrieval are the same.

Autobiographical Memory: recollection of events that happened in our life and when those events took place.

Childhood Amnesia: the inability of adults to remember personally experienced events prior to the age of two.

Eidetic Memory: the ability to reproduce unusually sharp and detailed images of something one has seen; commonly called photographic memory.

Flashbulb Memories: experience of remembering vividly a certain event and the incidents surrounding it even after a long time has passed.

Source Error: misattribution of the source of a memory.

Déjà vu: the eerie feeling of knowing in a situation in which you are experiencing something totally new.

Chapter 8

Cognition

Outline

© Lightspring/Shutterstock.com

Introduction to the Chapter (Summary)

In this chapter we will look at thinking, language, and intelligence which fall under the umbrella of cognition. There are three main building blocks of thought: language, images, and concepts. We use language, images, and concepts to help us formulate thoughts but cognition involves more than passively thinking about things, it involves actively using words, images, and concepts to understand the world, solve problems, and to make decisions.

Whenever we are faced with a problem to solve, we follow the three stages of the problem-solving process: 1) Interpreting the Problem 2) Implementing Strategies and 3) Evaluation of Progress. One way that we solve problems is through insight or a sudden and often novel realization of the solution to a problem. Insight contrasts with strategy-based solutions such as algorithms and also heuristics. Many factors can either help or hinder the problem solving process such as our level of motivation, and tendencies such as mental set and functional fixedness. One possible solution to these issues is brainstorming which emphasizes the value of looking for new ways to represent or tackle a difficult problem.

A large focus of cognition is intelligence; a general term referring to the ability involved in learning and adaptive behavior or a mental quality consisting of the ability to learn from experience, solve problems, and use knowledge to adapt to new situations. There are several theories of Intelligence. Theorists such as Charles Spearman believed that intelligence is very general like a well or spring of mental energy that flows through every action which he called general intelligence (g). Another theory coined by Howard Gardner is the theory of multiple intelligences which states that we possess many types (eight to be specific), each of which is relatively independent of the others. Finally, there is emotional intelligence which according to Daniel Goldman, is a form of intelligence that refers to how effectively people perceive and understand their own emotions and the emotions of others, and can regulate and manage their emotional behavior.

Psychologists use intelligence tests to assess an individual's mental aptitudes and compare them with those of others using numerical scores. The most common ways of testing intelligence involve individual IQ tests and there are two main tests that are typically used and those are the Wechsler Adult Intelligence Scale (WAIS) and the Stanford-Binet Tests (SB). The average score on an IQ test is 100 and nearly 70% of people have IQs between 85 and 115. What makes a good test? In order to be widely accepted, a test must be standardized, reliable, and valid.

There are two extremes of intelligence and the first one is Intellectual Developmental Disorder; a condition of significantly sub-average intelligence combined with deficiencies in behavior. The other extreme of intelligence is Giftedness which refers to superior IQ combined with demonstrated or potential ability in such areas as academic aptitude, creativity, and leadership. Often related to giftedness is creativity which is the ability to produce novel and socially valued ideas or objects. Our intelligence is thought to depend on both our biology and also our environment and experiences.

Cognition and The Building Blocks of Thought

This chapter focuses on **Cognition** or the processes whereby we acquire and use knowledge; the mental activities associated with thinking, knowing, remembering, and communicating. There are three key **Building Blocks of Thought** that help us with our cognitive processes; *language, images,* and *concepts.* **Language** is a flexible system of communication that uses sounds, rules, gestures, or symbols to convey information; our spoken, written, or signed words and the ways we combine them to communicate meaning. Language plays a key role in our understanding of others, encoding and memory of information, and in interpreting the world around us. **Images** are mental representations of a sensory experience which help us to think about things in our world. For example, if you were to think of a thunderstorm, you might picture wind, rain, and lightning. **Concepts** are mental categories for classifying objects, people, or experiences such as animals, books, mountains, plants, and so on. We use concepts, language, and images to help us formulate thoughts but cognition involves more than passively thinking about things, it involves actively using words, images, and concepts to understand the world, solve problems, and to make decisions.

© Gouraud Studio/Shutterstock.com

Problem Solving

We encounter countless problems in our every day lives! Problems can range from struggling to make small choices to trying to tackle elaborate situations that involve multiple subgoals. When we attempt to solve a problem, we go through three general stages of the problem-solving process: 1) Interpreting the Problem, 2) Implementing Strategies, and 3) Evaluation of our progress. In order to effectively solve a problem, we have to first interpret and define it. This process sets the stage for effectively implementing strategies to get us closer to solving the problem (which we will get to in a moment). Finally, we have to evaluate our progess toward our end goal. If the solutions that we implemented were unsuccessful, we may have to go back and redefine the problem or possibly just try different solutions!

Problem Solving Strategies

One way that we solve problems is through **Insight** or a sudden and often novel realization of the solution to a problem. Insight is an "Aha" moment that tends to give us a sense of happiness and satisfaction. It contrasts with strategy-based solutions such as **Algorithms** which are a step-by-step method of problem solving that guarantees a correct solution if it is appropriate for the problem and correctly carried out. Algorithms are often used in math such as with formulas for solving equations. Another strategy involves **Heuristics** or rules of thumb that help in simplifying and solving problems, although they do not guarantee a correct solution. There are several different types of heuristics that people use to try and solve problems. One example is called **Hill Climbing** which is a problem solving strategy in which each step moves you progressively closer to the final goal. You might use this heuristic on a multiple choice test to first eliminate the alternatives that are obviously incorrect in order to get closer to the right answer. Another heuristic involves creating **Subgoals** which are intermediate, more manageable goals used in one heuristic strategy to make it easier to reach the final goal. Using subgoals involves breaking a problem into smaller, more

manageable pieces that are easier to solve individually than the problem as a whole. When I was writing my 80+ pages thesis in graduate school, I created small subgoals so that the project wouldn't feel so intimidating. The thought of eighty pages was overwhelming but writing a ten page introduction didn't feel so impossible! Finally, sometime the best method is **Working Backward** which is a heuristic strategy in which one works backward from the desired goal to the given conditions. For example, if you have $100 to buy some clothes, you buy one item and subtract that from the total and continue doing so until you have spent the money.

Obstacles to Problem Solving

Many factors can either help or hinder the problem solving process such as our level of motivation or emotional arousal along with our approach to problem solving. One common obstacle is **Mental Set** which is the tendency to perceive and to approach problems in certain ways. This can be helpful if we have learned information that applies to the current situation but can create obstacles when a different or new approach is needed. The best problem solvers are those that can think flexibly and choose from many different sets. Another obstacle is **Functional Fixedness** or the tendency to perceive only a limited number of uses for an object, thus interfering with the process of problem solving. It is important for the learning process to assign correct functions to objects but also important that we are open to seeing that an object can be used for an entirely different function. One possible solution to these issues is **Brainstorming** which is a problem-solving strategy in which an individual or group produces numerous ideas and evaluates them only after all ideas have been collected. This technique emphasizes the value of looking for new ways to represent or tackle a difficult problem.

Intelligence and Mental Abilities

Psychologists have studied intelligence almost since the beginning of psychology itself and yet still struggle to fully understand it. So what is intelligence? Is there just one type of intelligence such as general intelligence or is it made up of many separate abilities? **Intelligence** is a general term referring to the ability involved in learning and adaptive behavior; a mental quality consisting of the ability to learn from experience, solve problems, and use knowledge to adapt to new situations.

Theories of Intelligence

There are several different theories of intelligence. The early theorists such as Charles Spearman believed that intelligence was very general like a well or spring of mental energy that flows through every action. He defined **General Intelligence (g)** as a general intelligence factor that underlies specific mental abilities and is therefore measured by every task on an intelligence test. A general intelligence score is like an overall rating of a city, it doesn't give you much specific information about its schools, streets, or nightlife but it gives you a general idea of the city. Another theory is the **Theory of Multiple Intelligences** which is Howard Gardner's theory that there is not one intelligence, but rather many intelligences, each of which is relatively independent of the others. Gardner lists eight different types: logical-mathematical, linguistic, spatial, musical, bodily-kinesthetic, interpersonal, intrapersonal, and naturalistic. Finally, there is **Emotional Intelligence** which according to Daniel Goleman, is a form of intelligence that refers to how effectively people perceive and understand their own emotions and the emotions of others, and can regulate and manage their emotional behavior.

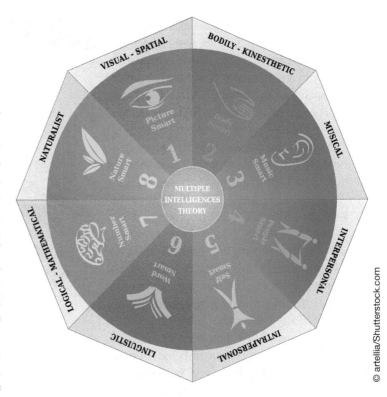

© artellia/Shutterstock.com

Assessing Intelligence

Psychologists use **Intelligence Tests** which are methods for assessing an individual's mental aptitudes and comparing them with those of others, using numerical scores. The most common ways of testing intelligence involve individual IQ tests. IQ or an **Intelligence Quotient** is a person's chronological age/mental age x 100. This numerical indicator allows for the direct comparison of scores between individuals; an average IQ score is 100. There are two main tests that are typically used and those are the Wechsler Adult Intelligence Scale (WAIS) and Stanford-Binet Tests (SB). The WAIS is probably the best test out there and the most commonly used to evaluate intelligence.

© Tashatuvango/Shutterstock.com

What Makes a Good Test?

So what makes the Wechsler Adult Intelligence Scale or the Stanford-Binet a good test? In order to be widely accepted, a test must be standardized, reliable, and valid. **Standardization** involves defining meaningful scores by comparison with the performance of a pretested standardization group. In other words, because it is standardized, one score can be compared accurately to another score. Some big examples of standardized tests are the SATs, ACTs, and GREs. A score of 1200 on the SATs means the same thing across people whereas something like GPA can be incredibly subjective depending on the standards of a class or even an institution (it might be easier to get an A in some versions of a class than in others). **Reliability** (consistency) is the ability of a test to produce stable and dependable scores. If something is reliable, you can count on it being consistent. Small variations and changes are to be expected but big differences in scores between administrations of a test, might indicate a reliability issue. Finally, **Validity** (accuracy) is the ability of a test to measure what it has been designed to measure. The best way to remember all of these is to think of a scale which is an assessment of weight. When you step on a scale you want it to be valid or accurate (it says what you actually weight), reliable or consistent (your weight

doesn't change drastically from minute to minute such as weighing 150 in the morning and 200 the next day), and standardized (your weight should be the same no matter what scale you get on).

Heredity, Environment, and Intelligence

Is intelligence inherited or is it the product of our experiences and the environment? This question is sometimes called *the IQ debate* and a useful analogy comes from studies of plants. If we grow one group of randomly assigned plants in enriched soil and another group in poor soil, the enriched group will grow to be taller and stronger than the nonenriched group. The differences between the two groups is due entirely to differences in the environment (in this case, the soil). Within each group of plants however, some plants are going to grow taller than others. Differences among individual plants in the same field are likely to be due to genetics because all plants in the group share the same environment. We can therefore conclude that the height and strength of any single plant depends on both heredity and environment. We are born with a biological predisposition for our potentials in terms of intelligence but whether or not we reach those potentials depends on environmental influences.

Extremes of Intelligence

As mentioned earlier, the average score on an IQ test is 100 and nearly 70% of people have IQs between 85 and 115. There are two extremes of intelligence and the first one is **Intellectual Developmental Disorder**;

formerly called mental retardation. IDD is a condition of significantly subaverage intelligence combined with deficiencies in behavior. There is also a distinction made within the category of Intellectual Developmental Disorder and it includes Mild IDD (IQ of 50–70), Moderate IDD (IQ of 35–49), Severe IDD (IQ of (20–34), and Profound IDD (IQ of below 20). In most cases, the causes of Intellectual Developmental Disorder (IDD) are unknown though having genetic or biological roots is a commonly proposed explanation. The other extreme of intelligence is **Giftedness** which refers to superior IQ combined with demonstrated or potential ability in such areas as academic aptitude, creativity, and leadership. Globally gifted people are rare, it is more common that giftedness is displayed in only a few areas.

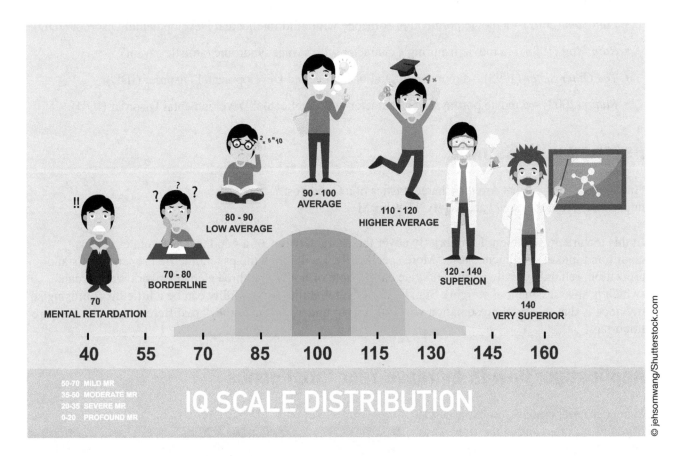

Creativity

Finally, often related to intelligence is **Creativity** which is the ability to produce novel and socially valued ideas or objects. Creativity is a phenomenon whereby something new and somehow valuable is formed. The created item may be intangible (such as an idea, a scientific theory, a musical composition, or a joke) or a physical object (such as an invention, a literary work, or a painting). If I were to give you a common place object like a pencil, how many uses could you list for it? Five? Ten? Fifty? Creativity is not measured by most IQ tests but a relationship between creativity and intelligence is thought to exist and creative people are often viewed as being more intelligent than non-creative people.

In Popular Culture

- *Bambi* (1942) – a movie that shows some of the different stages of learning of language.

- *Apollo 13* (1995) – a movie highlighting the problem-solving process.

- *The Core* (2003) – a movie featuring brainstorming and problem solving to fix the planet.

- *Fast Five* (2011) – a movie featuring a scene where the group engages in brainstorming and problem solving for their upcoming heist.

- *I am Sam* (2001) – a movie portrayal of someone with mild Intellectual Developmental Disorder (IDD).

- *Rain Man* (1988) – a movie featuring a character with savant syndrome (autistic savant).

- *The Other Sister* (1999) – a movie portrayal of Intellectual Developmental Disorder (IDD).

- *Radio* (2003) – a movie portrayal of a character with Intellectual Developmental Disorder (IDD).

Psyched with Setmire

"Intelligence Tests: What Are the Characteristics of a Good Test?"
https://www.youtube.com/watch?v=ly9l3IWluRM

In this lecture presentation, I will briefly cover the characteristics of a good test as it relates to our cognition topic of intelligence tests. More specifically, I will cover the psychometric properties of standardization, reliability, and validity and give an example of how these three elements work with a scale (which is an assessment of weight). Standardization, reliability, and validity can be a little bit confusing so my hope is that this brief presentation will help you to understand how they are different and why they are important!

Application: How to Increase Your Intelligence

Your brain needs exercise just like a muscle. If you use it often and in the right ways, you will become a more skilled thinker and increase your ability to focus. But if you never use your brain, or abuse it with harmful chemicals, your ability to think and learn will deteriorate. Here are some tips to help you process information faster, improve your comprehension, and to make the most of your intelligence:

© ESB Professional/Shutterstock.com

- *Minimize Television Watching* – watching television doesn't use your mental capacity or allow it to recharge.

- *Exercise* – using your body clears your head, creates a wave of energy, helps relieve stress and anxiety.

- *Read Challenging Books* – read books that make you focus. Reading a classic novel can change your view of the world and will make you think in more precise, elegant English.

- *Get Enough Sleep* – "early to bed, early to rise, makes a man healthy, wealthy, and wise" (Benjamin Franklin). Nothing makes it harder to concentrate than sleep deprivation so be sure to get enough sleep each night. You can also take power naps during the day to recharge.

- *Take Time to Reflect* – spending some time alone in reflection gives you a chance organize your thoughts.

- *Play Mind Games for Creativity, Logic, and Processing Speed* – play mind games like Sudoku, crossword puzzles, and other brain teasers.

- *Abstain from Drugs, Alcohol and Caffeine* – these substances negatively affect your health. Smoking is especially bad because it lowers your oxygen intake.

- *Meditation* – meditating improves your brain power. Meditation relieves stress and it makes you more calm resulting in an increase in attentiveness. The more aware that you are the easier it is to learn.

- *Eat Complex Foods* – The brain needs glucose to operate at max power. Food high in glucose is harder for the body to break down and kind of drip feeds the brain.

Key Terms

Cognition or the processes whereby we acquire and use knowledge; the mental activities associated with thinking, knowing, remembering, and communicating.

Building Blocks of Thought: three factors that help us with our cognitive processes; *language*, *images*, and *concepts*.

Language: plays a key role in our understanding of others, encoding and memory of information, and in interpreting the world around us.

Images: mental representations of a sensory experience which help us to think about things in our world.

Concepts: mental categories for classifying objects, people, or experiences such as animals, books, mountains, plants, and so on.

Insight: a sudden and often novel realization of the solution to a problem.

Algorithms: a step-by-step method of problem solving that guarantees a correct solution if it is appropriate for the problem and correctly carried out.

Heuristics: rules of thumb that help in simplifying and solving problems, although they do not guarantee a correct solution.

Hill Climbing: a problem solving strategy (heuristic) in which each step moves you progressively closer to the final goal.

Subgoals: intermediate, more manageable goals used to make it easier to reach the final goal.

Working Backward which is a heuristic strategy in which one works backward from the desired goal to the given conditions.

Mental Set: the tendency to perceive and to approach problems in certain ways.

Functional Fixedness: the tendency to perceive only a limited number of uses for an object, thus interfering with the process of problem solving.

Brainstorming: a problem-solving strategy in which an individual or group produces numerous ideas and evaluates them only after all ideas have been collected.

Intelligence: a general term referring to the ability involved in learning and adaptive behavior; mental quality consisting of the ability to learn from experience, solve problems, and use knowledge to adapt to new situations.

General Intelligence (g): a general intelligence factor that, according to Charles Spearman and others, underlies specific mental abilities and is therefore measured by every task on an intelligence test.

Theory of Multiple Intelligences: Howard Gardner's theory that there is not one intelligence, but rather many intelligences, each of which is relatively independent of the others.

Emotional Intelligence: according to Daniel Goleman, a form of intelligence that refers to how effectively people perceive and understand their own emotions and the emotions of others, and can regulate and manage their emotional behavior.

Intelligence Tests: methods for assessing an individual's mental aptitudes and comparing them with those of others, using numerical scores.

Intelligence Quotient (IQ): a numerical indicator for intelligence; a person's chronological age/mental age x 100.

Standardization: defining meaningful scores by comparison with the performance of a pretested standardization group.

Reliability: (consistency) is the ability of a test to produce stable/dependable scores.

Validity: (accuracy) is the ability of a test to measure what it has been designed to measure.

Intellectual Disability Disorder: formerly called mental retardation; a condition of significantly subaverage intelligence combined with deficiencies in behavior.

Giftedness: refers to superior IQ combined with demonstrated or potential ability in such areas as academic aptitude, creativity, and leadership.

Creativity: the ability to produce novel and socially valued ideas or objects.

Outline

© Trueffelpix/Shutterstock.com

Introduction to the Chapter (Summary)

This chapter will cover the ways in which motives affect behavior and are affected by the external environment. Motives are specific needs or desires, such as hunger, thirst, or achievement that prompt goal-directed behavior. All motives are triggered by some kind of stimulus such as a bodily condition or a feeling. When the stimulus induces goal-directed behavior, we say that it has motivated the person. There are several perspectives and theories that psychologists use to understand motivated behaviors.

Early in the 20th century, psychologists generally attributed behavior to instincts which are inborn, inflexible, goal-directed behaviors that are characteristic of an entire species. After instinct theory fell out of favor, drive reduction theory was proposed and states that bodily needs create a state of tension or arousal called a drive and that motivated behavior is aimed at reducing the bodily tension and returning the organism to homeostasis. Another theory of motivation is arousal theory which proposes that organisms seek an optimal level of arousal. Another distinction regarding motivation is whether it is intrinsically or extrinsically motivated. A final approach to explaining motivation is Abraham Maslow's Hierarchy of Needs which holds that higher order motives involving social and personal growth only emerge after lower level motives related to survival have been satisfied.

A very strong motive we possess is hunger. There is a difference between the psychological state of hunger and the biological need for food. The hypothalamus is the brain center involved in hunger and eating. Psychological factors can sometimes overwhelm our biological wisdom and two examples of this are Anorexia Nervosa and Bulimia Nervosa. Both of these disorders are more prevalent in women than men and are notoriously difficult to treat. On the opposite end of the spectrum, obesity is one of the most pressing health problems in America. Some people inherit a tendency to be overweight but other factors influencing obesity include a sedentary lifestyles, portion size, and poor diet. Body Mass Index (BMI) is a numerical index calculated from a person's height and weight and is used to indicate health status, predict disease risk, and to help determine obesity. When trying to lose weight, if our weight drops below a certain point called a set point, our hunger actually increases. Our bodies are genetically predisposed to maintain a certain weight by changing our metabolic rate and activity level in response to caloric intake which can make it incredibly difficult to lose weight.

Another important topic in motivation involves the need to belong. As people, we have a deeply rooted need to form relationships and be connected with others. Finally, we can look at motivation in the workplace. For most people, work consumes the majority of our waking time and can greatly influence our quality of life, financial stability, and level of happiness. Industrial-Organizational Psychology is a subfield of psychology that involves the application of psychological concepts and methods to optimizing human behavior in workplaces. The two main divisions of I-O Psychology include Personnel Psychology (focuses on employee recruitment, selection, placement, training, appraisal, and development) and Organizational Psychology (examines organizational influences on worker satisfaction and productivity and facilitates organizational change).

Motivation and Motivation Theories

A **Motive** is a specific need or desire, such as hunger, thirst, or achievement that prompts some kind of goal-directed behavior. All motives are triggered by some kind of stimulus or a bodily condition or a feeling. When the stimulus induces goal-directed behavior, we say that it has motivated the person. For example, as I was sitting here writing this chapter, I was feeling an internal pull toward food so I ran out to In-N-Out, ate a hamburger and fries, and now am back at my computer free from bodily signals of hunger! **Motivation** is the driving force which help causes us to achieve goals.

© Jirsak/Shutterstock.com

Motives and emotions (which we will cover next) push us to take some kind of action. Ever wonder why some people seem to be very successful, highly motivated individuals? Where does that energy, drive, or direction come from? From here we will look at some general concepts and theories of motivation and then a couple of specific motives that play an important role in human behavior.

Drive Reduction Theory

One view of motivation holds that bodily needs create a state of tension or arousal. This perspective focuses on **Drives**; a state of tension or arousal that motivates behavior. Common drives would include the need for food or water creating a drive such as hunger or thirst. **Drive Reduction Theory** states that motivated behavior is aimed at reducing a state of bodily tension or arousal and returning the organism to **Homeostasis** or a state of balance and stability in which the organism functions effectively. When we are hungry we find something to eat, when we are thirsty we find something to drink; our behavior is directed at reducing the state of bodily tension or arousal. My example a moment ago of running to In-N-Out to get lunch is perfect here! I was hungry, ate lunch, and now that state of tension is gone and I'm back to neutral homeostasis.

Need
(Food, Water) ➡ **Drive**
(Hunger, Thirst) ➡ **Drive-Reducing behaviors**
(Eating, Drinking)

Drive reduction theory is appealing but can't explain all kinds of behavior. From this perspective, people would do very little once all their drives were satisfied (we would have no motivation to act). Some psychologists then suggest that motivation might have to do with other factors such as our state of alertness or arousal.

Arousal Theory

The **Arousal Theory** theory of motivation proposes that organisms seek an optimal level of arousal and that we are driven to maintain a certain level of arousal in order to feel comfortable. Arousal refers to a state of emotional, intellectual, and physical activity and from this perspective, we perform behaviors to reduce or increase arousal. So for example, if we are bored we might turn on the television or call a friend. If we are sleepy we might turn off the light and go to sleep or maybe we grab a coffee to wake up instead. We are motivated

to maintain an optimal level of arousal not only for the given moment or task but also just in general. Some people tend to be more laid back and relaxed while others might be constantly in motion and dislike sitting still. People who are mellow will prefer to maintain that mellow level of energy while those that are constantly in motion, will be motivated to maintain that level of energy. Psychologists agree that there is no "best" level of arousal necessary to perform all tasks but rather different tasks require different levels of arousal for optimal performance. Think of this very moment that you are in as you read this chapter. If you are under aroused and sleepy, you will struggle to pay attention and stay awake enough to read. If you have too much arousal or energy, you might have a hard time sitting still or focusing. There is an optimal level somewhere in-between where you are able to stay awake and focus on the materials you are reading.

Intrinsic vs Extrinsic Motivation

Neither drive reduction theory or arousal theory accounts for all types of behaviors so we have additional theories to fill in the remaining gaps! One distinction that is often made in motivation is whether a behavior is intrinsically or extrinsically motivated. **Intrinsic Motivation** involves a desire to perform a behavior that stems from the enjoyment derived from the behavior itself. In other words, the motivation and enjoyment exists within the individual rather than relying on any external pressure or consequence. A child playing is a good example of intrinsic motivation. Children play because playing is fun and motivating by itself. Another example would be someone who reads because they enjoy reading.

Extrinsic Motivation on the other hand involves a desire to perform a behavior to obtain an external reward or punishment. Common extrinsic motivations are rewards like money, praise, or candy, or maybe even trying to avoid the threat of punishment. When people are extrinsically motivated, they perform a behavior because of an outside factor. One example would be a child does their chores not because he/she enjoys them but rather for the money they get when they finish. Another example might be someone reading a chapter in a textbook because they want to do well on the upcoming exam. Of course intrinsic and extrinsic motivation can work together and a person might be driven both instrinscally and extrinsically to perform a behavior. I always think of my teaching job as an example! I love to teach and genuinely enjoy the opportunity to inspire and share knowledge with my students (which is instrinsic motivation) but I also teach and work because I need to earn a paycheck so I can support my family (which is extrinsic motivation). When you can both internal and external factors working together, that is always a good thing!

EXTRINSIC MOTIVATION

© BadBrother/Shutterstock.com

Maslow's Hierarchy of Needs

Another theory of motivation is Maslow's **Hierarchy of Needs**. Abraham Maslow was an American Psychologist who proposed that higher order motives involving social and personal growth only emerge after lower level motives related to survival have been satisfied. Maslow believed that

Maslow's hierarchy of needs

morality, creativity, spontaneity, problem solving, lack of prejudice, acceptance of facts	5
self-esteem, confidence, achievement, respect of others, respect by others	4
friendship, family, sexual intimacy, sense of connection	3
security of body, employment, resources, morality, family, health, property	2
breathing, food, sex, sleep, homeostasis, excretion	1

Self-actualization
Self-esteem
Love and belonging
Safety and security
Physiological needs

© Pyty/Shutterstock.com

since our needs are many, they are arranged in order of importance, from the basic to the complex and a person advances to the next level of needs only after the lower level need is at least minimally satisfied. The further they progress up the hierarchy, the more individuality and psychological health a person will show.

The order of Maslow's hierarchy is not universally fixed and culture might play a prominent role in the order of needs. A frequently mentioned criticism of this theory is that it is based primarily on white males in western society when many people in simpler societies live on the edge of survival but still form strong and meaningful social ties. The basic idea that some motives and needs are more compelling than others makes a lot of common sense and is fairly well supported despite not being universal.

Instinct and Psychoanlytic Theory

Finally, we can approach motivation by examining **Instincts**. All creatures are born with instincts which are inborn and unlearned goal-directed behaviors characteristic of an entire species. Instincts involve specific innate and unlearned knowledge about how to survive. These innate tendencies are preprogrammed at birth; they are in our genes. We are born with the ability to cry as a signal for attention and are also born with particular reflexes which promote survival (include sucking, swallowing, coughing, and blinking). We also sometimes reference maternal instincts as a powerful driving force for the relationship between a mom and their children. Early in the 20th century, psychologists attributed quite a few behaviors to instincts but this approach fell out of favor for several key reasons: 1) most important human behavior is learned, 2) human behavior is rarely rigid, inflexibile and unchanging, and 3) ascribing every concivable human behavior to a corresponding instinct explains nothing; it only names the behavior rather than explaining the origins.

Influential psychologist Sigmund Freud also believed that instincts play a prominent role in human behavior and motivation. Freud's psychoanalytic theory proposed that humans have only two basic drives: **Eros** and **Thanatos**, or the Life and Death drives. According to psychoanalytic theory, everything we do, every thought we have, and every emotion we experience has one of two goals: to help us survive or to prevent our destruction. The life drive (libido or Eros) is in charge of survival, propagation, hunger, thirst, sex and expended energy in pursuit of our goals. The death drive is aggression or protecting our own interests. Freud believed that these two baisc instinctual drives function in a complementary manner.

Hunger

Now having looked at some of the basic concepts and theories of motivation, let's look at the specific motive of hunger (my personal favorite motive)! There is a difference between the psychological state of hunger and the biological need for food and external cues can influence our desire to eat or drink. If we look at the *biology of hunger*, the hypothalamus is the brain center involved in hunger and eating. How do areas of the brain know when to stimulate hunger? The brain monitors the blood levels of fats, carbohydrates, and insulin. Changes in the blood levels of these substances (glucose, leptin, and ghrelin) signal the need for food. The brain also monitors the amount of food that we have eaten through specialized cells in the stomach and upper part of the digestive system that measure the volume of food. All of these signals assist in letting us know when we physically need food.

APPETITE & HUNGER
(hormones)

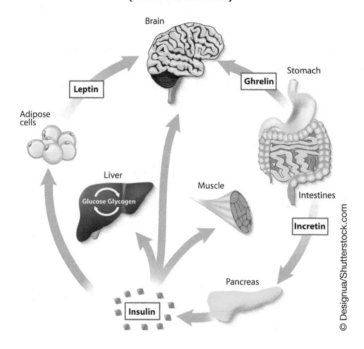

Biology is not the only determining factor in when we eat; other things outside of what is going on in the body can affect our hunger. Looking at the *psychology of hunger,* cultural and even individually learned preferences and eating habits can influence hunger. For example, some of us eat regular meals and rarely snack, while others just nibble throughout the day. Every culture has its collection of foods that are preferred and those that are avoided; many taste preferences involve conditioning and norms. Even looking at the clock and realizing that it is your typical dinner time might cause us to feel hungry even though you don't physically need food. Family cultures also play a role in when and what we might eat. My family

has a deeply entrenched custom of having dessert every night after dinner to the point where I almost can't move on in my evening without eating something sweet following dinner! My partner's family has quite a few people who battle diabetes and so they don't tend to eat dessert. When my partner and I first started dating, I remember waiting anxiously after dinner for the desserts to emerge and was dissappointed when they never came! Every family has different norms and customs around food which might directly shape when, what, and how often you eat. Oh and as a side note, after almost thirteen years of marriage, now my partner likes to have dessert after dinner too!

Eating Disorders

Our bodies are naturally disposed to maintain a normal weight but sometimes psychological influences might overwhelm our biological wisdom. One example of this can be found in **Anorexia Nervosa** which is a serious eating disorder that is associated with an intense fear of weight gain and a distorted body image. People with anorexia nervosa perceive themselves as overweight and strive to lose weight by severely limiting their intake of food. Part of the presentation of anorexia is a refusal to maintain a body weight at or above a minimal normal weight for their age and height. The restricted diet and refusal to maintain a typical weight can often have health correlates as people might suffer nutritional deficiencies, long-term consequences such as heart problems, and other health related problems including a loss of menstrual cycles for females.

Another commonly occuring eating disorder is **Bulimia Nervosa** which is characterized by binges of eating followed by compensatory behaviors such as self-induced vomiting or purging. With this disorder, there are recurrent episodes of binge eating (rapid consumption of a large amount of food usually in less than 2 hours), recurrent inappropriate behaviors to try and prevent weight gain such as self-induced vomiting, and body shape and weight excessively influencing a person's self-image. Bulimia nervosa is much more prevalent in women than men but over the past decade, the number of men struggling with weight and eating disorder issues has almost doubled. Both anorexia and bulimia are notoriously hard to treat. Think how many times a day the feeling of being hungry comes up for a person and then add to that the extra difficultly of our cultural expectations of weight and beauty.

Obesity and Weight Control

According to the Surgeon General, obesity is one of the most pressing health problems in America. **Obesity** is an excess of body fat in relation to lean body mass or a medical condition in which excess body fat has accumulated to the extent that it may have an adverse effect on health, leading to reduced life expectancy and/or increased health problems. Some people inherit a tendency to be overweight but other factors influencing obesity include sedentary lifestyles, portion size, and poor diet. **Body Mass Index (BMI)** is a numerical index calculated from a person's height and weight that is used to indicate health status and predict disease risk. This is a screening tool used to identify weight problems and elevated numbers correlate with increased risk for hypertension, stroke, heart disease, type 2 diabetes, and sleep apnea.

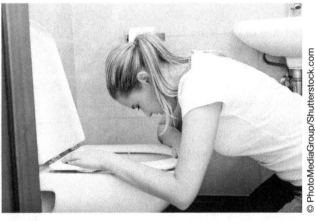

If we look briefly at the physiology of obesity, breaking it down very simply, people gain weight by consuming more calories than they expend; a pound of fat is equal to 3500 calories. Body fat is determined by the size and number of fat cells a person possesses and once the number of fat cells increases, it never decreases. You might be able to shrink these cells through dieting but they will not disappear. Once we are overweight we actually require less food to maintain our weight than we did to gain it because fat cells have a lower metabolic rate. Making it even more difficult, when our weight drops below a certain point, our hunger actually increases. **Set Point Theory** is a theory that our bodies are genetically predisposed to maintaining a certain weight by changing our metabolic rate and activity level in response to caloric intake. The specifics of our genes predispose the size of our jeans but don't tell the whole story; lack of exercise also plays a contributing role along with food and eating habits. In addition to health effects, there are also social effects of obesity. Being obese can affect how you feel about yourself and also how you are treated. Obese people are often stereotyped as slow, lazy, sloppy, meaner, and more obnoxious than their thin counterparts.

Permanent weight loss is not easy and over 66% of women and 50% of men report wanting to lose weight. Those who do manage to lose weight set realistic goals and change their lifestyles to lose weight gradually. I once heard someone recommend that in order to lose weight, you should eat crispy greens rather than Krispy Kremes! That stuck with me for some reason; most likely because I thought that the doughnuts sounded amazing! While there are countless different theories about the best way to lose weight, let's look at some of the common suggestions. One of the most important suggestions is to set realistic goals for weight loss; healthy weight loss means losing 1–2 pounds per week. To lose more than that each week is not realistic or possible under reasonable efforts. Other things that you can do to lose weight include adding exercise to your daily routine, practicing portion control with meals, making good choices with the foods that you eat, being motivated and committing to

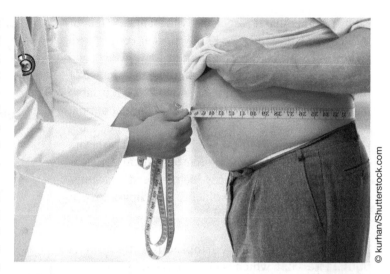

your diet, having a weight loss buddy, and allowing yourself to slip up every now and then. Weight loss can be incredibly difficult and take time but being realistic and making small life changes can go a long way to helping you reach your goal.

Box: Fad Diets

Most popular diets are considered **Fad Diets**. There is no clear definition for what constitutes a fad diet but they generally promise quick results with a short time commitment. Unfortunately, fad diets don't tend to be successful for long-term changes in a person's weight. Long-term success requires permanent changes in behavior, diet, and activity.

Ways to spot a fad diet:

- It claims fast weight loss

- Claims that sound too good to be true

- Foods defined as "good" and "bad"

- Less than 1,000 calories daily

- A required vitamin/mineral supplement or food product

- Elimination of a major food group (grains, fats, meats, dairy, fruit, vegetables)

- Lack of long-term randomized scientific studies proving the diet works and is safe.

- Elimination of an essential nutrient (carbohydrates, fats, proteins)

- No activity or exercise needed

- It's written by someone with no expertise in weight management

© Cozy Home/Shutterstock.com

The Need to Belong

Another powerful motive that we possess as people is the need to belong which is referred to as belongingness or our **Affiliation Need**. As people, we are social animals and want to have the feeling of belonging. Our need to affiliate captures our deeply rooted need to build relationships and to feel like we are part of a group. While some people are more private and enjoy solitude more than others, the vast majority of people seek to become strongly attached to others and to form close and enduring relationships. When this need is not being met, many people experience psycholgical discomfort and their wellbeing suffers.

© Rawpixel.com/Shutterstock.com

Our need to belong is thought to be instinctual; we are born feeling this way. It may even serve an evolutionary purpose as we have strength in numbers (espeically if you think about it from a hunters and gatherers perspective). There are an incredible number of benefits to

belonging and affiliation with others. Relationships tend to improve the quality of our lives nourishing us not only emotionally but also physically. Our connections with friends, family, partners, co-workers and so on provide us with a sense of identity, security, and a feeling of being valued. Relationships and connections with others also provide us with valuable support to deal with the difficulties of life and to manage stress and anxiety. On the flip side, being socially excluded or finding yourself in situations where you feel like an outsider can have strong negative effects. Isolation, lonliness, and having a low social status can harm a person's subjective sense of well-being as well as a number of other things like immune system and health, academic performance, mood, and motivation.

Because we are social animals and want to connect with others, social networking and social media are incredibly popular methods for people to reach out to others. Before classes begin each day, I can see the vast majority of

my students on their phones texting, posting, tweeting, and connecting with othes via technology. There is considerable debate about whether or not technology helps or hinders our connectedness with others with some arguing that it increases sociability and others that it only faciliates connectedness with those we already know.

Motivation at Work

For most people, work consumes the majority of our waking time and can greatly influence our quality of life, financial stability, and level of happiness and overall satisfaction. There is a subfield of psychology that deals with the workplace called **Industrial-Organizational Psychology**. Industrial-Organizational (I-O) psychology involves the application of psychological concepts and methods to optimizing human behavior in workplaces. This area specializes in deriving principles of individual, group, and organizational behavior and then applying that knowledge to the solution of problems at work. Individuals working in this subfield have specialized knowledge and traning in organizational development, attitudes, carerer development, decision theory, human performance and human factors, and task analysis. With that knowledge, they address issues of recruitment, selection and placement, training and development, performance measurment, quality of worklife, organizational development, and workplace motivation and reward systems.

Within this subfield, there are two main divisions each with their own focus; **Personnel Psychology** and **Organizational Psychology**. Personnel psychology is a subfield of Industrial-Organization Psychology that

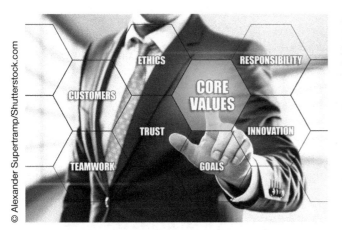

focuses on employee recruitment, selection, placement, training, appraisal, and development. Organizational Psychology is a subfield of Industrial-Organization Psychology that examines organizational influences on worker satisfaction and productivity and facilitates organizational change.

In Popular Culture

- *Thin* (2006) – a documentary about a group of young women in treatment for eating disorders.

- *Shallow Hal* (2001) – deals with the topic of weight along with showing cultural attitudes toward obesity.

- *Saw* (2004–2011) – a great example of motivation related to life and death instincts.

- *The Hunger Games* (2012 and on) – great example of survival instincts.

- *Office Space* (1999) – the "Bobs" are a great example of I-O psychologists.

- Countless Television Shows – *Heavy*, *Too Fat for Fifteen*, *The Biggest Loser*, *Shedding for the Wedding*, and *Dance Your Ass Off* – all of these shows focus on losing weight.

- *The Walking Dead* – a popular television show constantly featuring examples of the survival instinct at work!

- *All About That Bass* (2014) – a popular culture song by Meghan Trainor about heavier women being attractive and sexy.

- *Try* (2014) – a popular culture song by Colbie Caillat highlighting the idea of accepting yourself as you are.

Psyched with Setmire

"Survival Instinct (Motivational Theories)"
https://www.youtube.com/watch?v=cWtSgioYKpo

What would you do to survive? How would you react in a life or death circumstance? You might not be happy with the answers to those questions! We all possess a very powerful survival instinct or an instinct for self-preservation that can override our natural inclinations and tendencies. In this lecture presentation, I will review the instinct theory of motivation focusing specifically on our survival instinct. I will cover some of the big contributions to topic along with providing a few popular culture examples from the media; specifically referencing the Hunger Games movies, The Walking Dead television show, and the Saw movies. I hope you enjoy!

"May the odds be ever in your favor." (*Hunger Games*)

"You step outside; you risk your life . . . Every moment now you don't have a choice. The only thing you can choose is what you're risking it for." (*The Walking Dead*)

"Live or die, make your choice". (*Saw*)

Application: Eating Disorder Help and Treatments

While there is nothing wrong with wanting to lose some weight to be healthier, sometimes weight loss can become an unhealthy obsession that requires psychological assistance. Treatment for eating disorders can depend on the severity, duration, and type of disorder that a person is struggling with. In general, with anorexia, the first goal is to restore a person's weight to a healthy point. This can be incredibly difficult to do given the nature of the disorder but it is crucial for a person's health. With bulimia, the main focus is to break the cycle of binging and purging behavior; which is also a difficult task to do. After restoring typical weight and/ or breaking the binge and purge cycle, people then often undergo group or individual therapy to help find the root of the disorder and to brainstorm strategies to prevent relapse. Unfortunately relapse rates are quite high with eating disorders so it is important for someone struggling with one of them to have help and access to a multitude of different resources.

Here are some online resources to explore if you think you or someone you know might have an eating disorder:

- *National Eating Disorder Association* - http://www.nationaleatingdisorders.org/
- *Something Fishy* - http://www.something-fishy.org/
- *Mirror Mirror Eating Disorders* - http://www.mirror-mirror.org/resources.htm

Key Terms

Motive: is a specific need or desire, such as hunger, thirst, or achievement that prompts goal-directed behavior.

Motivation: the process that initiates, guides, and maintains goal-oriented behaviors.

Drives: a state of tension or arousal that motivates behavior.

Drive Reduction Theory: the theory of motivation that states that motivated behavior is aimed at reducing a state of bodily tension or arousal and returning the organism to homeostasis.

Homeostasis: or a state of balance and stability in which the organism functions effectively.

Arousal Theory: the theory of motivation proposes that organisms seek an optimal level of arousal and that we are driven to maintain a certain level of arousal in order to feel comfortable.

Intrinsic Motivation: involves a desire to perform a behavior that stems from the enjoyment derived from the behavior itself; behavior is driven by internal rewards.

Extrinsic Motivation: involves a desire to perform a behavior to obtain an external reward or punishment; behavior is driven by external rewards.

Hierarchy of Needs: the theory of motivation that proposes a five tier model of human needs depicted as hierarchical levels within a pyramid.

Instincts: are inborn and unlearned goal-directed behaviors characteristic of an entire species.

Eros: according to Sigmund Freud, the instinctual drive toward life and pleasure.

Thanatos: according to Sigmund Freud, the instinctual drive toward aggression and death.

Anorexia Nervosa: a serious eating disorder that is associated with an intense fear of weight gain and a distorted body image.

Bulimia Nervosa: a serious eating disorder characterized by binges of eating followed by compensatory behaviors such as self-induced vomiting or purging.

Obesity: an excess of body fat in relation to lean body mass or a medical condition in which excess body fat has accumulated to the extent that it may have an adverse effect on health, leading to reduced life expectancy and/or increased health problems.

Body Mass Index (BMI): a numerical index calculated from a person's height and weight that is used to indicate health status and predict disease risk.

Set Point Theory: a theory that our bodies are genetically predisposed to maintaining a certain weight by changing our metabolic rate and activity level in response to caloric intake.

Fad Diets: diets that promise quick results with a short time commitment.

Affiliation Need: our deeply rooted need to build relationships and to feel like we are part of a group.

Industrial-Organizational (I-O) Psychology: the application of psychological concepts and methods to optimizing human behavior in workplaces.

Personnel Psychology: a subfield of Industrial-Organization Psychology that focuses on employee recruitment, selection, placement, training, appraisal, and development.

Organizational Psychology: a subfield of Industrial-Organization Psychology that examines organizational influences on worker satisfaction and productivity and facilitates organizational change.

Chapter 10

Emotions

Outline

© g-stockstudio/Shutterstock.com

Introduction to the Chapter (Summary)

In this chapter we will discuss the various theories, physiological respones, experiences, and expressions of human emotions. Emotions, which are feelings such as fear, joy, or surprise that underly behavior, often motivate us toward some type of action or reflect a state of mind. When it comes to emotions, there is a chicken or the egg debate when we try to figure out which comes first, the physiological arousal or the emotional experience. Several theories have been proposed trying to answer this question and examine the order in which our mind and body responds to stimuli. These theories include the James-Lange Theory, the Cannon-Bard Theory, and the Two-Factor Theory; none of which are perfect. There are also a handful of smaller theories that have gained contemporary attention including the cognitive-mediational theory by Lazarus and also the facial-feedback theory. One common thread among these three theories is the fact that emotions involve several systems within the body that work together allowing us to process and respond to the various environmental demands that we face on a daily basis. The two main systems involved are the limbic system and the autonomic nervous system; more specifically the sympathetic and parasympathetic nervous systems which help to arouse us in cases of stress and then calm us down once the threat has subsided. Whenever we react emotionally to the environment, the chains of physiological events occuring within our body and the subsequent bodily reactions can be measured and used to tell us valuable information. One such piece of information, which is measured by a machine called a polygraph, is whether or not a person is lying or telling the truth!

Although emotions can often be expressed in words, much of the time we communicate our feelings nonverbally through things such as voice quality, facial expression, body language, personal space, and explicit acts. These emotional expressions have a strong cultural component and while facial expressions tend to be relatively universal, gestures and the degree of emotional expression can vary greatly by culture and region of the world. For example, a thumbs up gesture in the United States signifies that we are good or that everything is alright whereas it is considered rude in other cultures.

Psychologists tend to disagree on the number of basic and complex emotions that people are capable of expressing with some proposing only a few basic emotions and others theorizing dozens. A few emotions that tend to get a lot of attention are anger, fear, and happiness. Anger can be caused by countless environmental triggers and while it can fuel physically or verbally aggressive acts, anger can be also constructive when people learn to handle it in a balanced manner. Fear is our response to a perceived threat and can be incredibly adaptive when appropriate and protect us from harmful stimuli in the environment. Happiness has been shown to fuel upward spirals. In other words, people who are happy perceive the world as safer, make decisions more easily, are more cooperative and likely to help others as noted by the feel good do good phenomenon, and also live healthier, more energized and satisfied lives. Luckily, there are many things that we can do to increase our levels of happiness including giving priority to close relationships, getting good sleep, acting happy, laughing, and trying to appreciate and focus on what we have versus what we lack.

© Gearstd/Shutterstock.com

Emotions

Emotions can exert an incredibly powerful force on human behavior. Strong emotions can cause you to take actions you might not normally perform or avoid situations that you generally enjoy. Emotions are considered to be essential to survival and a major source of personal enrichment and resilience. But why exactly do we have emotions? What causes us to have these feelings? Researchers, philosophers, and psychologists have proposed a number of different theories to explain the how and why behind human emotions but first, we have to define emotions; which isn't necessarily an easy task!

Defining Emotion

In psychology, **Emotion** is generally defined as a complex state of feeling that results in physical and psychological changes that influence thought and behavior. The word emotion first appeared in our language in the mid-16th century, adapted from the French word émouvoir, which literally means, "to stir up". There isn't one universal definition for emotion just as there isn't one theory that explains how they occur. Despite the lack of agreement, in general, most definitions of emotion assert that emotions involve multiple components; physiological arousal, expressive behaviors, conscious experience, and an expressive response.

© lassedesignen/Shutterstock.com

Theories of Emotion

As mentioned above, there is much disagreement about defining and explaining emotions which has lead to the proposal of several different theories of the chain of events involved when we experience them. There is a bit of a chicken or the egg debate with emotions when we try to figure out which comes first, the physiological arousal or the emotional experience. Looking at the various theories of emotion, in the

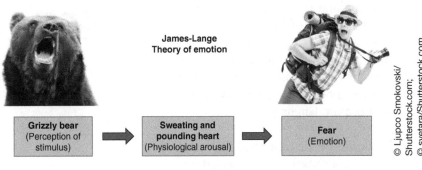

James-Lange Theory of emotion

Grizzly bear (Perception of stimulus) → Sweating and pounding heart (Physiological arousal) → Fear (Emotion)

© Ljupco Smokovski/Shutterstock.com; © svetara/Shutterstock.com

1880's American Psychologist William James formulated the first modern theory of emotion which was also reached by Danish Psychologist Carl Lange. Because the two came to the same independent conclusion, the theory became known as the **James-Lange Theory** and suggests that emotions occur as a result of physiological reactions to events. According to this theory, you see an external stimulus that leads to a physiological reaction. For example, suppose you are walking in the woods and you see a grizzly bear causing you to sweat and your heart to pound which then results in fear. From this perspective, stimuli in the environment cause physiological changes to occur and then emotions result from those physiological changes. The major flaw of this theory is that sensory information flows to the brain through the spinal cord so if bodily changes are the source of emotions, people with severe spinal cord injuries should experience fewer and less intense emotions but this is not the case. Also, this theory is often criticized because it is thought that the body's responses are not distinct enough to evoke different emotions. For example, does a racing heart trigger fear, anger, or love?

A second theory is the **Cannon-Bard Theory** which was proposed by Walter Cannon and Philip Bard in the 1920's. The Cannon-Bard theory states that we feel emotions and experience physiological reactions such as sweating, trembling and muscle tension simultaneously. More specifically, it is suggested that emotions result when the thalamus sends a message to the brain in response to a stimulus, resulting in a physiological reaction; the emotion and the arousal are simultaneous. Going back to the grizzly bear example, with this theory, when you saw the grizzly bear you would sweat, have your heart be pounding, and feel fear all at the same time. Because this theory discusses the role of the thalamus, it is sometimes also referred to as the thalamic theory of emotion. One common criticism is that there is general agreement that most emotions involve some level of cognition. In order to account for this, we have another theory!

The **Schachter-Singer or Two-Factor Theory** is the third major theory of emotion and was coined by Stanley Schachter and Jerome Singer in the 1960s. The Schachter-Singer or two-factor theory suggests that the physiological arousal occurs first, and then the individual must identify the reason behind this arousal in order to experience and label it as an emotion. This theory is sometimes called the two-factor theory of emotion; the experience of emotion depends on two factors: physiological arousal and cognitive processing. In other words, the situation gives us clues as to how we should interpret our state of arousal but only when we cognitively recognize that we are in danger do we experience those bodily changes as fear; arousal fuels emotion and cognition changes it! The main criticism of this theory is that we have the ability to respond to situations instantaneously without taking the time to interpret and evaluate them and infants can imitate emotional expressions well before they acquire language.

While the theories discussed above are the three big perspectives in the field, there are a couple of smaller theoretical contributions to the realm of emotion theories. One of the smaller theories was proposed by Psychologist Richard Lazarus and is known as the **Cognitive-Mediational Theory**. According to this theory, a stimulus leads to an immediate appraisal and that cognitive appraisal results in an emotional response which is then followed by the appropriate bodily response. At the heart of Lazarus's theory is what he called appraisal. Before an emotion occurs, Lazarus argued that people make an automatic, often unconscious, assessment of what is happening and what it may mean for them or those they care about. From this perspective, emotion becomes not just rational but a

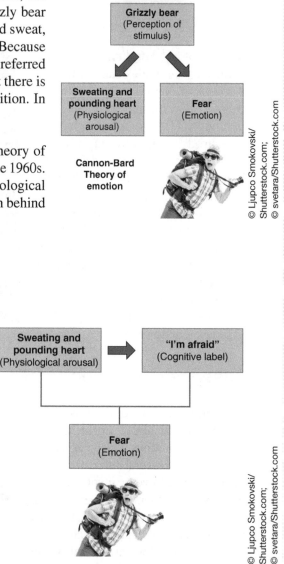

© Ljupco Smokovski/Shutterstock.com; © svetara/Shutterstock.com

necessary component of survival. The sound of a gunshot, for example, is interpreted as something potentially dangerous and leads to both the physiological responses like a rapid heart rate and trembling and the subjective experience of fear. A common criticism of this theory is that emotional reactions to situations are often so fast that there is little room for a cognitive appraisal to occur and that we often respond to physical stimuli before conscious thought enters into the picture.

Finally, according to the **Facial Feedback Theory**, emotion is the experience of changes in our facial muscles. In other words, when we smile, we then experience pleasure, or happiness. When we frown, we then experience sadness. It is the changes in our facial muscles that cue our brains and provide the basis of our emotions. Just as there are an unlimited number of muscle configurations in our face, so to are there a seemingly unlimited number of emotions. The sound of a gunshot, for example causes your eyes to widen, your teeth clench and your brain interprets these facial changes as the expression of fear. Therefore, you experience the emotion of fear. A problem or criticism of this approach is that if it were in fact true, shouldn't people with facial paralysis be unable to experience emotion in a normal or typical way? In case studies conducted on individuals with facial paralysis, no unusual or stunted emotional reactions were found to be present.

Embodied Emotions

Emotions involve the body and feeling without a body could be compared to breathing without lungs. In a crisis your **Sympathetic Nervous System** mobilizes your body for action through the flight or flight response. The sympathetic nervous systems is one of two divisions of the autonomic nervous system which is responsible for regulating involuntary body functions such as heartbeat, blood flow, breathing and digestion. When there is any form of stressor or threat, the sympathetic nervous system mobilizes your body for action (fight or flight response) by releasing adrenaline and norepinephrine. After the stressor, crisis, or emotion has subsided, your **Parasympathetic Nervous System** helps to calm you down and decrease arousal. The parasympathetic nervous system is the other branch of the autonomic nervous system and works to conserve energy as it slows the heart rate, increases intestinal and gland activity, and returns the body back to more of a resting state (in charge of resting and digesting). Emotions can activate different areas of the brain, lead to different bodily changes, and also facial expressions. These changes can be noticed by EEG recordings, heart rate monitors, and observation and can have practical applications like detecting lies.

Polygraphs

The **Polygraph** or lie detector test is a machine, commonly used in attempts to detect lies, that measures several of the physiological responses accompanying emotion (such as perspiration, cardiovascular changes, and breathing changes). Rather than detecting lies, a polygraph notices changes in physiological responses. When taking a lie detector test, you are first asked control questions to establish a baseline and maybe provoke slight levels of anxiety which are then compared to answers to later questions. The belief underlying

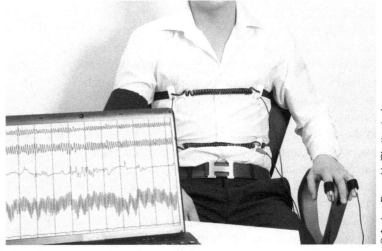

© Andrey Burmakin/Shutterstock.com

the use of the polygraph is that deceptive answers (lies) will produce physiological responses that can be differentiated from those associated with non-deceptive answers (true answers). If you're like most people, lying makes your heart race and makes you breathe differently. It drives up your blood pressure and makes you sweat. A polygraph machine detects lies by looking for signs of these physiological changes; it is basically a combination of medical devices that are used to monitor physiological changes occurring in the body. There are some problems with polygraphs which limit their usage. First, physiological arousal may look the same from one emotion to the next which might make it difficult to determine if someone is actually lying. Second, exam results are open to interpretation by the examiner. While someone might display fluctuations in bodily reactions, it is up to the examiner to interpret the results and determine whether or not it might indicate a lie. In the end, lie detector tests are inaccurate 1/3 of the time. In a way, lie detectors themselves can lie!

Box: Liar, Liar, Pants on Fire –

Have you ever heard the phrase "Liar, liar, pants on fire. Hanging from a telephone wire"? This expression is commonly used with accusations of dishonesty! If you have ever wondered, the origins of this phrase are well-debated but it is often attributed to a poem written by William Blake. The poem is entitled "The Liar"; here is the last stanza:

Deceiver, dissembler
Your trousers are alight
From what pole or gallows
Do they dangle in the night?

Just a fun fact for those of you who might have wondered where this phrase originated!

Communicating Emotion

Nonverbal Communication

Although emotions can often be expressed in words, much of the time we communicate our feelings through **Nonverbal Communication**. When we communicate nonverbally, we relay information through things such as voice quality, facial expression, body language, personal space and explicit acts. Voice quality refers to the way that words are expressed. *"Yeah I totally understand"* can have multiple meanings ranging from sincere understanding to sarcasm depending on the tone in which it is said. Facial expressions can tell you a good deal about a person's emotional state. If you see someone that is laughing, crying, smiling, frowning, etc., that can very easily convey their mood. Body language can also relay emotion. I love to people watch and couples are probably the most fascinating to observe! The body language of partners on a date can speak volumes

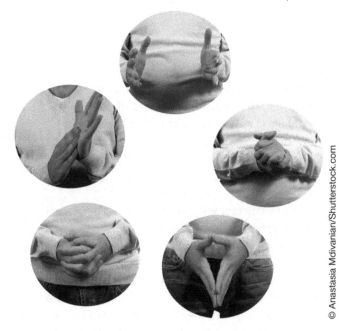

about how interested or disinterested they are in the relationship, their level of comfort, and whether or not the date is going well! Personal space or the distance between ourselves and others and can also mean something. When we are comfortable or know someone well, we tend to stand closer to that person than when it is a stranger. There are also cultural and gender differences with personal space. Women tend to be more comfortable being physically close to each other than men (stereotypically). My favorite observation of this is in a movie theater! Men, especially younger men, tend to put a seat or two between them at movie theaters versus female friends will often sit directly next to each other. Finally, explicit acts can also speak volumes. It is pretty clear what someone is trying to express when they flip you off or slam a door. Without even opening our mouth, we can say quite a bit about our mood and emotional state.

Gestures

Nonverbal communications, specifically gestures, can vary from culture to culture. Here are some common American gestures and their meanings in other cultures:

- *The "thumbs up" sign* - In the United States, the gesture indicates "I'm ok or everything's ok." Yet it is considered rude in Australia, Iran and other Muslim countries translating to "up yours."

- *The "OK" sign* - Often used in America to mean approval, it is considered vulgar and obscene in Brazil, southern Italy, Germany and Greece. In Japan, this gesture signifies money while in southern France it is used to convey that something is worthless.

- *The pointed index finger* - A pointed index finger is used to emphasize a point in our culture. However, it is impolite in the Middle East, Russia and Asia. Rather than pointing with a finger, it is suggested that you point with an open palm instead.

- *Shaking your head from side to side* - In the United States, shaking your head from side to side means "no." In Bulgaria the same gesture means "yes"; moving the head up and down translates to "no"!

- *The beckoning gesture* - This gesture is formed by curling and uncurling the index finger. It is common in most countries and means "come here." However, the gesture is offensive to Mexican, Filipino, and Vietnamese cultures.

- *Sitting with the soles of your shoes showing* - In many cultures this sends a rude message. In Thailand, Japan and France as well as countries of the Middle and Near East showing the soles of the feet demonstrates disrespect. You are exposing the lowest and dirtiest part of your body so this is insulting.

There are countless other gestures that are used by people so be sure to be careful with your nonverbal communication when you travel to other areas of the world!

Basic Emotions

How Many Emotions Do We Have?

There are many different theories when it comes to trying to explain how many emotions we have as people. The debate about the number of basic emotions has been present since the days of Aristotle but the most prominent current theory is that of Psychologist Robert Plutchik who proposed that there are eight basic emotions: *fear, surprise, sadness, disgust, anger, anticipation, joy,* and *acceptance.* Plutchik proposed that while there are eight basic emotions, they can combine and mix to form a wide variety of feelings

such as anticipation and joy together equaling optimism. There are other theories proposing that we have six universal emotions: *happiness, sadness, surprise, fear, anger,* and *disgust* (*contempt* is also sometimes added as a seventh emotion). Other theories assert that we might only have four basic emotions: *happiness, sadness, anger,* and *fear.* Whether it is four, six, seven, eight, or dozens, emotions have received quite a bit of attention over time and the number of them that we possess continues to be debated today. We will look a little more at three common emotions that tend to get a lot of attention: anger, fear, and happiness.

Anger

Anger is a strong feeling of annoyance, displeasure, hostility, or rage and is a completely normal and typically healthy human emotion. Anything can cause us to become angry. We can become angry from both internal and external events, we can be angry at a person, multiple people, at an event or situation, or even from memories and worrying. Anger can be constructive but when it fuels physically or verbally aggressive acts it can become maladaptive leading to violence, prejudice, or intolerance. Western cultures tend to believe in venting your anger presuming that through aggressive action or fantasy we can achieve emotional release or **Catharsis**. While catharsis might make one feel better

it typically does not get rid of one's rage and might breed more anger. The best way to handle anger is to wait and let yourself calm down. If you can wait and let time pass, the body will lower its level of physiological arousal and you will calm down. You should also deal with anger in a balanced way; don't get angry about every little thing but also don't not express anger and internalize it. Overly expressing anger can get you into trouble but so can repressing or internalizing it. People who don't express anger offer suffer from stomach aches, headaches, muscle tension, and even heart problems. Some common techniques for dealing with anger including changing your environment, giving yourself a break from the situation, using humor, physical releases such as exercise, and also finding ways to calm down or relax through counting, imagery, or deep breathing exercises.

Fear

Fear is a feeling caused by a perceived threat or danger and can be a vital response to physical and/or emotional danger. Fear is a chain reaction in the brain that starts with a stressful stimulus causing the release of chemicals which lead to physical changes such as causing your heart to race, breating faster, and other fight or flight reactions controlled by the sympathetic nervous system. There are multiple parts of the brain that are activated when a person is afraid including the thalamus, hypothalamus, hippocampus, and the amygdala. The hypothalamus activates the sympathtic nervous system and the endocrine system resulting in a release of neurotransmitters and hormones like adrenaline (epinephrine) and noradrenaline (norepinephrine) which then cause all the changes in your body mentioned above. The fight or flight response is intended to help you to survive dangrous situations by preparing you to either fight for your life or run for your life.

People can be afraid of anything! We will talk more about excessive and unreasonable fears called phobias in a later chapter but most people do have things that they are afraid of; and sometimes for good reason! Some of the most common fears include spiders, snakes, heights, open or crowded spaces, flying, public speaking, the dark, and countless other things. There are many techniques for conquering and facing your fears that we will get to in just a few chapters.

Happiness

Happiness is a mental and/or emotional state defined by positive or pleasant emotions. People who are happy perceive the world as safer, make decisions more easily, are more cooperative, and live healthier more energized and satisfied lives. It seems that positive emotions fuel upward spirals of positivity. Also, if we feel happy we are more likely to help others which is called the **Feel Good, Do Good Phenomenon**. When we are in a bad mood, we aren't nearly as likely to want to improve or make better someone else's day. But when we are happy, we have a much stronger tendency to be helpful.

There are two phenomena often discussed as we try to determine what makes us happy; the **Adaptation-Level Phenomenon** and **Relative Deprivation**. Adaptation-level phenomenon is our tendency to form judgments relative to a neutral level defined by our prior experience. We have a neutral level of something (neither hot nor cold or neither rich nor poor) that we then notice and react to variations up or down from that level. We use our past to calibrate our present experience and to form expectations for the future; satisfaction and dissatisfaction are relative to our prior experience. If our achievements rise above those expectations, we experience satisfaction. If our achievements fall below a neutral point defined by prior experience, we feel dissatisfied. For example, if you are an "A" student and always receive A's on exams, you will be disssappointed and unhappy if you earned a "B" on a test. On the other side, a "C" student who earns a "B" on a test might be thrilled! Our happiness is directly determined by our past experiences and expectations.

The other factor helping us to determine whether or not we are happy about something is called relative deprivation which is the perception that one is better or worse off relative to those with whom one compares oneself. Not ony do we compare within ourselves but we are constantly comparing ourselves and what we have to other people. Most of us have had that moment where we envy the amount of money another person makes or maybe wish that our relationship was more like another one in our life. A great example from my life of this concept was with my youngest brother. Several Christmases ago, my brother wanted a bike. All year long we heard about how much he wanted this bike and Christmas morning, there it was for him. He was so excited and despite the cold and snowy conditions outside (he lives in Wisconsin), he went out and rode it in the street. He was so happy with his bike until his neighbor came outside with his brand new snow mobile that he had received for Christmas. All of a sudden, the bike lost its appeal and my brother wasn't happy. This is relative deprivation at work. A great quote I once heard that also sums up this idea is "I cried because I had no shoes until I met a man who had no feet". So much of our happiness has to do with our perspective.

Happiness is thought to be slightly influenced by your genes but more influenced by things such as self-esteem, the perspective you have on life, the presence and quality of relationships you maintain, overall health, and many other factors. Many people often wonder how to be happier and there are several common tips that can help to improve your happiness levels. One thing that can be done is to realize that certain things (such as money) don't equal happiness. Too often we focus on the idea that if we only had money or some other item, that we will be happy when studies indicate that after a certain point, money doesn't increase happiness levels. Directly connected to this idea is to find ways to focus on and be grateful for what you have rather than focusing on what you don't have.

Other things that can make you happier are to act happy! This sounds silly, but in general, if you act happy, you are more likely to be happy. This is like the idea of faking it until you make it; act happy and you will be happy. Maintain good health which includes getting adequate sleep and eating a proper diet. Spirituality is also often linked to happiness and many find comfort and happiness in believing in something greater than themselves. Many people also find happiness in not only focusing on themselves but rather in helping and caring for others. Give priority to close relationships like family, friendships, and so on. Finally, do things that you enjoy! Find a small chunk of time every day to do something that is fun or rewarding to you. Go on a walk, play a video game, read a chapter in a book. Whatever it is, find time for the things that you love!

© Jacob Lund/Shutterstock.com

Box: The Power of Laughter –

More than just brightening up your day, having a good laugh can improve your health. The sound of laughter draws people together in ways that trigger healthy physical and emotional changes in the body. Laughter can reduce stress, anxiety, and depression, strengthen your immune system, and diminish pain. As children, we used to laugh hundreds of times a day, but as adults, our lives tend to be more serious and laughter more infrequent. By seeking out more opportunities for humor and laughter, though, you can improve your emotional health, strengthen your relationships, find greater happiness and even add years to your life.

© Sergey Furtaev/Shutterstock.com

- *Laughter relaxes the whole body* - A good, hearty laugh relieves physical tension and stress, leaving your muscles relaxed for up to 45 minutes.

- *Laughter boosts the immune system* – Laughter decreases stress hormones and increases immune cells and infection-fighting antibodies, thus improving your here resistance to disease.

- *Laughter triggers the release of endorphins* - the body's natural feel-good chemicals. Endorphins promote an overall sense of well-being and can temporarily relieve pain.

- *Laughter protects the heart* – Laughter improves the function of blood vessels and increases blood flow, which can help protect you against a heart attack and other cardiovascular problems.

- *Laughter burns calories* - laughing for 10 to 15 minutes a day can burn about 40 calories.

- *Laughter may even help you to live longer* - A study in Norway found that people with a strong sense of humor outlived those who don't laugh as much.

In Popular Culture

- *Inside Out* (2015) – a movie set in the mind of a young girl that follows five personified emotions (joy, sadness, anger, fear, and disgust) as they lead her through life.

- *Happy* (2013) – a popular culture song by Pharrell Williams about the emotion of happiness.

- *Lie to Me* (2009-2011) – a television show with private detectives who assist in investigations and reaching the truth by interpreting micro expressions and body language.

- *The Moment of Truth* (2008-2009) – a television show where contestants answer personal questions for cash prizes and are monitored with a polygraph.

- *Meet the Parents* (2000) – a comedy movie about a man meeting his girlfriends' parents; contains a funny scene depicting an old-school polygraph machine.

- *Liar Liar* (1997) – a comedy movie featuring a main character who struggles with keeping his promises and eventually falls under a curse of not being able to lie.

- *The Invention of Lying* (2009) – a romantic comedy movie set in an alternate reality where there is no such thing as lying (everyone tells the truth).

- *Anger Management* (2003) – a comedy movie featuring various strategies for coping with anger.

- *Fried Green Tomatoes* (1991) – a comedy/drama movie depicting the story of friendship between two women with a great cathartic release scene.

Psyched with Setmire

"Emotion Theories"
https://www.youtube.com/watch?v=xja5fZAQKnU

In this lecture presentation, I will define emotions and then cover the three theories of emotion (along with mentioning a couple additional smaller theories). I will also provide multiple graphics and examples to help illustrate and clarify these sometimes confusing theories! I hope this is helpful!

Application: How to Spot a Lie

some people are better liars than others! I am a horrible liar and tend to giggle and smile when I'm trying to deceive others. There are many signs that you can look for to try and spot a lie. In general, if you know someone well, you probably know whether they are telling you the truth but even with strangers, there are little signs and tells that give people away. Here are a few signs that a person might be lying:

- A person who is lying will often avoid eye contact or look away.

- When a person lies, they often will touch some portion of their face.

- Timing of speed and gestures may be off of normal patterns when someone is lying.

- People who are lying often giggle, laugh, or smile.

- People often get quite defensive when they lie.

- Sometimes people who are lying will quickly change the subject.

- Inconsistencies in stories can indicate a lie.

- Insincere emotions or a sense of unease or anxiety might indicate that someone is lying to you.

- Watch for micro-expressions.

- People often provide too many details when they are lying.

- Speech hesitations are common during lies.

- Fidgeting or other body language could indicate anxiety from lying.

Again, some people are much better at hiding the truth than others. After almost fourteen years of being together, I can't pull off lying to my partner about even the smallest of things. I start to smile before I even start talking and she knows! The better you know someone, the easier it might be to catch them in a lie.

Key Terms

Emotion: a complex state of feeling that results in physical and psychological changes that influence thought and behavior.

James-Lange Theory: a theory of emotion that suggests that emotions occur as a result of physiological reactions to events.

Cannon-Bard Theory: a theory of emotion that states that we feel emotions and experience physiological reactions such as sweating, trembling and muscle tension simultaneously.

Schachter-Singer or Two-Factor Theory: a theory of emotion that suggests that physiological arousal occurs first, and then the individual must identify the reason behind this arousal in order to experience and label it as an emotion.

Cognitive-Mediational Theory: a theory of emotion that proposes that a stimulus leads to an immediate appraisal and that cognitive appraisal results in an emotional response which is then followed by the appropriate bodily response.

Facial Feedback Theory: a theory of emotion proposing that emotion is the experience of changes in our facial muscles.

Sympathetic Nervous System: a division of the autonomic nervous system in charge of mobilizing the body for action via the fight or flight response.

Parasympathetic Nervous System: a division of the autonomic nervous system in charge of calming down the body and decreasing arousal (resting and digesting).

Polygraph: commonly called a lie detector test; a machine, commonly used in attempts to detect lies, that measures several of the physiological responses accompanying emotion.

Nonverbal Communication: relaying information through things such as voice quality, facial expression, body language, personal space and explicit acts.

Catharsis: an emotional release.

Feel Good, Do Good Phenomenon: our tendency to be helpful to others when we are happy ourselves.

Adaptation-Level Phenomenon: our tendency to form judgments relative to a neutral level defined by our prior experience.

Relative Deprivation: the perception that one is worse off relative to those with whom one compares oneself.

Chapter 11

Human Development

Outline

© Tatyana Pogorelova/Shutterstock.com

In Popular Culture

Psyched with Setmire

Application

• Keeping Your Mind Sharp and Improving Mental Fitness

Key Terms

Introduction to the Chapter (Summary)

Developmental Psychology studies physical, cognitive, and social changes throughout the lifespan. If we start at the very beginning, we can examine the development of a new fertilized cell called a zygote and folllow the incredible prenatal developmental journey all the way to the roughly nine month mark when a neonate (newborn baby) comes into the world. Newborns are incredibly fragile and dependent on others for care but do come equipped with reflexes which are natural instincts or abilities that are often critical to life outside of the uterus.

When we are born we have most of the brain cells that we will ever have but our nervous system is immature. In order to help continue our brain and neuron growth, stimulation is crucial during this early period. Motor development is also taking place during the early years of life and refers to the acquisition of skills involving movement such as sitting, crawling, and walking. Another big focus of childhood development is on cognition. Psychologist Jean Piaget proposed that children progress through four stages of cognitive development: 1) Sensorimotor Stage, 2) Preoperational Stage, 3) Concrete-Operational Stage, and 4) Formal-Operational Stage. The transitions between stages are not abrupt but rather tend to take place gradually. Socialization and attachment are also important social milestones during childhood.

Adolescence is a period of life roughly between the ages of 10-20 when a person is transitioning from being a child to an adult. Adolescence begins with puberty which causes a surge of hormones leading to a growth spurt. A teenager's brain is also continuing to develop. Teens can begin to reason abstractly and also begin imagining what other people are thinking about them leading to two common fallacies which are imaginary audience and personal fable. One of the chief tasks of adolescence is identity formation or the development of a stable sense of self necessary to make the transition from dependence on others to dependence on oneself.

Adulthood is much less predictable than childhood and is more a function of decisions, circumstances, and even luck. The main developmental concerns of adulthood are developing intimacy and finding a career or pusuit through which we can contribute to the world around us. Our physical abilities crest in our mid-twenties and then decline slowly at a rate that most people don't notice. For most people, cognitive skills such as vocabulary and verbal memory increase steadily through the 60's while reasoning and spatial orientation generally peak during the 40's and then slowly start to decline. Although some decline is inevitable with age, it can be minimized if people stay mentally active. For some, feelings of boredom and stagnation in adulthood may be part of a midlife crisis or a midlife transition. One common problem in late life is dementia with the most common type being Alzheimer's Disease; a neurological disorder, characterized by progressive loses in memory and cognition and by changes in personality. All of us have to face the very difficult reality that we will die at some point. Elisabeth Kubler-Ross' proposed five stages that people pass through as they react to their own impending death: denial, anger, bargaining, depression, and acceptance.

Developmental Psychology

Developmental Psychology is a branch of psychology that studies physical, cognitive, and social changes throughout the lifespan. Developmental or lifespan psychologists examine the changes that occur in people from birth through old age along with why and how people change. Some developmental psychologists are generalists and focus their energies on studying people across the lifespan while others might choose a specific developmental phase of life, such as childhood or adolescence, and then specialize in that specific area. From here, we will review the major phases of development across the lifespan highlighting the milestones and physical, cognitive, and social changes that come with each stage of life.

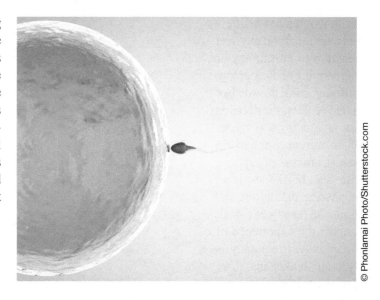

Prenatal Development

Prenatal Development covers the developmental process from conception to birth. The term "Prenatal" is from Latin *pre* meaning "before" and *nasci* meaning "to be born". If we start at the moment of **Conception** a new cell is formed as an egg is fertilized by a sperm cell. A woman's ovaries release a mature egg each month that travels down the fallopian tube toward the uterus. If sperm is introduced into a woman's system either through intercourse or an assisted reproductive method and it makes the long journey to the egg, a single sperm cell can penetrate the outer surface of the egg to create a new cell called a **Zygote**. A zygote is a fertilized egg which has a 2 week period of rapid cell division. The

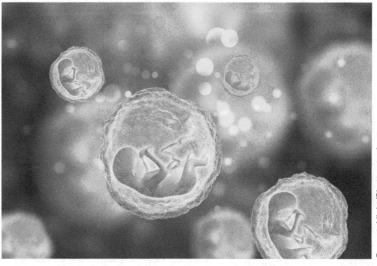

zygote divides and forms a hollow ball called a **Blastocyst** which implants into the uterine wall. Once the blastocyst impants into the uterine wall, hormones are released signaling the woman's body to not shed the endometrium (lining of the uterus) so that the pregnancy will be maintained. The fertilized cell continues to develop rapidly and in a very short timeframe, is no longer just an undifferentiated mass of cells but rather becomes what we call an **Embryo** or a developing human between 2 weeks and 3 months after conception. The cells begin to specialize to form the baby's organs, bones, muscles, the skin, and nervous system. The embryo stage ends three months after conception and the fetal stage begins. After the three month point and up until birth, the developing human is known as a **Fetus** which is Latin for "offspring" or "young one".

While the fetus is growing, an organ called the **Placenta** nourishes the fetus. Within the placenta the mother's blood vessels transmit nutritive substances to the embryo or fetus and carry waste products away from it. The placenta is connected to fetus by the umbilical cord which is cut after birth and the placenta is expelled from the birth canal shortly after a baby is delivered. This is also how toxic agents known as **Teratogens** can cross the placenta and compromise the baby's development. Pregnancy is most likely to have a favorable outcome when the mother gets good nutrition and good medical care and avoids exposing her baby to substances that can be harmful such as alcohol and nicotine.

Each woman has a different emotional and physical reaction to **Pregnancy** or the carrying of one or more offspring inside the womb of a female. How the decision for pregnancy was made, their current relationship status, amount of support, lifestyle, hormones, level of physical discomfort, and financial resources can all impact the experience of pregnancy. Pregnancy is typically broken into three periods, or **Trimesters**, each of about three months. While there are no hard and fast rules, these distinctions are useful in describing the changes that take place over time. Childbirth usually occurs about 38 weeks after conception (The World Health.Organization defines normal term for delivery as between 37 weeks and 42 weeks). As parents prepare for the birth of their little one(s), many people will enroll in some form of prepared childbirth classes which provide information about the process of labor including birthing exercises, breathing, and information about pain control options during labor.

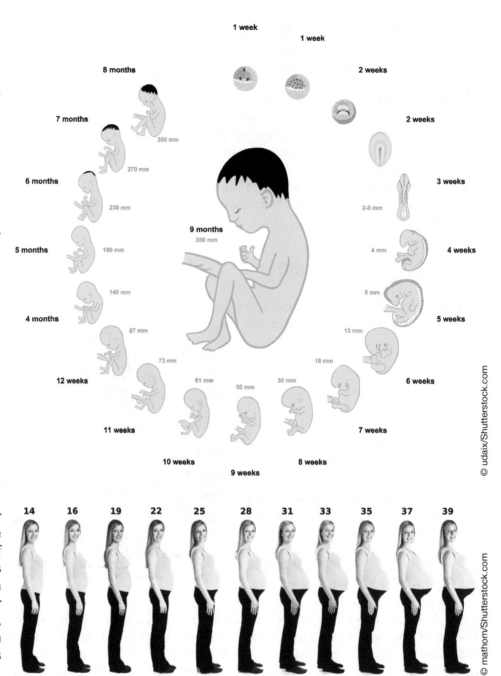

The Competent Newborn

After roughly nine months of pregnancy, a beautiful little neonate (Latin for newborn) comes into the world. Newborn babies are incredibly fragile and dependent on others for care but they do come into the world equipped with **Reflexes**; involuntary or automatic actions that your body does in response to something without you even having to think about it. These reflexes are incredibly basic but they are critical to life outside of the uterus. Here are some of the reflexes that newborns demonstrate:

- *Rooting Reflex* – when a baby's cheek is touched, they will turn their head and mouth in that direction.

- *Sucking Reflex* – a newborn will suck on anything that enters the mouth.

- *Swallowing Reflex* – babies know to and are able to swallow milk and liquids without choking on them.

- *Grasping Reflex* – babies will cling to any object placed in their hand. Even newborns have a very strong grip!

- *Stepping Reflex* – very young babies take what look like walking steps if held upright with their feet barely touching a flat surface.

- *Moro (Startle) Reflex* – in response to an unexpected loud noise or when an infant feels like they are falling, they will throw our their arms and spread their fingers.

These reflexes are again crucial to survival in the early months but tend to fade somewhere between the two month to one year mark as the brain matures.

Childhood

Brain and Neurological Development

In the womb, the body forms nerve cells at an explosive rate. When we are born we have most of the brain cells that we will ever have but our nervous system is im-

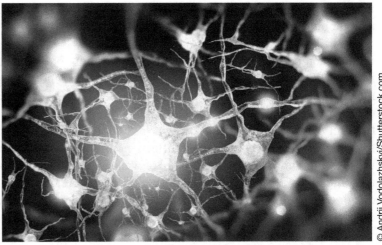

mature. During the first two years of life, dendrites begin to bloom and branch out and there is a rapid growth of myelin sheaths which are the fatty coverings that encases the neurons to provide insulation and increase the speed of conduction. The density of synaptic connections in the brain also increases. All of these patterns of neurological growth can be inhibited by a lack of stimulation during this early period which can negatively impact the growth of the neurons and the number of connections between them. Our brain is going though the process of **Maturation**; a biological growth processes that enables orderly changes in behavior, relatively uninfluenced by experience.

Motor Development

Motor development refers to the acquisition of skills involving movement such as sitting, crawling, and walking. The developing brain helps to enable physical coordination and allows for more complicated skills to develop. When a baby is born, their ability to move around and be mobile is incredibly limited. While they move their arms, legs, and head, if you put a newborn baby down in the middle of a bed, they will be in the exact same spot when you return! Not that I am reccommending leaving your newborn baby unattended! Babies progress through a series of stages of motor development and while the average age for each motor skill might vary, babies typically progress through the same sequence of development. After a couple of months, babies start to be able to support their heads. Newborns are not able to exercise this muscle control meaning that you have to support their heads very carefully when you hold them! As they learn to hold their heads up they start trying to roll over. This typically begins with little mini-pushup like movements and can be furthered and strengthened by having your little one practice tummy time to strengthen their core and neck muscles. Babies will often roll over around the four month mark (on average). Once they can roll over, the next motor task is sitting without support which happens on average around the six

© FamVeld/Shutterstock.com

month mark. After sitting, babies start working on crawling and becoming mobile! The average age for crawling is somewhere around seven to eight months old.

Infants then begin to start standing up while holding onto something. Infants will pull themselves to a stand somewhere around the eight to nine month mark on average. Once they can stand, they begin cruising or walking around objects that they are holding onto. Eventually, as they get the confidence and body control, children will take their first steps anywhere between the ten to fifteen month mark and by fourteen to fifteen months, on average, there are walking on their own. Again, these numbers are all averages. Every child is different! I have three daughters and they all crawled and walked at different times. My oldest took her first steps at eleven months (it was on the 4th of July), my middle daughter walked at ten months, and my youngest didn't take her first steps until close to thirteen months. While parents can become concerned when children don't meet these milestones as quick as their peers, most of the time there isn't a need for concern as every child tends to develop and progress at their own speed and in their own timeframe!

© Paul Hakimata Photography/Shutterstock.com

Cognitive Development

We talked previously about cognition which is all of the mental activities associated with thinking, knowing, remembering, and communicating. Swiss Psychologist Jean Piaget observed children playing and performing everyday tasks and concluded that children are intrinsically motivated to explore and understand things and that their mind is not a miniature model of an adult's mind but rather that they reason differently. Piaget believed that children progressed through four stages of cognitive development. The first stage is the **Sensorimotor Stage** from birth to 2 years of age. In this stage of cognitive development, children acquire the ability to form mental representations and are focused on taking in the world through their sensory and motor interactions with objects (looking, hearing, touching, mouthing, and grasping). Most babies live in the present and what is out of sight is also out of mind resulting in a lack of **Object Permanence** which is the concept that things continue to exist even when they are out of sight. For newborns, when objects go out of sight, they cease to exist. By about seven months children have gained enough experience with the world to develop object permanence but prior to that, you can use this to your advantage with peek-a-boo! If you are watching a young child, peek-a-boo is a great game of choice! When you put your hands over your eyes and face, you literally disappear from the world to a young child. And then when you move your hands and magically reappear, they are often surprised and will laugh or squeal! I have spent many hours entertaining my little ones with this simple game due to their lack of object permanence!

The **Preoperational Stage** from 2 to 7 years old is the second stage of cognitive development in which the individual becomes able to use mental representations and language to describe, remember, and reason about the world. Kids learn quite a bit in this stage through pretend play but they struggle with logic and taking the view of other people. In this way, children in this stage are very **Egocentric** meaning they are unable to see things from another's point of view. Children here are also mislead by appearances as they don't yet have conservation which they gain in the next stage. The third stage is the **Concrete-Operational** stage from 7 to 11 years of age. In the third stage of cognitive development, the individual can attend to more than one thing at a time and understand someone else's point of view. A person's thinking in this stage is limited to concrete matters; they can think logically but their thinking is very rigid. Children in this stage learn principles of **Conservation** which is the concept that the quantity of a substance is not altered by reversible changes in it's appearance. Children who have conservation understand that if you take a cup of liquid and pour it into another cup, that you haven't changed the amount of liquid, just the cup it is in. Finally, the **Formal-Operational Stage** lasting from adolescence through adulthood is the stage of cognitive development in which the individual becomes capable of abstract thought. They can formulate hypothesis and accept or reject them on the outcome of experiments. In this stage, people can understand cause and effect and develop general rules and theories along with thinking more scientifically in general about the world around them.

According to Piaget, the transitions between stages are not abrupt but rather tend to take place gradually. Piaget also believed that children don't just acquire more knowledge as they age but that they actually have a fundamental change in how they think about the world as they age. Overall, this is a useful schematic road of cognitive development despite some criticisms (Piaget underplayed the role of social interaction). In general his ideas have been supported through research and have provided valuable insights to the field and those who work with children such as parents and teachers.

Social Development

Children must learn to interact with others along with learning **Socialization** which is the process by which children learn the behaviors and attitudes appropriate to their family and culture. Early in life the most important interactions are with parents and caregivers but the social world expands when children start school. Children begin to learn what behaviors are acceptable and not from their family and then from their peers. An embarassing example of this happened in my family growing up with my younger brother. My brother used to pick his nose and smear it on the wall when he was little! Super gross! My parents would put him in timeout, take things away from him, and generally try to punish him but to no avail. He picked his nose and smeared it on the wall just once at school and all his peers made fun of him. He never did it again! Our peers can be very power influences in our lives.

Attachment, the emotional bond that develops in the first year of life that makes human babies cling to their caregivers, is another social task that we accomplish during childhood. Our attachment with our caregivers is built on many hours of interaction in which baby and parent come to form a close relationship. When an infant begins to crawl and walk they begin to use attachment figures (familiar people) as a secure base to explore from and return to. Parental responses lead to the development of patterns of attachment; these, in turn, lead to internal working models which will guide the individual's perceptions, emotions, thoughts and expectations in later relationships. There have been many famous psychological studies related to attachment such as the 1950's Harry Harlow experiment with monkeys and later research by developmental psychologist Mary Ainsworth in the 1960s and 70s. Ainsworth's strange situation research lead to the development of a number of attachment patterns in infants such as secure, anxious, avoidant, and disorganized styles.

Gender-Role Development

Another important process in childhood is the development of a **Gender Identity**. By about age 3, children have developed a perception of having a certain gender; a little girl's knowledge that she is a girl and a little boy's knowledge that he is a boy. Very rarely at this young of an age do children experience an incongruence with gender and feel that their gender does not match their physical sex. However, while children may have a perception of gender, they often have no idea what it actually means on a deeper level. Children also begin to acquire gender-role awareness which is the knowledge of what behavior is appropriate for each gender; what is expected of males and females in our society. Gender-role awareness leads to the development of gender stereotypes which are general beliefs about characteristics that men and women are presumed to have. In addition to parents and peers, the media and television have a significant influence on children's development by presenting both good and bad models for them to copy.

Adolescence

Adolescence is a period of life roughly between the ages of 10-20 when a person is transitioning from being a child to an adult starting with the physical beginnings of sexual maturity and ending with the social achievement of independent adult status. Psychologist G. Stanley Hall was one of the first psychologists to describe adolescence which he called the period of "storm and stress" after the many trials and tribulations faced by teens.

Physical Development

Adolescence begins with **Puberty**; the onset of sexual maturation. Puberty involves an incredible amount of physical and sexual development with boys experiencing growth of the testes occurring and girls experiencing the first menstrual cycle. During puberty there is a surge of hormones causing a **Growth Spurt** or a rapid increase in height and weight commonly ocurring around 10 ½ to 11 in girls and 12 ½ to 13 in boys. The pituitary gland releases hormones like testosterone and estrogen which lead to numerous physical and sexual changes in the body. During the growth spurt, the **Primary Sex Characteristics** (reproductive organs and external genitalia) develop dramatically along with the **Secondary Sex Characteristics** (non-reproductive traits such as female breast and hips, male voice quality and body hair). Landmarks for puberty include the first ejaculation for males (usually by age 14) and the first menstrual period (menarche) in females usually by 12).

Cognitive Development

Teenager's brains are also continuing to develop; especially in the frontal lobe which will bring improved judgment, impulse control, and planning ability. Teenagers can begin to reason abstractly (Piaget's formal-operational stage) and as they begin to think more about other people's thinking, they also begin imagining what other people are thinking about them. As a result, two common fallacies that characterize adolescent thinking can occur; **Imaginary Audience** and **Personal Fable**. Imaginary Audience is the delusion that an adolescent is constantly being observed by others. Here the person feels like others are constantly judging their appearance and behavior. This causes a person to feel as if they are perpetually on-stage or in the spotlight. People fighting this feel like you are being scrutinized; that every facial blemish or misstep will be noticed. That bad hair day you are having is what everyone is talking about and focusing on. The ironic thing about this is that because most teenagers are so worried about being in the spotlight and what everyone else it thinking about them, quite a bit of the things we worry about go unnoticed!

Personal Fable on the other hand is an adolescents' delusion that they are unique, very important, and invulnerable. As teenagers, we insist that others couldn't possibly understand our feelings because we are so unique and special. "You just don't know how it feels" or "nobody could ever experience the heartache I'm going through" are common phrases uttered by teenagers. I remember yelling something very similar to that at my parents when I was in high school; some assertion that they would never know what it was like to be me. In reality, our parents were teenagers once too and probably have a decent idea about what we are going through (as much as we would never want to admit).

Identity Formation and Social Development

Adolescents are eager to establish independence from their parents but simultaneously fear the responsibilities of adulthood which can make this is a stormy time of great instability and strong emotions. One of the chief tasks of adolescence is **Identity Formation** or the development of a stable sense of self necessary to make the transition from dependence on others to dependence on oneself. Part of this includes a period of intense exploration where teens explore a variety of role options. Most teenagers try on several "hats" as they try to figure out where they belong, what

their interests are, and who they want to be. I went through several phases in high school, like most teenagers. In my freshman year, I was incredibly into school. I was in all honors classes, on the academic team, played soccer, basketball, and cross-country running, and was an incredibly strong student. My sophomore and junior years, I struggled in all my classes, hung out with people who played Dungeons and Dragons and Magic cards at lunch, and went through a long phase of dying my hair, painting my nails, and wearing very gothic clothes to school. My poor parents! In my senior year, I found a little bit of balance between all my high school roles. I improved my grades to somewhere between the freshman 4.9 GPA and the failing grades of my sophomore year. I said goodbye to some of the stranger friends I made and spent a lot of time in band. Many of us go through similar journeys of trying to figure out who we are and where we belong.

As people near the end of the teenage years and enter into young adulthood, a period of time from around eighteen to the mid-twenties where a person is no longer an adolescent but hasn't yet taken on the responsibilities of adulthood. The main developmental concern according to Erikson in this stage is developing **Intimacy** whih is the ability to form close, loving relationships. Other milestones in this period of life commonly include entering the workforce, going off to college, or leaving home.

Adulthood

Adulthood development is much less predictable and is more a function of decisions, circumstances, and even luck.

Adulthood's Commitments

The stage of adulthood typically begins around the age of twenty as people shift their focus from forming an identity to friendships, romance, having children, and careers. Nearly all adults form a long-term, loving partnership with another adult in their lives. Ninety percent of Americans eventually get married and while heterosexual marriage is still the norm, other types of partnerships also exist. For many parents, loving and being loved by their children is an unparalleled source of fulfillment despite the fact that the birth of the first child tends to be a major turning point

in a couple's relationship and tends to require many adjustments. Work is also a large part of the identity of many adults. Happiness is most likely if you have a job that fits your interests and provides you with a sense of competence and accomplishment.

Physical Changes

Our physical abilities crest in our mid-twenties and then decline slowly at a rate that most people don't notice. At middle age, the level of physical ability is often more a result of health and exercise habits than age. For women, the foremost biological sign of aging is **Menopause** or a time of natural cessation of menstruation. Menopause can also refer to the biological changes a woman experiences as her ability to reproduce declines. Menopause typically happens around the age of 45 to 50 and while the sterotype is raging hormones and hot flashes, many women experince few to no noticeable symptoms.

While there is no comparable thing in men, men do experience more of a gradual decline in hormone levels that is sometimes called **Andropause**.

Cognitive Changes

For most people, cognitive skills such as vocabulary and verbal memory increase steadily through the 60's while reasoning and spatial orientation generally peak during the 40's and then slowly start to decline. Although some decline is inevitable with age, it can be minimized if people stay mentally active. There is a difference between

Crystallized Intelligence and **Fluid Intelligence**. Crystallized intelliigence is one's accumulated knowledge and verbal skills. This type of intelligence tends to increase with age and we sometimes refer to it as wisdom. Fluid Intelligence is one's ability to reason speedily and abstractly which tends to decrease during late adulthood. So while we do experience a slowing in our reactions and processing, our accumulated wisdom increases from life experiences.

Midlife

Psychological health tends to improve with adulthood as we learn better coping skills and there is often a strengthening of identity, confidence, and self-esteem that comes with age. For some, feelings of boredom and stagnation in adulthood may be part of **Midlife Crisis**. A midlife crisis is a time when adults discover they no longer feel fulfilled in their jobs or personal lives and attempt to make a decisive shift in career or lifestyle. This is not typical; most people do not make sudden and dramatic changes in their lives in mid-adulthood (only about 10%). Much more common is a **Midlife Transition** or a process whereby adults assess the past and formulate new goals for the future. When confronted with the first signs of aging, many will begin to think about the finite nature of life and may gradually reset their life priorities or establish new goals based on their insights.

Late Adulthood

Older adults constitute the fastest growing segment of the Uinted States population due primarily to the aging of the large baby-boom generation and advances in health care and nutrition. As a society, we have quite negative societal views of older adults often thinking they are lonely, poor, ill, or senile when in reality, the majority of people over 65 are healthy, productive, and able.

Physical Changes

There are physical changes that occur as we age. The hair thins and turns white or gray, the skin wrinkles, bones become more fragile, circulation slows, body shape and posture change, and reaction times are slower along with vision, hearing, and smell becoming less acute.

The body's immune system weakens but those that are older tend to experience fewer colds and viruses due to years of accumulating antibodies. These physical changes occur gradually and we hypothesize why they occur with several theories. Our bodies are genetically directed to age and deteriorate. Telemeres, which are special protective structures located on the chromosomal tips, become shorter with each replication until they are no longer capable of replicating. Aging is also thought to be related to free radicals. Unstable oxygen molecules ricochet within cells and damage the cellular components over time causing them to age. Many factors effect adults' physical well-being. A few we can control are diet, exercise, health care, smoking, drug-use, and over-exposure to sun. Attitudes also matter "You're only as old as you feel".

Social Development and Cognitive Changes

Most people over 65 are satisfied with their autonomous lifestyles. A large portion of the later years of life is spent in retirement for many people. Reactions to ceasing paid employment vary largely because our society has no clear idea of what retired people should do. Most see it as a time to slow down or to explore new possibilities but it can often depend on a person's financial status.

Cognitively, healthy people who remain intellectually active tend to maintain a high level of mental functioning in old age. In fact, a sizable number of adults lose only a small amount of cognitive ability. Some people do however face problems such as **Alzheimer's Disease,** a neurological disorder, most commonly found in late adulthood, characterized by progressive loses in memory and cognition and by changes in personality. Alzheimer's occurs in about 10% of adults over 65 and causal factors include genetic predisposition, family history of dementia, being born to a woman over 40, suffering head trauma, and a lack of physical and intellectual activity. Alzheimer's usually begins with minor memory loss and then progresses to personality changes like being withdrawn, flat, and even suffering delusions. Eventually the person loses the ability to speak and care for themselves. Alzheimer's is fatal and while we have some treatments to slow the progression, there is no known cure.

Facing the End of Life

All of us have to face the very difficult reality that we will die at some point. Fear of death is more common in young adulthood or middle age than in late adulthood when we are more concerned with pain, indignity, terminal illness, or dying alone. Elisabeth Kubler-Ross proposed five stages that people pass

through as they react to their own impending death: denial, anger, bargaining, depression, and acceptance. Most of us tend to live in a state of denial when it comes to the idea of death; especially when we are young. Denial is the refusal to believe that we will die one day or even refusing to think about it. When confronted with the idea or reality that we are going to die, after denial, people will often become angry and express hostility or envy at those who are healthy or will live a fuller life. Bargaining is when a person desperately tries to buy more time by negotiating with doctors or a higher power. Many will hit a point of depression when bargaining has failed and time is running out. The final stage is acceptance and while not everyone reaches this state, those who do submit themselves to fate and enter into a state of quiet expectation. Again, not everyone will progress through all of these stages and we might even revery back to an earlier phase of coping but they do tend to be relatively universal and highly accepted.

In Popular Culture

- *Baby Mama* (2008) – a movie that follows the experience of pregnancy, highlights the topic of infertility treatments, and has a few funny scenes involving prepared childbirth classes.

- *Knocked Up* (2007) – a movie about getting pregnant unexpectedly and the experience of pregnancy and childbirth.

- *Juno* (2007) – a movie about the experience of teenage pregnancy and prenatal development.

- *What to Expect When Expecting* (2012) – a movie that follows several couples through their journeys to get pregnant, pregnancy, adoption, and also childbirth.

- *Life's Greatest Miracle* (2001) – a wonderful documentary about prenatal development.

- *Breakfast Club* (1985) – a movie about five high school students meet in Saturday detention and discover how they have a lot more in common than they thought.

- *Mean Girls* (2004) – a movie about high school cliques and the pressures of fitting in.

- *Napoleon Dynamite* (2004) – a movie about a socially awkward 16-year-old by in high school.

- *Juno* (2007) – a movie about a teenage girl facing an unplanned pregnancy.

- *Easy A* (2010) – a movie involving a clean-cut high school student relying on the school's rumor mill to advance her social and financial standing.

- *17 Again* (2009) – a movie about a 37-year-old man who becomes a 17-year-old-boy after an accident.

- *Clueless* (1995) – a coming of age movie about a high school student.

- *American Pie* (1999) – a movie about four teenage boys that make a pact to lose their virginity by prom night.

- *The Bucket List* (2007) – a movie about two men coping with terminal diagnoses by completing items on a bucket list; great example of the progression through these five stages of coping.

- *Fifteen* (2008) – a popular culture song by Taylor Swift about the pressures of being a fifteen-year-old girl.

- *Letter to Me* (2007) – a popular culture song by Brad Paisley about being a teenage boy.

- *Live Like You Were Dying* (2004) – a popular culture song by Tim McGraw" which highlights how someone might react to their impending death.

- *If Today Was Your Last Day* (2011) – a popular culture song by Nickelback which is about living each day like it was your last.

Psyched with Setmire

"Human Development: 100 Years"
https://www.youtube.com/
watch?v=h6eM_9eNgXw

In this video introduction to the topic
of human development, I will introduce
some of the key developmental tasks for
each age range across the lifespan set to
the song "100 Years" by Five for Fighting.
The main focus will be on Erik Erikson's
eight stage theory of development but other
developmental milestones related to the
lyrics of the song will also be mentioned.

© Jne Valokuvaus/Shutterstock.com

Application

Keeping Your Mind Sharp: Improving Mental Fitness

Growing older does not necessarily mean that your mental abilities will drastically decline. Just as muscles get
flabby from sitting around and doing nothing, so does the brain. There's a lot you can do to keep your mind
sharp and alert. Below are some websites that provide tips and advice on keeping your mind and body sharp
along with brain teasers, puzzles, and games:

- *Alzheimer's Association* (www.alz.org) – website providing tips to staying mentally active.

- *Web MD* (www.webmd.com/healthy-aging/) – website provides information about aging and advice on
  ways to stay healthy both physically and mentally as you age.

- *Luminosity* (www.luminosity.com) – provides exercises and games to improve your mental fitness.

- *Mind Games* (www.mindgames.com) – provides links to countless mind games and puzzles to increase
  mental fitness. My favorite is the rapid math!

- *Sharp Brain* (www.sharpbrain.com) – provides quizzes and interactive games for improving mental
  abilities.

Key Terms

Developmental Psychology: a branch of psychology that studies physical, cognitive, and social change
throughout the lifespan.

Prenatal Development: development from conception to birth; from Latin *pre* "before" and *nasci* "to be born".

Conception: in pregnancy, the fertilization of an egg with a sperm.

Zygote: a cell formed as a result of egg and sperm joining; a fertilized egg which has a 2 week period of rapid
cell division.

Blastocyst: A cell that has developed for five to seven days after fertilization and has 2 distinct cell types and a central cavity filled with fluid; implants in the uterine wall.

Embryo: a developing human between 2 weeks and 3 months after conception; starts at implantation.

Fetus: the developing human organism from around 10 weeks after conception (3 months) to birth; Latin for "offspring" or "young one".

Placenta: an organ that connects the developing fetus to the uterine wall to allow nutrient uptake, provide waste elimination, and gas exchange via the mother's blood supply, and produce hormones to support pregnancy.

Teratogens: Any agent that can disturb the development of an embryo or fetus.

Pregnancy: the carrying of one or more offspring inside the womb of a female.

Trimesters: a period of three months, especially as a division of the duration of pregnancy.

Reflexes: involuntary or automatic actions that your body does in response to something without you even having to think about it.

Maturation: biological growth processes that enable orderly changes in behavior, relatively uninfluenced by experience.

Sensorimotor Stage: from birth to 2 years of age; the stage of cognitive development in which the individual develops object permanence and acquires the ability to form mental representations.

Object Permanence: the concept that things continue to exist even when they are out of sight.

Preoperational Stage: from 2 to 7 years of age; the stage of cognitive development in which the individual becomes able to use mental representations and language to describe, remember, and reason about the world, though only in an egotistical fashion.

Egocentric: the inability of a child see things from another's point of view.

Concrete-Operational Stage: from 7 to 11 years of age; the stage of cognitive development in which the individual can attend to more than one thing at a time and understand someone else's point of view, though thinking is limited to concrete matters.

Conservation: the concept that the quantity of a substance is not altered by reversible changes in it's appearance.

Formal-Operational Stage: from adolescence through adulthood; the stage of cognitive development in which the individual becomes capable of abstract thought.

Socialization: the process by which children learn the behaviors and attitudes appropriate to their family and culture.

Attachment: the emotional bond that develops in the first year of life that makes human babies cling to their caregivers.

Gender Identity: a person's perception of having a certain gender.

Adolescence: a period of life roughly between the ages of 10-20 when a person is transitioning from a child to an adult starting with the physical beginnings of sexual maturity and ending with the social achievement of independent adult status.

Puberty: the onset of sexual maturation.

Growth Spurt: a rapid increase in height and weight that occurs during adolescence.

Primary sex characteristics: the reproductive organs and external genitalia.

Secondary sex characteristics: the non-reproductive traits such as female breast and hips, male voice quality and body hair.

Imaginary Audience: the delusion that an adolescent is constantly being observed by others.

Personal Fable: adolescents' delusion that they are unique, very important, and invulnerable.

Identity Formation: the development of a stable sense of self necessary to make the transition from dependence on others to dependence on oneself.

Intimacy: the ability to form close, loving relationships.

Menopause: the time of natural cessation of menstruation; also refers to the biological changes a woman experiences as her ability to reproduce declines.

Andropause: aging-related hormone changes in men.

Crystallized Intelligence: one's accumulated knowledge and verbal skills; tends to increase with age.

Fluid Intelligence: one's ability to reason speedily and abstractly; tends to decrease with age.

Midlife Crisis: a time when adults discover they no longer feel fulfilled in their jobs or personal lives and attempt to make a decisive shift in career or lifestyle.

Midlife Transition: a process whereby adults assess the past and formulate new goals for the future.

Alzheimer's Disease: a neurological disorder, most commonly found in late adulthood, characterized by progressive loses in memory and cognition and by changes in personality.

Chapter 12
Personality

Outline

Introduction to the Chapter (Summary)

Personality is an individual's unique pattern of thoughts, feelings, and behaviors, that persists over time and across situations. There are several theories of personality (both classic and contemporary) which we will cover in this chapter.

One classic theory of personality is the Psychodynamic Theory which contends that behavior results from psychological forces that interact within an individual outside conscious awareness. Sigmund Freud was the best known and most influential of the psychodynamic theorists. Freud believed that human behavior is based on unconscious instincts or drives. According to Freud the personality is formed around three structures: the id, ego, and the superego. Freud's theory also focuses on the way in which we satisfy the sexual instinct (libido) during various courses of life. Freud believed that as infants mature, their libido becomes focused on various sensitive parts of the body during sequential stages of development and children's experiences at each of these stages results in tendencies that persist into adulthood. The five different stages of psychosexual development are the oral, anal, phallic, latency, and genital stages.

Following psychoanalytic theorists were the Neo-Analysts like psychologist Carl Jung who was a student of Freud's and agreed with many of Freud's tenets (especially the role of the unconscious) but believed that the libido represented all life forces not just sexual ones. Jung divided the unconscious in two parts the personal unconscious and the collective unconscious. Another psychoanalytic theorist is Erik Erikson who proposed eight stages that we progress through as we age and our personality develops.

Biological theories assert that our personality is the result of genetics and that much of who we are is present at birth. Behavioral theories take the opposite stance and propose that we are born a blank slate and that the environment dictates our personality. Cognitive personality theories examine our expectations and ideas about the world and believe that the essence of personality is found in the way that we think. One of the more contemporary theories of personality is the trait perspective which tries to describe personality using adjectives or traits. Within this perspective, the Big Five is the most dominant theory and proposes that personality can be boiled down to five different dimensions: conscientiousness, agreeableness, neuroticism, openness to experience, and extraversion. Humanistic and existentialist personality theories are another branch of classic theories and assert the fundamental goodness of people and their striving toward higher levels of functioning. Finally, person-situation theories of personality discuss the impact of situational forces on our behavior along with taking a life-long approach to studying personality.

Personality psychologists are interested in the typical behaviors of a person and how they behave in ordinary situations. This testing focus is known as personality assessment. Just as psychologists disagree on their views of personality, they also disagree on the best way to measure it. This disagreement results in numerous methods of assessing personality including objective and subjective tests.

Personality

Personality is an individual's unique pattern of thoughts, feelings, and behaviors that persists over time and across situations. There are two parts to this definition, our unique differences (what sets us apart from others) and the fact that personality is relatively

stable and permanent (certain characteristics will most likely be evident over time). Our personality captures everything that makes us who we are and sets us apart from every other person in this world. It is all our preferences, experiences, biology, and all the situations that we find ourselves in and how we react to them. There are many different personality theories and each one takes a different approach in explaining the factors that contribute to our personality. There isn't one best theory and none of the theories explain everything on their own but together, they capture the richness and complexity of personality. From here, we will look at the main theories and perspectives highlighting the key ideas within each theory.

Psychodynamic Theories

The first theory of personality we will discuss is the oldest and original theory of personality; **Psychodynamic or Psychoanalytic Theory**. According to psychodynamic theories, people are unconsciously motivated beings seeking to fulfill (and balance) sexual and aggressive urges. This approach was founded by psychologist Sigmund Freud who is probably the best known and most influential of the psychodynamic theorists and maybe even of the psychologists in general. Freud created an entirely new perspective on the study of human behavior in his theories. Before Freud, psychology focused on consciousness; what we are currently aware of in our mind. Freud's focus was on the **Unconscious** which he defined as all the ideas, thoughts, and feelings of which we are not and normally cannot become aware. Freud believed that human behavior is based on unconscious instincts or drives with some being aggressive and destructive while others are necessary for the survival of the individual and the species. Freud held that these instincts, Eros and Thanatos, were a critical factor in the development of personality. Freud believed that the unconscious mind would reveal itself in daydreams, dreams, and also through Freudian slips; in fact, he called dreams the royal road to the unconscious.

© Janusz Pienkowski/Shutterstock.com

Three Structures of the Personality

Sigmund Freud proposed that our personality is formed around three structures, the **Id**, **Ego**, and **Superego**. The id (Latin for "it") is the collection of unconscious urges and desires that continually seek expression and is the only structure present at birth. The id is completely unconscious and operates on the pleasure principle; it wants what it wants and wants it right now; to hell with the consequences. We rarely give into our id! Our ego (Latin for "I") and meaning above or over the self, is the part of the personality that mediates between environmental demands, our conscience, and instinctual needs. Our ego operates on the reality principle as it tries to delay the satisfaction of the id's desires until it can do so safely and successfully. You can think of the ego as the great compromiser between the primal demands of the id and the restrictive standards of the superego. The superego is the social and parental standards an individual has internalized. It is our conscience and the ego ideal; all of the things we "should" do in life. Moral standards develop through interaction with parents and society rather than being present at birth and continue to develop as we mature. Ideally these three

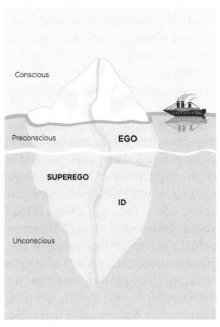

© Crystal Eye Studio/Shutterstock.com

"structures" work in harmony with the ego satisfying the demands of the id in a reasonable, moral manner that is approved by the superego. If the structures are out of balance, a person might struggle. If the id is dominant, then a person will act without thinking and solely on instinct. If the superego is dominant, then our ability to act or enjoy ourselves might be impaired.

Box: Freudian Slips

Freudian Slips are a psychological error in speaking or writing that reveals something about a person's unconscious. These slips of the tongue reveal a deeper motivation and/ or unconscious thoughts or wishes as Freud did not believe these occurrences were accidents. Freud believed that slips could be little windows into the unconscious mind and would look for meaning in even the most minor thoughts and behaviors. For example, if you couldn't find your keys, Freud would say that you didn't really want to go wherever you were headed. Or if you say the wrong name when talking to someone, they clearly were on your mind more than your current company. So, while a slip up could simply be just that, a mistake in the words we say, Freud thought they were quite a bit more meaningful than that!

© Minerva Studio/Shutterstock.com

Psychosexual Stages of Development

Another key concept in Freud's theory of personality is the psychosexual stages of development that he proposed. This part of Freud's theory focuses on the ways in which we satisfy our sexual instinct or **Libido** during various times in our life. Freud believed that as infants mature, their libido becomes focused on various sensitive parts of the body during sequential stages of development and that children's experiences in these stages results in personality tendencies that persist into adulthood. Freud believed that if a child is deprived of the required pleasure or allowed too much gratification then instead of moving on in a normal sequence, some of the sexual energy may become tied to that part of the body instead of allowing the child to move forward and develop an integrated personality. Freud called this issue **Fixation**; a partial or complete halt at some point in the individual's psychosexual development.

The first of Freud's five psychosexual stages is the **Oral Stage** which lasts from birth to 18 months. In the oral stage, an infant's erotic feelings center on the mouth, lips, and tongue. Infants relieve their sexual tension through sucking, swallowing, chewing, and biting. Freud believed that too much gratification in the oral stage could lead to a dependent adult while too little gratification could create a pessimistic or hostile adult. The second stage is the **Anal Stage** which is from roughly 18 months to about 3 ½ years of age. In this second stage, a child's erotic feelings center on the anus and on elimination. Freud believed that children derive pleasure from holding in and excreting feces and right about this time, toilet training is taking place forcing them to regulate this new pleasure. If parents are too strict in toilet training, then that child might grow up to be anal

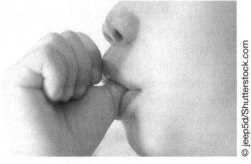

© jeep5d/Shutterstock.com

retentive or excessively orderly as an adult. If parents are too lenient in their potty training efforts, that child may grow up to be messy, disorganized, and sloppy.

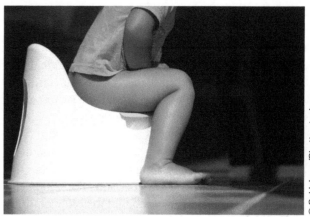

The third psychosexual stage is the **Phallic Stage** which lasts from age 3 to about 5 or 6 years of age. In this stage, erotic feelings center on the genitals. Freud believed that children here develop a marked attachment to the parent of the opposite sex while becoming jealous of the same-sex parent. In boys, Freud named this the **Oedipal Complex** after the Greek legend of Oedipus the King of Thebes who unknowingly kills his father and marries his mother. In girls, Freud named this the **Electra Complex**. Most children resolve this conflict through identifying with the same-sex parent though fixation can lead to vanity and egotism in men and flirtatiousness and promiscuity in women. Following the phallic stage is the **Latency Stage** which starts around age 5/6 and lasts until about 12 or 13 years old. The latency stage is a period in which the child appears to have no interest in the other sex. In this stage, sexual energies are channeled into activities such as going to school and making friends. Finally, the **Genital Stage** starts at puberty and is the final stage of normal adult sexual development which is usually marked by mature sexuality. Sexual impulses reawaken in the genital stage and ideally the quest for immediate gratification of these desires yields to sexual maturity.

These stages and Freud's theories in general are very controversial. Before Freud there were no theories of personality; he truly was a pioneer in the field. His ideas on the unconscious mind, the impact of childhood, and on sexual and aggressive urges where revolutionary but not without their critics. Freud's theories were very sexist in nature along with being very heterosexist in only discussing male/female relationships. His emphasis on sexuality was also not universally accepted and in general, his theories and tenants are hard to scientifically validate. Despite these limitations and issues, he was the first of his field and everyone who came after him built on his ideas.

Neo-Analytic Theories of Personality

After Freud came the **Neo-Analytic Theories** which viewed people as unconscious (and conscious) actors and goal-oriented strivers. Neo-Analytic means "new analysis" and was a different take on Freud's theories emphasizing the individual's sense of self as the core of personality. The most prominent individual in the Neo-Analytic approach was a psychologist named Carl Jung.

Carl Jung

Carl Jung was a colleague and close friend of Sigmund Freud. He agreed with many of Freud's tenets such as the prominent role of the unconscious but he also believed that the libido represented all life forces not just sexual ones. Jung believed that the unconscious was divided into two parts, the **Personal Unconscious** and the

Collective Unconscious. The personal unconscious, according to Jung, contains the individual's repressed thoughts, forgotten experiences, and undeveloped ideas. Jung believed that this included thoughts and feelings that weren't currently part of conscious awareness but could enter consciousness if an incident or sensation triggers their recall. He also discussed what he called the collective unconscious which is the level of the unconscious that is inherited and common to all members of a species. Jung thought that just as the body is the product of evolution, so is the mind. The collective unconscious was thought to hold memories and behavior patterns inherited from past generations; collective experiences of memories that people have had in common since prehistoric times. Within the collective unconscious, he proposed that we have numerous **Archetypes** or emotional symbols that are common to all people and have been formed since the beginning of time that therefore cause us to react in predictable ways to common reoccurring stimuli. Some of the most famous of these archetypes include the persona, the shadow, wise old man, the hero, and the mother.

Modern scientific psychology is skeptical at best on the idea of a collective unconscious and shared memories from ancestors. There is some validity to the idea that over time, people tend to struggle with the same issues repeatedly, and in this sense, we do seem to share certain interests, passions, conflicts, and feelings in a way that borders on instinctual. Jung stressed people's rational and spiritual qualities rather than the primacy of sexual instincts. His theories are often rejected due to his reputation of being more of a philosopher than a scientist and due to the mysticism and symbolism involved in his theories. Despite these shortcomings, he was the first person to challenge Freud and break new conceptual ground.

Erik Erikson

Another prominent Neo-Analytic psychologist is a man named Erik Erikson. Erikson believed in Freud's thinking on sexual development and the influence of libidinal needs on development but he also stressed the quality of parent-child relationships and identity in the formation of personality. Erikson believed that identity formation was a lifelong process rather than stopping after childhood as Freud believed. Erikson saw personality development occurring through eight stages of development. He believed that the outcome of each stage is dependent on the outcome of the previous

stage and that successful negotiation of each of the **Ego Crises** (conflicts of choice that must be resolved in sequence), was important for optimal psychological development.

In his theories, Erikson proposed eight stages of personality development over the lifespan. The first stage is *Trust vs. Mistrust* which occurs during infancy with the main developmental task being for an infant to develop a sense of trust and security. If an infant's needs aren't met at this stage, they might experience feelings of abandonment and mistrust in the world. Stage two of his model is *Autonomy vs. Shame and Doubt* which occurs during early childhood. In this stage, children are trying to learn control over their bodies and to control their impulse. Children in this stage tend to want to do things on their own to develop autonomy and may feel a sense of shame or doubt if not allowed that freedom. As I'm writing this book, my twin daughters are in the heart of this stage! One of them, Paisley, always

1) Trust vs. Mistrust
2) Autonomy vs. Shame and Doubt
3) Initiative vs. Guilt
4) Industry vs. Inferiority
5) Identity vs. Role Confusion
6) Intimacy vs. Isolation
7) Generativity vs. Stagnation
8) Integrity vs. Despair

tells me "I do"! I get it screamed at me at least once a day when I fail to let her take care of her own needs! My older daughter Kaiya, who is now four, used to yell "I do it the self" when she was in this stage! As difficult as it might be, letting little ones try to develop that autonomy is important for their development. The third stage is *Initiative vs. Guilt* which occurs in mid-childhood and is a time when children try to learn how to plan and carry out actions. Failure to plan and carry out actions can result in low self-esteem and guilt. The last childhood stage is *Industry vs. Inferiority* which is mid to late childhood. In this stage, children learn to derive pleasure from the completion of tasks and may feel inferior to their peers if unable to complete what they set out to accomplish.

The teenage years are marked by the fifth stage of *Identity vs. Role Confusion*. As teenagers, adolescents are experimenting with different roles and identities to figure out who they are and create a stable sense of self. The uncertainty about one's future or personality can lead to role confusion. In the young adult years, the sixth stage emerges focusing on *Intimacy vs. Isolation.* Young adults start developing companionships and entering long-term romantic relationships. Falling in love is a huge development task and priority for people in this stage of life and those that fail to do so can become lonely and adulthood. The focus of this stage is on giving to others and contributing to society either through having children or through a career. Those who become stagnant don't add to society but rather become or remain focused on their own needs. Finally, the eighth stage is *Integrity vs. Despair* and takes place in late adulthood. As people near the end of life, do they find meaning, integrity, and order in their life when reflecting or do they feel a sense of despair and regret?

© Amanda Carden/Shutterstock.com

Erikson emphasized reaching a balanced outcome for each of the stages; not going too far in either direction. Erikson was one of the first to emphasize personality changes throughout the lifespan and the role of culture, society, and families. Despite no formal training in Psychology, he was one of the most influential psychologists of the 20th century.

Biological Theories of Personality

© Nika Art/Shutterstock.com

From a biological perspective, a person is not born a blank slate that is then written on by the environment; we start with certain predispositions and abilities already in place. As people, we like to believe that success comes from hard work and determination and that any person can achieve almost anything that he/she desires but there is no doubt that biological factors affect a person's potentials and characteristic responses. **Biological Theories** see people as a bundle of genes, brains, and hormones. Our personality, from this perspective, is determined by our biological makeup and **DNA (*deoxyribonucleic acid*)** which is the main ingredient of chromosomes and genes that forms the code for all genetic information. Within a cell, DNA is organized into long structures called **Chromosomes**. A chromosome is an organized structure of DNA and protein found in cells. It is a single piece of coiled DNA containing many genes and other supporting elements. Chromosomes vary in size and shape and usually come in pairs; humans have 23 pairs of chromosomes. A **Gene** is the biochemical unit of heredity of a living organism. Living beings depend on genes as they specify all proteins and hold the information to build and maintain an organism's cells and pass genetic traits to offspring. Genes are segments of DNA capable of synthesizing a protein; the basic units of heredity.

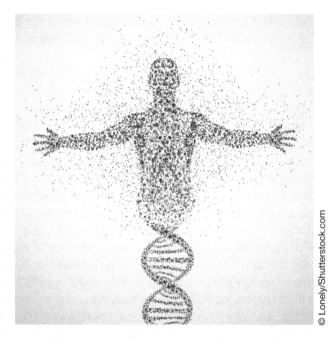

© Lonely/Shutterstock.com

Biological theories embrace the perspective of **Biological Determinism** which is the belief that an individual's personality is completely determined by biological factors (especially genetic ones).

The biological approach supports nature over nurture but of course it is limiting to describe behavior solely in terms of either nature or nurture; attempts to do this underestimate the complexity of human behavior. It is more likely that behavior is due to an interaction between biology) and the environment. A strength of the biological approach is that it provides clear predictions which can be scientifically tested. A limitation is that most biological explanations are reductionist and don't provide enough information to fully explain human behavior. Individuals may be predisposed to certain behaviors, but these behaviors may not be displayed unless they are triggered by factors in the environment.

Behavioral Theories of Personality

In direct contrast to biological theories of personality, **Behavioral Theories** view people as intelligent rats learning life mazes. Behaviorists reject such concepts as the unconscious, genetics, motivations, internal traits, and so on seeing people as controlled absolutely by their environments. In other words, our personality is learned. Behaviorism's roots were laid down by philosopher John Locke in the 1600's. Locke thought that infants were born as a blank slate which he called **Tabula Rasa**. Born with nothing written on our slate, Locke believed that the experiences of life would write our tale and create our personality. Russian Psychologist Ivan Pavlov took this mentality and laid the foundation for modern learning approaches with his theory of classical conditioning that we discussed in an earlier chapter. Around 1900, Freud and many others were studying psychology and unconscious processes in an approach fraught with methodological difficulties; there was no way of validating or verifying the data and conclusions that were being asserted. In response to these limitations, John B. Watson founded behaviorism which emphasized observable behaviors and a more scientific approach. Pavlov and Watson later inspired behavioral

© Georgios Kollidas/Shutterstock.com

psychologists Thorndike and Skinner who developed the operant conditioning theories that we covered earlier as well. Through a combination of classical conditioning, operant conditioning, and learning by observation, from this perspective we are shaped into the person that we become because of experiences and learning.

Just like with the biological perspective, this theory ignores the nature side of influences on our personality which is probably overly simplistic. Another common criticism of behavioral theories is that they are overly deterministic in nature and eliminate the idea of free will. From a behavioral perspective, we are simply stimulus and response or the product of conditioning which doesn't leave a lot of room for free will. An obvious advantage of behaviorism is its ability to clearly define behavior and to measure changes in behavior. Behaviorism looks for simple explanations of human behavior from a very scientific standpoint. Other advantages are that it is a highly applicable branch of psychology and that there are numerous experiments that support its assertions.

Cognitive Theories of Personality

As people, we think about and try to understand the world around us. Cognitive psychologists view perceptions of the environment and cognition as the core of what it means to be a person; the essence of personality is found in the way that we think. From a **Cognitive Theories** perspective, people are scientists and information processors. Cognitive theories focus on a myriad of factors that shape our personality ranging from expectations, schemas, intelligence, learning and cognitive styles, and explanatory styles. From this perspective, the way that we think about the world and our expectations about events will directly shape our mentality and therefore personality.

© ESB Professional/Shutterstock.com

One of the larger perspectives within this branch of personality psychology is the **Cognitive Social Learning Theories** of Albert Bandura. We talked about Bandura back in the learning chapter but his view that behavior is the product of the interaction of cognitions, learning, past experiences, and the immediate environment is a central tenant to this approach. Bandura is well known for his experiment on Bobo dolls that we covered earlier but also for his concept of **Self-Efficacy** which is the expectancy that one's efforts will be successful. Self-efficacy is the expectancy or belief about how competently one will be able to enact a behavior in a particular situation. If we don't believe that we can accomplish what we

© Olivier Le Moal/Shutterstock.com

desire to accomplish, we might perceive very little will to act. Our self-efficacy in any given situation is generally the result of four factors: 1) our experiences trying to perform the target behavior or other similar behaviors (our past successes and failures), 2) watching others perform that or similar behaviors (vicarious experiences), 3) verbal persuasion (people encouraging or discouraging our behavior through the things they say), and 4) how we feel about the behavior (our emotional reactions). Think of the situation of taking an exam in a class. Your self-efficacy or expectation about how well you will do on the test, is shaped by the four factors above. You expect to earn a certain score depending on how you generally do on exams, how others have done on exams in the class, what your family, parents, or others have said to you about your exam taking capabilities, and how you feel going into the test. Bandura believed that our behaviors and cognitions are constantly being shaped by the environment and that these evaluations play a large role in our expectancies and in our personality.

Trait Theories of Personality

A very different approach to personality theories can be found in **Trait Theories** which see people as clusters of temperaments, traits, and skills. While all the theories we have discussed so far try to explain why we have become the person that we are today, this theory in contrast, tries to accurately describe the person you are today. Trait theories focus more on explaining and describing who you are rather than focusing on how you got there. **Personality Traits** are dimensions or characteristics on which people differ in distinctive ways. Traits are basically adjectives such as selfish, friendly, dependent, loyal, and so on; they are words used to describe people. For thousands of years we have characterized people using traits with the first systematic approach being used in Greece. Hippocrates described human temperament in terms of bodily fluids or humors and the predominance of one type determined a person's typical reaction patterns. While modern science has shown this theory to be biologically groundless, it is still intriguing! Carl Jung, who we talked about earlier in this chapter, also focused some of his energy on traits to describe people. Jung coined terms like extrovert and introvert which are commonly used adjective s to describe personality tendencies.

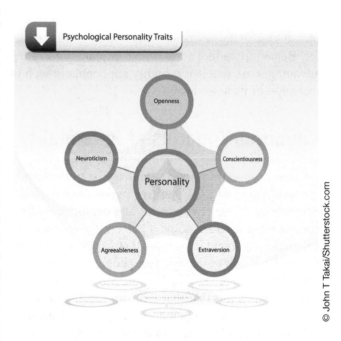

The Big Five

Within this perspective, a contemporary and popular theory called the **Big Five** can be discussed. The Big Five is a trait approach to personality that is supported by a great deal of research and suggests that personality can be captured in five dimensions. The five broad factors were discovered and defined by several independent sets of researchers who began by studying known personality traits and then factor-analyzing hundreds of measures of these traits (in self-report and questionnaire data, peer ratings, and objective measures from experimental settings) in order to find the underlying factors of personality. After all that research, we end up with the following five factors:

1. **Conscientiousness:** personality dimension that includes dependability, cautiousness, organization, and responsibility. Low scores on this are impulsive, careless, disorderly, and undependable.

2. **Agreeableness:** personality dimension that includes friendliness, cooperation, and warmth. People scoring low on this are cold, quarrelsome, and unkind.

3. **Neuroticism:** personality dimension including nervousness, tension, and anxiety. Low score on this are emotionally stable, calm, and contented.

4. **Openness:** personality dimension including imagination, wit, originality, and creativity. Low scores here are shallow, plain, and simple.

5. **Extroversion:** personality dimension that includes enthusiasm, dominance, and sociability. People scoring low on this dimension are considered introverted.

A common mnemonic device for remembering the Big Five is to use the acronym of "CANOE" (which is why the first letter of each factor is underlined). While popular, many people wonder, are 5 dimensions enough to summarize common traits? We don't yet know. Even proponents of the Big 5 approach generally add additional trait descriptions known as **Facets** which are sub-factors that underlie each of the Big Five factors.

Humanistic and Existential Personality Theories

Humanistic and Existential theories of personality look at resolutions of basic human conflicts about value and meaning along with the nature of being, realizing our potentials, happiness, and positive psychology. **Humanistic Personality Theories** see people as free and responsive beings seeking fulfillment of our spirituality and potentials; it asserts the fundamental goodness of people and their striving toward higher levels of functioning. Humanism is a philosophical movement that emphasizes the personal worth of the individual and the importance of human values. This approach attends to ethics and human worth, gives credit to the "human spirit", and emphasizes the creative, spontaneous, and active nature of human beings. Humanism is often called the "3rd force" (after behaviorism and psychoanalysis). Often clumped together with humanistic theories is **Existentialism** which is an area of philosophy concerned with the meaning of human existence.

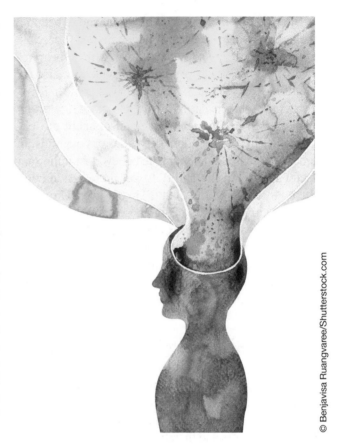
© Benjavisa Ruangvaree/Shutterstock.com

Abraham Maslow

If you think back to the chapter on motivation, we talked about humanistic psychologist Abraham Maslow and his hierarchy of needs. Maslow asserted that we are motivated by a hierarchy of needs and ultimately seek **Self-Actualization** which is the ultimate psychological need that arises after basic physical and psychological needs are met and self-esteem is achieved; our motivation to fulfill our potential. Maslow believed that we have a natural tendency coming from inside ourselves toward self-actualization. He argued that we must largely meet our more basic or **Deficiency Needs** (needs that are essential for survival) including physiological (food, water, shelter, sex), safety (necessity of a generally predictable world), belonging and love (intimate relationships with other people), and esteem needs (respect for oneself and others) before we can move to higher level needs or self-actualization.

© Elenarts/Shutterstock.com

Carl Rogers

A key part of humanistic and existential approaches is the idea that each person is responsible for his/her own life and maturity. This idea is best exemplified in the work of humanistic psychologist Carl Rogers. Rogers believed that every organism is born with innate capacities, capabilities, or potentialities. He believed the goal of life is to fulfill our genetic blueprint and to become the best of whatever each of us is inherently capable of becoming. Rogers felt that human beings form images of themselves or self-concepts which we also try to fulfill. Rogers thought that one of our goals in life is to become what he called a **Fully Functioning Person** which is an individual whose self-concept closely resembles his or her inborn capacities or potentials. In order to reach that potential, he believed an important factor in having the ability to get there was having **Unconditional Positive Regard** in our lives. Unconditional positive regard is the full acceptance and love of another person regardless of his or her behavior and is typically something that we receive from our parents. Rogers' theories and beliefs are most commonly used in Rogerian or Client-Centered therapy which we will cover in the therapies chapter!

© vvvita/Shutterstock.com

Person-Situation Theories of Personality

The last group of personality theories is the **Person-Situation Theory** which views people as an ongoing dialogue between self and environment. People are inconsistent in their behaviors and therefore, how can we study personality if people change their behavior from situation to situation? One way to counter this is to use **Aggregation** or the averaging of behaviors across situations (or over time) to improve the reliability of behavior assessments. Personality and the situation interact to affect behaviors and person-situation interactionist approaches look directly at different social situations and their impact on our personality.

One prominent psychologist within this approach is Harry Stack Sullivan who believed that personality is tied to social situations. Sullivan coined the **Interpersonal Theory of Psychiatry** which focuses on the recurring social situations faced by an individual. Sullivan thought that we become different people in different social situations; we imagine how others think of us and act accordingly and personality therefore is a combination of our individual inclinations and the social situation. He even went as far as to term the idea that a person has a single, fixed personality the **Illusion of Individuality**. Sullivan's ideas have heavily influences of social psychology and interpersonal relations.

© Victor Tondee/Shutterstock.com

Other concepts often examined in this perspective include the power of situational forces and a focus on the lifespan. Personality is sometimes a poor predictor of behavior because the power of a situation can be so strong that it overrides our natural inclinations. In life or death scenarios, people might act very out of character in order to survive. On a lesser level, even just being with different groups of people can bring out different parts of our personality. The power of the situation can sometimes be stronger than our natural tendencies. Focusing on the lifespan also gets attention in this perspective. Because we don't stop growing, changing, and responding to the environment, it becomes important to study people's changes over time. This can be accomplished through what are called **Longitudinal Studies** or the close, comprehensive, systematic, objective, and sustained study of individuals over significant portions of the lifespan; following people over time.

Overall, Person-situation Interactionist approaches try to consider the many ways that personality unfolds in, is realized in, and interacts with the situational context. It is also important to note that to some extent human behavior is unpredictable and part of what makes us human.

Personality Assessment

Personality psychologists are interested in the typical behaviors of a person and how they behave in ordinary situations. This testing focus is known as **Personality Assessment**. Just as psychologists disagree on their views of personality, they also disagree on the best way to measure it. This disagreement results in numerous methods of assessing personality. For the purposes of this class, we will examine two groups of personality assessments; objective and projective tests.

Objective vs Projective Tests

If a psychologist is interested in the typical behaviors of a person (how they behave in ordinary situations) they would use some sort of personality assessment to gather that information. There are two main categories of personality assessments; **Objective Tests** and **Projective Tests**. Objective tests are generally written tests that are administered and scored in a standard way or according to procedure. They are usually yes or no answers or choosing one answer among many choices and are the most widely used tool for assessing personality. One example of an objective test is the MMPI-2 which is the most widely used objective personality test. It was originally developed as an aide in diagnosing psychiatric disorders as it is helpful in distinguishing between different disorders and detecting malingering (faking). Another great example of an objective test is the Myers-Briggs Type Indicator (MBTI) invented by Carl Jung. Projective Tests are personality tests consisting of ambiguous or unstructured material that can elicit an unlimited number of responses. The test-taker looks at an essentially meaningless graphic or a vague picture and then explains what the material means. The best example of a projective test is the **Rorschach Ink Blot Test** named after Hermann Rorschach a Swiss Psychiatrist who published his research on the findings of inkblot interpreting in 1921. Each inkblot is printed on a separate card and is unique in form, color, shading, and white space. People are asked to specify what they see in each blot and are given very minimal test instructions. Psychologists look for patterns and for abnormal perspectives on the ink blots. Similar to the Rorschach is the **Thematic Apperception Test** which involves ambiguous pictures for which the test-taker must make up a storyline which might reveal some unconscious materials to psychologists administering the test.

Overall, objective tests are much more reliable and valid than projective ones. In general, it is best to use a combination of tests when trying to gather information about one's personality; sometimes we refer to this as having a battery of assessments. Clinicians often use several tests along with interviewing family, friends, and possibly conducting some naturalistic observations in order to come to more comprehensive and accurate conclusions.

In Popular Culture

- *Emperor's New Groove* (2000) – a movie featuring a scene where the character Kronk is talking with his shoulder angel and devil which can be compared to the id and superego in Freud's theory.

- *Snow White* (1937) – a movie featuring seven dwarves; while personality is never as simple as one trait, the basic concept of people having distinct personalities can be captured in the seven dwarves who are all defined by one trait or attribute.

- *The Simpsons* (1989 to present) – an episode of the television show The Simpsons entitled "Stark Raving Dad" features an Ink Blot test and a few different methods of personality assessment.

- *Armageddon* (1998) – a movie featuring a scene with an Ink Blot test which is a great example of looking for themes in personality assessment.

- *Crazy* by Gnarles Barkley (2006) – a popular culture song with a music video representation of ink blots.

Psyched with Setmire

"Personality Theories: Eight Major Approaches"
https://www.youtube.com/watch?v=ythHWudrG80&t=5s

The lecture presentation video will cover the different psychological perspectives related to personality. I will provide a brief overview of the eight major approaches to studying personality psychology: Psychoanalytic, Neo-Analytic, Biological, Behavioral, Cognitive, Trait, Humanistic/Existential, and Person-Situation Theories. Major concepts and theorists will be covered for each approach!

Application: Personality Tests

In general, people love to learn more about their personalities! One great way to do that is through taking personality tests. There are a ton of free personality tests online; here are a couple of websites that you can explore for fun! Most of these tests are entertaining but are largely inaccurate (poor reliability, validity, and standardization) so be sure to take the results lightly!

© kenary820/Shutterstock.com

© Amir Ridhwan/Shutterstock.com

© Marilyn Volan/Shutterstock.com

- http://www.outofservice.com/ – example of online tests you can take for free (finding out your Star Wars twin and other fun examples). Unreliable and invalid; but fun!

- http://www.personalityquiz.net/ – site contains numerous personality quizzes such as love tests, food and personality, and many others.

- http://www.humanmetrics.com/cgi-win/jtypes1.htm – Jung Typology personality test and several others.

- http://www.personalitypathways.com – Cognitive Style Inventory (based on the MBTI)

Key Terms

Personality: an individual's unique pattern of thoughts, feelings, and behaviors, that persists over time and across situations.

Psychodynamic (Psychoanalytic) Theory: the theory of personality proposed by Sigmund Freud asserting that humans are unconsciously motivated beings seeking to fulfill (and balance) sexual and aggressive urges.

Unconscious: in Freud's theory of personality, all the ideas, thoughts, and feelings of which we are not and normally cannot become aware.

Id: the collection of unconscious urges and desires that continually seek expression; operates according to the pleasure principle.

Ego: part of the personality that mediates between environmental demands, conscience, and instinctual needs; operates on the reality principle.

Superego: the social and parental standards the individual has internalized; the conscience and the ego ideal.

Freudian Slips: a psychological error in speaking or writing that reveals something about a person's unconscious.

Libido: according to Freud, our sexual instinct or energy.

Fixation: a partial or complete halt at some point in the individual's psychosexual development.

Oral Stage: the first of Freud's psychosexual stages in which an infant's erotic feelings center on the mouth, lips, and tongue.

Anal Stage: the second stage of Freud's psychosexual stages in which a child's erotic feelings center on the anus and on elimination.

Phallic Stage: the third stage of Freud's psychosexual stages in which erotic feelings center on the genitals.

Oedipal Complex: in Freud's theory, a boy who is fixated on his mother and competes with his father for maternal attention.

Electra Complex: in Freud's theory, a girl who is fixated on her father and competes with her mother for paternal attention.

Latency Stage: the fourth stage of Freud's psychosexual stages in which a child appears to have no interest in the other sex; sexual energies are channeled into activities such as going to school and making friends.

Genital Stage: the fifth and final stage of Freud's psychosexual stages in which sexual impulses reawaken and the quest for immediate gratification of these desires yields to sexual maturity.

Neo-Analytic Theories: theories of personality which view people as unconscious (and conscious) actors and goal-oriented strivers; a new-analysis.

Personal Unconscious: according to Jung, an individual's repressed thoughts, forgotten experiences, and undeveloped ideas.

Collective Unconscious: according to Jung, the level of the unconscious that is inherited and common to all members of a species.

Archetypes: emotional symbols that are common to all people and have been formed since the beginning of time that therefore cause us to react in predictable ways to common reoccurring stimuli.

Ego Crises: according to Erikson, conflicts of choice that must be resolved in sequence.

Biological Theories: theories of personality that see people as a bundle of genes, brains, and hormones.

DNA (*deoxyribonucleic acid*): the main ingredient of chromosomes and genes that forms the code for all genetic information.

Chromosomes: an organized structure of DNA and protein found in cells; humans have 23 pairs of chromosomes.

Gene: the biochemical unit of heredity of a living organism.

Biological Determinism: the belief that an individual's personality is completely determined by biological factors (especially genetic ones).

Behavioral Theories: theories of personality that view people as intelligent rats learning life mazes; rejects such concepts as the unconscious, genetics, motivations, internal traits, and so on seeing people as controlled absolutely by their environments.

Tabula Rasa: the idea, according to John Locke, that we are born with a blank slate upon which experience will write.

Cognitive Theories: theories of personality that see people as scientists and information processors; the essence of personality is found in what we think.

Cognitive Social Learning Theories: theories of personality that view behavior as the product of the interaction of cognitions, learning, past experiences, and the immediate environment.

Self-Efficacy: the expectancy that one's efforts will be successful.

Trait Theories: theories of personality which see people as clusters of temperaments, traits, and skills.

Personality Traits: dimensions or characteristics on which people differ in distinctive ways.

Big Five: a trait approach to personality that is supported by a great deal of research and suggests that personality can be captured in five dimensions

Facets: sub-factors that underlie each of the Big Five factors.

Humanistic Personality Theories: theories of personality that see people as free and responsive beings seeking fulfillment of our spirituality and potentials; it asserts the fundamental goodness of people and their striving toward higher levels of functioning.

Existentialism: an area of philosophy concerned with the meaning of human existence.

Self-Actualization: according to Maslow, the ultimate psychological need that arises after basic physical and psychological needs are met and self-esteem is achieved; our motivation to fulfill our potential.

Deficiency Needs: according to Maslow, needs that are essential for survival such as food and water.

Fully Functioning Person: according to Rogers, an individual whose self-concept closely resembles his or her inborn capacities or potentials.

Unconditional Positive Regard: according to Rogers, the full acceptance and love of another person regardless of his or her behavior.

Person-Situation Theory: theory of personality which views people as an ongoing dialogue between self and environment.

Aggregation: the averaging of behaviors across situations (or over time) to improve the reliability of behavior assessments.

Interpersonal Theory of Psychiatry: according to Sullivan, the recurring social situations faced by an individual.

Illusion of Individuality: according to Sullivan, the idea that we have a single, fixed personality being an illusion.

Longitudinal Studies: the close, comprehensive, systematic, objective, and sustained study of individuals over significant portions of the lifespan; following people over time.

Personality Assessment: the measuring of the typical behaviors of a person and how they behave in ordinary situations.

Objective Tests: generally written tests that are administered and scored in a standard way or according to procedure.

Projective Tests: personality tests consisting of ambiguous or unstructured material that can elicit an unlimited number of responses.

Rorschach Ink Blot Test: a projective test of personality involving inkblots each printed on a separate card with unique forms, colors, shading, and white space.

Thematic Apperception Test: a projective test of personality which involves ambiguous pictures for which the test-taker must make up a storyline.

Chapter 13
Stress and Health

Outline

© donskarpo/Shutterstock.com

Introduction to the Chapter (Summary)

Stress is a state of psychological tension or strain and also the process by which we perceive and respond to certain events called stressors which are any environmental demand that creates tension or strain. Stress doesn't always have to be bad, there is also good stress which can motivate us to grow and be better people. Stress arises more from how we appraise events rather than the events themselves! While most stressors come and go, sometimes people experience extreme stress which is a radical departure from everyday life such that a person cannot continue life as before. Extreme stress can lead to Post-Traumatic Stress Disorder which is a psychological disorder marked by episodes of anxiety, sleeplessness, and nightmares resulting from some disturbing past event. In general, extreme forms of stress such as PTSD require intense therapy and support from family, friends, and the community.

Our body reacts to stress much like it reacts to danger. Our reaction to perceived danger is commonly thought of as fight or flight, but extending that farther, Hans Selye proposed that we react to physical and psychological stress in three stages (alarm reaction, resistance, and exhaustion) that he collectively called the General Adaptation Syndrome indicator (GAS). Living in a state of exhaustion for extended periods of time can lead to health correlates. Stress is a major contributing factor in the development of coronary heart disease which is the clogging of the vessels that nourish the heart muscles. Stress can also impair health by disrupting the functioning of the immune system. It takes energy to fight infection, produce inflammations, and maintain fevers and stress also requires energy creating a competing energy need. When the fight or flight response is triggered, it diverts that energy to the muscles and brain which makes us more vulnerable to illness. Stress and negative emotions are also thought to exacerbate the progression from HIV infection to AIDS and have also been linked to cancer's rate of progression because it weakens the body's natural defenses. Finally, stress can lead to psychophysiological Illnesses such as hypertension, ulcers, and some headaches.

Stress arouses and motivates us and a life without stress would hardly be challenging or productive. When stress is short-lived, the costs are minimal but when uncontrollable stress or aggravation persists, the cost can become considerable. Stress requires that we cope or in other words, make behavioral efforts to manage and reduce our stress. We can cope with our stress directly by either confronting it, finding a compromise, or even withdrawing from the situation or we can cope defensively through defense mechanisms such as denial or repression. In addition to different coping mechanisms, there are several factors that influence our ability to cope with stress such as our perceived control over the stressor, our explanatory style (optimistic or pessimistic), and also our degree of social support. There are proven ways to reduce the negative impact of stress on your body and your health. Some things that you can do are learn ways to calm down (such as doing relaxation exercises, breathing exercises, yoga, or meditation), reach out to others, religion and altruism, learning to cope effectively (manage your time, prioritize, and learn how to deal with your stress), and adopting a healthy lifestyle which includes eating right, getting the right amount of sleep, and aerobic exercise. Exercise has been shown to not only improve the quality of your life but also the quantity!

Stress

Stress is a state of psychological tension or strain; the process by which we perceive and respond to certain events, called stressors that we appraise as threatening or challenging. Stress is the body's reaction to difficult situations that disrupt a person's normal functioning and state of being. Stress arises more from how we appraise events than the events themselves! There is a branch of psychology called **Health Psychology** which examines the relationship between psychological factors and physical health and illness. As a group, health psychologists look specifically at how psychological factors influence wellness and illness.

Sources of Stress

Stressors are any environmental demand that creates a state of tension or threat and requires change or adaptation. Not everything causes stress though many situations prompt us to change our behavior in some way. Stress is not limited to dangerous or unpleasant situations; sometimes stress can be a positive thing like a wedding. Everyday events can also cause stress because they necessitate change and/or adaptation. Some of the more common stressors are change, everyday hassles, and even self-imposed stress. Most people have a strong preference for order and predictability therefore anything that requires change has the potential to be stressful. Significant life changes such as the death of a loved one, loss of a job or marriage, or other life transitions can also lead to stress for people. Small daily things and everyday hassles can result in stress when they annoy or irritate us. We can also create stress for ourselves by having irrational or self-defeating beliefs. As mentioned before, stress is more about how we perceive an event. Two people can experience the exact same event, such as traffic for example, and it might stress out one person and not the other.

© Nadya_Art/Shutterstock.com

The Stress Response System

Whenever we experience stress, a structure in the brain called the **Hypothalamus** is activated. The hypothalamus regulates body homeostasis by controlling thirst, hunger, body temperature, and blood pressure along with linking the nervous system to the endocrine system. When our brain interprets something as dangerous, the hypothalamus triggers the firing of neurons throughout the brain and the release of hormones by activating two important systems, the autonomic nervous system and the endocrine system. The **Autonomic Nervous System** is a network of fibers that connects the nervous system to all the other organs of the body. This system controls many of the involuntary activities of the organs such as breathing, heartbeat, blood pressure, and perspiration. More specifically, within the autonomic nervous system, the **Sympathetic Nervous System** pathway is activated which then arouses us preparing for us to face danger by

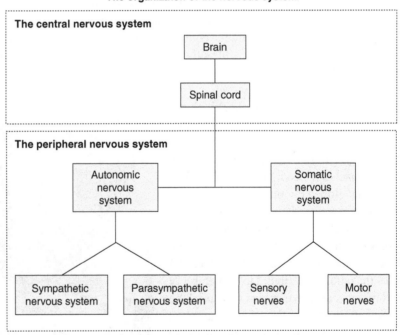

The organizaton of the nervous system

releasing epinephrine and norepinephrine. The sympathetic nervous system oversees fight-or-flight reactions and once a threat or stressor has passed, the **Parasympathetic Nervous System** then helps us to calm down as it is in charge of resting and digesting.

The other side of the stress response is controlled by the **Endocrine System** which includes all the glands located throughout the body that help control important activities such as growth and sexuality activity. Within this pathway, stress signals the pituitary gland which in turn signals the adrenal glands causing the release of stress hormones to various body organs. The body releases ACTH or adrenocorticotropic hormone which is the body's major stress hormone which in turn triggers the release of other stress hormones such as cortisol into the various parts of the body causing arousal. This chain of events is sometimes referred to as the hypothalamic-pituitary-adrenal (HPA) pathway.

Stress and Health

Our reaction to perceived danger is commonly thought of as fight or flight, but extending that farther, psychologist Hans Selye proposed that we react to physical and psychological stress in three stages he collectively called the **General Adaptation Syndrome (GAS)**. According to Selye, the three stages the body passes through as it adapts to are: *alarm reaction*, *resistance*, and *exhaustion*. *Alarm reaction* is our first response to stress when the body recognizes that it must fend off a physical or psychological danger. In this stage, emotions run high and activity of the sympathetic nervous system is increased

as it works to mobilize our coping resources. If we are unable to reduce the stress we move to the second stage which is *resistance* where physical symptoms and other signs of strain appear. In this stage, we intensify our coping strategies but if they don't work or if the stress is extreme or prolonged, we progress into stage three of *exhaustion*. If we hit exhaustion, we draw on increasingly ineffective defense mechanisms in a desperate attempt to bring the stress under control. Some people lose touch with reality and show signs of emotional disorders or mental illness while others show signs of burnout or physical symptoms such as headaches or stomach aches.

Stress can directly affect our health. Stress is a major contributing factor in the development of **Coronary Heart Disease** which is the clogging of the vessels that nourish the heart muscle; the leading cause of death in many developed countries. Frequent and/or chronic stress damages the heart and blood vessels and cortisol increases blood pressure and increases cholesterol which leads to blockages of the arteries. To test the idea that stress contributes to vulnerability to heart disease, researchers measured the blood cholesterol level and clotting speed of forty tax accountants and their rates were normal until right before the tax deadline of April 15 when they began scrambling causing their measures to go to dangerous levels. In another study, conducted by researchers

Friedman and Rosenman, 3000 healthy men were followed for nine years. During their research, they noticed some behavioral patterns in the participants in the interviews before their experiment and divided people into two groups termed **Type A Personality** and **Type B Personality**. Type A personalities were hard-driving, impatient, verbally aggressive, and anger-prone people while Type B personalities were easygoing, relaxed people. The research results were enormous in that 257 of the men experienced a heart attack and 69% of those men were Type A. Unfortunately, the research was heavily funded by tobacco companies and the results and claims of this study have been deemed invalid. While we have found a correlation between Type A characteristic ad heart problems, it isn't causal. Recent research has revealed that the core of Type A is negative emotions especially anger and aggression which contributed to greater levels of arousal which related to greater strain on the heart and increased likelihood of heart attacks.

Stress also impacts the immune system. **Psychophysiological Illness** literally, "mind-body" illness involves any stress-related physical illness, such as hypertension and some types of headaches. When psychologists look at stress and the immune system they are in the realm of **Psychoneuroimmunology (PNI)** which is a relatively new field that studies the interaction between stress on the one hand and immune, endocrine, and nervous system activity on the other. Stress impairs health by disrupting the functioning of the immune system. It takes energy to fight infection and stress also requires energy creating a competing energy need. When the fight or

flight response is triggered, it diverts that energy to the muscles and brain which makes us more vulnerable to illness. The bottom line is that stress does not make us sick, but it restrains our immune functioning, making us vulnerable to foreign invaders. Stress and negative emotions can accelerate the progression from HIV infection to AIDS (Acquired Immune Deficiency Syndrome) along with the speed of decline. Stress and negative emotions have also been linked to cancer's rate of progression. To be clear, stress is not thought to cause cancer but rather to affect its growth by weakening the body's natural defenses.

Stress arouses and motivates us and a life without stress would hardly be challenging or productive. When stress is short-lived, the costs are minimal but when uncontrollable stress or aggravation persists, the cost can become considerable as there is a constant interplay between our heads and our health.

Extreme Stress

Extreme stress is a radical departure from everyday life such that a person cannot continue life as before and in some cases, never fully recover. Sometimes, in cases of extreme stress, the reactions to an event can persist even after the event is over. One example of that is **Post-Traumatic Stress Disorder**; a psychological disorder marked by episodes of anxiety, sleeplessness, and nightmares resulting from some disturbing past event. PTSD often causes dramatic nightmares in which a person re-experiences the event exactly as it happened or has vivid daydreams or flashbacks in which the person relives the

trauma. It also tends to result in avoidance of any activities that remind the individual of the traumatic event along with any related thoughts, feelings, or conversations in addition to reduced responsiveness and a feeling of being detached or dissociated from others. This disorder can happen immediately or years after the traumatic event. In general, extreme forms of stress such as PTSD require therapy and support from family, friends, and the community to improve. Common treatment techniques include drug therapy, exposure techniques, insight therapy, family therapy, group therapy, and behavioral exposure techniques like eye movement and desensitization and reprocessing (EMDR).

Coping with Stress

Stress requires that we cope or make behavioral efforts to manage the psychological stress. There are two general categories of coping mechanisms; **Direct Coping** and **Defensive Coping**. Direct coping refers to intentional efforts to change an uncomfortable situation and tends to be problem oriented and to focus on the immediate issue. When we are threatened, frustrated, or in conflict, we have three basic choices for coping directly: **Confrontation**, **Compromise**, and **Withdrawal**. Confrontation involves acknowledging a stressful situation directly and attempting to find a solution to the problem or to attain the difficult

goal. Compromise is deciding on a more realistic solution or goal when an ideal solution or goal is not practical. Finally, withdrawal is avoiding a situation when other forms of coping are not practical. We might also cope defensively when we can't identify or can't directly deal with the source of our stress. In such situations, people turn to **Defense Mechanisms** which are self-deceptive techniques for reducing stress. We deceive ourselves about the causes of a stressful situation in order to reduce pressure, frustration, conflict, and anxiety. Common defense mechanisms include denial, repression, displacement, projection, sublimation, and rationalization.

Factors Influencing Our Ability to Cope Successfully with Stress

In addition to the strategies that we use to cope with stress, there are other factors that can influence our ability to cope successfully. One factor is *perceived control*. Uncontrollable events tend to trigger more intense stress responses and often perceiving a loss of control can cause us to become vulnerable to poor health because losing control provokes an outpouring of stress hormones. Our *explanatory style*, whether we are generally optimistic or pessimistic, can also greatly influence our ability to cope with stress. Do you tend to view the glass as half empty or half full? People who are optimistic tend to perceive more control, cope better with stressful events, and enjoy better health than their pessimistic counterparts. Finally, *social support* plays a role in coping with stress. People who are in committed relationships tend to live longer

and healthier lives and having social support seems to help with coping with stress. People supported by close relationships (family, friends, fellow workers, and members of a faith community or other support groups) are less likely to die prematurely and tend to have better success coping with their stress.

Staying Healthy

There are proven ways to reduce the negative impact of stress on our body and health. One thing that can be done is to *calm down*. Exercise lowers resting heart rate and blood pressure so your body doesn't react as strongly to stress and recovers quicker. Also, relaxation techniques can reduce muscle tension and breathing exercises can help with calming down. Even just taking a few slow deep breaths can be enough to help someone calm down when they are stressed or anxious. Another thing that can be done is to *reach out* to others. Having a strong network of family and friends (social support) can help to maintain good health.

Other ways to reduce stress include embracing *religion and altruism*; reaching out and giving to others because it brings you pleasure. Religiously active people tend to have healthier lifestyles (might smoke and drink less) and tend to have great social support networks. *Learning to cope effectively* can also reduce stress as how you appraise events in your environment and how you appraise your ability to cope with them can minimize or maximize stress. Also, *adopting a healthy lifestyle* can go a long way in helping to combat stress. A good diet of nutritious food provides the energy necessary to sustain a vigorous lifestyle. Avoiding smoking (linked to chronic lung disease, heart disease, and cancer) and avoid high-risk behaviors (wear a seatbelt, protect yourself during sex, and make safer choices) can all go a long way in staying healthy and reducing stress.

Another component of a healthy lifestyle is engaging in regular **Aerobic Exercise**; sustained exercise that increases heart and lung fitness. Exercise not only boosts our mood, but also strengthens the heart, increases blood flow, keeps blood vessels open, and lowers blood pressure. Exercise makes the muscles hungry for bad fats which contribute to clogged arteries. Exercise adds not only to the quality of life (more energy and a better mood) but also the quantity of life (on average it adds an additional two years to a person's lifespan).

Complementary and Alternative Medicine

Complementary and Alternative Medicine are another area that might help with stress relief and health. Complementary and alternative medicines are as yet unproven health care treatments intended to supplement/complement or serve as alternatives to conventional medicine. These methods are typically not widely taught in medical schools, used in hospitals, or reimbursed by insurance companies but they do tend to be widely used. There are five different domains of complementary and alternative medicines. The first domain is *alternative medical systems* which includes homeopathy or often plant-based medicines and home remedies. The second domain is *mind-body interventions* which include meditation, prayer, and therapies with creative outlets such as art, music, or dance. *Biologically based therapies* are the third domain and include embracing certain herbs, foods, and vitamins for medicinal purposes. Fourth are the *manipulative and body-based methods* such as chiropractic manipulation, acupuncture, and/or massage. Finally, the fifth domain involves *energy therapies* like Reiki and therapeutic touch which has the goal of affecting energy fields that surround and penetrate the human body.

In Popular Culture

- *Stressed Out* by Twenty-One Pilots (2015) – a popular culture song highlighting the topics of stress and aging.

- *American Sniper* (2014) – a movie featuring a character struggling with PTSD because of traumatic combat experiences.

- *Office Space* (1999) – this movie highlights several different kinds of stress and ways of coping with stress!

- *Brothers* (2009) – a movie featuring a character that suffers from PTSD because of combat experiences.

- *Boundin'* (2004) – an animated short by Pixar related to explanatory style and the impact of your perspective on events.

- *Hunger Games* (2012–2015) – popular culture movies and books featuring a character named Katnis who experiences PTSD in response to her experiences in the Hunger Games.

Psyched with Setmire

"How Stress Affects the Body"
https://www.youtube.com/watch?v=dv440mijyyM

In this lecture presentation video (adapted from my Introduction to Psychology course lecture), I will briefly discuss how stress affects the body. I will cover the physiological chain of events starting with the hypothalamus and how it triggers the activation of the autonomic nervous system and the endocrine system.

Application: Guided Relaxation Exercises

One of the best ways to reduce your stress level is to simply calm down by doing guided breathing or relaxation exercises (you can even just take a few deep breaths if you are short on time). Through deep breathing, meditation, or relaxation exercises, you lower your level of physiological arousal which puts less strain on your body and results in feeling calmer and less stressed. When we are stressed, our heart beats faster, our blood pressure goes up, digestion shuts down, our muscles tense, and we breathe harder. Guided relaxation or meditation exercises can help us to calm our stress response and reduce the physical effects of stress. There are tons of these exercises available for free on the Internet. Try to find a quiet place to do these, sit or lie down in a comfortable position, and don't get frustrated if you struggle the first time you try!

© EpicStockMedia/Shutterstock.com

Key Terms

Stress: a state of psychological tension or strain; the process by which we perceive and respond to certain events, called stressors.

Health Psychology: a subfield of psychology concerned with the relationship between psychological factors and physical health and illness.

Stressor: any environmental demand that creates a state of tension or threat and requires change or adaptation.

Hypothalamus: a structure in the brain that regulates body homeostasis along with linking the nervous system to the endocrine system.

Autonomic Nervous System: a division of the peripheral nervous system; a network of fibers that connects the nervous system to all the other organs of the body.

Sympathetic Nervous System: a division of the autonomic nervous system that is activated preparing for us to face danger through the fight-or-flight response.

Parasympathetic Nervous System: a division of the autonomic nervous system that helps us to calm down after a stressor or threat; in charge of resting and digesting.

Endocrine System: a system in the body that includes all the glands located throughout the body that help control important activities such as growth and sexuality activity.

General Adaptation Syndrome (GAS): according to Selye, the three stages the body passes through as it adapts to stress.

Coronary Heart Disease: the clogging of the vessels that nourish the heart muscle; the leading cause of death in many developed countries.

Type A Personality: according to Freidman and Rosenman, a personality type defined by being hard-driving, impatient, verbally aggressive, and anger-prone.

Type B Personality: according to Friedman and Rosenman, a personality type defined by being easygoing and relaxed.

Psychophysiological Illness: literally, "mind-body" illness; any stress-related physical illness, such as hypertension and some headaches.

Psychoneuroimmunology (PNI): a new field that studies the interaction between stress on the one hand and immune, endocrine, and nervous system activity on the other.

Post-Traumatic Stress Disorder: psychological disorder marked by episodes of anxiety, sleeplessness, and nightmares resulting from some disturbing past event.

Direct Coping: refers to intentional efforts to change an uncomfortable situation.

Defensive Coping: coping mechanisms used when we either can't identify or can't directly deal with the source of our stress.

Confrontation: acknowledging a stressful situation directly and attempting to find a solution to the problem or to attain the difficult goal.

Compromise: deciding on a more realistic solution or goal when an ideal solution or goal is not practical.

Withdrawal: avoiding a situation when other forms of coping are not practical.

Defense Mechanisms: self-deceptive techniques for reducing stress.

Aerobic Exercise: sustained exercise that increases heart and lung fitness.

Complementary and Alternative Medicine: unproven health care treatments intended to supplement (complement) or serve as alternatives to conventional medicine, and which typically are not widely taught in medical schools, used in hospitals, or reimbursed by insurance companies.

© igorstevanovic/Shutterstock.com

Outline

Introduction to the Chapter (Summary)

It isn't always easy to determine when a person's behavior is abnormal. Society's main standard of abnormality is whether the behavior fails to conform to prevailing ideas about what is socially acceptable but psychologists in general tend to view abnormality as a psychological disorder when it is deviant, distressful, dangerous, and includes dysfunctional behavior patterns. The place and time also contributes to how we define mental disorders. Mysterious behaviors were once attributed to the supernatural or possession by demons. We currently have several models of abnormal behavior including the biological (medical) model, psychoanalytic model, cognitive-behavioral model, diathesis-stress model, and the systems approach (biopsychosocial) model. Each model explains abnormality from a different perspective and dictates the course of treatment. The American Psychiatric Association (APA) has a manual called the Diagnostic and Statistical Manual of Mental Disorders (DSM-5) which provides a complete list of mental disorders. The DSM is the most widely used classification system. Some critics of the DSM speak about the dangers of labeling. When we label a person, we may view the person differently and often make judgments about that person along with possibly changing reality. Labels can also be helpful as they can help lead to effective treatments.

Everyone experiences anxiety; something caused by an appropriate and identifiable stimulus that passes with time. Anxiety disorders differ in that they are disorders in which the person either doesn't know why he or she is afraid or the anxiety is inappropriate to the circumstances. A few common anxiety disorders include specific phobias, panic attacks, and obsessive compulsive disorder. Psychosomatic and somatoform disorders are another smaller category of disorders that involve an interplay between the mind and the body. Dissociative disorders are another group of disorders in which some aspect of the personality is separated from the rest. These disorders usually involve some form of memory loss and a complete though generally temporary, change of identity. The most common of this group is dissociative identity disorder. Personality disorders are disorders in which inflexible and maladaptive ways of thinking and behaving learned early in life cause distress to the person or conflicts with others. Personality disorders range from harmless eccentrics to cold-blooded killers. There are several personality disorders covered in the DSM, the two most dramatic and severe are borderline personality disorder and antisocial personality disorder.

Everyone experiences fluctuations in mood from happy to sad and everything in-between. In contrast, mood disorders are disturbances in mood or prolonged emotional states and are characterized by emotional extremes. The most common mood disorders are major depressive disorder and bipolar disorder. Schizophrenia is another disorder and involves a break with reality and symptoms such as hallucinations and delusions. It is a common misconception that schizophrenia is the same thing as having multiple personalities but what is split in schizophrenia is not the personality as much as it is the connection among thoughts. There are also disorders of childhood such as attention-deficit hyperactivity disorder (ADHD) and autistic spectrum disorder along with disorders of aging like neurocognitive disorders such as Alzheimer's.

Perspectives on Psychological Disorders

It isn't always easy to determine when a person's behavior is abnormal. Is someone who wears strange clothing or has bizarre mannerisms eccentric or suffering from a disorder? It can be a fine line between the two! Abnormality can depend on many factors such as culture, perspective, norms, the time, and even the location. Society's main standard of abnormality is whether the behavior fails to conform to prevailing ideas about what is socially acceptable of people but individuals may evaluate things on different criteria

such as whether or not it causes unhappiness and/or a lack of well-being. In general, we can define a **Psychological Disorder** or mental illness as a pattern of behavioral and psychological symptoms that impact several areas of a person's life causing significant distress and impairment. A general rule of thumb for determining abnormality is sometimes found in the four D's of abnormality: *deviance*, *distress*, *danger*, and *dysfunction*. If a person is exhibiting deviance, their attitudes or behaviors differ markedly from what is typical. This might manifest in the way a person acts, dresses, speaks, or in their expression of something like anxiety or mood. Disorders also cause distress to the individual and/or the people in their life. Sometimes disorders can also be dangerous. This can be in the form of danger to self as in suicidality or it can appear as danger to others like we might see with Antisocial Personality Disorder (which we will get to later). Disorders also result in dysfunction meaning that a person's life is impaired by their maladaptive emotions and/or behaviors. There are no hard and fast rules for determining abnormality but we do have diagnostic criteria that we can rely on to help make those difficult decisions.

Historical Views of Psychological Disorders

As mentioned above, the place and time also contribute to how we define mental disorders. Mysterious behaviors were once attributed to the supernatural, witchcraft, or even possession by demons. If we go back hundreds of years or more, the prevailing explanation for mental illness was demonic possession. It was believed that the body and soul were a battleground between good and evil and someone manifesting signs of mental illness, was possessed by evil spirits or even the devil himself. The treatment for possession was typically to perform an exorcism to drive the evil spirits out of the body. Sometimes we even performed procedures called trephinations where a circular section of the skull was cut away to allow the spirits to escape. As you can imagine, many people died during these procedures.

Another early theory of mental illness viewed it as the result of bodily fluids that Hippocrates called humors. Hippocrates proposed that we have four bodily fluids: blood, phlegm, black bile, and yellow bile that if out of balance, could cause mental illness. While biologically groundless, it was a decisive shift away from the idea of demonic possession. Other theories over time have blamed biology, learning, the unconscious mind, and countless other factors for causing mental illness. While psychology has a shocking history of viewing and treating mental illness, we have come an incredibly long way in the last hundred or so years!

Models of Abnormality

Within the field of psychology, we currently have several models of abnormality. A **Model** is a set of assumptions and concepts that helps scientists explain and interpret

©Alex Malikov/Shutterstock.com

© udra11/Shutterstock.com

observations; also sometimes called a paradigm. Models spell out basic assumptions and set guidelines for investigation along with treatment. These models can directly conflict with each other and some have better support than others especially for certain disorders. Together, they likely capture the complexity of what can cause a mental illness.

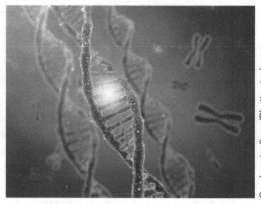

One very common model of abnormality is the **Biological (Medical) Model** which views disorders as having a biochemical or physiological basis. The biological or medical model often looks at factors like genetics, hormones, neurotransmitters, and brain anatomy to explain the causes of mental illness. Many disorders do have a genetic element to them and countless disorders have been blamed on imbalances of certain neurotransmitters. From this model or perspective, mental illness is biologically caused and therefore should be biologically treated through methods like medication, brain stimulation, and surgery. Another model of abnormality is the **Psychoanalytic Model** which views disorders as a result of unconscious internal conflicts. This is Freud's perspective and examines the role of early childhood, the unconscious, and sexual and aggressive urges. If a disorder has roots in early childhood experiences, from this perspective, treatment would involve going back in time, through therapy, and working through those issues.

The **Cognitive-Behavioral Model** views abnormality and mental illness as the result of learning maladaptive ways of thinking and behaving. Cognitive-behavioral approaches combine two popular perspectives together. We can view mental illness solely as the result of cognitive influences like illogical thinking patterns and cognitive distortions (which are very common in depression) or as the result of only behavioral factors like conditioning (which are very common with anxiety disorders). This perspective is popular in a contemporary sense and combines all of these elements together in viewing the causes of mental illness along with strategies for treatment. The **Diathesis-Stress Model** asserts that people are biologically predisposed to a mental disorder and will tend to exhibit that disorder when particularly affected by stress. This involves a combination of elements; a biological predisposition along with an environmental trigger. Commonly referenced with disorders like schizophrenia, a person is born with the biological tendency in place but it takes an environmental element like combat or a bad drug trip to trigger that predisposition. Finally, the **Systems (Biopsychosocial) Approach** combines biological, psychological, and social risk factors when examining the causes of psychological disorders. This brilliant and yet incredibly common sense approach asserts that it is a combination of multiple factors that causes mental illness and therefore a combination of elements in treating disorders are often used.

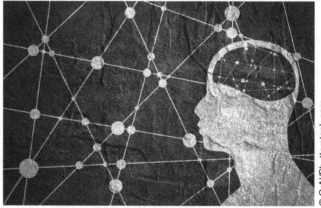

Classifying Abnormal Behavior

The American Psychiatric Association (APA) has a manual called the Diagnostic and Statistical Manual of Mental Disorders (DSM-5) which provides a complete list of mental disorders that are recognized. The DSM is currently in its 5th edition and provides all of the diagnostic criteria for each mental illness but nothing about causes or treatment. The DSM is the most widely used classification of psychological disorders and most people find it very helpful along with being necessary for insurance companies. In order to treat a disorder, we must first name and describe it which are the main goals of the DSM. Unfortunately, labeling a person is one of the biggest criticisms of the DSM and the mental health field in general. Critics of the DSM speak about the dangers of labeling someone including viewing the person differently, making judgments about that person, and possibly changing reality; sometimes if you expect something out of someone you might create it or treat them in a way that will create it (self-fulfilling prophecies). Labels however are often helpful as they can help lead to effective treatments. If I know that someone has depression, then I can use common depression treatments to help that person. The system of diagnosing and labeling is far from perfect but the DSM and our classification system is the best that we currently have.

Box: Slang Terms for Mental Illness

Our society has an incredible number of slang terms for people suffering from mental illness. Here are a few of them:

- Basket case
- Mental
- Belong in a Looney Bin
- Disturbed
- Nuts
- Crazy
- Psycho
- Spastic
- Schizo
- Mad
- Insane
- Looney
- Different
- Freak
- Bananas
- Waco
- Odd Ball
- Retard
- Wears a strait jacket

- She's off her rocker
- Not firing on all Cylinders
- Has a screw loose
- Not playing with a full deck
- Mad as a hatter
- The lights are on but there's nobody home
- Lost his marbles
- The elevator doesn't go all the way to the top floor
- Cookie doesn't crumble the right way
- Few fries short of a happy meal

Anxiety Disorders

From here we will look at some of the common mental illnesses. We won't be covering all of them but we can look at some of the more frequently occurring disorders and their symptoms. The most common group of disorders that people struggle with are the anxiety disorders. Anxiety disorders are different from experiencing **Anxiety** which are feelings of fear and apprehension. Experiencing anxiety is completely healthy and normal. Anxiety is caused by something appropriate and identifiable and passes with time. In contrast to anxiety, **Anxiety Disorders** are disorders in which the person either doesn't know why he or she is afraid or the anxiety is inappropriate to the circumstances such as the level of fear and anxiety just not making sense. Anxiety disorders are characterized by distressing, persistent anxiety or maladaptive behaviors that reduce anxiety. There are quite a few different anxiety disorders. We will cover specific phobias, panic attacks, and obsessive compulsive disorder.

© Asier Romero/Shutterstock.com

Specific Phobias

Most of us have things that scare us. Fear, like anxiety, can be healthy and adaptive! More intense than fear is a **Specific Phobia** which is an intense and paralyzing fear of something that perhaps should be feared but the fear is excessive and unreasonable. With a phobia, the fear is so great that it leads a person to avoid routine activities and thus interferes with life functioning. People can literally have a phobia of anything and it is estimated that about 10% of people struggle with phobias. Common phobias include *Arachnophobia (*fear of spiders), *Claustrophobia* (fear of confined spaces), *Acrophobia* (fear of heights), and *Mysophobia* (fear of germs or dirt). Another very common phobia is **Social Anxiety Disorder (*formerly called Social Phobia*)**. People with this disorder have excessive and inappropriate fears connected with social situations or performances in front of other people in which embarrassment may occur. This fear is incredibly common and probably one of the reasons why speech classes are so unpopular!

© lassedesignen/Shutterstock.com

Phobias are typically thought to be caused by learning and conditioning. Through classical conditioning, two events can become associated with each other and we learn to fear something like spiders, heights, snakes, or the dark. Most people can trace their phobias back to a frightening experience, typically in childhood. I have a terrible phobia of spiders and can trace it back to preschool when I was locked in a bathroom filled with daddy long leg spiders. I was probably only stuck in there for a matter of seconds but it felt like an eternity and with all the spiders in this bathroom, something about that situation must have caused my phobia. That is the earliest memory I have of my fear of spiders! It has also been proposed that people might be more prone to develop certain phobias as there are some that occur more commonly than others.

Panic Attacks

Panic Attacks are another commonly experienced anxiety disorder. Panic attacks are short periodic bouts of panic that occur suddenly, reach a peak within minutes, and then gradually pass. Common symptoms of a panic attack include heart palpitations, tingling in the hands or feet, shortness of breath, sweating, hot or cold flashes, trembling, chest pain, faintness, dizziness, feelings of unreality, and choking sensations. People often become more panicked by the symptoms which can just make things worse. Panic attacks can be brought on by something specific or without apparent reason. When panic attacks happen recurrently, we say a person has **Panic Disorder**; recurrent panic attacks in which the person suddenly experiences intense fear or terror without any reasonable cause. The dread of having another panic attack can cause people to avoid situations that might cause anxiety. Sometimes panic disorder can be accompanied by **Agoraphobia** which involves multiple intense fears of crowds, public places, and other situations that require separation from a source of security

such as the home or in which escape might be difficult. People become afraid to leave their home or place of comfort out of fear that they can't control their environment and might have a panic attack. Common causes of panic attacks are genetics, abnormalities in norepinephrine, activity in a brain area called the locus ceruleus, misinterpreting physiological events within the body, and people having anxiety sensitivity or a tendency to focus on bodily sensations and assess them illogically.

Obsessive Compulsive Disorder

Finally, **Obsessive Compulsive Disorder** is an anxiety disorder in which person feels driven to think disturbing thoughts or to perform senseless rituals. OCD has roots in superstitions and superstitious thinking; a belief or notion not based on reason or knowledge that future events can be influenced or foretold by specific unrelated prior events. Superstitious beliefs are incredibly common and while not problematic, they can go too far and become an issue for someone. In obsessive-compulsive disorder, a person experiences **Obsessions** which are thoughts, images, or impulses that occur over and over again and feel out of their control. A person does not want to have these ideas, finds them disturbing and intrusive, and usually recognizes that they don't really make sense. People with OCD may worry excessively about dirt and germs and be obsessed with the idea that they are contaminated or may contaminate others. Or they may have obsessive fears of having inadvertently harmed

someone else (perhaps while pulling the car out of the driveway), even though they usually know this is not realistic. Obsessions are accompanied by feelings, such as fear, disgust, and doubt.

People with OCD typically try to make their obsessions go away by performing **Compulsions** which are acts a person performs repeatedly, often according to certain "rules." People with an obsession about contamination may wash constantly to the point that their hands become raw and inflamed. A person may repeatedly check that the stove is off because of an obsessive fear of burning the house down. OCD compulsions do not give the person pleasure but are performed to obtain relief from the discomfort caused by the obsessions. In this way, obsessive compulsive disorder is an anxiety disorder because if a person tries to stop their irrational behavior and/or thoughts they experience severe anxiety; the OCD behavior developed to keep anxiety under control.

Obsessive compulsive disorder has several proposed causes. One small contribution to causal factors is Freud's Psychodynamic perspective that asserts OCD is the result of overly harsh toilet training during childhood. While there isn't direct support to this concept, it is a commonly discussed notion and relates to the idea of control in childhood carrying over to control issues in adulthood. Much more supported is the behavioral perspective which explains OCD as the result of learned associations and conditioning. From a cognitive perspective, OCD happens when people begin to blame themselves for superstitious and/or unwanted thoughts and begin expecting that terrible things will happen. Finally, from a biological model, abnormally low levels of serotonin are thought to play a role along with abnormal functioning of the orbitofrontal cortex just above each eye.

Psychosomatic and Somatoform Disorders (Disorders Featuring Somatic Symptoms)

Another group of disorders involve interplay between the psyche (mind) and the soma (body). **Psychosomatic Disorders** are disorders in which there is a real physical illness that is largely caused by psychological factors such as stress and anxiety. Tension headaches are a good example of this in that they are caused by muscle contractions brought on by stress; the headache is real but caused by psychological factors. **Somatoform Disorders** (also commonly referred to as Disorders Featuring Somatic Symptoms) on the other hand are disorders in which there is an apparent physical illness for which there is no organic cause. In other words, physical symptoms are occurring without an identifiable physical cause. People seek help for these symptoms but aren't doing it to consciously mislead others about their physical condition; the symptoms are real to them and not under voluntary control. What is so fascinating about disorders featuring somatic symptoms is that the person is not doing it on purpose! There

have been documented cases where people lose feeling in a limb, go blind, or even make themselves sick without conscious intent! The key again with somatoform disorders is that there is no sense of wanting or guiding the symptoms. Another disorder in this category is **Illness Anxiety Disorder (*formerly Hypochondriasis*)** which is a disorder in which people mistakenly fear that minor changes in their physical functioning indicate a serious disease. All of these psychosomatic and somatoform disorders are thought to be caused by stress and trauma.

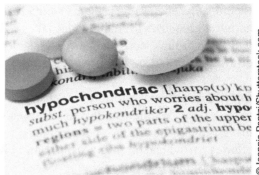

Dissociative Disorders

As a group, dissociative disorders involve some aspect of the personality being separated from the rest and typically involve some form of memory loss and a complete though generally temporary, change of identity. The most well-known disorder in this category is **Dissociative Identity Disorder** which is characterized by the separation of the personality into two or more distinct personalities that routinely take control of a person's behavior and result in memory loss. Dissociative identity disorder is commonly known as Multiple Personality Disorder. With this disorder, personalities are distinct people with their own names, identities, memories, mannerisms, speaking voices, and even IQs and sometimes they are so separate that they don't even know that they inhabit a body with other "people". The relationship between the personalities dictates how difficult this disorder can be to live with. When all of the personalities know about each other, there is drastically less memory loss than when the personalities are unaware of each other or there is one dominant personality.

The origins of this disorder are still not understood. The most common proposal is that this disorder develops as a response to childhood abuse. The thought here is that a traumatic childhood experience is fought off by unconsciously trying to disown and assign those memories to other personalities. Others say it isn't a real disorder at all but rather an elaborate kind of role playing but biological data seems to indicate that it isn't being faked. Though commonly confused, this disorder is different from schizophrenia where there isn't a split in personality but rather in the connections among thoughts.

Personality Disorders

Personality, as discussed previously, is an individual's unique and enduring pattern of thoughts, feelings, and behavior; a unique and long-term pattern of inner experience and outward behavior. We tend to respond in certain ways but we are also flexible, learning from experiences and interacting with our surroundings. **Personality Disorders** are inflexible and maladaptive ways of thinking and behaving learned early in life that cause distress to the person or conflicts with others. These disorders are enduring and rigid patterns of inner experience and outward behavior that impair the sense of self, emotional experiences, goals, capacity

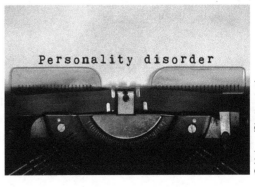

for empathy, and even a person's ability to have intimacy with other people. Personality disorders range from harmless eccentrics to cold-blooded killers. There are ten different personality disorders in the DSM-5 separated into three groups: odd, dramatic, and anxious types. We will focus on two of the most dramatic personality disorders; **Borderline Personality Disorder** and **Antisocial Personality Disorder**.

Borderline personality disorder is characterized by marked instability in self-image, mood, and interpersonal relationships. People with this disorder tend to act impulsively and often self-destructively. Other symptoms that go along with this disorder are frantic efforts to avoid real or imagined abandonment, unstable and intense interpersonal relationships characterized by alternating between extremes of idealization and devaluation, an unstable sense of self, recurrent suicidal behaviors, gestures, threats, or self-mutilation, and inappropriate or intense anger or chronic feelings of emptiness.

© pathdoc/Shutterstock.com

Antisocial personality disorder involves a pattern of violent, criminal, or unethical and exploitative behavior and an inability to feel affection for others. People with this disorder lie, steal, cheat, and show little or no sense of responsibility, guilt, or remorse; they are likely to blame society or even their victims. People with Antisocial personality disorder often seem intelligent and charming but it is often a superficial charm. In order to be diagnosed with this disorder, a person must be at least 18 and have shown a pervasive pattern of disregard for and violation of the rights of others since age 15. Other symptoms include a failure to conform to social norms which often includes repeatedly breaking the law, a reckless disregard for the safety of others, and a lack of remorse.

Personality disorders are thought to be related to a multidimensional risk perspective meaning that multiple factors build upon each other to cause a disorder. Cognitive factors include having broad maladaptive assumptions and dichotomous thinking patterns. Psychoanalytic factors include poor early interactions with parents, loss of abandonment by a parent, early traumas, and absence of parental love during infancy leading to a lack of basic trust in the world. Biological contributors to personality disorders are thought to include genetics, imbalances in neurotransmitters, and slower or decreased autonomic nervous system arousal which might lead people to take risks and seek thrills. Behavioral factors are things such as family dysfunction and conflicts, modeling, being treated too positively or negatively leading to an inferiority or superiority complex, and ridicule or embarrassing moments in childhood leading to a negative self-image. It is thought to be some combination of all these factors in addition to social and cultural ones that build upon each other to make someone at risk for personality disorders.

Mood Disorders

Most people's moods come and go but sometimes moods persist. Mood disorders are disturbances in mood or prolonged emotional states; psychological disorders characterized by emotional extremes. There are two ends or poles to the mood spectrum, the low end (depression) and the high end (mania) with a range of normal or typical mood in between. People can struggle with one or both ends of mood leading to several different disorders depending on the symptoms being displayed. We will focus on two of the more common mood disorders; **Major Depressive Disorder** and **Bipolar Disorder**.

Major depressive disorder is a mood disorder characterized by overwhelming feelings of sadness, lack of interest in activities, and possibly excessive guilt or feelings of worthlessness. People with depression lose interest in things they used to enjoy, they are tired, apathetic, and

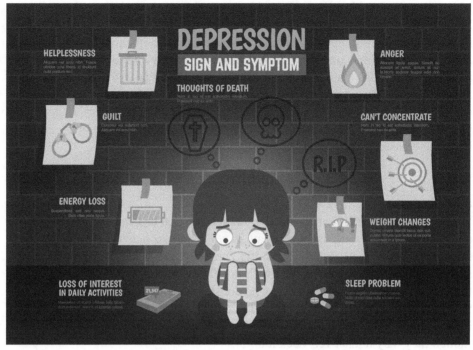

often unable to make even the simplest of decisions. Other symptoms people often suffer from include insomnia, loss of interest in food and sex, having trouble thinking or concentrating, and the possibility of becoming suicidal. Depression is different from feeling down or having the blues and psychologists and counselors are trained to diagnose and distinguish between the two. I once heard a psychologist describe major depression as feeling like the anguish of grief combined with the sluggishness of jet lag and that stuck with me as an amazing description of this very low state of mood.

Mania is a state of mood characterized by euphoric states, extreme physical activity, excessive talkativeness, distractedness, and sometimes grandiosity. Someone in a manic state might have unlimited hopes and schemes but no interest in realistically carrying them out. They might also become wild, incomprehensible, or violent until they collapse from exhaustion. The mood disorder in which both mania and depression are present is known as bipolar disorder. In bipolar disorder, periods of mania and depression can alternate with periods of normal mood intervening. Bipolar disorder can be very challenging not only for the person struggling with it, but also for the people in their life. It can almost feel like two different people

as a person alternates between depression and mania. In a depressed state, a person feels worthless, might sleep all the time, and is overcome with hopelessness. When they switch to mania, that same person now has grandiosity, sleeps very little, they are full of energy, talk all the time and rapidly, and have unlimited hopes and schemes.

Mood disorders are thought to result from a combination of biological, psychological, and social risk factors. Some of the biological factors thought to play a role in mood disorders are genetics and chemical imbalances in the brain of certain neurotransmitters like serotonin, dopamine, and norepinephrine. Psychological factors include illogical and maladaptive responses to events called **Cognitive Distortions**. These illogical and maladaptive responses are often learned early in life and lead to feelings of incompetence and unworthiness that are reactivated whenever a new situation arises that resembles the original events. People who are depressed tend to think very in very illogical ways which only contributes to more depression; depression can be a very vicious cycle. Social factors might also contribute as people struggle in interpersonal relationships which might lead to increased feelings of loneliness and/or isolation.

Suicide

Suicidality is very commonly linked to depression and bipolar disorder. Suicide is a self-inflicted death in which a person acts intentionally or directly to take their life. People who consider suicide are typically overwhelmed with hopelessness and feel that things cannot get better. People who consider suicide often see no way out of their difficulties and don't feel like things will ever change or get better. Most suicidal people want help even though they may not actively seek it out.

© pimchawee/Shutterstock.com

There are quite a few warning signs to look for that might indicate that someone is contemplating suicide. Some of the signs to worry about include: talking about dying, recent losses, changes in personality, changes in behavior, changes in sleep patterns, low self-esteem, no hope for the future, and giving away prized possessions. If someone that you know is showing some of these signs, it is important to react and take it seriously. I think that it is always better to overreact than to underreact; someone will forgive you for caring too much about them but can you forgive yourself for not doing enough if something were to happen? Some of the things you can to do help someone who is suicidal are to let them know that they matter, give them a hug, don't leave them alone, connect them with resources such as a suicide prevention hotline, therapist, or counselor, and to try and keep them busy. Unfortunately, sometimes there is only so much that you can do so it is important to remember that and always keep your safety in mind as well.

Schizophrenia

it is a common misconception that schizophrenia is the same as having multiple personalities which is under the category of dissociative disorders covered earlier. What is split in schizophrenia is not the personality as much as it is the connection among thoughts. **Schizophrenia** is a severe disorder, in which there are disturbances of thoughts, communications, emotions, and delusions and hallucinations. Someone struggling with schizophrenia is typically out of touch with reality (psychotic) and has a wide variety of symptoms from three main categories: *positive*, *negative*, and *psychomotor* symptoms. *Positive symptoms* are symptoms of schizophrenia that seem to be excesses of or bizarre additions to normal thoughts, emotions, or

© Cherednychenko Ihor/Shutterstock.com

behaviors. One common positive symptom are **Hallucinations** or sensory experiences in the absence of external stimuli with hearing voices that aren't there being the most common. The other common positive symptom are **Delusions** which are false beliefs about reality that have no basis in facts. Most commonly these delusions are paranoid (believe that someone is out to harm them) though people can also have delusions of grandeur believing they are someone of great importance.

Negative symptoms of schizophrenia are symptoms that seem to be deficits in normal thought, emotions, or behaviors. Common negative symptoms include alogia (poverty of speech), flat or blunted affect, loss of volition (feeling drained of energy and interest), and also social withdrawal. *Psychomotor symptoms* of schizophrenia are awkward movements, repeated grimaces, or odd gestures which often have a private purpose. Sometimes people with extreme psychomotor symptoms will exhibit a catatonic state including rigidity or posturing.

Because schizophrenia is such a serious disorder, considerable research has been conducted trying to discover its causes. Many studies indicate a genetic component that may relate to a faulty regulation of the neurotransmitters dopamine and glutamate in the central nervous system, pathology in various structures of the brain, or prenatal disturbance. Environmental factors are also believed to contribute and include disturbed family relations, the level of expressed emotions in households, drug use, etc. It is commonly believed that schizophrenia is the result of an interaction of factors.

Disorders of Childhood

People tend to think of childhood as a very happy and carefree time but it can also be very upsetting and marked by difficulties. Adolescence can also be incredibly difficult and various pressures can lead to depression, anxiety, and several other issues. It is estimated that 1 out of 5 children and adolescents have a diagnosable disorder. While there are several childhood disorders, we will focus on two of the more common ones, attention-deficit hyperactivity disorder and autistic spectrum disorder.

Attention-Deficit Hyperactivity Disorder is a childhood disorder characterized by inattention, impulsiveness, and hyperactivity. Children with this disorder are easily distracted, often fidgety, and impulsive and almost constantly in motion. This disorder typically manifests itself in the school age child as school demands that children sit quietly, pay attention as instructed, follow directions, and inhibit their urges to yell and run around; children with ADHD cannot conform to these demands. ADHD can also sometimes include communication or learning problems or lead to anxiety or mood issues. For many people with this disorder, symptoms tend to decrease with age though some adults continue to have ADHD. ADHD is also more common in boys than girls. Some of the proposed causes of attention-deficit hyperactive disorder are biological contributors like abnormal dopamine levels, deficiencies in the frontal lobe, and genetics.

Another childhood disorder is **Autistic Spectrum Disorder**; a group of disorders marked by impaired social interactions, unusual communications, and inappropriate responses to stimuli in the environment. Autistic spectrum disorder is a pervasive developmental disorder marked by extreme unresponsiveness to others, poor communication skills, and highly repetitive and rigid behavior. This disorder tends to appears before age three and is more common in boys than girls and as many as 90% remain severely impaired into adulthood having difficulty maintaining jobs, doing household tasks, and living independent lives. Symptoms of autistic spectrum disorder include a *lack of responsiveness* (lack of interest in other people and inability to share attention with other people), *language and communication problems* (failing to speak, echoing of phrases spoken by others, pronoun reversals, using abstract language, or difficulty understanding speech), *repetitive and rigid behavior* (become very upset by minor changes in routine, objects, or people or may become

© nito/Shutterstock.com

fascinated by a movement or object for hours), and *motor movements* (engage in self-stimulatory behaviors or self-injurious behaviors such as banging their head against the wall). In terms of causes, it was originally thought that family dysfunction and social stress were the primary causes but research has not supported these notions. From a psychological viewpoint, it is thought that people with autistic spectrum disorder fail to develop theory of mind which is the awareness that other people base their behaviors on their own beliefs, intentions, and other mental states, not on information that they have no way of knowing. By age 3 to 5 most children can take another person's perspective. It is thought that children with autistic spectrum disorder fail to develop this possibly as a result of biological problems that may result from a genetic factor or chromosomal abnormalities, birth complications, or biological abnormalities (abnormalities in the cerebellum which deals with movement and attention or neurotransmitter abnormalities).

Disorders of Aging

Old age in our society is usually defined as the years past the age of 65. Like childhood, old age brings special pressures, unique upsets, and major biological changes. People become more prone to illness and injury, and suffer more losses of former activities and roles along with spouses and friends. One common category of disorders of aging include the **Dementias (Neurocognitive Disorders)** which are syndromes marked by severe problems in memory and in at least one other cognitive function. There are several different types of neurocognitive disorders but the

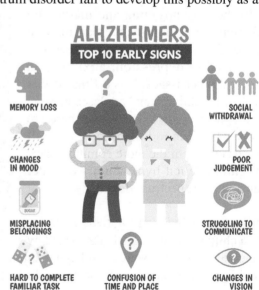

© Falara/Shutterstock.com

most common type is **Alzheimer's Disease**; named after Alois Alzheimer who identified the first case in 1901. Alzheimer's disease is the most common neurocognitive disorder, usually occurring after the age of 65. The timeframe between onset and death is typically 8 to 10 years. Alzheimer's usually begins with mild memory problems, lapses of attention, and difficulties in language and communication but as symptoms worsen, people eventually have trouble with simple tasks and changes in personality often become noticeable. People tend to be unaware of their difficulties as they worsen and sometimes withdraw from others and may become confused about the time and place. They may even lose all recognition of familiar faces and become completely reliant on others for care.

Alzheimer's can only be diagnosed with certainty after death when structural changes in the person's brain can be fully examined. The disorder is thought to be caused by **Neurofibrillary Tangles** which are twisted protein fibers that form within certain brain cells as people age. People with Alzheimer's disease have an excessive number of such tangles. **Senile Plaques** or sphere-shaped deposits of beta-amyloid protein that form in spaces between certain brain cells and in certain blood vessels as people age are also thought to play a role as people with Alzheimer's disease have an excessive number. Alzheimer's is thought to have a genetic component if it occurs before the age of 65. Abnormalities in proteins in key brain cells and in neurotransmitters such as Acetylcholine (ACH) and Glutamate are linked to the disease. Other causal factors look at the role of toxins in the environment and damage to the brain.

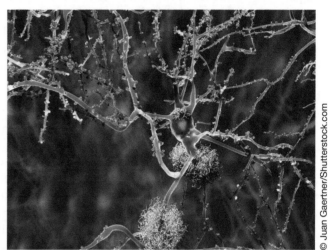

© Juan Gaertner/Shutterstock.com

In Popular Culture

- *As Good As It Gets* (1997) – a movie about a character suffering from obsessive compulsive disorder.

- *Matchstick Men* (2003) – a movie with a character suffering from obsessive compulsive disorder.

- *Arachnophobia* (1990) – a classic movie portraying someone with a specific phobia of spiders.

- *Girl, Interrupted* (1999) – a movie and book about a young woman with borderline personality disorder.

- *Shutter Island* (2010) – a movie featuring a portrayal of dissociative identity disorder.

- *The Number 23* (2007) – a movie highlighting delusions around the number 23.

- *The Soloist* (2009) – a movie about a man suffering from schizophrenia.

- *A Beautiful Mind* (2001) – a movie showing a portrayal of schizophrenia.

- *Black Swan* (2010) – a movie about a ballet dancer struggling with schizophrenia.

- *Silver Linings Playbook* (2012) – a movie featuring a main character suffering from bipolar disorder and several other characters also struggling with mental illness.

- *Split* (2016) – a movie about a character with 23 different personalities (dissociative identity disorder).

- *United States of Tara* (2009–2011) – a television show about a mom with multiple personalities.

- *Hoarders* (2009–2013) – a television show about OCD and hoarding behaviors.

- *Dexter* (2006–2013) – a television show about a character with antisocial personality disorder.
- *Bates Motel* (2013–2017) – a television show about Norman Bates and his battle with dissociative identity disorder.

Psyched with Setmire

"Models of Abnormality (Explaining Mental Illness)"
https://www.youtube.com/watch?v=6LcmcYQ5wBI&t=1s

In this lecture presentation video (adapted from my Introduction to Psychology course lecture), I will cover the concept of models of abnormality including a definition of models and how they set the stage for treatment along with a discussion of the medical model, psychoanalytic model, cognitive-behavioral model, diathesis-stress model, and the systems (biopsychosocial) model.

Application: Suicidality and Getting Help

There is often a relationship between mood disorders and suicidality. People who consider suicide are overwhelmed with hopelessness feeling that things cannot get better and seeing no way out of their difficulties. If you know someone who may be suicidal, getting them professional help is urgent. Some warning signs for suicidality include talking about dying, recent loss, change in personality, change in behavior, low self-esteem, no hope for the future, and many others. Below are links to two websites that discuss suicide in detail, if you or someone you know might be suicidal, this is a good place to start for further information:

- www.sprc.org – Suicide Prevention Resource Center's website with tips for suicide prevention along with resources and training programs.
- http://www.cdc.gov/ViolencePrevention/suicide/ – a website from the Center for Disease Control discussing statistics, resources, and prevention information related to suicide.
- https://www.nimh.nih.gov/health/topics/suicide-prevention/index.shtml – National Institute of Mental Health's website filled with information and resources for people struggling with suicidality.
- *National Suicide Prevention Lifeline*: 1-800-273-8255 – a 24-hour suicide prevention hotline.

The best thing you can do if you suspect that someone may be suicidal is to not leave them alone and to contact someone who can help you to ensure their safety! Most college campuses have a health center with a licensed psychologist or nurses who are trained to recognize signs of suicidality or to provide assistance for people dealing with psychological disorders. You can also call the friend, partner, or parents of someone you are concerned about and express your concern. If all else fails or if you feel the person is in serious immediate danger, you can call the police.

Key Terms

Psychological Disorder: patterns of behavioral or psychological symptoms that impact multiple areas of life creating distress for the person experiencing these symptoms.

Model: a set of assumptions and concepts that helps scientists explain and interpret observations; also called a paradigm.

Biological (Medical) Model: the model of abnormality that views disorders as having a biochemical or physiological basis.

Psychoanalytic Model: the model of abnormality that views disorders as a result of unconscious internal conflicts mainly occurring during early childhood.

Cognitive-Behavioral Model: the model of abnormality that views disorders as a result of learning maladaptive ways of thinking and behaving.

Diathesis-Stress Model: the model of abnormality that views disorders resulting from a biological predisposition to a mental disorder that is triggered by an environmental stressor.

Systems Approach (Biopsychosocial): the model of abnormality that views disorders as a result of biological, psychological, and social risk factors.

Diagnostic and Statistical Manual of Mental Disorders (DSM-5): the most widely used classification of psychological disorders; provides a complete list of all recognized mental illnesses.

Anxiety: feelings of fear and apprehension that are identifiable, appropriate, and pass with time.

Anxiety Disorders: disorders in which the person either doesn't know why he or she is afraid, or the anxiety is inappropriate to the circumstances.

Specific Phobia: intense and paralyzing fear of something that perhaps should be feared but the fear is excessive and unreasonable.

Social Anxiety Disorder (*formerly Social Phobia*): excessive and inappropriate fears connected with social situations or performances in front of other people in which embarrassment may occur.

Panic Attacks: short periodic bouts of panic that occur suddenly, reach a peak within minutes, and then gradually pass.

Panic Disorder: recurrent panic attacks in which the person suddenly experiences intense fear or terror without any reasonable cause.

Agoraphobia: involves multiple intense fears of crowds, public places, and other situations that require separation from a source of security such as the home or in which escape might be difficult.

Obsessive Compulsive Disorder: anxiety disorder in which person feels driven to think disturbing thoughts or to perform senseless rituals.

Obsessions are thoughts, images, or impulses that occur over and over again and feel out of your control.

Compulsions acts the person performs over and over again, often according to certain "rules."

Psychosomatic Disorders: a disorder in which there is real physical illness that is largely caused by psychological factors such as stress and anxiety.

Somatoform Disorders (Disorders Featuring Somatic Symptoms): disorders in which there is an apparent physical illness for which there is no organic cause; a physical illness or ailment that is explained largely by psychosocial causes, in which the patient experiences no sense of wanting or guiding the symptoms.

Illness Anxiety Disorder (*formerly Hypochondriasis*): a disorder in which people mistakenly fear that minor changes in their physical functioning indicate a serious disease.

Dissociative Identity Disorder: Disorder characterized by the separation of the personality into two or more distinct personalities that routinely take control of a person's behavior and memory loss.

Personality: individual's unique and enduring pattern of thoughts, feelings, and behavior.

Personality Disorders: disorders in which inflexible and maladaptive ways of thinking and behaving learned early in life cause distress to the person or conflicts with others.

Borderline Personality Disorder: a personality disorder characterized by marked instability in self-image, mood, and interpersonal relationships.

Antisocial Personality Disorder: a personality disorder characterized by a pattern of violent, criminal, or unethical and exploitative behavior and an inability to feel affection for others.

Major Depressive Disorder: a mood disorder characterized by overwhelming feelings of sadness, lack of interest in activities, and possibly excessive guilt or feelings of worthlessness.

Mania: a mood disorder characterized by euphoric states, extreme physical activity, excessive talkativeness, distractedness, and sometimes grandiosity.

Bipolar Disorder: a mood disorder in which periods of mania and depression alternate, sometimes with periods of normal mood intervening.

Cognitive Distortions: an illogical and maladaptive response to early negative life events that leads to feelings of incompetence and unworthiness that are reactivated whenever a new situation arises that resembles the original events.

Schizophrenic Disorders: severe disorders, in which there are disturbances of thoughts, communications, and emotions, including delusions and hallucinations.

Hallucinations: sensory experience in the absence of external stimuli.

Delusions: false beliefs about reality that have no basis in facts.

Attention-Deficit Hyperactivity Disorder: a disorder of childhood characterized by inattention, impulsiveness, and hyperactivity.

Autistic Spectrum Disorder: a disorder of childhood; a group of disorders marked by impaired social interactions, unusual communications, and inappropriate responses to stimuli in the environment.

Dementia (Neurocognitive Disorder): a syndrome marked by severe problems in memory and in at least one other cognitive function.

Alzheimer's Disease: the most common neurocognitive disorder, usually occurring after the age of 65.

Neurofibrillary Tangles: twisted protein fibers that form within certain brain cells as people age.

Senile Plaques: sphere-shaped deposits of beta-amyloid protein that form in spaces between certain brain cells and in certain blood vessels as people age.

Chapter 15

Therapies

Outline

Introduction to the Chapter (Summary)

In the past, we have treated psychological disorders through a variety of methods such as cutting holes in the head, controlled bleeding, administering drugs, electric shock, giving continuous baths and massages, and even through exorcisms. Luckily a growing sentiment that people should be treated with respect and dignity became popular throughout the 1900's and helped lead to more humane (and successful) treatments such as psychotherapy.

One group of therapies are the insight therapies which are designed to give people a better awareness and understanding of their feelings, motivations, and actions in the hope that this will help them to adjust. There are three major insight therapies: Psychoanalysis, Client-Centered (Person-Centered) therapy, and Gestalt Therapy. Another group of therapies are the behavioral therapies which are based on the belief that all behavior, normal and abnormal, is learned and therefore the objective of therapy is to teach people new, more satisfying ways of behaving. There are many techniques used by behaviorists to treat clients including token economy, exposure therapy (flooding), and systematic desensitization. Cognitive therapies are another branch and emphasize changing clients' perceptions of their life situation as a way of modifying their behavior. Therapists examine dysfunctional thoughts in a supportive but objective manner by looking for evidence to help the person be more realistic and flexible in their thinking. A last cluster of therapies are ones that involve more than one person receiving treatment including group therapy, and couples therapy. Group therapies embrace the notion that it is our interactions with other people that can create or maintain dysfunction so it is therefore important to treat all people involved rather than just one individual.

Therapy has been shown to be helpful (roughly twice as many people improve with therapy than with no treatment at all) and appears to be most helpful for people with relatively mild psychological problems, those who are motivated to change, and those who have long-term vs. short-term therapy. In general, it doesn't appear that one type of therapy is better than another. More important than the type is the instillation of hope, therapeutic alliance, and providing an explanation for problems that comes with all types of therapy. Certain types of therapies are better for certain types of problems but the current trend in therapy is toward eclecticism. There are a couple of alternative therapies worth mentioning such as EMDR which stands for eye movement desensitization and reprocessing and also light exposure therapy.

Biological (Biomedical) treatments are a group of approaches including medication, brain stimulation techniques, and psychosurgery that are sometimes used to treat psychological disorders in conjunction with, or instead of, psychotherapy. Sometimes people are too agitated, disoriented, or unresponsive to be helped by therapy. Drug therapies often cost less than therapy and often take effect faster. There are several classes of drugs such as antipsychotic drugs, antianxiety drugs, antidepressant drugs, mood-stabilizers, and several others such as sedatives, and psychostimulants. Electroconvulsive therapy (ECT) involves a mild electrical current being passed through the brain for a short period, often producing convulsions and temporary coma. ECT and other brain stimulation methods like transcranial magnetic stimulation are often used to treat severe, prolonged depression when medications and therapy have failed. It is also common for people with intense psychological disorders to be hospitalized for treatment though the current trend is deinstitutionalization.

History of Treatment

Just like with viewing mental illness, there is a dark history of treating mental illness. Throughout time we have treated psychological disorders through a variety of methods such as cutting holes in the head, by restraining people, by bleeding people with leeches, by administering drugs or electric shock, giving warm baths and massages, exorcisms, throwing people into asylums without care, and eventually through therapy. Because mental illness was viewed as the work of evil spirits, exorcisms and trephinations were commonly practiced for many years with the goal of coaxing

© MichyD/Shutterstock.com

spirits out of the body. The **Asylum**, a type of institution that first became popular in the 16th century to provide care for persons with mental disorders, was invented with good intentions to help combat some of the cruel and ineffective treatments of mental illness. While asylums began with good intentions of providing care, most became prisons where patients were held in filthy conditions and subject to cruelty. The idea behind them was to take people away from their stressors and put them in a large house out in the country where they could be at peace. Unfortunately, a lack of funding, resources, and knowledge to treat mental illness lead to horrible conditions

and all the negative associations most of us have with the word asylum. The most infamous of the asylums was Bethlehem Hospital in London. The name Bethlehem evolved over time to "Bedlam" which means madness or chaos. This massive hospital was the first hospital in London used for the "insane" or the "mad".

In wasn't until the late 1800s that we saw a shift away from massive hospitals and asylums to a smaller one on one approach. Freud helped to advance the idea of the "talking cure" which later became known as **Psychotherapy** or the use of psychological techniques to treat psychological disorders. In this chapter, we will explore several different types of therapies and therapeutic techniques that are commonly used today.

Types of Clinicians

There are many different modalities of treatment and many different types of clinicians. It can sometimes be a bit overwhelming trying to decide what type of services to seek and from whom! In general, most people seeking counseling services will see one of the following types of professionals: counseling psychologists, clinical psychologists, psychiatrists, social workers, or medical doctors. **Counseling Psychologists** generally have a master's degree and are often marriage and family therapists (MFTs) who help people with problems of everyday life such as stress, relationships, anxiety, and so on. **Clinical Psychologists** typically have a Ph.D. and have expertise in assessment and psycho-

logical disorders. Clinical psychologists often work with populations suffering from more severe disorders such as schizophrenia or bipolar disorder. **Psychiatrists** specialize in prescribing medications for the treatment of psychological disorders. Psychiatrists have a M.D. and are therefore trained in physiology. Appointments with Psychiatrists are often shorter and are focused around medications and discussing side effects that go along with them. **Social Workers** typically have a master's degree and work with the institutions of society helping to mediate the relationships between people, families, school systems, and legal systems. Finally, **Medical Doctors** have a medical degree and specialize in physical treatments. People often start here and are then referred to counseling services by their primary physician. General family doctors can prescribe medications but often will refer to someone with more specialized knowledge.

Box: Common Stereotypes of Therapy and Therapists

As a culture, we often have very negative connotations and attitudes about therapy and therapists. Here are some common stereotypes about therapy and therapists:

- Therapists always ask "How does that make you feel?" or "Tell me more about that . . ."
- In therapy, you will be laying on a couch
- There is a fountain or Zen garden somewhere in the office
- Therapists wear glasses
- Therapists are always taking notes
- Therapists have baggage or problems themselves which is why they became a therapist
- Therapists are bobble heads (always nodding)
- Therapists only care about money
- There are probably lots of college degrees on the wall
- Therapists are always analyzing people even off the job
- You are going to talk about your mother and childhood at some point in therapy
- Only people with problems go to therapy

These are all very commonly held stereotypes and opinions about therapy! As a side note, many people call therapists "shrinks". If you were ever curious, the term "shrink" originates from headshrinker and is a disparaging reference comparing the process of psychotherapy to primitive tribal practices of shrinking the heads of enemies!

Every clinician will have their own theoretical orientation for how they provide services. Some therapists are very direct and give a high amount of guidance. Others sit back and let you control the sessions and your treatment. It is important to find someone whose approach matches your needs so feel free to look around and even try out a couple of clinicians before settling on the one that you like best!

© Max4e Photo/Shutterstock.com

Insight Therapies

The first group of therapies that we will discuss are the **Insight Therapies** which are a variety of individual psychotherapies designed to give people a better awareness and understanding of their feelings, motivations, and actions in the hope that this will help them to adjust. There are three major insight therapies: **Psychoanalysis**, **Client-Centered Therapy**, and **Gestalt Therapy**.

Psychoanalysis is a theory of personality and a form of therapy invented by Freud designed to bring hidden feelings and motives to conscious awareness so that the person can deal with them more effectively. Freud invented therapy and this was the type of therapy that he practiced with his clients. One of the techniques that Freud used heavily is **Free Association** which is a technique that encourages the person to talk without inhibition about whatever thoughts or fantasies come to mind. Freud believed that this stream of consciousness would provide insight into the client's mind. In therapy, clients would lay on a couch with the therapist seated behind them out of sight. The client is encouraged to talk about anything that comes to mind without editing or censoring it in any way. This type of therapy is still practiced today but doesn't tend to be popular with insurance companies as it can be very lengthy in nature.

Client-Centered (Person-Centered) Therapy is non-directional form of insight therapy developed by Carl Rogers that calls for unconditional positive regard of the client by the therapist with the goal of helping the client become a fully functioning person. The focus of client-centered therapy is on insight into current feelings rather than unconscious past wishes or feelings. Rogers believed that responsibility for change is on the person with the problem while the therapist tries to understand things from the client's point of view. This type of therapy is incredibly non-directive in nature which sometimes proves frustrating for those who go to therapy seeking active guidance or advice. The last insight therapy is Gestalt Therapy which emphasizes the wholeness of the personality and attempts to reawaken people to their emotions and sensations in the present. Gestalt therapy emphasizes the here and now and trying to help people become more genuine in their daily interactions. The therapist's goal is to fill in the holes in personality to help make the person complete again. This type of therapy is much more direct than client-centered therapy as the clinician will often "skillfully frustrate" the client to challenge their nonverbal versus verbal reactions.

Behavioral Therapies

Another approach, completely different from focusing on gaining insight, are the **Behavior Therapies**; therapeutic approaches that are based on the belief that all behavior, normal and abnormal, is learned and that the objective of therapy is to teach people new, more satisfying ways of behaving. The focus here is on changing behaviors rather than insights, thoughts, or feelings, in other words, maladaptive behaviors are the problem not symptoms of deeper underlying causes. One technique commonly used for treatment in this framework is a **Token Economy**. Token economies are an operant conditioning therapy in which people earn tokens or points (reinforcers) for desired behaviors and exchange them for desired items or privileges. This technique is often used in schools or hospitals though the positive changes in behavior don't always generalize to everyday life. When I was growing up, my brother and I used to fight horribly! He would dig his fingers into his arm and tell our parents that I did it so I would get into trouble and I would break things and tell them he did it so that he got into trouble. We hated each other as kids (thankfully that has changed drastically now that we are adults). My parents created

a token economy to try and help us to stop fighting. Every day that we didn't fight we would get a sticker and once we had a certain number of stickers, we could trade them in for a prize that we wanted. Five stickers was enough to earn a trip to get ice cream so I never made it beyond five stickers! One day, my brother and I, thinking we were brilliant and beating the system, decided that we wouldn't fight anymore so that we could get more stickers. We thought we were beating the system when the system was working perfectly!

Behavioral therapies are often used to help treat anxiety disorders such as phobias. There are two different methods that can be used to treat phobias, **Exposure Therapy (Flooding)** and **Systematic Desensitization**. Exposure therapies or flooding are full-intensity exposures to a feared stimulus for a prolonged period. Flooding is a very intense and sometimes massive exposure to a phobic stimulus with the goal of teaching people that anxiety levels will reach a peak and then gradually decrease. If someone had a phobia of heights for example, flooding therapy would have them climb to the top of the tallest building that we can find to face that fear head on. Clients will experience great anxiety, cry, swear, and be incredibly upset but at some point, during the treatment, their anxiety peaks and then starts to come back down. The theory is that if you can endure going up fifty stories, then two or three stories shouldn't bother you! I had a student a few years ago, who decided to try and do flooding on her own! She was also terrified of heights so she decided to face that fear by going sky diving. She shared with the class that she had to literally be thrown out of the plane and that she was screaming, swearing, and crying the entire way down toward the earth. She went back and jumped out of a plane a second and third time and with each jump, her fear of heights was lessened. Impressive! I'm terrified of spiders and I don't think that I would be willing to face that fear through flooding, let alone on my own!

The other technique is Systematic Desensitization which is a technique for reducing a person's fear and anxiety by gradually associating a new response (relaxation) with stimuli that have been causing the fear and anxiety. In this approach, a therapist creates a hierarchy of fears from the least to the most anxiety provoking and then teaches client relaxation techniques. From there, the two are paired together and they move up the hierarchy. Sticking with the heights example, rather than facing the fear massively and head on, from this approach you would gradually move up the fear hierarchy. The therapist would take the client up to three stories and have them rate their anxiety and fear level on a scale of 0–100. Then there would be deep breathing and relaxation exercises to lower that anxiety level. Once a person can handle three stories, they would move up to four, then five, and so on. This approach is much slower than flooding but more people tend to be willing to give it a try since it is much less intense and invasive.

Cognitive Therapies

Another approach to treatment are the **Cognitive Therapies** which are psychotherapies that emphasize changing clients' perceptions of their life situation as a way of modifying their behavior. If people can change their distorted ideas about themselves and the world, then they can also change their problems to make life more enjoyable. This approach looks at erroneous and illogical ways of thinking and then how to correct them. Therapists examine dysfunctional thoughts in a supportive but objective manner looking for evidence to help the person be more realistic and flexible in their thinking.

Group Therapies

There are a few different therapies that involve more than one person being in treatment. Most of the ones we have discussed so far are conducted one on one whereas group, family, and couples therapy all involve multiple people in the therapy sessions. **Group Therapy** is a type of psychotherapy in which clients meet regularly to interact and help one another achieve insight into their feelings and behavior. There are several advantages to group therapy over individual therapy. Meeting in groups can offer social support and the opportunity for group members to help each other learn useful new behaviors. Group therapy can also be less expensive than individual therapy since several clients are sharing a therapist. Take for example a group that meets for the treatment of

eating disorders. As the people in that group share their stories, all the members can relate and understand the gravity of what they are saying. When a group member shares that they ate a piece of pizza and didn't throw it up, all the other members understand the significance of that action which can lead to a feeling of not being alone with an issue.

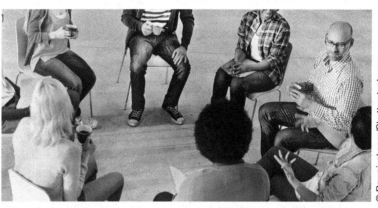

Family Therapy is another form of group therapy that sees the family as at least partly responsible for the individual's problems and that seeks to change all the family members' behaviors to the benefit of the family unit as well as the troubled individual. Some of the most common trouble spots and areas of focus for family therapists are improving family communication, encouraging empathy, getting family members to share responsibilities, and reducing conflict. A family might even be in therapy just to get help with coping with the impact of a disorder on the unit. While this type of therapy is notoriously unpopular

with children and teenagers, it can prove helpful for those willing to consider it.

Finally, **Couples Therapy** is a form of group therapy intended to help troubled partners improve their problems of communication and interaction. This type of therapy might carry one of the biggest stigmas of all therapy modalities with a common stereotype of couples only going as a last-ditch effort to save their relationship. In reality, most couples could benefit from couples counseling and having a neutral third party as a bit of a mediator and sometimes translator. Common issues that bring people into couples therapy are communication problems, issues around sex, and also struggles with the division of responsibilities. Often times a couples therapist will begin by having the partners describe how they first met as a way of softening and easing into therapy. There are also typically questionnaires or inventories that might be given in-person or to take home that will help the therapist to evaluate what the problem areas are in the relationship. When I was training to be a marriage and family therapist, I loved and yet feared this type of counseling. I found it incredibly interesting but when we love someone, things can get very heated for better or for worse. I always worried

slightly that the couple might kill each other before the next session! I am joking of course but it is important to lay down boundaries as things can quickly get escalated and there isn't always time to work through an issue before the session ends!

The Effectiveness of Psychotherapy

In general, therapy has been shown to be helpful; roughly twice as many people improve with therapy than with no treatment at all. What we have noticed is that therapy appears to be most helpful for people with relatively mild psychological problems, those who are motivated to change, and those who have access to long-term vs. short-term therapy. If you go into therapy with the mindset that it won't help you, then it likely won't help you. Motivation and a desire to make improvements can go a long way in increasing the likelihood of progress.

A common question people ask is "Is there a best type of therapy?" In general, it doesn't appear that one type of therapy is better than another. More important than the type are certain factors involved in the therapeutic relationship such as an instillation of hope, the therapeutic alliance, and helping to provide an explanation for problems. It is true though that certain types of therapies are better for certain types of problems. For example, cognitive therapy tends to be successful for treating depression and behavioral therapies tend to be successful in the treatment of phobias. So more than being one best type, there are better types for certain disorders and for certain people. The current trend in therapy is toward **Eclecticism** which is a psychotherapeutic approach that recognizes the value of a broad treatment package over a rigid commitment to one form of therapy.

Alternative Therapies

There are a handful of alternative therapies worth mentioning. These therapeutic approaches are either not commonly used and/or they might lack the evidence needed to make them a more standard method of treatment. Once such example is **Eye Movement Desensitization and**

Reprocessing (EMDR) which is a psychotherapy technique designed to help alleviate the symptoms of PTSD. The goal of EMDR is to reduce the long-lasting effects of distressing memories by engaging the brain's natural adaptive information processing mechanisms, thereby relieving present symptoms. The therapy uses a multiple phase approach that includes having the patient recall distressing images while receiving one of several types of bilateral sensory input, such as side to side eye movements. This is typically accomplished using a small machine that has a light moving from side to side that patients are instructed to follow with their eyes while thinking about their traumatic experiences. The working mechanisms that underlie the effectiveness of the eye movements in EMDR therapy are still under investigation and there is as yet no definitive finding.

Another alternative therapy is **Light Exposure Therapy** which is often used to treat Seasonal Affective Disorder (SAD). SAD, which is the best acronym you could ask for with a disorder, is thought to result from the dark and overcast period of winter. In some portions of the world, the sun rarely comes out during the winter months and there are people who are more sensitive to that change and might develop a seasonal depression. In order to treat SAD, clinicians give clients a dose of intense light from a light box for a prescribed period of time each day. The results show that it is often helpful in improving SAD symptoms.

Biological Treatments

In addition to the more therapy based options we have talked about so far, there are also several **Biological (Biomedical) Treatments** available to people struggling with mental illness. The biological treatments are a group of approaches, including medication, electroconvulsive therapy, and psychosurgery, that are sometimes used to treat psychological disorders in conjunction with, or instead of, psychotherapy. Sometimes people are too agitated, disoriented, or unresponsive to be helped by therapy. Biological treatments are almost always used for disorders with a biological component and also for people who are a danger to themselves and to others.

Drug Therapies

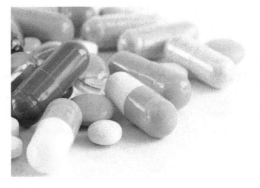

© areeya_ann/Shutterstock.com

An incredibly common modality of treatment in our culture is the use of medications or drugs to help with mental illness. Drug treatments often cost less than therapy and can be faster if the right drug and dosage are found quickly. Currently there are several very effective medications that are prescribed to help alleviate the symptoms associated with psychological disorders. **Psychopharmacology** is the study of the effects of drugs on mind and behavior and in this case, is examining the effects of drugs such as antidepressant drugs, antipsychotic drugs, mood stabilizers, benzodiazepines, psychostimulants, and several other categories of medications.

One of the most commonly prescribed groups of medications are the **Antidepressant Drugs** which are used primarily to combat depression though they have many other uses as well including helping with anxiety disorders. There are four main categories of antidepressant drugs: MAOIs, Tricyclics, SSRIs, and SNRIs. **Monoamine Oxidase Inhibitors (MAOIs)** are the oldest and least commonly used group of antidepressant drugs. MAOIs work by preventing the action of the enzyme monoamine oxidase. They slow the body's production of MAO which then influences several neurotransmitters; it increases the amount of dopamine, serotonin, and norepinephrine in our system. Because of potentially lethal dietary and drug interactions, monoamine oxidase inhibitors have historically been reserved as a last line of treatment, used only when other classes of antidepressant drugs have failed. A second category of drugs are the **Tricyclics**, an antidepressant drug that has three rings in its molecular structure. Tricyclics work by blocking the reuptake process of serotonin, dopamine, and norepinephrine which in turn increases neurotransmitter activity. These are still an older category of antidepressants and are the most commonly prescribed. The most common example of Tricyclics is a drug called Elavil. A third category of antidepressants are the **Selective Serotonin Reuptake Inhibitors (SSRIs)** which are a group of second-generation antidepressant drugs that increase serotonin activity specifically without affecting other neurotransmitters. This is one of the newer and more popular groups of antidepressants because they are more targeted which results in less side effects. Some common examples of SSRIs include Prozac, Zoloft, Celexa, and Lexapro. Finally, **Serotonin-Norepinephrine Reuptake Inhibitors (SNRIs)** are a fourth category of antidepressants that work by increasing the levels of serotonin and norepinephrine in the brain. Like SSRIs, these tend to be more targeted and therefore result in less side effects. Some of the commonly prescribed SNRIs are Cymbalta, Effexor, and Prestiq.

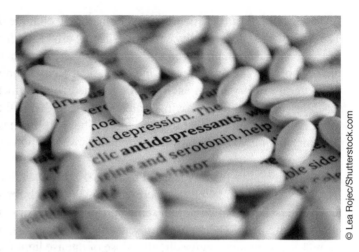

© Lea Rojec/Shutterstock.com

Another category of drugs are **Mood-Stabilizers**. Mood stabilizers are commonly prescribed for people struggling with bipolar disorder and work by stabilizing and maintaining a remission of manic symptoms. Common mood-stabilizing drugs include Lithium, Tegretol, and Depakote. Lithium is a naturally occurring salt that helps level out the wild and unpredictable mood swings of bipolar disorder. We don't know exactly how it works but the sodium element to it is possibly connected to ion activity which can directly affect the firing of our nerve cells.

© Angel Soler Gollonet/Shutterstock.com

Antipsychotic Drugs are another category of drugs used to treat very severe psychological disorders, particularly schizophrenia. Antipsychotic drugs are very effective for treating the positive symptoms of schizophrenia such as hallucinations but not as helpful with negative symptoms. As a group, these drugs can often have dramatic effects which can lead to discomfort and extensive side effects. Antipsychotic drugs work to reduce dopamine by blocking its release which in turn reduces the dopamine induced symptoms associated with schizophrenia.

Sedatives such as the **Benzodiazepines** and **Psychostimulants** are some of the other commonly prescribed groups of medications. Benzodiazepines are a class of psychoactive drugs that enhance the effect of the neurotransmitter gamma-aminobutyric acid (GABA). As a group, benzodiazepines are useful in treating anxiety, insomnia, seizures, muscle spasms, and alcohol withdrawal. The benzodiazepines are generally viewed as safe and effective for short- term use but long-term use can lead to dependence and withdrawal. The most common examples of benzodiazepines are Xanax and Valium. Psychostimulants are a broad category of drugs

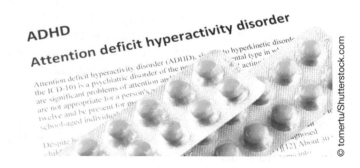

© tomertu/Shutterstock.com

that reduce fatigue, promote alertness and wakefulness, and have possible mood-enhancing properties. In contemporary practice, psychostimulants have a limited but important and well-identified role. Drugs such as dexamphetamine and methylphenidate are used to treat attention-deficit hyperactivity disorder (ADHD) in both children and adults. A newer psychostimulant, modafinil is sometimes used for reducing sleepiness in obstructive sleep apnea and narcolepsy. Common side effects associated with psychostimulants include insomnia, agitation, anxiety and confusion.

Brain Stimulation Methods and Psychosurgery

In some cases, people don't respond to or can't tolerate medications. In severe cases of depression or other disorders, brain stimulation methods might be considered as a line of treatment. Brain stimulation methods can be much more invasive than medication so they aren't used as a first line of defense but can be helpful for those who aren't responding to or can't tolerate other treatment options. The old standby of brain stimulation methods is **Electroconvulsive Therapy (ECT)** which is a biological therapy in which a mild electrical current is passed through the brain for a short period, often producing convulsions and a loss of consciousness. The aim of electroconvulsive therapy is to induce a therapeutic clonic seizure (a seizure where the person loses consciousness and has convulsions) lasting for at least 15 seconds. Although a large amount of research has been carried out, the exact mechanism of action of ECT remains elusive. A person undergoing ECT typically receives 6–12 treatments over a 2–4 week period. Side effects include confusion, disorientation, and memory impairment. Again, this is typically considered a last resort treatment after all others have failed.

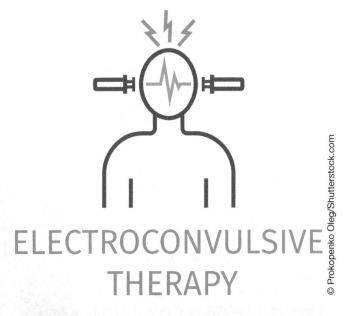

ELECTROCONVULSIVE THERAPY

© Prokopenko Oleg/Shutterstock.com

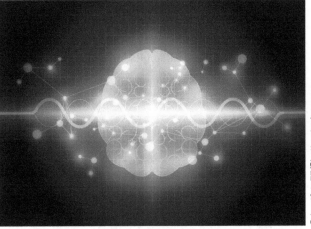

© bestfoto77/Shutterstock.com

Other methods of brain stimulation include **Vagus Nerve Stimulation, Transcranial Magnetic Stimulation (TMS),** and **Deep Brain Stimulation (DBS)**. In vagas nerve stimulation, an implanted pulse generator sends electrical signals to a person's vagus nerve which in turn stimulates the brain. A surgeon implants a small pulse generator under the skin of the chest with a wire attached to the left vagus nerve. An electrical signal travels through the wire to the nerve every five minutes and the stimulated nerve then sends electrical signals to the brain. This is thought to help by possibility altering GABA and norepinephrine levels but it still isn't fully understood. Much more promising is transcranial magnetic stimulation (TMS) in which an electromagnetic coil, placed on or above a person's head, sends a current into the brain. The coil sends a current into the prefrontal cortex (which is often underactive in depressed patients) and appears to increase neuron activity. This is much less invasive than ECT and is likely the direction we are headed as the future of brain stimulation. Deep brain stimulation (DBS) involves a pacemaker which powers electrodes implanted in Brodmann Area 25 thus stimulating that brain area. Depression has been linked to high activity level in Brodmann Area 25 so two holes are drilled into a patient's skull and electrodes are implanted and connected to a battery operated pacemaker implanted in the person's chest/stomach. The pacemaker sends low-voltage electricity to Area 25 and this repeated stimulation is thought to recalibrate the depressed brain circuit. This is generally not considered a viable option of treatment as it is incredibly invasive.

Even more rare than brain stimulation methods is a **Psychosurgery**; brain surgery performed to change a person's behavior and emotional state; a biological therapy rarely used today. One example is a prefrontal lobotomy where the frontal lobes of the brain are severed from the deeper emotion controlling centers beneath them. The effects of these surgeries are difficult to predict and are rarely used today. In the past, these procedures typically resulted in the patient becoming permanently lethargic, immature, and/or impulsive.

Institutionalization and its Alternatives

People with severe mental illness are often hospitalized. As mentioned previously, the idea behind "mental hospitals" originally was that a country setting would calm patients down helping them to restore their mental health. Despite these intentions, state mental hospitals in general have not provided adequate care for their residents. Large state hospitals are perpetually under-funded and under-staffed and historically became warehouses for patients who didn't get better due to lack of adequate treatment. Rather than removing people from their typical setting and lives, current trends focus on **Deinstitutionalization** which is a policy of treating people with severe psychological disorders in the larger community or in small residential centers such as halfway houses, rather than large public hospitals. Outpatient therapy and treatments dominate the therapeutic landscape and most of the mammoth state hospitals have actually been shut down, abandoned, or converted into other facilities.

In Popular Culture

- *Skyfall* (2013) – a movie featuring a short scene highlighting the Psychoanalysis technique of free association.

- *Divergent* (2014) – a movie featuring the concept of facing your fears through virtual fear landscapes which could be compared to exposure treatments like flooding.

- *Shutter Island* (2010) – a movie that takes place at a psychiatric institution and highlights a few different older treatment methods.

- *Analyze This* and *Analyze That* (1999/2002) – two movies that feature extensive therapy examples.

- *Couples Retreat* (2009) – a movie featuring several examples of couples counseling by different therapists.

- *Mr. and Mrs. Smith* (2005) – this movie shows several scenes of couples counseling between Angelina Jolie and Brad Pitt's characters. Never has counseling looked so good!

- *What About Bob* (1991) – a great example of poor therapeutic boundaries; a must see for any future therapist!

- *From Hell* (2001) – a movie set during the time of Jack the Ripper that features a few scenes highlighting ancient treatment methods such as trephination and asylums.

- *Gothica* (2003) – a movie that takes place in a psychiatric hospital and has several examples of therapeutic approaches.

- *One Flew Over the Cookoo's Nest* (1975) – a classic psychology movie that features a mental hospital and electroconvulsive therapy.

Psyched with Setmire

"Different Types of Clinicians: Choosing a Therapist"
https://www.youtube.com/watch?v=BdLT-IDMNh0

In this lecture presentation video adapted from my Introduction to Psychology courses, I will cover some of the common types of clinicians in the mental health profession (counselors, clinical psychologists, psychiatrists, social workers, and medical doctors) along with some tips and suggestions for how to choose a therapist.

Application: What Makes a Good Therapist?

This can be a very difficult question to answer as it often depends on the person seeking therapy, the disorders(s) they are struggling with, and their financial situation! Some people prefer to have a therapist of the same sex as them while others might prefer an opposite sex therapist. If you are more comfortable talking to one sex over the other, this might be something that you keep in mind. Do you want someone who is direct and gives advice or would you prefer someone who lets you guide your progress? Again, very individualistic preferences! I touched on some these things in the "Psyched with Setmire" video referenced above.

In general, there are several characteristics that define a "good therapist". A good therapist isn't that different from a good listener, in fact that is one of the most commonly referenced positive descriptors of a therapist. Other things that are consistently reported as desired traits in a therapist include: someone who actually cares about your life, that they offer advice, that the therapist  has some life experience that can help them to see your perspective but not so much that it interferes, that the person is insightful and able to see deeper meanings in the things you share, that they are someone you feel you can trust, they are flexible, sensitive, and able to instill hope that change and/or progress can occur. Again, these are general traits or descriptors; be sure to think about what is important to you when choosing a therapist!

Key Terms

Asylum: a type of institution that first became popular in the 16th century to provide care for persons with mental disorders.

Psychotherapy: the use of psychological techniques to treat mental illness.

Counseling Psychologists: typically have a master's degree and are often marriage and family therapists (MFTs) who help people with problems of everyday life such as stress, relationships, anxiety, and so on.

Clinical Psychologists: typically have a Ph.D. and have expertise in assessment and psychological disorders; often work with populations suffering from more severe disorders.

Psychiatrists: specialize in prescribing medications for the treatment of psychological disorders.

Social Workers: typically have a master's degree and work with the institutions of society helping to mediate the relationships between people, families, school systems, and legal systems.

Medical Doctors: have a medical degree and specialize in physical treatments.

Insight Therapies: a variety of individual psychotherapies designed to give people a better awareness and understanding of their feelings, motivations, and actions in the hope that this will help them to adjust.

Psychoanalysis: a theory of personality and a form of therapy invented by Freud designed to bring hidden feelings and motives to conscious awareness so that the person can deal with them more effectively.

Free Association: a technique that encourages the person to talk without inhibition about whatever thoughts or fantasies come to mind.

Client-Centered (Person-Centered) Therapy: a non-directional form of insight therapy developed by Carl Rogers that calls for unconditional positive regard of the client by the therapist with the goal of helping the client become a fully functioning person.

Behavior Therapies: therapeutic approaches that are based on the belief that all behavior, normal and abnormal, is learned and that the objective of therapy is to teach people new, more satisfying ways of behaving.

Token Economy: an operant conditioning therapy in which people earn tokens or points (reinforcers) for desired behaviors and exchange them for desired items or privileges.

Exposure Therapies (Flooding): full-intensity exposures to a feared stimulus for a prolonged period of time.

Systematic Desensitization: a technique for reducing a person's fear and anxiety by gradually associating a new response (relaxation) with stimuli that have been causing the fear and anxiety.

Cognitive Therapies: psychotherapies that emphasize changing clients' perceptions of their life situation as a way of modifying their behavior.

Group Therapy: a type of psychotherapy in which clients meet regularly to interact and help one another achieve insight into their feelings and behavior.

Family Therapy: a form of group therapy that sees the family as at least partly responsible for the individual's problems and that seeks to change all the family members' behaviors to the benefit of the family unit as well as the troubled individual.

Couples Therapy: a form of group therapy intended to help troubled partners improve their problems of communication and interaction.

Eclecticism: a psychotherapeutic approach that recognizes the value of a broad treatment package over a rigid commitment to one particular form of therapy.

Eye Movement Desensitization and Reprocessing (EMDR): a psychotherapy technique designed to help alleviate the symptoms of PTSD.

Light Exposure Therapy: consists of exposure to artificial light administered for a prescribed amount of time and, in some cases, at a specific time of day.

Biological (Biomedical) Treatments: a group of approaches, including medication, electroconvulsive therapy, and psychosurgery, that are sometimes used to treat psychological disorders in conjunction with, or instead of, psychotherapy.

Psychopharmacology: the study of the effects of drugs on mind and behavior.

Antidepressant Drugs: a group of drugs used primarily to combat depression though have many other uses as well including helping with anxiety disorders.

Monoamine Oxidase Inhibitors (MAOIs): a group of antidepressant drugs that work by preventing the action of the enzyme monoamine oxidase.

Tricyclics: a group of antidepressant drugs that have three rings in its molecular structure and work to increase levels of serotonin, dopamine, and norepinephrine.

Selective Serotonin Reuptake Inhibitors (SSRIs): a group of antidepressant drugs that increase serotonin activity specifically without affecting other neurotransmitters.

Serotonin-Norepinephrine Reuptake Inhibitors (SNRIs): a group of antidepressant drugs that work by increasing the levels of serotonin and norepinephrine in the brain.

Mood Stabilizers: a group of drugs commonly prescribed for people struggling with bipolar disorder and work by stabilizing and maintaining a remission of manic symptoms.

Antipsychotic Drugs: a category of drugs used to treat very severe psychological disorders, particularly schizophrenia.

Benzodiazepines: a class of psychoactive drugs enhance the effect of the neurotransmitter gamma-aminobutyric acid (GABA).

Psychostimulants: a broad category of drugs that reduce fatigue, promote alertness and wakefulness, and have possible mood-enhancing properties.

Electroconvulsive Therapy (ECT): a biological therapy in which a mild electrical current is passed through the brain for a short period, often producing convulsions and a loss of consciousness.

Psychosurgery: brain surgery performed to change a person's behavior and emotional state; a biological therapy rarely used today.

Deinstitutionalization: a policy of treating people with severe psychological disorders in the larger community or in small residential centers such as halfway houses, rather than large public hospitals.

Chapter 16
Social Psychology

Outline

© Lightspring/Shutterstock.com

Introduction to the Chapter (Summary)

Social psychology is the scientific study of the ways in which the thoughts, feelings, and behaviors of one individual are influenced by the real, imagined, or inferred behavior or characteristics of other people. Part of the process of being influenced by other people involves organizing and interpreting information about others to form first impressions, to try to understand the behavior of others, and maybe even to determine to what extent we are attracted to someone. Attribution theory is the theory that addresses the question of how people make judgments about the causes of behavior. We tend to attribute behavior to either internal causes or external causes; we decide if a behavior is typical of someone's personality or if it is a result of situational factors. Unfortunately, our causal attributions are often vulnerable to biases with the most common being the fundamental attribution error.

Looking at social influence (the process by which others individually or collectively affect one's perceptions, attitudes, and actions), our culture exerts enormous influence on our attitudes and behavior. We are reinforced for going along with the crowd and often punished for deviating from norms or shared ideas about how to behave. Related to norms there are several yielding behaviors where people give up their personal preferences that are studied by social psychologists such as conformity, compliance, and obedience. Social psychologists also examine the processes that occur when people interact in groups. There is a tendency in our culture to turn important decisions over to groups and many people trust these group decisions more than those made by individuals but sometimes the social interaction components of groups make the decisions less sound than if they were made by someone acting alone. Some of the observed group phenomenon include the risky shift, groupthink, and deindividuation. Groups can be incredibly effective under certain circumstances and generally effective groups involve people who are motivated and have a clear task to accomplish.

Social cognition is the knowledge and understanding concerning the social world and the people in it (including oneself). When we are forming our first impressions or meeting someone for the first time we notice all sorts of things (clothes, gestures, facial features, etc.) and then categorize people which then influences what we notice and remember. Over time as we interact with people we add new information about them to our mental files but early information about someone weighs more heavily than later information in influencing one's impression of that person which is called the primacy effect. People also tend to not take in all details but rather the minimal amount of information in our first impressions which can lead us to stereotypes which can result in prejudice, discrimination, and even racism.

Other forces examined by social psychologists are aggression and attraction. There are five factors of interpersonal attraction: proximity, physical attractiveness, similarity, exchange/reciprocity, and intimacy. Related to attraction is the concept of love which can take many forms including passionate love and companionate love. One final group of topics that social psychologists spend considerable time on is helping behaviors such as altruism (helping behavior not linked to personal gain) and the bystander effect (the tendency for an individual's helpfulness in an emergency to decrease as the number of passive bystanders increases). Obviously, you should worry about your safety and maybe someone else has already done something, but be aware of this tendency and challenge it when possible and appropriate!

Social Psychology

Social Psychology the scientific study of the ways in which the thoughts, feelings, and behaviors of one individual are influenced by the real, imagined, or inferred behavior or characteristics of other people. Social psychology seeks to understand and explain how the thoughts, feelings, and behavior of individuals are influenced by the actual, imagined, or implied presence of other people. Essentially, social psychology is all about understanding how each person's individual behavior is influenced by the social environment in which that behavior takes place. Social psychology covers a wide range of topics including

attitudes, conformity, group behaviors, aggression, prejudice, attraction, love, and helping behaviors like altruism and the bystander effect.

Attribution Theory and the Fundamental Attribution Error

Part of the process of being influenced by other people involves organizing and interpreting information about them to form first impressions and to try to understand their behavior. Social interaction is also filled with occasions that invite us to make judgments about the cause of behavior. So how do we decide why people act the way that they do?

A very important part of our interactions with other people and the attributions we make involve **Attitudes** which are relatively stable organizations of beliefs, feelings, and behavior tendencies directed toward something or someone. Attitudes are important because they often influence our emotions and behavior. For example, if we believe that someone is mean, we may feel dislike for them and act unfriendly toward them. In this way, it is easy to create self-fulfilling prophecies. Many of our basic attitudes come from direct early personal experiences from parents or caregivers, through reinforcement for certain behaviors, and also through imitation. Attitudes can also be heavily influenced by many other factors including our peers, life experiences, and the media. Attitudes can be very difficult to change and tend to play a large role in our social interactions.

Attribution Theory is the theory that addresses the question of how people make judgments about the causes of behavior. We tend to attribute behavior to either internal causes or external causes (personality or situational factors). Unfortunately, our causal attributions are often vulnerable to biases. The most common bias or error we can make is called the **Fundamental Attribution Error** which is the tendency for observers, when analyzing another's behavior, to underestimate the impact of the situation and to overestimate the impact of personal disposition (personality); or the tendency of people to overemphasize personal causes for other people's behavior and to underemphasize personal causes for their own behavior. This is an easy mistake to make! Before becoming a parent, I used to make this mistake with other people and their kids all the time. I would see a parent yelling at their child at Target and my first thought or assumption would be to think that they are a horrible parent. By doing that, I completely underestimated the situation and overestimated that parent's personality. It is completely possible that the child had been horrible in Target and it wasn't a case of bad parenting at all. Another example might be thinking that a student in my class who never speaks is shy when it might just be my class that makes them uncomfortable and unwilling to talk. Situation forces can be quite powerful and social psychology considers them in explaining behavior.

Social Influence

The next topic we will look at in the realm of social psychology is **Social Influence** which is the process by which others individually or collectively affect one's perceptions, attitudes, and actions. In the previous section, we looked at attitudes, now we will look at how the presence or actions of others can control behavior without regard to underlying attitudes.

Our culture exerts enormous influence on our attitudes and behavior, we are natural mimics and behavior is often contagious (one person laughs and others follow). We learn cultural lessons about what is considered normal or the

© Crystal Home/Shutterstock.com

right way of doing things and we are reinforced for going along with the crowd and often punished for deviating. When we compare our behavior to that of others we often learn the norms for our culture. **Norms** are shared ideas or expectations about how to behave. There are norms for classroom behavior such as raising your hand when you want to say something or sitting in your seat rather than standing on your desk. There are even norms for what we eat and don't eat. If you went into an American restaurant you would not see dog meat on the menu. We, as a culture, don't eat dogs; we instead have them for pets. This is not true in all countries.

Conformity, Compliance, and Obedience

Accepting cultural norms should not be confused with conformity. Millions of people drink coffee in the morning because they enjoy it not because they are conforming to a societal norm. **Conformity** involves voluntarily yielding to social norms, even at the expense of one's preferences. There were some famous experiments done by a man named Solomon Asch's on people's tendencies to conform. In Asch's experiment, groups of eight male college students participated in a simple "perceptual" task. In reality, all but one of the participants were "confederates" (actors), and the true focus of the study was about how the one subject would react to the confederates' behavior. The actors were introduced as research participants but knew the true goal of the experiment. Participants were shown a set of vertical lines and were then asked to say aloud which line matched the length of the first line they were shown. Prior to the experiment, the confederates were given specific instructions to unanimously nominate one of the lines. The group was seated such that the real participant always responded last. Asch found that in the vast majority of the trials, the participant would go along with the group even if they believed that the group was wrong. So why do we conform? We typically conform because we desire to gain approval or avoid disapproval, because of one's willingness to accept other's opinions about reality, and often due to cultural norms and influences. Conformity is a response to pressure exerted by norms that are generally left unstated.

In contrast, **Compliance** involves a change of behavior in response to an explicit request from another person or group. There are several techniques to induce compliance including the **Foot-in-the-Door Effect**, the **Lowball Procedure**, and the **Door-in-the-Face Effect**. The foot-in-the-door effect is a technique for helping to induce compliance that operates on the idea that once someone has granted a small request they are more likely to

comply with a larger one. The idea here is that a person lets you through the door once so they then have a hard time closing the door on you later. Let's say you borrow a small amount of money from someone and then pay them back (this would probably only work if you paid them back). Then the next time, you ask them if you can borrow more money and then more and more. That person will have a hard time telling you no because they said yes to you initially. The door-in-the-face effect is the opposite situation. With this technique, a person who has refused to comply with one request may be more likely to comply with a second one because they might feel guilty. So if you were to ask someone for a really big favor and they say no to you, they might be more willing to say yes to your next request because they feel guilty about saying no last time. Another way of thinking about this might be to say that they slam the door in your face, feel badly about it, and therefore are more likely to open the door for you next time! The lowball procedure gets a person to agree to something and then slowly raises the cost of compliance. This is a very commonly used technique at car dealerships as they slowly add more and more to the cost of a car that you are interested in buying.

The last type of yielding behavior is called **Obedience** which is a change of behavior in response to a command from another person, typically an authority figure. Stanley Milgram conducted a famous experiment on obedience and the administration of electric shocks. The subject was told to read a list of words to the "learner" and then ask them to recall them at a later point. If the learner was incorrect, the subject was told to administer a shock that would increase in intensity. The electric shocks were clearly labeled and the highest ones were marked with an "xxx" to indicate that they would be deadly. 65% of the subjects delivered all the way up to the deadly levels of shocks simply because they were told to do so by the researcher. Luckily, the subject wasn't actually being shocked but the subject did not learn this until after the experiment had ended. Why would someone obey even if it violates their own principles? Many of the subjects in Milgram's experiment obeyed because they saw themselves as agents of another person's wishes (the researcher) and therefore were not responsible for their obedient actions or the consequences of those actions. Others reported getting caught up in the power of the situation or not believing that the researcher would allow any real harm to come to the learner. Another big reason why people obey is out of fear or necessity or because they fail to perceive the situation accurately.

Groups and Decision Making

So far we have talked about various kinds of social influence that may take place even when nobody else is physically present. Now we turn to processes that occur when people interact in groups. There is a tendency in our culture to turn important decisions over to groups (committees, business, government, etc.) and many people trust these group decisions more than those made by individuals but sometimes the social interaction components of groups make the decisions less sound than if they were made by someone acting alone.

One thing that tends to occur in groups is known as the **Risky Shift** which is the greater willingness of a group than an individual to take substantial risks. Group members may not feel as vulnerable or accountable as they would have been individually so they are more likely to up the stakes. Related to this is something called **Groupthink** which is the mode of thinking that occurs when the desire for harmony in a decision-making group overrides a realistic appraisal of alternatives. Groupthink is common as members may go along with an idea that they don't like just to avoid conflict. I guarantee that you have been in a group and someone has proposed an idea that you think is the worst idea ever, but you said nothing because you didn't want to create conflict! That is an example of groupthink.

Another tendency with groups is for Deindividuation to occur. **Deindividuation** is a loss of personal sense of responsibility in a group. In general the more anonymous that people feel in a group, the less responsible they feel as individuals. An example of this is mob behavior where people lose a personal sense of responsibility combined with peer pressure and anxiety. It is important to note that deindividuation and the notion that people become more destructive and irresponsible when they get together is not as common as the instances of cooperation and mutual assistance that occur when people get together. Groups can be incredibly effective under certain circumstances and generally effective groups involve people who are motivated and having a clear task to accomplish.

Social Cognition

Social Cognition is the knowledge and understanding concerning the social world and the people in it (including oneself). When we are forming our first impressions or meeting someone for the first time we notice all sorts of things (clothes, gestures, facial features, etc.) and then categorize people which then influences what we notice and remember. Over time as we interact with people we add new information about them to our mental files but early information about someone weighs more heavily than later information in influencing one's impression of that person which is called the **Primacy Effect**. People also tend to not take in all details but rather the minimal amount of information in our first impressions which can lead us astray and cause us to see things in a person that aren't accurate. Another way this minimal effort can be a problem is through stereotyping. A **Stereotype** is a set of characteristics presumed to be shared by all members of a social category. When our first impression of a person is governed by a stereotype we tend to infer things about that person based on some key distinguishing feature and ignore facts that are inconsistent with the stereotype. Stereotypes can result in **Prejudice** which is an unfair, intolerant, or unfavorable attitude toward a group of people. Prejudice often involves negative stereotypes paired with strong emotions such as dislike, fear, hatred, etc. Another thing that can happen is **Discrimination** which is an unfair series of acts taken toward an entire group of people or individual members of that group. **Racism** is prejudice and discrimination directed at a particular racial group. Blatant forms of racism have declined during the past decades but subtle forms still exist.

Box: Strategies for Reducing Prejudice and Discrimination

Here are some strategies for reducing prejudice are discrimination:

- *Recategorization* – expanding our schema of a particular group such as viewing people from different genders as sharing similar qualities.

- *Controlled Processing* – training ourselves to be more mindful of people who differ from us allowing us to suppress and challenge prejudiced beliefs.

- *Improved Group Contact* – bring groups together and have all group members have an equal status, have one-on-one contact with members of other groups.

- *Broadening horizons* – take a random class, participate in events that you might not normally, and push yourself to broaden your horizons.

Aggression and Interpersonal Attraction

The most destructive force in social relations is **Aggression** which is any physical or verbal behavior intended to hurt or destroy. For a gun to fire, the trigger must be pulled. Social psychologists look at the forces that might contribute to aggressive tendencies and also look at patterns of aggression and violence. Aggression can be motivated by a wide variety of factors, is more common in men than women, and takes a variety of forms, including being physical, verbal, mental, and emotional.

In the opposite spirit of aggression, social psychologists also spend considerable time looking at attraction. When people meet what determines whether they will like each other? There are five factors of interpersonal attraction: 1) *Proximity,* 2) *Physical Attractiveness,* 3) *Similarity,* 4) *Exchange or Reciprocity,* and 5) *Intimacy.* Proximity has to do with the geographical nearness of two people to each other. We tend to be attracted to people that we are near and have contact with on a regular basis. We also tend to be drawn toward people that we find physically attractive. People are generally drawn to each other when they perceive similarities with each other. The more attitudes and opinions two people share, the greater the probability that they

will like each other. Paula Abdul may have said that opposites attract but people who are similar tend to stay together. Exchange or reciprocity has to do with equity or fairness in a relationship. We tend to want equity in our relationships; both people giving and taking in equal amounts. When the giving or effort in a relationship is lopsided, the relationship tends to fail. Finally, intimacy plays a role in attraction and relationships. Intimacy is not just a physical exchange but also an emotion bond that brings closeness between two people.

Love is difficult to define and measure. It has strong emotional and behavioral components and often means different things to different people. Love can take many forms, but one very common distinction is **Passionate Love** versus **Companionate Love**. Passionate Love is state of extreme absorption in another person; also known as romantic love or infatuation. Passionate love is typically short lived and measured in months rather than years. It usually occurs at the beginnings of relationships and includes sexual desire, anxiety, and intense feelings. Companionate Love is a type of love characterized by friendly affection and deep attachment based on extensive familiarity with the loved one. This type of love is enduring and includes a tolerance or acceptance of one's shortcomings; loving someone despite their shortcomings.

Box: The Colors of Love

Another very famous categorization of types of love comes from John Alan Lee who proposed six basic ways to love. Lee termed these the "Colors of Love" and his ideas and theory were gathered from literature, interviews, statements, philosophy, and the social sciences.

1. *Eros*: The Romantic Lover – immediate attraction

2. *Ludus*: The Game-Playing Lover – enjoy the act of seduction

3. *Storge*: The Quiet, Calm Lover – goal of comfort and companionate love

4. *Mania*: The Crazy Lover – possessive and dependent

5. *Pragma*: The Practical Lover – planners and have a shopping list of qualities

6. *Agape*: The Selfless Lover – patient and true

Lee thought that we tend to be happier or more content when we are with lovers of the same type as ourselves and that different colors tend to contrast and lead to conflict.

Helping Behaviors

One final topic that social psychologists spend considerable time on is **Altruistic Behavior** or helping behavior that is not linked to personal gain. Most of the time when we help someone it is because we expect something in return. Altruism is an unselfish regard for the welfare of others or giving without the expectation of getting anything back in return. Altruism is one aspect of what social psychologists refer to as prosocial behavior. Prosocial behavior refers to any action that benefits other people, no matter what the motive or how the giver benefits from the action. Can you imagine what a better world this would be if we all just did one random act of kindness each day (which we will talk about more in a moment)?

Related to this helping behavior is the **Bystander Effect** which is the tendency for an individual's helpfulness in an emergency to decrease as the number of passive bystanders increases. Unfortunately, we have a tendency as people to not help the more people are present. How many times have you driven past someone on the side of the road with a flat tire or a broken down car and not stopped? Have you ever seen someone in need of help and not done anything? If you have done either of these things, don't beat yourself up over it, it is a natural human tendency. There are countless reasons why people don't help. Maybe you fear for your own safety. Many people decide

that someone else must have already called for help by now. Finally, many people don't help because they don't feel they have the knowledge or ability to do so. Obviously you should worry about your safety and maybe someone else has already done something, but be aware of this tendency and challenge it when appropriate!

In Popular Culture

- *What Would You Do?* (2008 to present) – a television show with hidden cameras exploring ethical dilemmas.

- *Crash* (2004) – a movie set in Los Angeles about racism, prejudice, and discrimination.

- *Gran Torino* (2008) – a movie that highlights the topics of prejudice, discrimination, and racism.

- *42* (2013) – a movie about the story of Jackie Robinson and his struggles with racism.

- *American History X* (1998) – a movie about the story of two brothers who become involved in the neo-Nazi movement.

- *The Help* (2011) – a movie about a young white woman and her relationship with two black maids during the Civil Rights era in 1963 Jackson, Mississippi.

- *12 Years A Slave* (2013) – a movie about a New York State-born free African-American man who was kidnapped in Washington, D.C., in 1841 and sold into slavery.

- *Higher Learning* (1995) – a movie following the changing lives of three incoming freshmen at the fictional Columbus University dealing with issues of prejudice and discrimination.

- *Boys Don't Cry* (1999) – a movie about the real-life story of Brandon Teena, a transsexual man who is beaten, raped and murdered by his male acquaintances after they discover he is anatomically female.

Psyched with Setmire

"Reducing Prejudice and Discrimination"
https://www.youtube.com/watch?v=SmUwf1SBIgQ

In this lecture presentation video (adapted from my Introduction to Psychology course lecture) I will briefly discuss some strategies for reducing prejudice and discrimination. Most of these strategies and/or suggestions are aimed at reducing prejudice and discrimination on a personal level but can obviously have far reaching implications if we could all make an effort to challenge ourselves!

Application: A Random Act of Kindness

One of the helping behaviors that we discussed in this chapter was altruism;

giving without the expectation of getting anything in return. Often discussed in relation to altruism is the concept of a random act of kindness which can be defined as is a non-premeditated, inconsistent action designed to offer kindness towards the outside world. There are countless organizations that encourage people to perform a random act of kindness each day or even each week. These organizations encourage us to help or cheer up a random stranger, for no reason other than to make people happier. Common suggestions for little things you can do include: opening a door for someone, putting a coin in an expired meter, bringing doughnuts for co-workers (I like this idea), smile at someone just because, compliment someone you know, and even randomly donating to a cause.

Not only will you be engaging in a positive pay it forward kind of behavior but there are demonstrated health benefits to being kind and altruistic. An act of kindness creates emotional warmth, which releases a hormone known as oxytocin. Oxytocin causes multiple physiological effects on our body with one of them being to dilate the blood vessels. Dilating the blood vessels reduces blood pressure and strain on the heart. Also, remember back to the section on happiness. People who engage in kind acts tend to be happier as positivity tends to fuel upward spirals. When you are kind to others, you feel good as a person, more moral, optimistic, and positive. It can be hard to take time out of our busy days and lives to give to others but I challenge and encourage you to take a few seconds, if you have it, and perform a random act of kindness to a stranger whenever you have the chance!

Key Terms

Social Psychology: the scientific study of the ways in which the thoughts, feelings, and behaviors of one individual are influenced by the real, imagined, or inferred behavior or characteristics of other people.

Attitudes: relatively stable organizations of beliefs, feelings, and behavior tendencies directed toward something or someone.

Attribution Theory: the theory that addresses the question of how people make judgments about the causes of behavior.

Fundamental Attribution Error: the tendency for observers, when analyzing another's behavior, to underestimate the impact of the situation and to overestimate the impact of personal disposition (personality); or the tendency of people to overemphasize personal causes for other people's behavior and to underemphasize personal causes for their own behavior.

Social Influence: the process by which others individually or collectively affect one's perceptions, attitudes, and actions.

Norm: a shared idea or expectation about how to behave.

Conformity: voluntarily yielding to social norms, even at the expense of one's preferences.

Compliance: change of behavior in response to an explicit request from another person or group.

Foot-in-the-Door Effect: a compliance technique in which once you get a person to grant a small request they are more likely to comply with a larger one.

Lowball Procedure: a compliance technique in which you get a person to agree to something and then slowly raise the cost of compliance.

Door-in-the-Face Effect: a compliance technique in which once person has refused to comply with one request may be more likely to comply with a second one because they might feel guilty.

Obedience: change of behavior in response to a command from another person, typically an authority figure.

Risky Shift: greater willingness of a group than an individual to take substantial risks.

Groupthink: the mode of thinking that occurs when the desire for harmony in a decision-making group overrides a realistic appraisal of alternatives.

Deindividuation: a loss of personal sense of responsibility in a group.

Social Cognition: the knowledge and understanding concerning the social world and the people in it (including oneself).

Primacy Effect: early information about someone weighs more heavily than later information in influencing one's impression of that person.

Stereotype: a set of characteristics presumed to be shared by all members of a social category.

Prejudice: an unfair, intolerant, or unfavorable attitude toward a group of people.

Discrimination: an unfair series of acts taken toward an entire group of people or individual members of that group.

Racism: prejudice and discrimination directed at a racial group.

Aggression: any physical or verbal behavior intended to hurt or destroy.

Love: an intense feeling of deep affection with emotional and behavioral components; often means different things to different people.

Passionate Love: a state of extreme absorption in another person; also known as romantic love or infatuation.

Companionate Love: a type of love characterized by friendly affection and deep attachment based on extensive familiarity with the loved one.

Altruistic Behavior: helping behavior that is not linked to personal gain.

Bystander Effect: the tendency for an individual's helpfulness in an emergency to decrease as the number of passive bystanders increases.

POWERPOINT SLIDES

Chapter 1: History and Scope of Psychology

- Psychology's Roots
- The History of Psychology
- Psychology's Subfields
- Truths and Myths about Psychology
- Careers in Psychology

Psychology's Roots

- Roots in Philosophy

- Greek words *psyche* (soul, spirit, or mind) and *logos* (study of a subject matter)

- Aristotle, a naturalist and philosopher, suggested that the soul and body are not separate and that knowledge grows from experience.

Aristotle (384-322 B.C.)

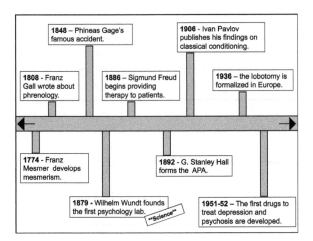

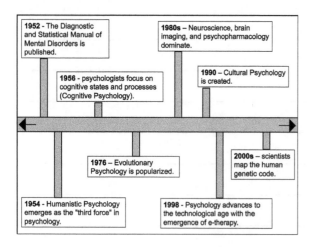

1952 - The Diagnostic and Statistical Manual of Mental Disorders is published.

1956 - psychologists focus on cognitive states and processes (Cognitive Psychology).

1954 - Humanistic Psychology emerges as the "third force" in psychology.

1976 – Evolutionary Psychology is popularized.

1980s – Neuroscience, brain imaging, and psychopharmacology dominate.

1990 – Cultural Psychology is created.

2000s – scientists map the human genetic code.

1998 - Psychology advances to the technological age with the emergence of e-therapy.

Contemporary Psychology

Today, we define psychology as the scientific study of behavior (what we do) and mental processes (inner thoughts and feelings).

Psychology's Famous Faces

Psychology's Big Question

Nature vs. Nurture

The controversy over the relative contributions of biology and experience.

_____

_____

_____

_____

_____

_____

Psychology's Three Main Levels of Analysis

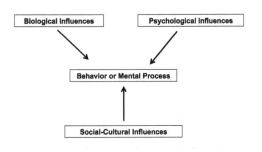

_____

_____

_____

_____

_____

_____

The Subfields of Psychology

· Developmental Psychology

· Physiological Psychology

· Experimental Psychology

· Personality Psychology

· I-O Psychology

· Social Psychology

· Clinical and Counseling Psychology

_____

_____

_____

_____

_____

_____

Clinical Psychology vs. Counseling Psychology vs. Psychiatry

A <u>Clinical Psychologist</u> studies, assesses, and treats people with psychological disorders through psychotherapy.

A <u>Counseling Psychologist</u> assists people with everyday problems in living.

<u>Psychiatrists</u> are medical professionals (M.D.) who use treatments like drugs and psychotherapy to treat patients.

Psychological Associations & Societies

The American Psychological Association is the largest organization of psychology with over 200,000 members world-wide.

The Truth About Psychology

Myths	Facts
Psychology is simply common sense	Psychology is scientific and uses scientific methods
Psychology only focuses on abnormal behavior	Psychology studies both normal and abnormal behavior
Psychologists all share a similar perspectives and approaches to analyzing information	Psychology embraces many different perspectives and has numerous subfields
Psychology is all old theories in textbooks	Psychology is ever-changing and is all around you
If you are interested in working in the field of psychology, you must want to be a therapist	Psychology is not just therapy; psychology offers a wide range of career options

Careers in Psychology

<u>Associates Degrees</u> – paraprofessional positions in state hospitals and other human service settings.

<u>Bachelor's Degrees</u> – work in correctional centers, assisting psychologists in mental health centers, research assistants, teach psychology in high school, or work with the government or in business.

<u>Master's Degrees and Doctorates</u> – work in colleges and universities as professors, researchers, educational psychologists, management and consulting positions, and counselors or therapists.

Chapter 2: Research Strategies

■Imperfect Methods: Intuition, Common Sense, and Pseudoscience

■Embracing a Scientific Attitude and Critical Thinking

■Research Methods

■Ethical Concerns and Guidelines

Intuition & Common Sense

- Many believe that Intuition and Common Sense are enough to bring forth answers regarding human nature.

- Intuition and common sense may aid queries, but they are not free of error.

- *For Example*: personal interviewers may rely too much on their "gut feelings" when meeting with job applicants.

Intuition & Common Sense

Other Limits to Intuition and Common Sense:

- Hindsight Bias: the "I-knew-it-all-along" phenomenon.

- Overconfidence: sometimes we think we know more than we actually know.

Pseudoscience: a body of knowledge, methodology, belief, or practice that is claimed to be scientific or made to appear scientific, but does not adhere to the scientific method, lacks supporting evidence or plausibility, or otherwise lacks scientific status.

- Astrology, Aliens, Ghosts, etc.

In Contrast to Intuition: What is Science?

Science (from Latin *scientia*, meaning "knowledge") is a systematic enterprise that builds and organizes knowledge in the form of testable explanations and predictions about the universe. Science is:

- Observable

- Objective

- Empirical

- Testable

- Falsifiable

- Replicable

- Systematic

- Peer-reviewed

The Scientific Attitude: composed of curiosity, skepticism, and humility.

Critical Thinking: not accepting arguments and conclusions blindly.

Principles of Critical Thinking

1. Be Skeptical

2. Examine Definition of Terms

3. Be Cautious in Drawing Conclusions from Evidence

4. Consider Alternative Interpretations of Research Findings

5. Do Not Oversimplify

6. Do Not Overgeneralize

7. Avoid Making Belief Changes Based on the Findings from One Study

---

Psychology as Science

Psychologists rely on the scientific method when seeking to answer questions.

Scientific Method: an approach to knowledge that relies on collecting data, generating a theory to explain the data, producing testable hypotheses based on the theory, and testing those hypotheses empirically.

- Fact: an objective and verifiable observation.

- Theory: systematic explanation of a phenomenon.

- Hypotheses: specific, testable predictions derived from a theory.

Facts 🔘 Theories 🔘 Hypotheses 🔘 Tested by Psychologists (through a variety of methods) to examine claims.

Research Methods in Psychology

Naturalistic Observation: systematic study of animal or human behavior in natural settings rather than in the laboratory.

Case Study: intensive description and analysis of a single individual or just a few individuals.

Research Methods in Psychology

Survey Research: research technique in which questionnaires or interviews are administered to a selected group of people.

▪Population: the complete collection to be studied containing all subjects of interest.

▪Sample: a part of the population of interest.

▪Random Sampling: each member of a population has an equal chance of inclusion into a sample.

Research Methods

Correlational Research: examines the naturally occurring relationship between two or more variables.

Variable: anything that can have different values between different individuals or over time; an element, feature, or factor that is liable to vary or change.

Pearson product-moment correlation coefficient (Pearson's r): a measure of the linear correlation between two variables ranging between -1 and +1.

Variable List #1	Variable List #2
Intelligence (IQ)	# of boyfriends
Average Daily Blood Alcohol Concentration	GPA
$ earned/year	# of appliances owned
3 years smoking 1+ packs per day	# times arrested
Degree of extroversion	# of moldy containers in fridge
Hours spent studying	# lung problems

Correlation or Causation?

Need to prove something you already believe? Statistics are easy. All you need is two graphs and a leading question.

Correlation does not mean causation!

Research Methods

Experimental Method: technique in which an investigator deliberately manipulates selected events or circumstances and then measures the effects of those manipulations on subsequent behavior.

- Independent Variable

- Dependent Variable

- Experimental Group

- Control Group

Example: Does alcohol consumption have an effect on exam scores?

Research and Ethics

The American Psychological Association ensures that both human and animal subjects are treated with dignity.

APA Ethical Guidelines:

- Participation in research should be voluntary and based on informed consent

- Participants should not be exposed to harmful or dangerous research procedures

- If there is deception of participants involved in the study, the researcher must correct any misunderstandings as soon as possible (debriefing)

- Participant's right to privacy should never be violated

- Harmful or painful procedures imposed on animals must be thoroughly justified in terms of the knowledge to be gained

- Prior to conducting studies, approval should be gained from host institutions

Chapter 3: Biological Psychology

- Neurons
- The Neural Impulse
- The Nervous System
- The Endocrine System
- Older Brain Structures and the Limbic System
- The Cerebral Cortex
- Studying the Brain
- Our Divided Brain

Neurons: The Messengers

Neurons: individual cells that are the smallest unit of the nervous system.

- The brain of an average human contains as many as 100 billion neurons with billions more being found in other parts of the nervous system.

Parts of a Neuron

Neurons: The Messengers

Types of Neurons:

1. Sensory (Afferent) Neurons

2. Motor (Efferent) Neurons

3. Interneurons (Association) Neurons

Neurons: The Messengers

The nervous system also contains Glial Cells which:

– Hold neurons in place, provide nourishment, and remove waste

– Prevent harmful substances from passing from the bloodstream into the brain

– Form the myelin sheath

The Neural Impulse

Ions: electrically charged particles found both inside and outside the neuron.

Neural Impulse (Action Potential): the firing of a nerve cell.

- Threshold of Excitation
- All-or-None Law

_____

_____

_____

_____

_____

_____

_____

The Synapse

Synapse: the entire area composed of the axon terminals of one neuron, the synaptic space, and the dendrites and cell body of the next neuron.

_____

_____

_____

_____

_____

_____

_____

Neurotransmitters

Neurotransmitters (chemicals) released from the sending neuron travel across the synapse and bind to Receptor Sites on the receiving neuron, thereby influencing it to generate an action potential.

_____

_____

_____

_____

_____

_____

The Endocrine System

The Endocrine System is the body's "slow" chemical communication system.

Communication is carried out by Hormones synthesized by a set of glands.

Older Brain Structures

Brainstem: responsible for automatic survival functions including heart rate, breathing, maintaining consciousness, and regulating the sleep cycle.

•Pons: upper part of the brainstem; Latin for "bridge".

•Medulla: the lower half of the brainstem.

Cerebellum: regulates reflexes, balance, and coordinates movement.

The Limbic System

Limbic System: responsible for emotions and drives.

•Thalamus: relay station for sensory and motor information.

•Hypothalamus: responsible for many metabolic processes; links the nervous system to the endocrine system.

•Hippocampus: memory and spatial navigation.

•Amygdala: emotional reactions and memory.

The Cerebral Cortex

Cerebral Cortex: The intricate fabric of interconnected neural cells that covers the cerebral hemispheres.

Divided into four lobes that are separated by prominent fissures:

1. Frontal Lobe
2. Parietal Lobe
3. Occipital Lobe
4. Temporal Lobe

- Folds of the cerebral cortex – Gyrus and Sulcus

Tools for Studying the Brain

Four basic techniques for studying the brain:

1. Microelectrode Techniques: used to study the functions of individual neurons.

2. Macroelectrode Techniques: used to obtain a picture of the activity in a particular region of the brain.

- Electroencephalogram (EEG)

Tools for Studying the Brain

3. Structural Imaging: used to map structures in a living brain.

 – CAT/CT (Computerized Axial Tomography) Scan

 – MRI (Magnetic Resonance Imaging)

4. Functional Imaging: image activity in the brain as it responds to various stimuli such as pain, words, tone, etc.

 – Positron Emission Tomography (PET) Scan

Hemispheric Specialization

Corpus Callosum: thick band of nerve fibers connecting the left and right cerebral hemispheres allowing them to work as a coordinated unit.

• Severing the Corpus Callosum

• Left vs. Right Brain

Damage and Neural Plasticity

• Phineas Gage's Accident

Neural Plasticity: the ability of the brain to change in response to experience.

• Rosenzweig (1984)

Chapter 4: Sensation and Perception

- Sensation vs. Perception
- Receptor Cells, Thresholds, and Subliminal Messages
  - Our Five Senses
- Perceptual Organization

Sensation & Perception

How do we construct our representations of the external world?

To represent the world, we must detect physical energy from the environment and convert it into neural signals. This is a process called <u>Sensation</u>.

When we select, organize, and interpret our sensations, the process is called <u>Perception</u>.

The Nature of Sensation

<u>Absolute Threshold</u>: the least amount of energy that can be detected as a stimulation 50% of the time.

<u>Adaptation</u>: automatic adjustment of our senses to the overall level of stimulation in a particular setting.

Subliminal Messages

The Eye

Cornea: the transparent protective coating over the front part of the eye.

Pupil: a small opening in the iris through which light enters the eye.

Iris: the colored part of
the eye that regulates
the size of the pupil.

Lens: the transparent
part of the eye behind
the pupil that focuses
light onto the retina.

The Retina and Receptor Cells

Retina: the light-sensitive inner surface of the eye, containing the receptor cells that are sensitive to electromagnetic energy and process visual information.

Two types of receptors cells:

1. Rods: receptor cells in the retina
   responsible for night vision and
   perception of brightness.

2. Cones: receptor cells in the retina
   responsible for color vision.

From the Eye to the Brain

*Messages from the eye must travel to the brain
in order for a visual experience to occur.*

Optic Nerve: the bundles of axons of ganglion cells that carries neural messages from each eye to the brain.

Blind Spot: the place on the retina where
the axons of all the ganglion cells leave the
eye and where there are no receptors.

Optic Chiasm: the point near the base of the
brain where some fibers in the optic nerve
from each eye cross to the other side of the
brain.

Theories of Color Vision

1. <u>Trichromatic (Young-Helmholtz) Theory</u>: the theory of color vision that holds that all color perception derives from three different color receptors (red, green, and blue).

2. <u>Opponent-Process Theory:</u> theory of color vision that holds that three sets of color receptors (yellow-blue, red-green, and black-white) respond to determine the color you experience.

The Ear and Sound

Hearing begins when <u>Sound Waves</u> are gathered by the outer ear and passed along to the eardrum causing it to vibrate.

Touch

- Our largest sense organ *(A person who is 6 feet tall has 21 square feet of skin!)*

The sense of touch is a mix of four distinct skin senses:

1. Pressure

2. Warmth

3. Cold

4. Pain

Taste

Taste Buds: structures on the tongue that contain the receptor cells for taste (found on the tip, sides, and back of the tongue).

5 Basic Taste Qualities:

Sweet   **Sour**   **Salty**   **Bitter**   **Umami**

Smell

Like taste, smell is a chemical sense. Odorants enter the nasal cavity to stimulate 5 million receptors to sense smell.

Olfactory Bulb: the smell center in the brain.

• Smell and Memories

Kinesthetic and Vestibular Senses

Kinesthetic Senses: senses of muscle movement, posture, and strain on muscles and joints.

Vestibular Senses: the senses of equilibrium and body position in space; use this information to determine which way is up and which way is down.

• Motion Sickness

• Vertigo

Perceptual Organization

Gestalt Psychologists: showed that a figure can form a whole different from its surroundings; the whole is greater than the sum of its parts.

Figure-Ground: the tendency of the visual system to simplify a scene into the main object that we are looking at (the figure) and everything else that forms the background (or ground).

_____

_____

_____

_____

_____

_____

Perception and Grouping

Grouping: the perceptual tendency to organize stimuli into coherent groups. Four principles of perceptual organization/grouping:

_____

_____

_____

_____

_____

_____

Visual Illusions

Visual Illusions: result from false and misleading depth cues.

- Physical: cause of the illusion is in the behavior of the light before it reaches the eye causing us to see something that isn't physically there

- Perceptual: occur because the stimulus contains misleading cues that give rise to inaccurate or impossible perceptions.

_____

_____

_____

_____

_____

_____

Movement Illusions

Real Movement: physical displacement of an object from one position or location to another.

Apparent Movement: occurs when we perceive movement in objects that are actually standing still.

- Stroboscopic Motion: apparent movement that results from a series of still pictures in rapid succession as in a motion picture.

- Phi Phenomenon: apparent movement caused by flashing lights in sequence, as on theater marquees.

Perceptual Organization

How important is experience in shaping our perception?

Perceptual Set: A mental predisposition to perceive one thing and not another. Examples of perceptual set:

(a) Loch ness monster or a tree trunk?
(b) Flying saucers or clouds?

Extrasensory Perception (ESP)

The ability to perceive or acquire information without using the ordinary senses is called Extrasensory Perception (ESP).

Parapsychology: field of study focusing on ESP and other psychic phenomenon.

No clear scientific support for the existence of ESP (Pseudoscience)

Types of Extrasensory Perception

Telepathy: Mind-to-mind communication; one person sends thoughts and the other receives them.

Clairvoyance: Perception of remote events, such as sensing a friend's house on fire.

Precognition: Perceiving future events, such as a plane crash or accident.

Psychokinesis: mind over matter where people can levitate objects or influence the movement of an object.

_____

_____

_____

_____

_____

_____

_____

Chapter 5: Consciousness

- Consciousness
  - Sleep
  - Hypnosis
  - Drug Altered Consciousness

Conscious Experience

Consciousness: our awareness of various cognitive processes such as sleeping, dreaming, concentrating, and making decisions; refers to the relationship between the mind and the world with which it interacts.

Attention

Our conscious awareness processes only a small part of all that we experience.

Selective Attention: the focusing of conscious awareness on a particular stimulus.

- Inattentional Blindness

- Change Blindness

Conscious Experience

<u>Daydreams</u>: shifts in attention away from the here and now into a private world of make-believe.

- *Reasons?*

- *Helpful or harmful?*

Sleep and Sleep Theories

<u>Sleep</u>: a natural state of rest characterized by a reduction in voluntary body movement and decreased awareness of our surroundings.

- *Why Do We Sleep?*

  - Restorative Theories

  - Learning/Memory Theories

  - Developmental/Brain Plasticity Theories

  - Adaptive/Evolutionary/ Inactivity Theories

What Makes Us Sleepy?

<u>Circadian Rhythm</u>: a regular biological rhythm with a period of approximately 24 hours.

<u>Suprachiasmatic Nucleus (SCN):</u> a cluster of neurons in the hypothalamus that receives input from the retina regarding light and dark cycles and is involved in regulating the biological clock.

- <u>Melatonin</u>: hormone that contributes to the regulation of the sleep-wake cycle.

- <u>Adenosine</u>: a neurotransmitter that plays a role in promoting sleep and suppressing arousal.

The Stages of Sleep

Each stage of sleep is marked by characteristic patterns of brain waves, muscular activity, blood and body temperature.

- Misconceptions about sleep

- Brain waves and sleep stages

- Sleep cycles throughout the night

Dreams

Dreams: vivid visual and auditory experiences that occur primarily during REM periods of sleep.

Why Do We Dream?

1. Wish Fulfillment
2. Information Processing
3. Physiological Function
4. Activation-Synthesis
5. Cognitive Development
6. Extension of Waking Life

Sleep Disorders

- Sleep Talking and Sleepwalking

- Nightmares
  vs
- Night Terrors

- Insomnia: difficulty in falling asleep or remaining asleep throughout the night .

- Apnea: breathing difficulty during the night and feelings of exhaustion during the day.

- Narcolepsy: sudden nodding off during the day and sudden loss of muscle tone following moments of emotional arousal.

Hypnosis:

A trancelike state in which a person responds readily to suggestions; A social interaction in which one person (the hypnotist) suggests to another (the subject) that certain perceptions, feelings, thoughts, or behaviors will spontaneously occur.

Hypnos: Greek god of sleep

Facts and Myths

Can anyone experience hypnosis?	Yes, to some extent.
Can hypnosis enhance recall of forgotten events?	No.
Can hypnosis force people to act against their will?	No.
Can hypnosis be therapeutic?	Yes. Self-suggestion can heal too.
Can hypnosis alleviate pain?	Yes.

Hypnosis

- Controversial state!

- Posthypnotic Suggestions: a suggestion, made during a hypnosis session, to be carried out after the subject is no longer hypnotized.

Explaining the Hypnotized State

1. Social Influence Theory:
   Hypnotic subjects may
   simply be imaginative
   actors playing a social
   role.

2. Divided Consciousness
   Theory: Hypnosis is a
   special state of
   dissociated (divided)
   consciousness..

Drugs and Consciousness

Psychoactive Drugs:
chemical substances
that alter perception,
mood, and
consciousness.

Drug Altered Consciousness

Drug use is different today than from earlier times:

- Change in use from being
  spiritual, medicines and tonics
  to recreational use

- Drugs have changed to
  stronger and more addictive
  substances

- Know more about the harmful effects of drugs

Substance Disorders

Substance Use Disorders: a
problematic pattern of drug use;
combines the DSM-IV-R categories
of substance abuse and
substance dependence into a
single disorder measured on a
continuum from mild to severe.

Substance Induced Disorders:
disorders where the symptoms
are the direct result of substance use.

_____

_____

_____

_____

_____

_____

_____

Tolerance and Withdrawal

Tolerance: with repeated exposure to a
drug, the drug's effect lessens and it
takes greater quantities to get the
desired effect.

Withdrawal Symptoms: unpleasant
physical or psychological effects following
the discontinuance of a substance.

_____

_____

_____

_____

_____

_____

How Drugs Work in The Body

Many drugs can be grouped based on their method of action:

•Agonist: a chemical that binds to some receptor of a cell and triggers a
response by that cell; often mimic the effect of a neurotransmitter in the
brain. *Ex: morphine, which mimics the actions of endorphins.*

•Antagonist: a type of drug that does not
provoke a biological response itself upon
binding to a receptor, but blocks or
dampens neurotransmitters in the brain.
*Ex. Haloperidol which blocks dopamine
to help control symptoms of schizophrenia.*

***Not always simple to classify a drug – have to look at the specific
neurotransmitters and/or systems being affected.***

_____

_____

_____

_____

_____

_____

Three Main Categories of Drugs:

1. Depressants

2. Stimulants

3. Hallucinogens

_____

_____

_____

_____

_____

_____

_____

Depressants

Depressants: chemicals that slow down behavior or cognitive processes.

- Alcohol: a depressant that is the intoxicating ingredient in fermented or distilled liquors.

  - Benzodiazepines: a group of depressant drugs known as sedative-hypnotics, which generally describes their sleep-inducing and anxiety decreasing effects.

  - Barbiturates: a group of depressant drugs first used for their sedative and anticonvulsant properties, now used only to treat such conditions as epilepsy and arthritis.

- Opiates: depressant drugs, such as opium, and heroin, derived from the opium poppy, that dull the senses and include feelings of euphoria, well-being and relaxation.

_____

_____

_____

_____

_____

_____

Stimulants

Stimulants: drugs that stimulate the sympathetic nervous system and produce feelings of optimism and boundless energy.

- Caffeine: a stimulant that occurs naturally in coffee, tea, and cocoa, popularly believed to maintain alertness and wakefulness.

- Amphetamines: stimulant drugs that initially produce "rushes" of euphoria often followed by sudden crashes sometimes severe depression.

_____

_____

_____

_____

_____

_____

_____

Stimulants

Ecstasy (MDMA): a stimulant and mild hallucinogen; commonly used in rave settings.

Cocaine: drug derived from the coca plant that, although producing a sense of euphoria by stimulating the sympathetic nervous system, also leads to anxiety, depression, and addictive cravings.

_____

_____

_____

_____

_____

_____

_____

Stimulants

Nicotine: the psychoactive ingredient in tobacco.

• Probably the most dangerous and addictive stimulant in use today.

_____

_____

_____

_____

_____

_____

Hallucinogens

Hallucinogens: drugs that distort visual and auditory perception.

• LSD: psychedelic drug that produce hallucinations and delusions similar to those occurring in a psychotic state.

• Marijuana: a mild hallucinogen that produces a "high" often characterized by feelings of euphoria, a sense of well-being, and swings in mood from relaxation to anxiety and paranoia.

• Most frequently used illegal drug in U.S

_____

_____

_____

_____

_____

_____

Influences on Drug Use

The causes of substance abuse and dependence are a complex combination of biological, psychological, and social factors that vary for each individual and for each substance.

Biological influences
- genetic tendencies
- dopamine reward circuit

Psychological influences
- lacking sense of purpose
- signifigant stress
- psycological disorders, such as depression

Drug use

Social-cultural influences
- urban environment
- belonging to a drug-using cultural group
- peer influences

Chapter 6: Learning

- •Classical Conditioning
- •Operant Conditioning
- •Observational Learning

What is Learning?

Learning: The process by which experience or practice results in a relatively permanent change in behavior.

Classical Conditioning

Classical Conditioning: a form of learning in which a response naturally elicited by one stimulus comes to be elicited by a different, formerly neutral stimulus.

- Ivan Pavlov

1

Classical Conditioning

Unconditioned Stimulus (US): a stimulus that invariably causes an organism to respond in a specific way.

Unconditioned Response (UR): a response that takes place in an organism whenever an unconditioned stimulus occurs.

Conditioned Stimulus (CS): an originally neutral stimulus that is paired with an unconditioned stimulus and eventually produces the desired response in an organism when presented alone.

Conditioned Response (CR): after conditioning, the response an organism produces when a conditioned stimulus is present.

The Conditioning Process

Acquisition is the initial learning stage in classical conditioning in which an association between a neutral stimulus and an unconditioned stimulus takes place.

The Conditioning Process

Extinction: the diminishing of a conditioned response.

Spontaneous Recovery: the reappearance, after a pause, of an extinguished conditioned response.

Generalization: the tendency to respond to stimuli similar to the CS.

Discrimination: the learned ability to distinguish between a conditioned stimulus and other stimuli.

2

Extending Pavlov's Understanding

- John Watson and "Baby Albert"

- Pavlov and Watson considered consciousness, or the mind, unfit for the scientific study of psychology.

  Later behaviorists suggested that animals learn *expectancy* or *awareness* of a stimulus.

Operant Conditioning: the type of learning in which behaviors are emitted to earn rewards or avoid punishments.

Thorndike and Skinner

Edward Thorndike and the Puzzle Box

- Law of Effect: rewarded behavior is likely to occur again.

B.F. Skinner and the Operant Chamber (Skinner Box)

- Performed studies in conditioning and training through reward/punishment mechanisms.

Shaping

Shaping: reinforcers guide behavior toward the desired target behavior through successive approximations.

Consequences: events following a behavior.

Reinforcers: a stimuli that follows a behavior and increases the likelihood that the behavior will be repeated.

Punishers: stimuli that follows a behavior and decreases the likelihood that the behavior will be repeated.

- To be effective, punishment needs to be: swift, sufficient, and consistent.

- Although there may be some justification for occasional punishment, it often leads to negative effects.

Observational Learning

Observational (Vicarious) Learning: learning by observing other people's behavior.

Modeling: the process of observing and imitating a specific behavior.

Social Learning Theorists: psychologists whose view of learning emphasizes the ability to learn by observing a model or receiving instructions, without firsthand experience by the learner.

4

Mirror Neurons

Neuroscientists discovered <u>Mirror Neurons</u> (frontal lobe neurons that fire when performing certain actions or when observing another doing so) in the brains of animals and humans that are active during observational learning.

_____

_____

_____

_____

_____

_____

_____

Bandura's Experiments

Bandura's Bobo doll study (1961) indicated that individuals learn through imitating others who receive rewards and punishments.

_____

_____

_____

_____

_____

_____

_____

5

Chapter 7: Memory

- Memory
- Short-Term Memory
- Long-Term Memory
- The Biology of Memory
- Why Do We Forget?
- Special Topics in Memory
- How to Improve Your Memory

Memory

Memory: the ability to remember the things that we have experienced, imagined, and learned.

Information Processing Model: a computer-like model used to describe the way humans encode, store, and retrieve information.

Three process involved in memory:

1. Encoding
2. Storage
3. Retrieval

Short-Term Memory

Short-Term Memory: working memory; briefly stores and processes selected information from the sensory registers.

- Limited capacity – information that can be repeated in 1.5 to 2 seconds.

Example:

1. C X W
2. M N K T Y
3. R P J H B Z S
4. G B M P V Q F J D
5. E G Q W J P B R H K A

Short-Term Memory

Chunking: the grouping of information into meaningful units for easier handling by short-term memory.

Example:

6. T J Y F A V M C F K I B

TV FBI JFK YMCA

Short-Term Memory

Maintaining Short-Term Memory – STM is fleeting and lasts for only a few seconds so how do we hold information longer?

- Rote Rehearsal: repeating information over and over again either silently or out loud.

Long-Term Memory

Long-Term Memory: the portion of memory that is more or less permanent, corresponding to everything we "know".

Types of LTM:

1. Episodic:

2. Semantic

3. Procedural

4. Emotional

Long-Term Memory

Four processes used to hold information in LTM:

1. Rote Rehearsal

2. Elaborative Rehearsal: the linking of new information in STM to familiar material stored in LTM.

   - Mnemonics: techniques that make material easier to remember.

3. Schema: a set of beliefs or expectations about something that is based on past experience.

4. Spacing Effect: the tendency for distributed study or practice to yield better long-term retention.

The Biology of Memory

- How are memories stored?

  - Long-Term Potentiation (LTP): a long-lasting change in the structure or function of a synapse that increases the efficiency of neural transmission and is thought to be related to how information is stored by neurons.

- Where are memories stored?

Forgetting

What factors explain why we sometimes forget?

1. Biological Factors

2. Experience Related Factors

Biology and Forgetting

1. __Time__

   - Decay Theory

2. __Disruption of storage process__

   - Retrograde Amnesia

   - Head Injuries/Brain Damage

   - Alzheimer's Disease

Experiences and Forgetting

1. __Interference__: information mixed up or pushed aside by other information.

   Retroactive
   Interference

   Proactive
   Interference

Experiences and Forgetting

2. Situational Factors

   - __State-Dependent Memory__: people who learn material in a certain physiological state tend to recall that material better if they return to the same state they were in during learning.

Special Topics in Memory

Autobiographical Memory

- Childhood Amnesia

Extraordinary Memory

- Eidetic Memory

Flashbulb Memories: experience of remembering vividly a certain event and the incidents surrounding it even after a long time has passed.

Special Topics in Memory
Continued...

Source Error: involves the misattribution of the source of a memory.

Elizabeth Loftus and Eye Witness Testimony

Déjà Vu

Déjà Vu: the eerie feeling of "I've experienced this before."

How To Improve Your Memory

A strong memory depends on the health and vitality of your brain and there are many things you can do to improve your memory and mental performance.

Lifestyle Tips:

■Don't underestimate the importance of exercise and sleep

■Eat a brain-boosting diet

■Keep stress in check

■Give your brain a workout

_____

_____

_____

_____

_____

_____

_____

How To Improve Your Memory

Attention and Learning Tips:

■Be motivated

■Pay attention and minimize distractions

■Practice and rehearse

■Use multiple senses when possible

■Make it meaningful – mnemonic devices and relating information to things you already know

■Try explaining the ideas to someone else in your own words

_____

_____

_____

_____

_____

_____

Chapter 8: Cognition

- Cognition and The Building Blocks of Thought
- Problem Solving
- Intelligence and Mental Abilities
- Heredity, Environment, and Intelligence
- Extremes of Intelligence
- Creativity

Cognition and Mental Abilities

Cognition: the processes whereby we acquire and use knowledge.

Building Blocks of Thought – three most important:

1. Language

2. Images

3. Concepts

Problem Solving

Problem Solving: the three general aspects of the problem-solving process:

1. Interpreting the Problem

2. Implementing Strategies

3. Evaluation

Problem Solving Strategies

- _Insight_: a sudden and often novel realization of a solution to a problem.

- _Algorithms_: a step-by-step method of problem solving that guarantees a correct solution if it is appropriate for the problem and correctly carried out.

- _Heuristics_: rules of thumb that help in simplifying and solving problems, although they do not guarantee a correct solution.

Common Heuristics

- _Hill Climbing_: a heuristic, problem solving strategy in which each step moves you progressively closer to the final goal.

- _Subgoals_: intermediate, more manageable goals used in one heuristic strategy to make it easier to reach the final goal.

- _Working Backward_: a heuristic strategy in which one works backward from the desired goal to the given conditions.

Problem Solving: Obstacles and Solutions

Obstacles:

- _Mental Set_: the tendency to perceive and to approach problems in certain ways.

- _Functional Fixedness_: the tendency to perceive only a limited number of uses for an object, thus interfering with the process of problem solving.

Solutions:

- _Brainstorming_: a problem-solving strategy in which an individual or group produces numerous ideas and evaluates them only after all ideas have been collected.

Intelligence and Mental Abilities

What is intelligence?

Intelligence: a general term referring to the ability involved in learning and adaptive behavior; mental quality consisting of the ability to learn from experience, solve problems, and use knowledge to adapt to new situations.

Theories of Intelligence

- General Intelligence (g)

- Triarchic Theory of Intelligence

- Theory of Multiple Intelligences

- Emotional Intelligence

Assessing Intelligence

Psychologists define Intelligence Testing as a method for assessing an individual's mental aptitudes and comparing them with others using numerical scores.

Psychometric Properties:

What Makes a Good Test?

- Standardization: defining meaningful scores by comparison with the performance of a pretested standardization group.

- Reliability (consistency): ability of a test to produce stable and dependable scores.

- Validity (accuracy): ability of a test to measure what it has been designed to measure.

Heredity, Environment, and Intelligence

The IQ Debate -
A useful analogy
comes from
studies involving
plants.

Extremes of Intelligence

Intellectual Developmental Disorder (formerly Mental Retardation): condition of significantly sub-average intelligence combined with deficiencies in behavior.

Giftedness: refers to
superior IQ combined
with demonstrated or
potential ability in
such areas as academic
aptitude, creativity,
and leadership.

Creativity

Creativity: the ability
to produce novel
and socially valued
ideas or objects.

■ Difficult to Measure

Chapter 9: Motivation

- Motivation and Motivation Theories
  - Hunger
  - The Need to Belong
  - Motivation at Work

Motive: specific need or desire, such as hunger, thirst, or achievement, that prompts goal-directed behavior.

Perspectives on Motivation: Drives

Drive: state of tension or arousal that motivates behavior.

Drive Reduction Theory: states that motivated behavior is aimed at reducing a state of bodily tension or arousal and returning the organism to Homeostasis (balance).

Perspectives on Motivation: Arousal

Arousal Theory: theory of
motivation that proposes
that organisms seek
an optimal level of
arousal.

Perspectives on Motivation: Intrinsic vs. Extrinsic

Intrinsic Motivation: a desire to perform a behavior that
stems from the
enjoyment derived
from the behavior
itself.

Extrinsic Motivation: a
desire to perform a
behavior to obtain an
external reward or
punishment.

Perspectives on Motivation: Maslow's Hierarchy of Needs

Hierarchy of Needs: a
theory of motivation
advanced by Maslow
holding that higher
order motives only
emerge after lower
level motives have
been satisfied.

Perspectives on Motivation: Instincts

Instinct Theory: All creatures are born
with specific innate knowledge about how
to survive.

Psychoanalytic Theory:
Freud believed that humans
have only two basic drives:
Eros and *Thanatos*, or the
Life and Death drives.

Hunger

- There is a difference between the
  psychological state of hunger and the
  biological need for food.

- The hypothalamus is the brain center involved in hunger
  and eating.

- Psychological and Environmental
  Factors

Eating Disorders

Anorexia Nervosa: an eating disorder that is associated
with an intense fear of weight gain
and a distorted body image.

Bulimia Nervosa: an eating disorder characterized by binges of
eating followed by self-induced vomiting or purging.

Obesity and Weight Control

- Obesity is the most pressing health problem in America.

Obesity: excess of body fat in relation to lean body mass.

Body Mass Index (BMI): a numerical index calculated from a person's height and weight that is used to indicate health status and predict disease risk.

Losing Weight

Set Point Theory: a theory that our bodies are genetically predisposed to maintaining a certain weight by changing our metabolic rate and activity level in response to caloric intake.

- 2/3 of women and 1/2 of men report wanting to lose weight.

- Those who do manage to lose weight set realistic goals and change their lifestyles to lose weight gradually.

- Eat crispy greens rather than Krispy Kremes!

Losing Weight

Most popular diets are Fad Diets which often promise quick results with a short time commitment whereas long-term success requires permanent changes in behavior, diet, and activity.

Ways to spot a fad diet:

- It claims fast weight loss
- Claims that sound too good to be true
- Foods defined as "good" and "bad"
- Less than 1,000 calories daily
- A required vitamin/mineral supplement or food product
- Elimination of a major food group or an essential nutrient
- No activity or exercise needed
- It's written by someone with no expertise in weight management

The Need to Belong

- Another powerful motive that we possess as people is the need to belong which is referred to as belongingness or our Affiliation Need.

- While some people are more private and enjoy solitude more than others, the vast majority of people seek to become strongly attached to others and to form close and enduring relationships.

- Affiliation vs Social Exclusion – advantages and disadvantages

Motivation at Work

Industrial-Organizational Psychology: the application of psychological concepts and methods to optimizing human behavior in workplaces.

- Personnel Psychology: focuses on employee recruitment, selection, placement, training, appraisal, and development.

- Organizational Psychology: examines organizational influences on worker satisfaction and productivity and facilitates organizational change.

Chapter 10: Emotion

•Defining Emotion

•Theories of Emotion

•Embodied Emotions

•Communicating Emotions

•Basic Emotions

Emotions

- In psychology, emotion is often defined as a complex state of feeling that results in physical and psychological changes that influence thought and behavior.

- The word first appeared in our language in the mid-16th century, adapted from the French word émouvoir, which literally means, "to stir up".

- Human emotion involves "...physiological arousal, expressive behaviors, and conscious experience."

- Emotions are "a complex psychological state that involves three distinct components: a subjective experience, a physiological response, and an expressive response."

Theories of Emotion

- Independently proposed by psychologist William James and physiologist Carl Lange in the late 19th century.

- The James-Lange Theory of Emotion suggests that emotions occur as a result of physiological reactions to events.

- According to this theory, you see an external stimulus that leads to a physiological reaction. Your emotional reaction is dependent upon how you interpret those physical reactions.

Theories of Emotion

- Developed by Walter Cannon and Philip Bard.

- The Cannon-Bard Theory of Emotion states that we feel emotions and experience physiological reactions such as sweating, trembling and muscle tension simultaneously.

- More specifically, it is suggested that emotions result when the thalamus sends a message to the brain in response to a stimulus, resulting in a physiological reaction; the emotion and the arousal are simultaneous.

Theories of Emotion

- Coined by Stanley Schachter and Jerome Singer in the 1960s.

- The Schachter-Singer Theory of Emotion suggests that the physiological arousal occurs first, and then the individual must identify the reason behind this arousal in order to experience and label it as an emotion.

- Sometimes called the two-factor theory of emotion; the experience of emotion depends on two factors: physiological arousal and cognitive processing.

Theories of Emotion

Additional Theories:

- Facial Feedback Theory

- Lazarus Cognitive-Mediational Theory

Emotions and the Autonomic Nervous System

During an emotional experience, our autonomic nervous system mobilizes energy in the body that arouses us.

_____
_____
_____
_____
_____
_____
_____

Detecting Lies

Polygraph (Lie Detector): a machine, commonly used in attempts to detect lies, that measures several of the physiological responses accompanying emotion.

_____
_____
_____
_____
_____
_____
_____

Communicating Emotion

Although emotions can often be expressed in words, much of the time we communicate our feelings nonverbally through:

– Voice Quality

– Facial Expressions

– Body Language

– Personal Space

– Explicit Acts

_____
_____
_____
_____
_____
_____

Experienced Emotion

How Many Basic Emotions Do We Possess?

- Psychologist Robert Plutchik proposed eight basic emotions: fear, surprise, sadness, disgust, anger, anticipation, joy, and acceptance.

- Other theories propose that we have six basic or universal emotions: happiness, sadness, surprise, fear, anger, and disgust.

Anger

1. People generally become angry with friends and loved ones who commit wrongdoings, especially if they are willful, unjustified, and avoidable.

2. People are also angered by small things such as foul odors, high temperatures, traffic jams, and aches and pains.

Dealing with anger -

- Catharsis: emotional release.

- Other strategies...

Fear

- Fear is a feeling caused by a perceived threat or danger and can be a vital response to physical and/or emotional danger.

- Physical Changes (fight or flight reaction)

- Common fears include spiders, snakes, heights, open or crowded spaces, flying, public speaking, and the dark.

Happiness

People who are happy perceive the world as being safer, are able to make decisions easily, are more cooperative, and live healthier, energized, and more satisfied lives.

• <u>Feel-Good, Do-Good Phenomenon:</u> when we feel happy we are more willing to help others.

• Our satisfaction and dissatisfaction or success and failure are all relative to our recent experience.

Determining Our Happiness

<u>Adaptation-Level Phenomenon:</u> our tendency to form judgments relative to a neutral level defined by our prior experience.

<u>Relative Deprivation:</u> the perception that one is worse off relative to those with whom one compares oneself.

"I cried because I had no shoes until I met a man who had no feet"

How to be Happier

• Realize money doesn't equal happiness

• Take control of your time

• Act happy

• Seek work and leisure that engage your skills

• Give your body the sleep it wants

• Give priority to close relationships

• Focus beyond self

• Be grateful

• Nurture your spiritual self

• Laughter

Chapter 11: Human Development

·Developmental Psychology

·Prenatal Development

·Childhood

·Adolescence

·Adulthood

·Late Adulthood

Developmental Psychology

Developmental Psychology: a branch of psychology that studies physical, cognitive, and social change throughout the lifespan.

Conception

A single sperm cell (male) penetrates the outer coating of the egg (female) and fuses to form one fertilized cell.

Prenatal Development

Zygote

↓

Blastocyst

↓

Embryo

↓

Fetus

_____

_____

_____

_____

_____

_____

_____

Pregnancy

Pregnancy: the carrying of offspring inside the womb of a female.

- Typically broken into three periods, or Trimesters, each of about three months.

Placenta: an organ that connects the developing fetus to the uterine wall to allow nutrient uptake and waste elimination via the mother's blood supply.

Teratogens: toxic agents that can compromise the development of the fetus.

- Pregnancy is most likely to have a favorable outcome when the mother has good nutrition and good medical care and avoids exposing the fetus to harmful substances.

_____

_____

_____

_____

_____

The Competent Newborn

Neonate: newborn baby.

Reflexes: newborns come equipped with a number of useful reflexes which are critical to life outside the uterus.

- Rooting Reflex

- Sucking Reflex

- Swallowing Reflex

- Grasping Reflex

- Stepping Reflex

- Moro Reflex

_____

_____

_____

_____

_____

_____

Childhood - Physical Development

Brain and ***Neurological Development*** – high importance of stimulation to increase neural growth!

Maturation: biological growth processes that enable orderly changes in behavior, relatively uninfluenced by experience.

Sequence
of Motor
Development

Childhood - Cognitive Development

Jean Piaget's 4 Stages of Cognitive Development

Sensorimotor Stage
(0-2 years)

Babies take in the world by looking, hearing, touching, mouthing, and grasping.

Young children do not grasp Object Permanence, i.e., objects that are out of sight are also out of mind.

Preoperational Stage
(2-7 years)

Children are too young to perform mental operations.

Preoperational children are
<u>Egocentric</u>: they cannot perceive
things from another's point of view.

Do you get the impression your
child is constantly saying, "My
way or the highway!" At this
point, she probably is!

Concrete Operational Stage
(7-11 years)

In concrete operational stage, 6- to 7-year-olds grasp
<u>Conservation</u>: the concept that the quantity of a
substance is not altered by reversible changes in it's
appearance.

Formal Operational Stage
(12+ years)

Around age 12, our reasoning ability expands from
concrete thinking to *abstract thinking*. We can now use
symbols and imagined realities to systematically reason.
Piaget called this formal operational thinking.

Childhood - Social Development

Attachment: emotional bond that develops in the first year of life that makes human babies cling to their caregivers.

Socialization: process by which children learn the behaviors and attitudes appropriate to their family and culture.

_____

_____

_____

_____

_____

_____

Gender-Role Development

By about age 3, children have developed:

■ Gender Identity: a person's perception of being a certain gender; a little girl's knowledge that she is a girl and a little boy's knowledge that he is a boy.

At a young age children begin to acquire:

■ Gender-Role Awareness: a knowledge of what behavior is appropriate for each gender – what is expected of males and females in their society.

_____

_____

_____

_____

_____

Adolescence - Physical Development

Adolescence: a period of life roughly between the ages of 10-20 when a person is transitioning from a child to an adult.

- Starts with the physical beginnings of sexual maturity and ends with the social achievement of independent adult status.

Puberty: the onset of sexual maturation.

- Puberty occurs earlier in females (11 years) than males (13 years).

Growth Spurt: a rapid increase in height and weight that occurs during adolescence.

_____

_____

_____

_____

_____

_____

Sexual Characteristics

During puberty <u>Primary Sexual Characteristics</u> develop rapidly and include the reproductive organs and external genitalia.

<u>Secondary Sexual Characteristics</u>: the non-reproductive traits such as breasts and
hips in girls
and facial
hair and
deepening
of voice
in boys
develop.

Adolescence - Cognitive Development

Two common fallacies that characterize adolescent thinking:

1. <u>Imaginary Audience</u>: delusion that an adolescent is constantly being observed by others.

2. <u>Personal Fable</u>: adolescents' delusion that they are unique, very important, and invulnerable.

Forming an Identity

In Western cultures, many adolescents try out different selves before settling into a consistent and comfortable identity (stable sense of self).

Emerging Adulthood

Emerging adulthood spans ages 18-25. During this time, young adults may live with their parents and attend college or work.

The main developmental concern is Intimacy: the ability to form close, loving relationships. On average, emerging adults marry in their mid-twenties.

Adulthood's Commitments

Love, Partnerships, and Parenting

• Nearly all adults form long-term, loving partnership in their lives.

• For many parents, loving and being loved by their children is an unparalleled source of fulfillment.

Work

• Happiness stems from working in a job that fits your interests and provides you with a sense of competence and accomplishment.

Adulthood - Physical Changes

Muscular strength, reaction time, and sensory abilities begin to decline after the mid-twenties.

Around age 50, women go through Menopause: the time of natural cessation of menstruation; also refers to the biological changes a woman experiences as her ability to reproduce declines.

Men experience decreased levels of hormones and fertility often called Andropause.

Adulthood – Cognitive Changes

Fluid Intelligence: ability to reason speedily. ⇓

Crystalline Intelligence: accumulated knowledge ⇑ and skills.

We gain vocabulary and knowledge but lose recall memory and process more slowly.

Middle Adulthood

Midlife Crisis: a time when adults discover they no longer feel fulfilled in their jobs or personal lives and attempt to make a decisive shift in career or lifestyle.

Midlife Transition: a process whereby adults assess the past and formulate new goals for the future.

- Midlife transitions are much more common than a midlife crisis!

Late Adulthood

- Negative societal views of older adults – often think they are lonely, poor, ill, or senile, when in reality the majority of people over 65 are healthy, productive, and able.

Physical Changes

- Hair thins and turns white/grey
- Skin wrinkles
- Posture changes
- Senses dull
- Reaction times are slower

Attitudes also matter - You're only as old as you feel!

Late Adulthood

Social Development

- <u>Retirement</u> – most see it as a time to slow down and do less or a time to explore new possibilities.

Cognitive Changes

- Healthy people who remain intellectually active maintain a high level of mental functioning in old age

- <u>Alzheimer's Disease</u>: a neurological disorder, most commonly found in late adulthood, characterized by progressive loses in memory and cognition and by changes in personality.

_____

_____

_____

_____

_____

_____

_____

Late Adulthood

Facing the End of Life – Elisabeth Kubler-Ross' five stages that people pass through as they react to their own impending death:

1. Denial

2. Anger

3. Bargaining

4. Depression

5. Acceptance

_____

_____

_____

_____

_____

_____

_____

Chapter 12: Personality

- Personality
- Psychodynamic Theories
- Neo-Analytic Theories
- Biological Theories
- Behaviorist Theories
- Cognitive Theories
- Trait Theories
- Humanistic and Existentialist Theories
- Person-Situation Theories
- Personality Assessment

<u>Personality</u>: an individual's unique pattern of thoughts, feelings, and behaviors that persists over time and across situations.

Each one of us has a distinct personality.

Psychodynamic Theories

Quick Analogy: Humans as unconsciously motivated beings seeking to fulfill (and balance) sexual and aggressive urges.

Sigmund Freud - believed that human behavior is based on unconscious instincts and has strong roots in early childhood experiences.

- <u>Unconscious</u>: all the ideas, thoughts, and feelings of which we are not normally aware.

- <u>Psychoanalysis</u>: theory of personality and form of therapy invented by Freud.

3 Structures of Personality:

1. <u>id</u>
2. <u>ego</u>
3. <u>superego</u>

Psychosexual Stages of Development:

1. Oral Stage
2. Anal Stage
3. Phallic Stage
4. Latency Stage
5. Genital Stage

Neo-Analytic Theories

Quick Analogy: Humans as unconscious (and conscious) actors and goal-oriented strivers.

Carl Jung

- <u>Personal Unconscious</u>: contains the individual's repressed thoughts, forgotten experiences, and undeveloped ideas.

- <u>Collective Unconscious</u>: the level of the unconscious that is inherited and common to all members of a species.

Erik Erikson

- Eight stages of personality development over the lifespan

1. Trust vs. Mistrust
2. Autonomy vs. Shame and Doubt
3. Initiative vs. Guilt
4. Industry vs. Inferiority
5. Identity vs. Role Confusion
6. Intimacy vs. Isolation
7. Generativity vs. Stagnation
8. Integrity vs. Despair

Biological Personality Theories

Quick Analogy: Humans as a bundle of genes, brains, and hormones.

<u>DNA</u> (*deoxyribonucleic acid*): the main ingredient of chromosomes and genes that forms the code for all genetic information.

- Segments within DNA consist of <u>Genes</u> (the biochemical units of heredity) that make proteins to determine our development.

<u>Biological Determinism</u>: the belief that an individual's personality is completely determined by biological factors (especially genetic ones).

Behaviorist Personality Theories

Quick Analogy: Humans as intelligent rats learning life mazes.

- Behaviorists reject such concepts as the unconscious, genetics, motivations, internal traits, and so on seeing people as controlled absolutely by their environments; personality is learned.

- John Locke and *tabula rasa*

- Ivan Pavlov and classical conditioning

- John Watson and Baby Albert

- B.F. Skinner and operant conditioning

Cognitive Personality Theories

Quick Analogy: Humans as scientists and information processors.

■Cognitive psychologists view perceptions of the environment and cognition as the core of what it means to be a person. In other words, the essence of personality is found in the way that we think.

Cognitive Social Learning Theories: view behavior as the product of the interaction of cognitions, learning and past experiences, and the immediate environment.

■*Albert Bandura*

Self-Efficacy: the expectancy that one's efforts will be successful.

Trait Personality Theories

Quick Analogy: Humans as clusters of temperaments, traits, and skills.

Personality Traits: dimensions or characteristics on which people differ in distinctive ways; basically adjectives such as selfish, friendly, dependent, loyal, etc. (words used to describe people).

Trait Approach: use of a limited set of adjectives or adjective Dimensions to describe and scale individuals.

The Big Five: five traits or basic dimensions currently considered to be of central importance in describing personality.

1. *Conscientiousness*
2. *Agreeableness*
3. *Neuroticism*
4. *Openness to Experience*
5. *Extraversion*

Humanistic and Existential Personality Theories

Quick Analogy: Humans as free and responsive beings seeking fulfillment of our spirituality and potentials.

Humanistic Personality Theory: asserts the fundamental goodness of people and their striving toward higher levels of functioning.

Abraham Maslow

■ Self-Actualization: fulfilling our potential.

Carl Rogers

■ Fully Functioning Person: an individual whose self-concept closely resembles his or her inborn capacities or potentials.

■ Unconditional Positive Regard: the full acceptance and love of another person regardless of his or her behavior.

Person-Situation Personality Theories

Quick Analogy: Humans as an ongoing dialogue between self and environment.

- Person-Situation Interactionist approaches look directly at different social situations and their impact on behaviors.

The Power of the Situation

- Personality is sometimes a poor predictor of behavior because the power of a situation can be so strong that it overrides our natural inclinations.

Focus on the Lifespan

- Because we don't stop growing, changing, and responding to the environment, it becomes important to study people's changes over time.

Personality Assessment

Objective Tests

- Minnesota Multiphasic Personality Inventory (MMPI-2)

Projective Tests

- Rorschach Ink Blot Test: a projective test that asks the examinee to describe each of a series of inkblot images.

Projective Tests

Thematic Apperception Test: a projective test in which a participant is asked to make up a story (including what will happen in the future) about a picture that is presented.

Chapter 13: Stress and Health

•Stress and Stressors

•The Stress Response System

•Stress and Health

•Extreme Stress

•Coping with Stress

•Staying Healthy

Stress and Health Psychology

Stress: a state of psychological tension or strain.

Health Psychology: a subfield of psychology concerned with the relationship between psychological factors and physical health and illness.

Sources of Stress

Stressor: any environmental demand that creates a state of tension or threat and requires change or adaptation.

- Change

- Everyday Hassles

- Events

- Self Imposed Stress

The Stress Response System

Hypothalamus: regulates body homeostasis along with linking the nervous system to the endocrine system.

Sympathetic NS "Arouses"
(fight-or-flight)

Parasympathetic NS "Calms"
(rest and digest)

The stress response is marked by the outpouring of *epinephrine* and *norepinephrine* from the inner adrenal glands, increasing heart and respiration rates, mobilizing energy, and dulling pain.

How Stress Affects Health

General Adaptation Syndrome (GAS): According to Selye, the three stages the body passes through as it adapts to stress.

1. Alarm
    Reaction

2. Resistance

3. Exhaustion

Stress and the Body

Coronary Heart Disease: a clogging of the vessels that nourish the heart muscle.

Psychophysiological Illness: any stress-related physical illness such as hypertension and some headaches.

Psychoneuroimmunology (PNI): a developing field in which the health effects of psychological, neural, and endocrine processes on the immune system are studied.

• Stress and AIDS

• Stress and Cancer

Extreme Stress

Post-Traumatic Stress Disorder: psychological disorder marked by episodes of anxiety, sleeplessness, and nightmares resulting from some disturbing past event.

- – Exposure to (or witnessing) a traumatic event

- – Traumatic event is persistently re-experienced

- – Numbing of general responsiveness and avoidance of stimuli associated with the event

- – Symptoms of increased arousal – difficulty sleeping, irritability, hyper vigilance

- – Duration of at least a month

Coping with Stress

Two general types:

1. Direct Coping: refers to intentional efforts to change an uncomfortable situation.

- – Confrontation: acknowledging a stressful situation directly and attempting to find a solution.

- – Compromise: deciding on a more realistic solution or goal when an ideal solution or goal is not practical.

- – Withdrawal: avoiding a situation when other forms of coping are not practical.

2. Defensive Coping: there are times when we can't identify or can't directly deal with the source of our stress.

- – Defense Mechanisms: self-deceptive techniques for reducing stress.

Coping With Stress

- •Perceived Control Over the Stressor

- •Explanatory Style - optimistic vs. pessimistic

- •Social Support

Staying Healthy

- Calm Down

- Reach Out

- Religion and Altruism

- Learn to Cope Effectively

- Adopt a Healthy Lifestyle

  – <u>Aerobic Exercise</u>: sustained exercise that increases heart and lung fitness.

Complementary and Alternative Medicine

<u>Complementary and Alternative Medicine</u>: as yet unproven health care treatments intended to supplement (complement) or serve as alternatives to conventional medicine, and which typically are not widely taught in medical schools, used in hospitals, or reimbursed by insurance companies.

<u>5 Domains</u>:

  – Alternative Medical Systems

  – Mind-Body Interventions

  – Biologically Based Therapies

  – Manipulative and Body-Based Methods

  – Energy Therapies

Chapter 14: Psychological Disorders

- Perspectives on Psychological Disorders
- Anxiety Disorders
- Psychosomatic and Somatoform Disorders
- Dissociative Disorders
- Personality Disorders
- Mood Disorders and Suicide
- Schizophrenia
- Disorders of Childhood
- Disorders of Aging

Defining Psychological Disorders

Mental health workers view <u>Psychological Disorders</u> as persistently harmful thoughts, feelings, and actions.

When behavior is *deviant, distressful, dangerous, and dysfunctional* psychiatrists and psychologists label it as disordered.

In the Wodaabe tribe men wear costumes to attract women. In Western society this would be considered abnormal.

Perspectives on Psychological Disorders

<u>Medical (Biological) Model</u>: psychological disorders have a biochemical or physiological basis.

<u>Psychoanalytic Model</u>: psychological disorders result from unconscious internal conflicts.

<u>Cognitive-Behavioral Model</u>: psychological disorders result from learning maladaptive ways of thinking and behaving.

<u>Diathesis-Stress Model</u>: view that people biologically predisposed to a mental disorder (those with a certain diathesis) will tend to exhibit that disorder when particularly affected by stress.

<u>Systems Approach (Biopsychosocial)</u>: view that biological, psychological, and social risk factors combine to produce psychological disorders; also known as the biopsychosocial model of psychological disorders.

Classifying Psychological Disorders

The American Psychiatric Association rendered a <u>Diagnostic and Statistical Manual of Mental Disorders (DSM)</u> to describe psychological disorders.

The most recent edition, DSM-5 (2013), describes 400 psychological disorders compared to 60 in the 1950s.

Labeling

- Critics of the DSM speak about the dangers of labeling someone

  - we view the person differently

  - make judgments

  - possibly changing reality

- Labels however are often helpful as they can help lead to effective treatments.

Anxiety Disorders

<u>Anxiety</u>: Feelings of fear & apprehension caused by something appropriate and identifiable that pass with time.

<u>Anxiety Disorders</u>: A group of disorders primarily characterized by extreme, unrealistic, or debilitating anxiety.

Anxiety Disorders

Specific Phobias: intense paralyzing fear of
something that is excessive and
unreasonable.

- *Arachnophobia*: spiders

- *Acrophobia*: heights

- *Claustrophobia*: confined spaces

Social Anxiety Disorder (Social Phobia): social
situations and performances in front of other
people.

_____

_____

_____

_____

_____

_____

_____

Anxiety Disorders

Panic Attacks: periodic short bouts of panic
that occur suddenly, reach a peak within
minutes, and then gradually pass.

Panic Disorder: recurrent panic attacks in which
the person suddenly experiences intense fear
or terror without any reasonable cause.

Agoraphobia: multiple intense fears of crowds,
public places, and other situations that require
separation from a source of security.

_____

_____

_____

_____

_____

_____

_____

Anxiety Disorders

Obsessive Compulsive Disorder (OCD): anxiety disorder in which a
person feels driven to think disturbing thoughts or to perform senseless
rituals.

Obsessions: involuntary
thoughts or ideas that keep
recurring despite person's
attempts to stop them.

Compulsions: repetitive,
ritualistic behaviors that a
person feels compelled to
perform.

_____

_____

_____

_____

_____

_____

_____

Psychosomatic and Somatoform Disorders

<u>Psychosomatic Disorder</u>: A disorder in which there is real physical illness that is largely caused by psychological factors such as stress and anxiety.

<u>Somatoform Disorders (*Disorders Featuring Somatic Symptoms*)</u>: Disorders in which there is an apparent physical illness for which there is no organic cause.

- *Examples*: Conversion Disorder, Illness Anxiety Disorder (*formerly* Hypochondriasis)

Dissociative Disorders

<u>Dissociative Disorders</u>: disorders in which some aspect of the personality seems separated from the rest.

- Usually involves some form of memory loss and a complete though generally temporary, change of identity.

<u>Dissociative Identity Disorder</u>: disorder characterized by the separation of the personality into two or more distinct personalities.

Personality Disorders

<u>Personality</u>: individual's unique and enduring pattern of thoughts, feelings, and behavior.

<u>Personality Disorders</u>: disorders in which inflexible and maladaptive ways of thinking and behaving learned early in life cause distress to the person or conflicts with others.

Personality Disorders

Borderline Personality Disorder:
characterized by marked instability
in self-image, mood, and interpersonal
relationships.

Antisocial Personality Disorder: involves a
pattern of violent, criminal, or unethical and
exploitative behavior and an inability to
feel affection for others.

_____

_____

_____

_____

_____

_____

_____

Mood Disorders

Mood Disorders: disturbances in mood or prolonged emotional state;
psychological disorders characterized by emotional extremes.

Major Depressive Disorder: a mood disorder characterized by
overwhelming feelings of sadness, lack of interest in activities, and
possibly excessive guilt or feelings of
worthlessness.

Mania: a mood disorder characterized by
euphoric states, extreme physical activity,
excessive talkativeness, distractedness,
and sometimes grandiosity.

_____

_____

_____

_____

_____

Bipolar Disorder

A mood disorder in which periods of mania and
depression alternate, sometimes with periods of normal
mood intervening. Formerly called manic-depressive
disorder.

_____

_____

_____

_____

_____

_____

_____

Suicide

People who consider suicide are overwhelmed with hopelessness and feel that things cannot get better; they see no way out of their difficulties.

Warning signs:

- Talking About Dying
- Recent Losses
- Intense Depression
- Changes in Personality
- Giving Away Possessions
- Fear of losing control
- Low self esteem
- No hope for the future

Causes of Mood Disorders

Most believe that mood disorders result from a combination of risk factors:

- *Biological*
- *Social*
- *Psychological*

Cognitive Distortions: an illogical and maladaptive response to early negative life events that leads to feelings of incompetence and unworthiness that are reactivated whenever a new situation arises that resembles the original events.

Schizophrenia Disorders

Schizophrenia: a psychotic disorder in which there are disturbances of thoughts, communications, and emotions, including delusions and hallucinations.

1. *Positive Symptoms (Excesses)*

   - Hallucinations: sensory experience in the absence of external stimuli.
   - Delusions: false beliefs about reality that have no basis in facts.

2. *Negative Symptoms (Deficits)*

3. *Psychomotor Symptoms*

**Causes and Treatments

Disorders of Childhood

Attention-Deficit Hyperactivity Disorder (ADHD):
a childhood disorder characterized by
inattention, impulsiveness, and hyperactivity.

Autistic Spectrum Disorder: a pervasive
developmental disorder marked by extreme
unresponsiveness to others, poor communication
skills, and highly repetitive and rigid behavior.

- Lack of responsiveness
- Language and communication problems
- Repetitive and rigid behavior
- Motor movements

Disorders of Aging

Neurocognitive Disorders (*formerly Dementia*): a syndrome marked by
severe problems in memory and in at least one other cognitive function.

Alzheimer's Disease: the most common form of dementia, usually
occurring after the age of 65. The timeframe between onset and
death is typically 8 to 10 years.

- Neurofibrillary Tangles: twisted protein fibers that
  form within certain brain cells as people age.

- Senile Plaques: sphere-shaped deposits of
  beta-amyloid protein that form in spaces
  between certain brain cells and in certain
  blood vessels as people age.

Chapter 15: Therapies

- History of Treatment
- Types of Clinicians
- Insight Therapies
- Behavioral Therapies
- Cognitive Therapies
- Group Therapies
- The Effectiveness of Therapy
- Alternative Therapies
- Biological Treatments
- Institutionalization and Its Alternatives

History of the Treatment of Mental Illness

Maltreatment of the mentally ill throughout the ages was the result of irrational views. Many patients were subjected to strange, debilitating, and downright dangerous treatments.

Psychotherapies

Psychotherapy: the use of psychological techniques to treat mental illness.

Different Types of Clinicians

Counseling Psychologists - generally have a master's degree and help people with problems of everyday life.

Clinical Psychologists - typically have a Ph.D. and have expertise in assessment and psychological disorders.

Psychiatrists – have a M.D. and specialize in prescribing medications for the treatment of psychological disorders.

Social Workers - typically have a master's degree and work with the institutions of society.

Medical Doctors - have a medical degree and specialize in physical treatments.

Insight Therapies

Insight Therapies: a variety of individual psychotherapies designed to give people a better awareness and understanding of their feelings, motivations, and actions in the hope that this will help them to adjust.

Three major insight therapies:

– Psychoanalysis
– Client-Centered Therapy
– Gestalt Therapy

Insight Therapies

Psychoanalysis: theory of personality/form of therapy invented by Freud designed to bring hidden feelings and motives to conscious awareness so that the person can deal with them more effectively.

- Free Association: a psychoanalytic technique that encourages the person to talk without inhibition about whatever thoughts or fantasies come to mind.

Insight Therapies

Client-Centered (Person-Centered) Therapy: non-directional form of therapy developed by Carl Rogers that calls for unconditional positive regard of
the client by the
therapist with the
goal of helping
the client become
a fully functioning
person.

Gestalt Therapy: an insight therapy that emphasizes the wholeness of the personality and attempts to reawaken people to their emotions and sensations in the present.

Behavior Therapies

Behavior Therapies: therapeutic approaches that are based on the belief that all behavior, normal and abnormal, is learned and that the objective of therapy is to teach people new, more satisfying ways of behaving.

- Token Economy: an operant
  conditioning therapy in which
  people earn tokens
  (reinforcers) for desired
  behaviors and exchange them
  for desired items or privileges.

- Exposure Therapies (Flooding):
  a full intensity exposure to a feared
  stimulus for a prolonged period
  of time.

Systematic Desensitization

Systematic Desensitization: a behavioral technique for reducing a person's fear and anxiety by gradually associating a new response (relaxation) with stimuli that have been causing the fear and anxiety.

Cognitive Therapies

<u>Cognitive Therapies</u>: psychotherapies that emphasize changing clients' perceptions of their life situation as a way of modifying their behavior.

Group Therapies

<u>Group Therapy</u>: type of psychotherapy in which clients meet regularly to interact and help one another achieve insight into their feelings and behavior.

<u>Family Therapy</u>: a form of group therapy that sees the family as at least partly responsible for the individual's problems and that seeks to change all the family members' behaviors to the benefit of the family unit as well as the troubled individual.

<u>Couple Therapy</u>: a form of group therapy intended to help troubled partners improve their problems of communication and interaction.

Is Psychotherapy Effective?

It is difficult to gauge the effectiveness of psychotherapy because there are different levels upon which its effectiveness can be measured.

1. Does the patient sense improvement?

2. Does the therapist feel the patient has improved?

3. How do friends and family feel about the patient's improvement?

The Effectiveness of Different Therapies

There is not one best type of therapy but rather a best type for each disorder and each person.

Current trend toward Eclecticism: psychotherapeutic approach that recognizes the value of a broad treatment package over a rigid commitment to one particular form of therapy.

Disorder	Therapy
Depression	Behavioral, Cognitive
Anxiety	Cognitive, Exposure
Bulimia	Cognitive-behavioral
Phobia	Behavioral

Alternative Therapies

In Eye Movement Desensitization and Reprocessing (EMDR) Therapy, the therapist attempts to unlock and reprocess previous frozen traumatic memories by waving a finger in front of the eyes of the client.

** EMDR has not consistently held up under scientific testing.

Alternative Therapies

Seasonal Affective Disorder (SAD), a form of depression, has been effectively treated by Light Exposure Therapy. This form of therapy has been scientifically validated.

Biological Treatments

Biological (Biomedical) Treatments: a group of approaches, including medication, electroconvulsive therapy, and psychosurgery, that are sometimes used to treat psychological disorders in conjunction with, or instead of psychotherapy.

Drug Treatments

Psychopharmacology: the study of the effects of psychoactive drugs on the mind and behavior.

Antidepressant Drugs: used to combat depression. Four different types:

1. MAOIs
2. Tricyclics
3. SSRIs
4. SNRIs

Mood Stabilizers: regulate ups and downs.

Antipsychotic Drugs: drugs used to treat very severe psychological disorders, particularly schizophrenia.

Benzodiazepines: a class of drugs often used to reduce anxiety that enhance the effects of GABA.

Psychostimulants: a broad category of drugs that reduce fatigue, promote alertness, and have possible mood-enhancing properties.

Brain Stimulation

Electroconvulsive Therapy (ECT): is used for severely depressed patients who do not respond to drugs. The patient is anesthetized and given a muscle relaxant.

Newer Methods:

•Vagus Nerve Stimulation

•Transcranial Magnetic Stimulation (TMS)

•Deep Brain Stimulation (DBS)

Psychosurgery

Psychosurgery: brain surgery
performed to change a
person's behavior and
emotional state was popular
even in Neolithic times.

Although used sparingly
today, about 200 such
operations do take place in
the US alone.

Institutionalization and Alternatives

- People with severe mental
  illness are often hospitalized

Controversial:

- Perpetually under-funded
  and under-staffed becoming
  warehouses for patients who don't get better due to lack of
  adequate treatment.

Deinstitutionalization: policy of treating people with severe
psychological disorders in the larger community or in small
residential centers such as halfway houses, rather than large
public hospitals.

Chapter 16: Social Psychology

• Social Psychology
• Attribution Theory and the Fundamental Attribution Error
• Social Influence
• Groups and Decision Making
• Social Cognition
• Helping Behaviors

Social Psychology: the scientific study of the ways in which the thoughts, feelings, and behaviors of one individual are influenced by the real, imagined, or inferred behavior or characteristics of other people.

Attributing Behavior to a Person or to a Situation

Attribution Theory: Fritz Heider (1958) suggested that we have a tendency to give causal explanations for someone's behavior, often by crediting either the situation or the person's disposition.

Fritz Heider

Fundamental Attribution Error

The tendency to overestimate the impact of personal disposition and underestimate the impact of the situations in analyzing the behaviors of others leads to the Fundamental Attribution Error.

Example: We see Joe as quiet, shy, and introverted most of the time, but with friends he is very talkative, loud, and extroverted.

Social Influence

Social Influence: the process by which others individually or collectively affect one's perceptions, attitudes, and actions.

Social Influence

- Cultural Influences

- Norms: a shared idea or expectation about how to behave.

Social Influence

<u>Conformity</u>: Adjusting one's behavior or thinking to coincide with a group standard even at the expense of one's preferences.

Solomon Asch's experiments

Social Influence

<u>Compliance</u>: change of behavior in response to an explicit request from another person or group. Techniques to induce compliance:

- *Foot-in-the-door effect*

- *Lowball procedure*

- *Door-in-the-face effect*

<u>Obedience</u>: change of behavior in response to a command from another person, typically an authority figure.

- Stanley Milgram's experiment

- Why do people obey even if
  it violates their own principles?

Groups and Decision Making

<u>Risky Shift</u>: greater willingness of a group than an individual to take substantial risks.

Groups and Mob behavior

<u>Groupthink</u>: a mode of thinking that occurs when the desire for harmony in a decision-making group overrides the realistic appraisal of alternatives.

<u>Deindividuation</u>: a loss of personal sense of responsibility in a group.

Groups and <u>Lord of the Flies</u>

Social Relations

Primacy Effect: early information about someone weighs more heavily than later information in influencing one's impression of that person.

Stereotypes: a set of characteristics presumed to be shared by all members of a social category.

Social Relations

Prejudice: an unfair, intolerant, or unfavorable attitude toward a group of people.

Discrimination: an unfair series of acts taken toward an entire group of people or individual members of that group.

Racism: prejudice and discrimination directed at a particular racial group.

Strategies for Reducing Prejudice and Discrimination

- *Re-categorization*

- *Controlled Processing*

- *Broadening Horizons*

  - *Improved Group Contact*

Helping Behaviors

Altruistic Behavior:
helping behavior
that is not linked to
personal gain;
unselfish regard for
the welfare of
others.

Helping Behaviors

Bystander Effect: the tendency for an individual's helpfulness in an
emergency to decrease as the number of passive bystanders
increases.

The decision-making process for bystander intervention:

WARM-UPS

WARM-UPS INSTRUCTIONS AND GRADING RUBRIC

At the beginning of each class (except exam days), we will do a "warm-up". The goal of these warm-ups will be to either review a topic that we have covered or to preview a topic that we will be covering that day. At the beginning of class, I will announce the warm-up prompt for the day which can be found in your <u>Guide to Psychology</u> textbook. Once the warm-up has been announced, you will have roughly five minutes to answer the prompt using your notes, book, partner, or a small group depending on your personal preference. I am not looking for essay responses, just a few well-thought out sentences indicating that you have reflected on your given prompt. If you come unprepared (i.e. you don't have your textbook, notes, or haven't done the reading) you will struggle to get full points on many of the warm-ups so please come prepared! We will briefly discuss your responses, I will collect the warm-ups, and then we will move on.

You must turn your warm-up in when they are collected in order to receive credit; if you come in after I have collected the warm-ups, you will not be able to receive points for that day! Missing a couple of these will not hurt you. In fact, I will only be counting a certain number of warm-ups which allows you a couple of free days and gives me room in case I must cancel a class; see the syllabus for the specific number of warm-ups to be counted. Please make your best effort to arrive on time; if you are consistently late, the points will start to add up!

Grading Scale

5 points – you fully and/or correctly answered the prompt/questions on the warm-up. It is clear that you have given your response some thought and that you understand the material in question.

3 points – you adequately and/or somewhat correctly answered the prompt/questions on the warm-up. Your response indicates an average level of understanding, effort, or thoughtfulness.

1 point – your answers or responses were either incorrect or inadequate. Your response lacked effort and understanding but you were present for the warm-up and did attempt it.

0 points – you were either absent, came in late and missed the warm-up, or did not attempt to answer the provided question/prompt.

Chapter 1: *Nature and Nurture*

PROMPT: "Nurture works on what nature endows." Define *nature* and *nurture* and then describe what you think the quote means using your own words.

Chapter 2: *Science vs. Intuition and Common Sense*

PROMPT: Why are the answers that come from a scientific approach more reliable than those based on intuition and common sense? In other words, how does a scientific approach differ from other ways of gaining knowledge about behavior?

Chapter 2: *Babies Can Read*

PROMPT: After watching the brief product video, bring together what you have learned in Chapter 2 and critique the claims being made using a scientific lens.

Chapter 2: *Matching Research Methods*

PROMPT: **Match each of the following examples of research with the appropriate research method discussed in the lecture and textbook.** *Hint: Each method will only be used once.*

A)   Naturalistic Observation

B)   Case Study

C)   Survey

D)   Correlation

E)   Experiment

_____ Dena will be teaching an introductory psychology class for the first time next semester. Dena has chosen some films to show to her class of 50 students and is preparing a questionnaire to administer to her students after each film. She hopes that getting student reactions to the films will be helpful in deciding which films to show next time she teaches in the class.

_____ Josh is an undergraduate psychology major. For his senior thesis he is investigating the population of people who shop for pornography. This afternoon he is sitting in his car across the street from one of the adult/pornographic bookstores in the area taking notes on the sex, approximate age, gender, and ethnicity of the patrons as they enter and leave the store.

_____ A researcher is interested in whether people are more or less likely to help someone in distress when others are present. Some subjects were tested when they alone witnessed someone in distress, while others were tested when many people were present. The researcher discovered that witnesses were much more likely to help when they alone witnessed the person in distress.

_____ In an investigation of drug abuse, it was noted that there was a relationship between the age at which an individual first started experimenting with drugs and the severity of drug abuse patterns. Those who experimented with drugs at the earliest ages tended to be those with the most drug abuse problems.

_____ Rachel, a marriage and family therapist, is counseling Jessie at a psychiatric hospital. Jessie was admitted to the hospital when he came to the student health clinic complaining that he hears voices shouting obscenities at him and that he often sees things that aren't actually there. After each session with Jessie, Rachel writes a detailed report describing Jessie's verbal and nonverbal behavior along with her interpretations of Jessie's behavior.

Chapter 3: *What Are Neurons?*

PROMPT: In your own words, what are neurons, and how do they transmit information?

Chapter 3: *What Are Neurotransmitters?*

PROMPT: What are neurotransmitters, and how do they influence human behavior? Give one specific example.

Chapter 4: *Sensation vs. Perception*

PROMPT: What is the difference between sensation and perception? Give an example!

Chapter 5: *The Shoes on Your Feet*

PROMPT: Before reading this prompt, you probably didn't notice the sensation of your shoes touching your feet, yet it is likely you notice it now. Explain why this occurs from the perspectives of consciousness, attention, and perception.

Chapter 5: *Sleep Stages Matching*

PROMPT: Match each of the following stages of sleep with their corresponding element(s).
Hint: Each method will only be used once.

_____ Associated with being **awake**

_____ Associated with the **twilight stage**

_____ Associated with **stage 1** of sleep

_____ Associated with **stage 2** of sleep

_____ Associated with **stages 3/4** of sleep

A) **Delta waves**

B) **Theta waves**

C) **Beta waves**

D) **Alpha waves**

E) **K-complexes and sleep spindles**

Chapter 5: *Hypnosis*

PROMPT: How would you describe the state and/or process of hypnosis, *and* what are your thoughts, stereotypes, or opinions about it?

Chapter 5: *Drug Use*

PROMPT: Briefly explain why some people become regular users of consciousness-altering drugs by providing one possible contributing factor from each of the following perspectives:

Biological –

Psychological –

Social/Cultural –

Chapter 6: *Who Is Pavlov?*

PROMPT: **In your own words, who is Ivan Pavlov, and what influential research did he conduct?**

Chapter 6: *Identifying Classical Conditioning Components from a Clip*

PROMPT: Identify the following classical conditioning elements from the clip:

US =

UR =

CS =

CR =

Chapter 6: *Observational Learning*

PROMPT: What is observational learning? Explain *and* give one specific example of a behavior and how it could be learned through this approach.

Chapter 7: *Retaining Information*

PROMPT: **If you needed to retain a piece of information such as a phone number or street address (and you have no way of writing down or recording that information so you must rely solely on your memory) for 5 seconds, what would be the best strategy? What if you needed to retain it for 5 days?**

5 seconds:

5 days:

Chapter 7: *Memorize This!*

PROMPT: What was the 28-digit sequence of letters and numbers displayed last class? Describe what specific methods/techniques you used to remember it.

Chapter 7: *Exam Memory Tips*

PROMPT: **What are some strategies for improving memory that you could use to help remember content when studying for an exam?**

Chapter 8: *What Is Intelligence?*

PROMPT: How does the textbook define *intelligence*? What attributes, traits, behaviors, or characteristics do you personally associate with people who are intelligent?

Chapter 9: *Why Are You Here?*

PROMPT: Why are you here in this class today? In other words, what motivated you to come to our class this morning?

Chapter 9: Losing or Gaining Weight

PROMPT: Have you ever made an active attempt to lose or gain weight? If yes, then explain your methods and success or failure. If no, describe the methods and success or failure of someone you know.

Chapter 10: *Emotion Theories*

PROMPT: Christine is holding her 8-month-old baby when a fierce dog appears out of nowhere and, with teeth bared, leaps for the baby's face. Christine immediately ducks for cover to protect the baby, screams at the dog, and then notices that her heart is pounding in her chest and she's broken out in a cold sweat. How would you explain Christine's emotional reaction from each of the different theories of emotion discussed last class? *(Let's agree that Christine's emotion is fear.)*

Chapter 11: *Stuck at an Age*

PROMPT: **If you had to be stuck at one age for the rest of your life, what age would you select and why?**

Chapter 11: *Who Is Piaget?*

PROMPT: Who is Jean Piaget, and what four stages did he propose children progress through in terms of cognitive development?

Chapter 11: *Death*

PROMPT: What are the five stages we go through as we react to our own impending death, *and* if you were given the choice, would you want to know when and/or how you were going to die?

Chapter 12: The Big Five

PROMPT: List the Big Five personality traits.

Chapter 12: *Freud's Structures of Personality*

PROMPT: Who is Sigmund Freud, *and* what three main structures of personality did he propose?

Chapter 12: *Erikson's Eight Stages*

PROMPT: List Erik Erikson's *eight* stages of development. *Hint: In order to receive full credit, both parts of each stage must be provided and be correct!*

Chapter 13: *The Cup Is?*

PROMPT: Finish the following sentence: The cup is half _____. Would you describe yourself as an optimist, pessimist, or other? Explain.

Chapter 13: *Alternative Medicine*

PROMPT: Thinking back to Chapter 13 and the various tips discussed for staying healthy, what are complementary and alternative medicines? Define/describe and give at least one example.

Chapter 14: *Models of Abnormality*

PROMPT: Read the following short vignette and then briefly explain Greta's depression from the perspective of *two* of the models of abnormality discussed last class.

Greta suffers from depression and can't seem to find any reasons to like herself; she constantly thinks of herself as unattractive and not worth loving, and that she is responsible for everything that goes wrong in her life. To be fair, things have never been easy for Greta. When she was a child, her mother and father got a divorce, which made her feel different from other kids and made typical family life impossible. She lived with her mother and barely ever saw her father, who lived in another state. Greta sometimes felt that it may have been her fault that her parents separated. Things only got worse when she was a teenager and her best friend died of a drug overdose, triggering an intense downward spiral of depression that nearly ended in suicide. As an adult, Greta is still single and doesn't know what she wants to do with her life. She feels pressured to graduate from college, get a good job, and settle down and start a family—what she thinks all happy and successful people should do with their lives. Not having accomplished any of these typical adult milestones makes her feel like more of a failure and only makes her depression worse.

Chapter 14: *Suicide*

PROMPT: What are some of the warning signs that someone may be suicidal? If you suspected that someone was contemplating suicide, what are some things you could do to help that person?

Chapter 15: *Rico and Heights*

PROMPT: Rico is terrified of heights; anything over three floors high causes him to panic. Describe at least two different approaches that could be used to treat Rico's phobia.

Chapter 16: *Making an Error*

PROMPT: While driving to school one wintery day, Marco narrowly misses a car that slides through a red light. "Slow down! What a terrible driver," he thinks to himself. Moments later, Marco himself slips through an intersection and yelps, "Wow! These roads are awful. The city snow plows needs to get out here." What social psychology principle has Marco just demonstrated? *Explain.*

Chapter 16: *Racism*

PROMPT: In your opinion, do you think that racism is still present in the United States today? How do you think it has changed in the last 50 years? Is it getting better or getting worse?

HANDOUTS AND ACTIVITIES

Name: _____

Random Sampling with M&Ms

Instructions:

1) Open Your Bag of M&Ms and separate by color into piles.

2) Count the total number of M&Ms in your bag.

3) Count the total number of each color and record the results in the table below.

4) Calculate the percentage of each color and record the results in the table below.

5) Predict the percentage of each color in the total population of M&Ms and record the percentages in the table below.

Total =	Red	Brown	Yellow	Green	Orange	Blue
#						
%						
Predicted population %						

Creating a Research Design Activity

1) Generate a research study: What would you want to know? What is your research question?

2) How will you research your topic? What *specific* research method will you use to answer your question(s)?

3) What are some problems, limitations, or ethical concerns you might come across in your research, and how will you address them?

Drawing the Brain

With your group, draw and label the following elements of the brain:

- Four lobes

- Brainstem (pons and medulla)

- Spinal cord

- Cerebellum

- Gyri/sulci (folds of the brain)

- If you are feeling confident or finish quickly, you are welcome to add the structures of the limbic system!

Names of All Group Members (You only need to turn in one sheet per group):

Sensation and Perception Participation Worksheet

Go from station to station and answer the following questions to receive credit for this activity!

Station #1 Smell and Memories

1. Where is the smell center in the brain?

2. What are smell memories, and why do they occur?

3. Smell the various items and record any associations or memories that come to mind.

4. How could you use the connection between smell and memory in your life?

Station #2 Blind Spot and Color Afterimages

5. What is the blind spot, and why does it occur?

6. What are the two different theories of color vision?

7. What is a color afterimage, and why does it occur?

8. What are the two different types of visual illusions?

Station #3 ESP Experiment

9. What is ESP, and what is its scientific status?

10. Record the results of your experiment in the table below and then describe your results and reactions. Indicate a correct response with an "x" or check mark on the chart below.

	1	2	3	4	5	6	7	8	9	10	11	12	13	14	15	16	17	18	19	20
Person #1																				
Person #2																				
Person #3																				

11. Define/describe one specific type of ESP.

Station #4 Thresholds and Subliminal Perception

12. What is an absolute threshold, and how is it influenced by adaptation?

13. What are subliminal messages? Are they thought to be effective?

Name: _____

Why We Dream: Five Modern Theories for Dreams and Nightmares

Published on November 11, 2009, by Ilana Simons, Ph.D., in The Literary Mind

Freud said that whether we intend it or not, we're all poets. That's because on most nights, we dream. And dreams are lot like poetry, in that in both things, we express our internal life in similar ways. We use images more than words; we combine incongruent elements to evoke emotion in a more efficient way than wordier descriptions can; and we use unconscious associations rather than logic to tell a story.

Freud essentially called dreams those poems we tell ourselves at night in order to experience our unconscious wishes as real. Dreams allow us to be what we cannot be, and to say what we do not say, in our more repressed daily lives. For instance, if I dream about burning my workplace down, it's probably because I want to dominate the workplace but am too nervous to admit that aggressive drive when I'm awake and trying to be nice to the people who might give me a raise.

Freud certainly had a catchy theory about dreams, but it was also limited. For him, every single dream was the picture of an unconscious wish. But people who have had boring dreams or nightmares might feel something missing from that formulation. In turn, recent theorists have tried to give a more accurate account of why we dream. In the following post, I'll list some of the current theories on why, at night, our brains tell strange stories that feel a lot like literature. I'd like to know if any of these theories resonate with you, or if you have your own belief about why we dream.

(Many great literary minds were obsessed with their dreams. Samuel Coleridge wanted to write a book about dreams—that "night's dismay" which he said "stunned the coming day." Edgar Allan Poe knew dreams fed his literature, and he pushed himself to dream "dreams no mortal ever dared to dream before.")

Theory #1: The Evolutionary Theory: We Dream to Practice Responses to Threatening Situations

Ever notice that most dreams have a blood-surging urgency to them? In dreams, we often find ourselves naked in public, or being chased, or fighting an enemy, or sinking in quicksand. Antti Revonsuo, a Finnish cognitive scientist, has shown that our amygdala (the fight-or-flight piece of the brain) fires more than normal when we're in REM sleep (the time in sleep when we dream). In REM sleep, the brain fires in similar ways as it does when it's specifically threatened for survival. In addition to that, the part of the brain that practices motor activity (running, punching) fires increasingly during REM sleep, even though the limbs are still. In other words, Revonsuo and other evolutionary theorists argue that in dreams, we are actually rehearsing fight-and-flight responses, even though the legs and arms are not actually moving. They say that dreams are an evolutionary adaptation: We dream in order to rehearse behaviors of self-defense in the safety of nighttime isolation. In turn, get better at fight-or-flight in the real world.

Theory #2: Dreams Create Wisdom

If we remembered every image of our waking lives, it would clog our brains. So, dreams sort through memories, to determine which ones to retain and which to lose. Matt Wilson, at MIT's Center for Learning and Memory, largely defends this view. He put rats in mazes during the day, and recorded what neurons fired in what patterns as the rats negotiated the maze. When he watched the rats enter REM sleep, he saw that the same neuron patterns fired that had fired at choice turning points in the maze. In other words, he saw that the rats were dreaming of important junctures in their day. He argues that sleep is the process through which we separate the memories worth encoding in long-term memory from those worth losing. Sleep turns a flood of daily information into what we call wisdom: the stuff that makes us smart for when we come across future decisions.

Theory #3: Dreaming Is Like Defragmenting Your Hard Drive

Francis Crick (who co-discovered the structure of DNA) and Graeme Mitchison put forth a famously controversial theory about dreams in 1983 when they wrote that "we dream in order to forget." They meant that the brain is like a machine that gets in the groove of connecting its data in certain ways (obsessing or defending or retaining), and that those thinking pathways might not be the most useful for us. But, when we sleep, the brain fires much more randomly. And it is this random scouring for new connections that allows us to loosen certain pathways and create new, potentially useful, ones. Dreaming is a shuffling of old connections that allows us to keep the important connections and erase the inefficient links. A good analogy here is the defragmentation of a computer's hard drive: Dreams are a reordering of connections to streamline the system.

Theory #4: Dreams Are Like Psychotherapy

But what about the emotion in dreams? Aren't dreams principally the place to confront difficult and surprising emotions, and sit with those emotions in a new way? Ernest Hartmann, a doctor at Tufts, focuses on the emotional learning that happens in dreams. He has developed the theory that dreaming puts our difficult emotions into pictures. In dreams, we deal with emotional content in a safe place, making connections that we would not make if left to our more critical or defensive brains. In this sense, dreaming is like therapy on the couch: We think through emotional stuff in a less rational and defensive frame of mind. Through that process, we come to accept truths we might otherwise repress. Dreams are our nightly psychotherapy.

Theory #5: The Absence of Theory

Of course, others argue that dreams have no meaning at all—that they are the random firings of a brain that doesn't happen to be conscious at that time. The mind is still "functioning" insofar as it's producing images, but there's no conscious sense behind the film. Perhaps it's only consciousness itself that *wants* to see some deep meaning in our brains at all times.

On a separate piece of paper with your name on it, answer the following two questions:

1) Select one dream that you have had recently that you still remember with some detail and that you don't mind sharing. Briefly describe your dream and then *explain your dream from the perspective of a minimum of two of the dream theories* discussed in the lecture, article, and/or the book. In other words, how would those theories explain your dream and where it came from? *Be sure to describe the theories you have selected in order to receive full credit!*

2) Why do you, personally, think we dream?

Squirt Gun Exercise

As I conduct an experiment on classical conditioning with a volunteer, try to identify the following components and describe what happened with each.

Unconditioned Stimulus (US):

Unconditioned Response (UR):

Conditioned Stimulus (CS):

Conditioned Response (CR):

Generalization:

Discrimination:

Extinction:

Spontaneous Recovery:

Classical vs. Operant Conditioning

For each of the following examples, decide if the behavior in question was acquired through operant or classical conditioning. If you decide the behavior is operant, identify which type of consequence was responsible for the behavior change (i.e., positive/negative reinforcement or punishment). If you decide the behavior is classical, identify the US, UR, CS, and CR.

1) Every time someone flushes a toilet in the apartment building, the shower becomes very hot and causes the person to jump back. Over time, the person begins to jump back automatically after hearing the flush, before the water temperature changes.

2) A lion in a circus learns to stand up on a chair and jump through a hoop to receive a food treat.

3) Jacob's girlfriend was wearing perfume on their recent date. The date itself was quite passionate and Jacob felt very happy throughout the night. The following day when Jacob gets into his car he smells the lingering scent of her perfume and is instantly flooded with a feeling of happiness.

4) Shelly is in the grocery store with her dad. As they near the checkout lane, Shelly starts whining for a candy bar but her dad says no. Shelly begins to cry and cries louder when her dad continues to refuse. At the checkout lane, Shelly throws herself onto the floor and begins screaming. Her dad responds by grabbing a candy bar and giving it to her. She quickly quiets down and eats her candy. *Hint: there are two sides to this situation and therefore two behaviors occurring here! Try to analyze both Shelly's and her dad's behavior!*

5) Create Your Own: As a group, create your own example of *operant conditioning*, and be sure to explain the conditioning processes involved.

6) Create Your Own: As a group, create your own example of *classical conditioning*, and be sure to explain the different elements involved.

Cognition Homework

Answer the following questions related to the modules on cognition. Utilize your workbook and textbook and be sure to put your name at the top of this paper in order to receive credit.

(1) List the three building blocks of thoughts.

(2) List the three steps involved in problem-solving.

(3) _____ are step-by-step methods of problem-solving that guarantee a correct solution if it is appropriate for the problem and correctly carried out while _____ are rules of thumb that help in simplifying and solving problems but do not guarantee a, correct solution.

(4) Provide one example of a heuristic and how it might be used to solve a problem; *be specific in your example!*

(5) Define <u>Intelligence</u>.

(6) Several different theories of intelligence are mentioned in the slides and/or the textbook. Select one theory of intelligence and briefly describe it below.

(7) What does IQ stand for and how is it calculated?

(8) In order to be widely accepted, an intelligence test (and most tests in general) must have three psychometric properties. Provide and define those three properties.

1) _____:

2) _____:

3) _____:

(9) Explain the nature vs. nurture IQ debate.

(10) _____ is a condition of significantly subaverage intelligence combined with deficiencies in behavior, while _____ refers to superior IQ combined with demonstrated or potential ability in such areas as academic aptitude, creativity, and leadership.

(11) Define and describe *Creativity*.

Problem Solving

1) Can you name four days that start with the letter "T"?

2) Connecting the dots:

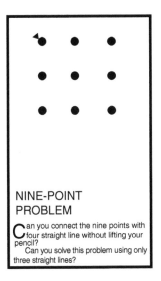

NINE-POINT PROBLEM

Can you connect the nine points with four straight line without lifting your pencil?

Can you solve this problem using only three straight lines?

3) The T-puzzle:

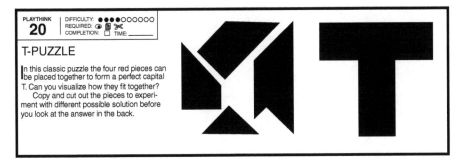

PLAYTHINK 20

DIFFICULTY: ●●●●○○○○○○
REQUIRED: ☺ 📄 ✂
COMPLETION: ☐ TIME: _____

T-PUZZLE

In this classic puzzle the four red pieces can be placed together to form a perfect capital T. Can you visualize how they fit together?

Copy and cut out the pieces to experiment with different possible solution before you look at the answer in the back.

Motivational Theories Scenarios

Read the following scenarios and then decide which theory of motivation best explains the person's behavior in each, and explain your decision. Note: Theories may be used more than once!

Drive Reduction Theory	Extrinsic Motivation
Arousal Theory	Maslow's Hierarchy of Needs
Intrinsic Motivation	Instinct Theory

1) Jaime was sitting at her office desk and suddenly felt slightly chilled. She reached behind her chair and pulled on her sweater.

2) Frank always disliked his 8:30 a.m. class because he was not a morning person. Today's lecture was particularly important, so he purchased a Red Bull to help him stay awake so that he could actually pay attention to the professor.

3) Leah has always enjoyed writing short stories. She is so excited to have a career as a writer!

4) Mike had no interest in being a doctor but went into medicine because of the salary and the prestige associated with the position.

5) Connie is between jobs and is struggling to find an apartment. When one landlord asked her if it would be just her moving in or if her boyfriend/husband would be joining her, she replied "I can't even fathom thinking about a relationship right now. I need to find a job and a place to live first!"

6) Susan just gave birth about 2 weeks ago to a beautiful baby girl. Last night she stayed up all night long rocking and singing to her infant to provide the baby with comfort.

7) Marco really wants to get straight A's this semester because his parents will give him $20 for every "A" that he earns in school.

8) A newborn baby is hungry, so she begins to cry.

9) Carlos loves crossword puzzles! Every Sunday morning he will sit for hours with the newspaper trying to solve the puzzle.

10) Luca enjoys lounging on the couch and watching movies, whereas Jack would rather be out skateboarding or doing something active.

Motivation and Emotion Worksheet

Answer the following questions related to the modules on motivation and emotion. Utilize your workbook and textbook to answer the questions and be sure to put your names at the top of this paper in order to receive credit.

(1) Describe the two main eating disorders presented in the book and slides.

(2) What is a BMI and how is it used?

(3) _____is a subfield of industrial-organization psychology that focuses on employee recruitment, selection, placement, training, appraisal, and development, while _____ is a subfield of industrial-organization psychology that examines organizational influences on worker satisfaction and facilitates organizational change.

(4) Describe and/or define each of the following theories of emotion:

James–Lange theory:

Cannon–Bard theory:

Two-Factor theory:

(5) Apply your knowledge to the following scenario by matching the emotion theory to the chain of events that occurs.

Lucas is driving to school and running late! While driving quickly to campus, the person in front of him suddenly slams on their brakes and comes to an abrupt stop. Lucas' heart starts pounding and he starts to sweat, but he responds quickly by slamming on his brakes. Angry and frazzled, Lucas expresses his emotions by screaming at the driver in front of him.

_____ Cognitive (two-factor) theory

_____ James–Lange theory

_____ Cannon–Bard theory

(A) Heart pounds/sweating → feel anger

(B) Heart pounds/sweating → label the reaction as anger → feel anger

(C) Heart pounds/sweating and anger occur at the same time

(6) Explain how emotions and the body can interact *and* provide one practical application of the interaction between emotions and the body.

(7) Describe some of the ways that the members of your group cope with their anger.

(8) _____ is our tendency to form judgments relative to a neutral level defined by our prior experience, while _____ is the perception that one is worse off relative to those with whom one compares oneself.

(9) What are some tips from the slides and book (feel free to also include personal tips) for how to be happier?

Greeting Cards

For our next class meeting, you will each bring one greeting card to class targeting the age group of 30, 40, 50, 60, 70, 80, 90, or aging in general. The card can be funny or serious and from anywhere that sells greeting cards but should reflect one of the age categories. You are welcome to keep the card when we are done analyzing or leave it with me!

In your small groups, answer the following:

1) What are some stereotypes of the elderly or aging? These can be stereotypes that you hold personally or those you have heard from others or from the media.

2) What are the messages about aging in the greeting cards?

Name(s): _____

Personality Homework

Answer the following questions related to the modules on personality. Utilize your textbook to answer the questions and be sure to put your names at the top of this paper in order to receive credit!

1) What are the three structures of personality according to Sigmund Freud?

2) What are the five psychosexual stages of development according to Freud?

3)_____is one of the two levels of the unconscious; it contains the individual's repressed thoughts, forgotten experiences, and undeveloped ideas while _____ is the level of the unconscious that is inherited and common to all members of a species.

4) What are the 8 stages of personality development according to Erik Erikson?

5) What does DNA stand for and what is it?

6) What does tabula rasa mean?

7) If you had to describe yourself in 4 to 6 traits (words), what would they be? List the 4 to 6 words for each group member.

8) What are the Big Five Personality Traits? List them.

9) What are the levels of Maslow's Hierarchy of Needs?

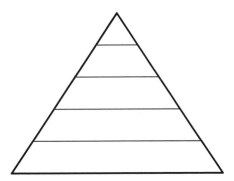

10) Give one example of an objective test of personality and one example of a projective test of personality.

Name: _____

Stress Test

_____ 1. Do you worry about the future?

_____ 2. Do you sometimes have trouble falling a sleep?

_____ 3. Do you often reach for a cigarette, a drink, or a tranquilizer in order to reduce tension?

_____ 4. Do you become irritated over basically insignificant matters?

_____ 5. Do you have less energy than you seem to need or would like to have?

_____ 6. Do you have too many things to do and not enough time to do them?

_____ 7. Do you have headaches or stomach problems?

_____ 8. Do you feel pressure to accomplish or to get things done?

_____ 9. Are you very concerned about being either well liked or successful?

_____ 10. Do you perform well enough in life to satisfy yourself?

_____ 11. Do you get satisfaction from the small joys or simple pleasures of life?

_____ 12. Are you able to really relax and have fun?

TOTAL # _____

Scoring: 1 point for a yes answer to 1–9 or no answer to 10–12. A score of 4 or more suggests that you may have above-average stress levels.

Source: Dr. Frank C. Richardson, Associate Professor, Department of Educational Psychology, and author of Stress, Sanity, and Survival.

1) List the current stressors in your life:

2) List some of the ways that you cope with your stress:

Therapy and Therapist Stereotypes

In your small group, answer the following questions:

1) What are some stereotypes of therapy and/or therapists? These can be stereotypes that you hold personally or those you have heard from others or from the media.

2) What makes for a good therapist? What makes someone a bad therapist?

Social Cognition

Find another person in the room whom you don't know well and go sit next to that person. Answer the questions about the individual solely based on his or her appearance. Once both of you have finished answering the questions about each other, compare your answers to see how you did!

1. Is your partner single, married/in a committed relationship, or dating someone?

2. What is your partner's major?

3. What type of job does your partner have?

4. What kind of car do they drive?

5. What type of music does your partner listen to?

6. What kind of activities or hobbies does your partner enjoy?

After comparing your answers, respond to the following:

7. How did you do? Were you close or way off from your partner's responses?

8. What clues did you use to draw your conclusions and answer the questions?

STUDY GUIDES
AND EXTRA CREDIT

Exam #1 Study Guide

Please remember that this test will not be open-note-book, or any other materials, so plan and study accordingly. Please remember to bring your scantron form 886-E and a number 2 pencil for use with your scantron.

Chapter 1: roots of psychology, demographics of early psychologists (characteristics of who dominated the field), definition of psychology, different professions within the field (psychiatrist vs. clinical vs. counseling), myths vs. facts about psychology, and the subfields of psychology (humanistic, psychodynamic, behaviorism, etc.).

Chapter 2: intuition, hindsight bias, pseudoscience, science, critical thinking and its principles, the scientific attitude, scientific method, theory, hypothesis, the different types of research methods (survey research, case study, naturalistic observation, experiment, etc.), Pearson's *r*, random sampling, correlation vs. causation, independent vs. dependent variables, and APA ethical guidelines.

Chapter 3: phrenology, neurons and their main parts (Know what they do and be able to label them), glial cells, ions and action potentials, electrochemical communication, synapse, neurotransmitters (Know what they are and be able to give an example and describe their primary function), central vs. peripheral nervous system, hormones, big parts of the brain (cerebellum, hypothalamus, etc.), cerebral cortex, gyri and sulci, lobes of the brain (Know what they do and be able to label them), spinal cord, corpus callosum, plasticity, neurotransmitters vs. hormones, left vs. right brain, and the three types of neurons.

Chapter 4: sensation vs. perception, sensory thresholds, subliminal messages, sensory adaptation, retina, blind spot, rods vs. cones, two theories of color vision, sound vibrations, locating sounds, taste buds and the five basic taste sensations, smell center of the brain, basic sensations of touch, kinesthetic senses, gestalt, retinal disparity, perceptual set, physical vs. perceptual illusions, apparent movement, ESP and its scientific status, types of ESP (telepathy, clairvoyance, psychokinesis), and parapsychology.

Good luck studying and remember that your completed study guide can be turned in for extra credit on the day of the test (can be typed or handwritten pages or in the form of index cards). You can receive up to five points depending on the comprehensiveness of completion.

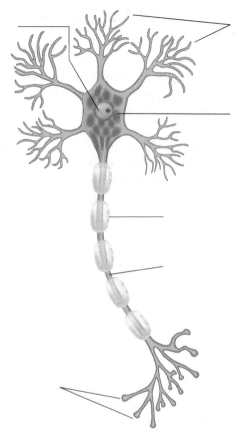

©Alila Medical Images, 2013. Used under license from Shutterstock, Inc.

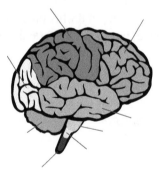

©Athanasia Nomikou, 2013. Used under license from Shutterstock, Inc.

Exam #2 Study Guide

Please remember that this test will not be open-note-book, or any other materials, so plan and study accordingly. Please remember to bring your scantron form 886-E and a number 2 pencil for use with your scantron.

Chapter 5: consciousness, role of daydreams, selective attention, inattentional blindness, circadian rhythms, what makes us sleepy, sleep and sleep stages (know the different rhythms and waves), REM, narcolepsy, sleep apnea, nightmares vs. night terrors, dream theories, hypnosis, hypnosis and memories/behaviors, psychoactive drugs, agonist and antagonist, withdrawal, tolerance, psychoactive ingredient in tobacco, effects of ecstasy, Marijuana side effects and psychoactive ingredient, alcohol, typical drug use results, substance use disorder vs. substance induced disorder and the three different categories of drugs and examples for each.

Chapter 6: learning, conditioning, classical conditioning, Pavlov's experiments and US, UR, CS, CR, extinction, generalization, spontaneous recovery, operant conditioning, law of effect, shaping, consequences, reinforcement and punishment, positive vs. negative reinforcers, negative effects of punishment, classical vs. operant conditioning, observational learning, and mirror neurons.

Chapter 7: memory, short-term memory and its capacity, rehearsal, chunking, serial position effect, spacing effect, long-term memory, four types of long-term memory, where memories are stored, the three processes involved in memory, decay theory, interference (proactive and retroactive), Elizabeth Loftus and her experiments, eidetic memory, childhood amnesia, déjà vu, state dependent learning, and strategies for improving memory.

Chapter 8: three building blocks of thought, algorithms, heuristics, subgoals, functional fixedness, three steps in the problem solving process, intelligence and intelligence tests, standardization, reliability, validity, extremes of intelligence (intellectual developmental disorder and giftedness), influences on intelligence, and creativity.

Good luck studying and remember that your completed study guide can be turned in for extra credit on the day of the test (can be typed or handwritten pages or in the form of index cards). You can receive up to five points depending on the comprehensiveness of completion.

Exam #3 Study Guide

Please remember that this test will not be open-note-book, or any other materials, so plan and study accordingly. Please remember to bring your scantron form 886-E and a number 2 pencil for use with your scantron.

Chapter 9: motives, drive reduction theory, instincts, arousal theory, Eros and Thanatos, intrinsic and extrinsic motivation, Maslow's hierarchy of needs (be able to list the five levels), psychological and physiological hunger, anorexia nervosa and bulimia nervosa and who they affect, obesity (what it is and its current status), body mass index, fad diets, industrial-organizational Psychology, and personnel & organizational psychologists.

Chapter 10: theories of emotion (James–Lange, Cannon–Bard, two-factor), emotions and the body, polygraphs, catharsis, people who are happy, adaptation level phenomenon, relative deprivation, and how to be happier.

Chapter 11: developmental psychology, conception, trimesters, stages of prenatal development (zygote, blastocyst, embryo, fetus), placenta, teratogens, reflexes, maturation, infant motor development, object permanence, conservation, socialization, attachment, gender identity, adolescence, personal fable and imaginary audience, menopause, men and middle adulthood, fluid vs. crystallized intelligence, midlife crisis and midlife transition, Alzheimer's disease, Piaget's four stages, and the five stages of death.

Chapter 12: personality, psychodynamic theory, Freud and psychic energy, unconscious, libido, three structures that make up the personality, five psychosexual stages of development, fixation, defense mechanisms, personal and collective unconscious, Erickson's 8 stages of development (be able to list them), humanistic theories, self-actualization and Maslow, Rogers and unconditional positive regard, traits, focus of trait theories, Big five personality traits, cognitive-social learning theory, Bandura and self-efficacy, objective tests of personality (MMPI), and projective tests of personality (TAT and Rorschach).

Good luck studying and remember that your completed study guide can be turned in for extra credit on the day of the test (can be typed or handwritten pages or in the form of index cards). You can receive up to five points depending on the comprehensiveness of completion.

Exam #4 Study Guide

Please remember that this test will not be open-note-book, or any other materials, so plan and study accordingly. Please remember to bring your scantron form 886-E and a number 2 pencil for use with your scantron.

Chapter 13: stress, stressors, stress and good or bad, health psychology, PTSD, sympathetic and parasympathetic nervous systems and their role in arousal, the stress response in the body, type A and B personalities, psychoneuroimmunology, coronary heart disease, stress and AIDS/cancer, factors influencing our ability to successfully cope with stress, locus of control (internal and external), two general strategies for coping with stress, and an example of complementary or alternative medicines.

Chapter 14: defining abnormal behavior, 4 D's of abnormality, DSM-5, views of mental disorders (diathesis-stress, medical, etc.), effects of labeling, anxiety disorders, specific phobia, panic attacks, generalized anxiety disorder, obsessive compulsive disorder, obsessions vs. compulsions, somatoform vs. psychosomatic disorders, personality disorders, borderline personality disorder, antisocial personality disorder, dissociative disorders, dissociative identity disorder, mood disorders, major depressive disorder, mania, bipolar disorder, suicide (warning signs and what you should do), schizophrenia and the three groups of symptoms, schizophrenia vs. dissociative identity disorder, hallucinations vs. delusions, ADHD, autistic spectrum disorder, and Alzheimer's disease.

Chapter 15: treatments through time, psychotherapy and types of therapists (social worker, counseling, clinical, and psychiatrists), insight therapies, free association, transference, goal of client-centered therapy, behavior therapy, systematic desensitization, cognitive therapy, eclecticism, EMDR, biological treatments, psychopharmacology, four types of antidepressants, lithium, ECT, effectiveness of therapy, and which therapy is best.

Chapter 16: social psychology, fundamental attribution error, social cognition, stereotypes, attitudes, racism, prejudice vs. discrimination, just–world-phenomenon, strategies for reducing prejudice, foot-in-the-door, conformity, Milgram and obedience, five factors influencing attraction, two types of love, group behaviors, primacy effect, altruistic behavior, and the bystander effect.

Good luck studying and remember that your completed study guide can be turned in for extra credit on the day of the test (can be typed or handwritten pages or in the form of index cards). You can receive up to five points depending on the comprehensiveness of completion.

.

Final Exam Cumulative Portion

Content

For this closing assignment, think back over all the topics that we have covered throughout the course of the semester and reflect on the following:

- Please discuss *five specific* ways that the content from this course can apply to your life. *Hint: Think of a specific topic and/or concept we've covered and discuss or describe how it can apply to your life or how that information might be helpful to you personally.*

- For each of the five examples, focus on a different concept covered in this course.

Formatting

- **Be sure to number your examples one through five** (rather than writing this out as an essay, think of it as five separate paragraphs each numbered for ease of identification).

- **Write as clearly as possible** (i.e., complete sentences, proper grammar, etc.).

- **Your paper should be roughly two typed pages** (single-spaced with standard font and margins).

Grading

Your paper will be worth a maximum of 15 points. Points will be awarded based on meeting the criteria above in addition to your ability to demonstrate your understanding and application of various course materials. These 15 points will be added directly to your final exam score.

Your paper will be submitted to me (inperson) on the day of our final exam; no late or email submissions will be accepted.

Extra Credit–Semester Long Option #1

If you are interested in earning up to 20 points of extra credit, you can complete the requirements of the optional assignment below.

Content

- Find *two* brief clips on YouTube (or that you record by other means) that illustrate a specific concept or topic covered in this class. Include the title, link, and length of time of the clip in your document. *Your clips must be current examples from popular culture (i.e., television shows or movies); don't give me the first thing you find on YouTube. Selecting clips that are not current or relevant may result in loss of points.*

- For each clip, describe the specific concept or topic that is being highlighted. *Your description should be specific.* Be sure to define and/or describe the concept/topic and how the clip demonstrates or illustrates that concept/topic. Each description should be at least a paragraph or two in length.

- Your clip must either be closed captioned or you must provide a typed transcript of the audio portions of your clip. If the clip has *accurate* closed captioning, that will save you some effort; otherwise, you can type the transcript yourself or use any program you might have at your disposal.

Logistics

- Your assignment should be typed, double-spaced, and in standard font size and format.

- Your document should be between one and two pages in length (without the transcripts).

- You must include the hyperlink to each of your two YouTube clips or an attached file if you recorded it by other means.

- Your submission must include the transcripts to your videos (failure to submit these will result in a heavy deduction of points).

- Your assignment should be *submitted online* through the *"Semester-Long Extra Credit Option #1" link* located on our online course homepage.

Due Date

All submissions should be done prior to the end of our class (the start of the final exam). *No late submissions will be accepted.*

Extra Credit–Semester Long Option #2

If you are interested in earning up to 20 points of extra credit, you can complete the requirements of the optional assignment below!

Content

- Create a short movie, montage, or media presentation about a specific concept, theory, or person that we have covered this semester that I can post on my YouTube channel. This media presentation can provide examples to aid in understanding, serve as an introduction to, or go into more depth than was covered in class on a concept, theory, or person.

- Your project should be effortful, well-made, accurate, and ideally something that could be shown in future semesters of this class or help other students who view it online. *Before submitting your final product, you must meet with me briefly or submit it to me for review; failing to submit your materials for review or selecting or creating material that is not historically or topically accurate will result in loss of points so do your research!*

- Your project must either be captioned or you must provide a typed transcript of the audio portions of your media.

Logistics

- The media presentation should be a minimum of two minutes in length and should include images and/or video, music or audio, and ideally be engaging, interesting, or funny! Make the images, audio, and other media relevant to the concept, theory, or person being presented.

- You will submit the video/presentation file to me and allow me to share it with my students via my YouTube channel.

- Your submission must include the transcripts to your video/presentation if it is not captioned (failure to submit these will result in a heavy deduction of points).

- Your assignment should be submitted online through the "Semester-Long Extra Credit Option #2" link located on our online course homepage.

Due Date

All submissions should be submitted prior to the end of our class (the final day)!! *No late submissions will be accepted.*

CPSIA information can be obtained
at www.ICGtesting.com
Printed in the USA
LVHW05s0354230518
578173LV00002B/4/P

9 781524 924034